BIOLOGICAL ANTHROPOLOGY
An Introductory Reader

Fifth Edition

Michael Alan Park
Central Connecticut State University

McGraw Hill

Boston   Burr Ridge, IL   Dubuque, IA   Madison, WI   New York   San Francisco   St. Louis
Bangkok   Bogotá   Caracas   Kuala Lumpur   Lisbon   London   Madrid   Mexico City
Milan   Montreal   New Delhi   Santiago   Seoul   Singapore   Sydney   Taipei   Toronto

Biological Anthropology: An Introductory Reader, Fifth Edition

Published by McGraw-Hill, a business unit of The McGraw-Hill Companies, Inc., 1221 Avenue of the Americas, New York, NY 10020. Copyright © 2008 by The McGraw-Hill Companies, Inc. All rights reserved. No part of this publication may be reproduced or distributed in any form or by any means, or stored in a database or retrieval system, without the prior written consent of The McGraw-Hill Companies, Inc., including, but not limited to, any network or other electronic storage or transmission, or broadcast for distance learning.

Some ancillaries, including electronic and print components, may not be available to customers outside the United States.

ISBN: 978-0-07-340519-3
MHID: 0-07-340519-1

1 2 3 4 5 6 7 8 9 0 QPD/QPD 0 9 8 7

Editor-in-chief: *Emily Barrosse*
Publisher: *Frank Mortimer*
Sponsoring editor: *Monica Eckman*
Marketing manager: *Lori DeShazo*
Production editor: *David Blatty*
Art director: *Jeanne M. Schreiber*
Design manager: *Cassandra Chu*
Cover designer: *Joan Greenfield*
Art manager: *Robin Mouat*
Illustrator: *John & Judy Waller*
Production supervisor: *Rich DeVitto*

The text was set in 10/12 Palatino by ICC Macmillan Inc. and printed on acid-free, 45# New Era Matte by Quebecor, Dubuque.

Cover image: Mouse lemur: © 2004 Frans Lanting/www.lanting.com

Library of Congress Cataloging-in-Publication Data

Biological anthropology : an introductory reader / [compiled by] Michael Alan Park—5th ed.
    p. cm
    Includes bibliographical references and index.
    ISBN-13: 978-0-07-340519-3 (alk. paper)
    ISBN-10: 0-07-340519-1 (alk. paper)
    1. Physical anthropology.   I. Park, Michael Alan.

GN60.B54 2007   2006048082
599.9—dc22

The Internet addresses listed in the text were accurate at the time of publication. The inclusion of a website does not indicate an endorsement by the authors or McGraw-Hill Higher Education, and McGraw-Hill does not guarantee the accuracy of the information presented at these sites.

www.mhhe.com

Preface

Introductory-level readers in biological anthropology tend to be, as one such volume put it, collections "of the best of the public press." They recognize the contributions of popular magazines, newspapers, and journals in "providing current, first-rate educational information."

While it is absolutely the case that the public press, at its best, provides up-to-the-minute, accurate articles that are informative and stimulating to the general public and the beginning student, it is also the case that other sources of information are important to a scholarly discipline and are relevant to a well-rounded introduction to that discipline. These include older writings, perhaps now outdated but of historical interest; technical articles; sections of important books; and relevant writings from outside the discipline—all of these are part of the canon of an academic field. Students in the process of becoming familiar with a field, even (and maybe especially) at the introductory level, will benefit from exposure to a broad sample of literature that expresses the ideas of that field.

This anthology provides such a sample of the spectrum of writing about biological anthropology. The array of selections includes

- **Articles from the "popular press"** (such as *Discover*, *The New Yorker*, and *Natural History*). These articles, specifically intended to introduce their readers to a subject, at the same time assume some basic background knowledge and degree of literacy. Because college students taking an introductory course may already be formally familiar with the subjects of these articles, reading them not only will serve to enhance and expand their knowledge of the subjects but may well provide a positive sense of recognition and encouragement.

- **Articles from semiprofessional journals** (such as *Scientific American* and *The Sciences*). These selections serve to enhance and encourage students' abilities to acquire and synthesize more technical information within the discipline.

- **Articles from professional journals** (such as *Evolutionary Anthropology*, *Nature*, and *Science*). Students will see what primary research and professional-level reporting look like and that the scientific method (a major theme of this reader) is not just a nice idea but is put into action by real scientists doing real science.

- **Sections from books** (for example, those by Johanson and Dettwyler). These pieces stand by themselves as readings but may also make some students want to read the books in their entirety and perhaps undertake further reading by those authors or on those subjects.

- **Excerpts from original works.** Although the work of Darwin, Wallace, Lamarck, Mendel, Linnaeus, and others can be summarized perfectly well, it is still instructive to students (and to us) to learn exactly what they said and how they said it. When one goes even a bit beyond the "quotable quotes" and reads the rest of the paragraphs around them, one often is surprised at what else these important figures had to say. We see that Lamarck, for example, clearly understood the scientific method and applied it to his own idea in a very modern manner.

- **Writings—in all the above categories—from outside anthropology.** Of all scholarly disciplines, anthropology is perhaps necessarily the least parochial. Because of our holistic perspective, we rely on—and contribute to—other fields, and we recognize that scholars in other fields may well have something to say about our subject and may do so in a way that is every bit as faithful to the anthropological perspective as is our own work. Stephen Jay Gould and Jared Diamond stand out as examples.

ADDITIONAL FEATURES

- More articles pertaining to modern human populations are included than in any other reader. See, for example, "Differential Mortality and the Donner Party Disaster" by Donald K. Grayson and "Are Humans Still Evolving?" by Michael Balter.

- The anthology begins with a section on the personal experiences of biological anthropologists and ends with seven examples of bioanthropology "in action"—applied to specific interesting and topical concerns.

- Unique to this collection is a section on the nature of science. The articles in this section provide concrete examples of the scientific method at work. This theme, however, is carried throughout the book.

- Several articles cover current debates in bioanthropology (the meaning and utility of new molecular data and of genetic tracing of ancestry, the presence of culture among nonhuman primates, and intelligent design). Introductions and articles together help students summarize and compare points of view.

- The reading selections are divided into ten thematic parts, each part briefly introduced and with a short statement as to the reason for the inclusion of each contained selection. Individual selections are introduced with a short biography of the author (longer in the case of historical figures so as to better provide the historical context), an introduction to the article itself, and a set of pre-reading questions. Terms that might require definition appear in a glossary at the end of the book. Also included are an annotated table of contents and an index.

- For the benefit of instructors, there is a list of major topics and which selections pertain to each, and a chart showing to which chapter(s) in major bioanthropology texts each selection is relevant. An accompanying Instructor's Manual contains selection rationale, key terms, and multiple-choice and essay questions.

WHAT'S NEW IN THIS EDITION

Ten of the forty-two articles are new to this edition, and the volume features these changes (in sequential order):

- Part 3: The Evolution of Evolution has a new article (13) on the intelligent design controversy.

- Part 5: The Primates and Primate Behavior has a new article (18) on behavioral flexibility as an adaptation among Madagascar lemurs.

- Part 6: Hominid Evolution has three new chapters (22, 24, and 25) on the evolution of bipedalism,

the "Hobbit" fossils from Indonesia, and the controversy over the emergence of the modern human mind.

- Part 7: The Bioanthropology of Modern Human Populations contains an article (28) on disease originally in another section of the previous edition.

- Part 8: Human Biodiversity now has the original article (29) on "The Five Sexes."

- Part 9: Bioanthropology and the Human Genome has two new chapters (34, 35) on the chimpanzee genome and the new services that purport to trace one's genetic ancestry.

- Part 10: Biological Anthropology: Applied and Considered has three new chapters (36, 40, 42) on the controversy of co-sleeping with infants, the ethics of research on great apes, and the question of ongoing human evolution.

ACKNOWLEDGMENTS

The staff at McGraw-Hill has, once again, expertly transformed my words and ideas into a finished product. Special thanks to my original editor Jan Beatty, my current editor Monica Eckman, production editor David Blatty, developmental editor Beth Ebenstein, editorial coordinators Jessica Badiner and Teresa Treacy, permissions editor Karyn Morrison, and copy editor Jamie Fuller.

The following colleagues reviewed the manuscript and choice articles and made many helpful suggestions. All choices and errors, of course, remain my responsibility.

Erin Browder, Southwestern College

Joanne Devlin, University of Tennessee

Debra Gold, St. Cloud State University

Mark Hartmann, University of Arkansas at Little Rock

Patricia M. Lambert, Utah State University

Lorena Madrigal, University of South Florida

Paul Stephen Mattson, Moorpark College

Anne R. Titelbaum, University of New Orleans

Finally, a long-overdue thank you to my parents for the gift of reading.

Contents

PART 3   *THE EVOLUTION OF EVOLUTION*   35

PART 4   *THE PROCESSES OF EVOLUTION*   63

List of Articles by Major Topic Areas

Race and Biodiversity

Scientific Method

Taxonomy

Concordance

What follows is a chart indicating to which chapters in ten major biological anthropology texts each part in this reader might best correspond. The following texts are included:

Boaz, Noel T., and Alan J. Almquist. 2002. *Biological Anthropology: A Synthetic Approach to Human Evolution*, 2 ed. Upper Saddle River, NJ: Prentice-Hall.

Boyd, Robert, and Joan B. Silk. 2006. *How Humans Evolved*, 4 ed. New York: Norton.

Campbell, Bernard G., James D. Loy, and Kathryn Cruz-Uribe. 2006. *Humankind Emerging*, 9 ed. New York: Allyn & Bacon.

Fuentes, Agustín. 2007. *Core Concepts in Biological Anthropology*. Boston: McGraw-Hill.

Jurmain, Robert, Harry Nelson, Lynn Kilgore, and Wenda Trevathan. 2006. *Essentials of Physical Anthropology*, 6 ed. Belmont, CA: Wadsworth. **[Jurmain (brief)]**

Jurmain, Robert, Harry Nelson, Lynn Kilgore, and Wenda Trevathan. 2006. *Introduction to Physical Anthropology*, 10 ed. Belmont, CA: Wadsworth. **[Jurmain (large)]**

Park, Michael Alan. 2007. *Biological Anthropology*, 5 ed. Boston: McGraw-Hill.

Relethford, John H. 2006. *The Human Species: An Introduction to Biological Anthropology*, 6 ed. Boston: McGraw-Hill.

Stanford, Craig, John S. Allen, and Susan C. Antón. 2006. *Biological Anthropology: The Natural History of Humankind*. Upper Saddle River, NJ: Prentice-Hall.

Stein, Philip L., and Bruce M. Rowe. 2006. *Physical Anthropology*, 9 ed. Boston: McGraw-Hill. **[Stein/Rowe (large)]**

Biological Anthropology Reader		Boaz/ Almquist	Campbell/ Loy/Cruz-Uribe	Jurmain (brief)	Jurmain (large)	Fuentes	Stein/Rowe (large)
Part 1:	Being a Biological Anthropologist	1	1	1	1	1	1
Part 2:	The Nature of Science	1	1	1	1	1	2
Part 3:	The Evolution of Evolution	3	1	2	2, 4	1	2, 3
Part 4:	The Processes of Evolution	4	2	4	4	4	4, 5
Part 5:	The Primates and Primate Behavior	6, 7, 9	3, 4, 9	5, 6	5, 6, 7	5	6, 9, 10
Part 6:	Hominid Evolution	8, 10, 11	5–17	7–11	7–13	6–9	11–15
Part 7:	The Bioanthropology of Modern Human Populations	14		12	14, 16	3, 10	16
Part 8:	Human Biodiversity		18	13	15	10	17
Part 9:	Bioanthropology and the Human Genome	3, 13	3	3	3	2	3
Part 10:	Biological Anthropology: Applied and Considered	15	18	15		11	Epilogue

PART 1

Being a Biological Anthropologist

Anthropology is defined as "the holistic study of the human species." A holistic study is one that assumes an interrelationship among all its parts. Thus, the human past is related to the human present. Human biology is related to human culture. One facet of a human cultural system—for example, economics—is related to any other—for example, religion.

The subject of anthropology—the human species, now and in the past—is, however, so broad and varied that the field of anthropology has traditionally been divided into four major subfields. *Cultural anthropology* focuses on cultural behavior as a species characteristic and on the nature of and variation among the world's cultural systems. *Linguistic anthropology* studies language as a facet of culture and examines the variation among languages. *Archaeology* looks at the human cultural past by locating, recovering, preserving, and interpreting the remains of past cultural systems and, ultimately, by trying to reconstruct those systems.

Biological anthropology (or physical anthropology)—our topic here—studies humans as a biological species, much the way, say, an entomologist would study insects or an ichthyologist would study fishes. A major difference, of course, is that part of our identity as a species is not only our large, complex brain but also the cultural behavior that it makes possible. Thus, even as anthropologists focusing on biology, we cannot ignore human culture. The holism of anthropology is the hallmark of the discipline.

Bioanthropology itself is divided into several specialties. Some anthropologists are primarily interested in human genetics and evolution. Others, paleoanthropologists, study the results of genetic and evolutionary changes—the human fossil record. Still others focus on living human populations—their demographics and genetic and physical variations.

Because we are all members of a single species, we need to look at ourselves within a larger biological context. Thus, primatologists study our closest relatives, the nonhuman primates. We also need to view ourselves relative to the environments in which we live and to which we have adapted. This is the study called human ecology.

Finally, anthropology is applied to matters of current social and political concern. This is known generally as applied anthropology; within bioanthropology, the best-known example is forensic anthropology, the application of anthropological knowledge to legal matters such as the identification of skeletal remains.

One of the things that attracts people to the field of anthropology is the possibility for travel and adventure—seeing exotic locales, learning about the behavior of our primate relatives, meeting peoples of different cultures, or discovering the fossils of some hitherto unknown human ancestor. The formal name for this is *fieldwork*—the data-collection stage of anthropology—but the romantic nature of how we gather our data cannot be denied.

The selections in this part are examples of this personal side of the field from diverse areas of bioanthropology. In "Finding Lucy," taken from the prologue of his book *Lucy: The Beginnings of Humankind*, paleoanthropologist Donald Johanson recounts how he and his team discovered the famous fossil skeleton that changed our knowledge of human evolution. Primatologist Agustín Fuentes, in "Monkey Business in Bali," describes the multiple facets of anthropological fieldwork: the data gathered about the subjects of the study (in this case, long-tailed macaques), the interactions between those subjects and the humans who live around them as well as those who study them, and the reactions of his students to a new environment and different cultural system. In "The Homegoing" I tell of one of my most personal and meaningful experiences, the exhumation of the remains of a native Hawaiian buried in Connecticut and the preparation for his return to his native land. And Katherine A. Dettwyler tells about her very personal reactions during a data-collection session among the Bambara of Mali in "Bad Breath, Gangrene, and God's Angels."

SUGGESTED WEBSITES FOR FURTHER STUDY

http://www.leakeyfoundation.org
http://www.asu.edu/clas/iho
http://www.eskeletons.org
http://physanth.org

1

Finding Lucy

Donald Johanson and Maitland Edey

Donald Johanson was curator of physical anthropology at the Cleveland Museum of Natural History while he was conducting the research in Ethiopia that led to the discovery of Lucy and other important fossils. He is now director of the Institute for Human Origins at Arizona State University in Phoenix. Maitland Edey is a well-known and widely published science writer.

The origins of the human branches of primate evolution have been, and remain, shrouded in mystery. Fossils documenting our past are rare and hard to find. Locating them involves a combination of good scientific background, some informed guesswork, and an ample helping of luck. Sometimes, however, when all these factors are at work, the result is a discovery that changes our entire picture of human evolution. In this selection, Donald Johanson, with Maitland Edey, tells how his knowledge, intuition, and luck led to finding the now-famous fossil called Lucy, still one of the most significant pieces of data in our evolutionary story. (More detail about this period of human evolution will be discussed in Part 6.)

As you read, consider the following questions:

1. Why were Johanson and his team looking for fossils in the desolate Hadar area in the first place? Why did they expect to find any hominid remains there?

2. How does Johanson define *hominid*? How does he define *human*?

3. What did Lucy look like, and how were things like her sex, size, and age of death determined?

4. Why were Lucy's fossil remains so significant to the study of human evolution?

In some older strata do the fossilized bones of an ape more anthropoid (manlike) or a man more pithecoid (apelike) than any yet known await the researches of some unborn paleontologist?

—T. H. Huxley

On the morning of November 30, 1974, I woke, as I usually do on a field expedition, at daybreak. I was in Ethiopia, camped on the edge of a small muddy river, the Awash, at a place called Hadar, about a hundred miles northeast of Addis Ababa. I had been there for several weeks, acting as coleader of a group of scientists looking for fossils.

For a few minutes I lay in my tent, looking up at the canvas above me, black at first but quickly turning to green as the sun shot straight up beyond the rim of

hills off to the east. Close to the Equator the sun does that; there is no long dawn as there is at home in the United States. It was still relatively cool, not more than 80 degrees. The air had the unmistakable crystalline smell of early morning on the desert, faintly touched with the smoke of cooking fires. Some of the Afar tribesmen who worked for the expedition had brought their families with them, and there was a small compound of dome-shaped huts made of sticks and grass mats about two hundred yards from the main camp. The Afar women had been up before daylight, tending their camels and goats, and talking quietly.

For most of the Americans in camp this was the best part of the day. The rocks and boulders that littered the landscape had bled away most of their heat during the night and no longer felt like stoves when you stood next to one of them. I stepped out of the tent and took a look at the sky. Another cloudless day; another flawless morning on the desert that would turn to a crisper later on. I washed my face and got a cup of coffee from the camp cook, Kabete. Mornings are not my favorite time. I am a slow starter and much prefer evenings and nights. At Hadar I feel best just as the sun is going down. I like to walk up one of the exposed ridges near the camp, feel the first stirrings of evening air and watch the hills turn purple. There I can sit alone for a while, think about the work of the day just ended, plan the next, and ponder the larger questions that have brought me to Ethiopia. Dry silent places are intensifiers of thought, and have been known to be since early Christian anchorites went out into the desert to face God and their own souls.

Tom Gray joined me for coffee. Tom was an American graduate student who had come out to Hadar to study the fossil animals and plants of the region, to reconstruct as accurately as possible the kinds and frequencies and relationships of what had lived there at various times in the remote past and what the climate had been like. My own target—the reason for our expedition—was hominid fossils: the bones of extinct human ancestors and their close relatives. I was interested in the evidence for human evolution. But to understand that, to interpret any hominid fossils we might find, we had to have the supporting work of other specialists like Tom.

"So, what's up for today?" I asked.

Tom said he was busy marking fossil sites on a map.

"When are you going to mark in Locality 162?"

"I'm not sure where 162 is," he said.

"Then I guess I'll have to show you." I wasn't eager to go out with Gray that morning. I had a tremendous amount of work to catch up on. We had had a number of visitors to the camp recently. Richard and Mary Leakey, two well-known experts on hominid fossils from Kenya, had left only the day before. During their stay I had not done any paperwork, any cataloguing. I had not written any letters or done detailed descriptions of any fossils. I *should* have stayed in camp that morning—but I didn't. I felt a strong subconscious urge to go with Tom, and I obeyed it. I wrote a note to myself in my daily diary: *Nov. 30, 1974. To Locality 162 with Gray in AM. Feel good.*

As a paleoanthropologist—one who studies the fossils of human ancestors—I am superstitious. Many of us are, because the work we do depends a great deal on luck. The fossils we study are extremely rare, and quite a few distinguished paleoanthropologists have gone a lifetime without finding a single one. I am one of the more fortunate. This was only my third year in the field at Hadar, and I had already found several. I know I am lucky, and I don't try to hide it. That is why I wrote "feel good" in my diary. When I got up that morning, I felt it was one of those days when you should press your luck. One of those days when something terrific might happen.

Throughout most of that morning, nothing did. Gray and I got into one of the expedition's four Land-Rovers and slowly jounced our way to Locality 162. This was one of several hundred sites that were in the process of being plotted on a master map of the Hadar area, with detailed information about geology and fossils being entered on it as fast as it was obtained. Although the spot we were headed for was only about four miles from camp, it took us half an hour to get there because of the rough terrain. When we arrived, it was already beginning to get hot.

At Hadar, which is a wasteland of bare rock, gravel and sand, the fossils that one finds are almost all exposed on the surface of the ground. Hadar is in the center of the Afar desert, an ancient lake bed now dry and filled with sediments that record the history of past geological events. You can trace volcanic-ash falls there, deposits of mud and silt washed down from distant mountains, episodes of volcanic dust, more mud, and so on. Those events reveal themselves like layers in a slice of cake in the gullies of new young rivers that recently have cut through the lake bed here and there. It seldom rains at Hadar, but when it does it comes in an overpowering gush—six months' worth overnight. The soil, which is bare of vegetation, cannot hold all that water. It roars down the gullies, cutting back their sides and bringing more fossils into view.

Gray and I parked the Land-Rover on the slope of one of those gullies. We were careful to face it in such a way that the canvas water bag that was hanging from the side mirror was in the shade. Gray plotted the locality on the map. Then we got out and began doing what most members of the expedition spent a great deal of their time doing: we began surveying, walking slowly about, looking for exposed fossils.

Some people are good at finding fossils. Others are hopelessly bad at it. It's a matter of practice, of training your eye to see what you need to see. I will never be as good as some of the Afar people. They spend all their time wandering around in the rocks and sand. They have to be sharp-eyed; their lives depend on it. Anything the least bit unusual they notice. One quick educated look at all those stones and pebbles, and they'll spot a couple of things a person not acquainted with the desert would miss.

Tom and I surveyed for a couple of hours. It was now close to noon, and the temperature was approaching 110. We hadn't found much: a few teeth of the small extinct horse *Hipparion*; part of the skull of an extinct pig; some antelope molars; a bit of a monkey jaw. We had large collections of all these things already, but Tom insisted on taking these also as added pieces in the overall jigsaw puzzle of what went where.

"I've had it," said Tom. "When do we head back to camp?"

"Right now. But let's go back this way and survey the bottom of that little gully over there."

The gully in question was just over the crest of the rise where we had been working all morning. It had been thoroughly checked out at least twice before by other workers, who had found nothing interesting. Nevertheless, conscious of the "lucky" feeling that had been with me since I woke, I decided to make that small final detour. There was virtually no bone in the gully. But as we turned to leave, I noticed something lying on the ground partway up the slope.

"That's a bit of a hominid arm," I said.

"Can't be. It's too small. Has to be a monkey of some kind."

We knelt to examine it.

"Much too small," said Gray again.

I shook my head. "Hominid."

"What makes you so sure?" he said.

"That piece right next to your hand. That's hominid too."

"Jesus Christ," said Gray. He picked it up. It was the back of a small skull. A few feet away was part of a femur: a thighbone. "Jesus Christ," he said again. We stood up, and began to see other bits of bone on the slope: a couple of vertebrae, part of a pelvis—all of them hominid. An unbelievable, impermissible thought flickered through my mind. Suppose all these fitted together? Could they be parts of a single, extremely primitive skeleton? No such skeleton had ever been found—anywhere.

"Look at that," said Gray. "Ribs."

A single individual?

"I can't believe it," I said. "I just can't believe it."

"By God, you'd better believe it!" shouted Gray. "Here it is. Right here!" His voice went up into a howl. I joined him. In that 110-degree heat we began jumping up and down. With nobody to share our feelings, we hugged each other, sweaty and smelly, howling and hugging in the heat-shimmering gravel, the small brown remains of what now seemed almost certain to be parts of a single hominid skeleton lying all around us.

"We've got to stop jumping around," I finally said. "We may step on something. Also, we've got to make sure."

"Aren't you sure, for Christ's sake?"

"I mean, suppose we find two left legs. There may be several individuals here, all mixed up. Let's play it cool until we can come back and make absolutely sure that it all fits together."

We collected a couple of pieces of jaw, marked the spot exactly and got into the blistering Land-Rover for the run back to camp. On the way we picked up two expedition geologists who were loaded down with rock samples they had been gathering.

"Something big," Gray kept saying to them. "Something big. Something *big.*"

"Cool it," I said.

But about a quarter of a mile from camp, Gray could not cool it. He pressed his thumb on the Land-Rover's horn, and the long blast brought a scurry of scientists who had been bathing in the river. "We've got it," he yelled. "Oh, Jesus, we've got it. We've got The Whole Thing!"

That afternoon everyone in camp was at the gully, sectioning off the site and preparing for a massive collecting job that ultimately took three weeks. When it was done, we had recovered several hundred pieces of bone (many of them fragments) representing about forty percent of the skeleton of a single individual. Tom's and my original hunch had been right. There was no bone duplication.

But a single individual of what? On preliminary examination it was very hard to say, for nothing quite like it had ever been discovered. The camp was rocking with excitement. That first night we never went to bed at all. We talked and talked. We drank beer after beer. There was a tape recorder in the camp, and a tape of the Beatles song "Lucy in the Sky with Diamonds" went belting out into the night sky, and was played at full volume over and over again out of sheer exuberance. At some point during that unforgettable evening—I no longer remember exactly when—the new fossil picked up the name of Lucy, and has been so known ever since, although its proper name—its acquisition number in the Hadar collection—is AL 288-1.

"Lucy?"

That is the question I always get from somebody who sees the fossil for the first time. I have to explain: "Yes, she was a female. And that Beatles song. We were sky-high, you must remember, from finding her."

Then comes the next question: "How did you know she was a female?"

"From her pelvis. We had one complete pelvic bone and her sacrum. Since the pelvic opening in hominids has to be proportionally larger in females than in males to allow for the birth of large-brained infants, you can tell a female."

And the next: "She was a hominid?"

"Oh, yes. She walked erect. She walked as well as you do."

"Hominids all walked erect?"

"Yes."

"Just exactly what is a hominid?"

That usually ends the questions, because that one has no simple answer. Science has had to leave the definition rather flexible because we do not yet know exactly when hominids first appeared. However, it is safe to say that a hominid is an erect-walking primate.

That is, it is either an extinct ancestor to man,* a collateral relative to man, or a true man. All human beings are hominids, but not all hominids are human beings.

We can picture human evolution as starting with a primitive apelike type that gradually, over a long period of time, began to be less and less apelike and more manlike. There was no abrupt crossover from ape to human, but probably a rather fuzzy time of in-between types that would be difficult to classify either way. We have no fossils yet that tell us what went on during that in-between time. Therefore, the handiest way of separating the newer types from their ape ancestors is to lump together all those that stood up on their hind legs. That group of men and near-men is called hominids.

I am a hominid. I am a human being. I belong to the genus *Homo* and to the species *sapiens:* thinking man. Perhaps I should say wise or knowing man— a man who is smart enough to recognize that he is a man. There have been other species of *Homo* who were not so smart, ancestors now extinct. *Homo sapiens* began to emerge a hundred thousand—perhaps two or three hundred thousand—years ago, depending on how one regards Neanderthal Man. He was another *Homo.* Some think he was the same species as ourselves. Others think he was an ancestor. There are a few who consider him a kind of cousin. That matter is unsettled because many of the best Neanderthal fossils were collected in Europe before anybody knew how to excavate sites properly or get good dates. Consequently, we do not have exact ages for most of the Neanderthal fossils in collections.

I consider Neanderthal conspecific with *sapiens,* with myself. One hears talk about putting him in a business suit and turning him loose in the subway. It is true; one could do it and he would never be noticed. He was just a little heavier-boned than people of today, more primitive in a few facial features. But he was a man. His brain was as big as a modern man's, but shaped in a slightly different way. Could he make change at the subway booth and recognize a token? He certainly could. He could do many things more complicated than that. He was doing them over much of Europe, Africa and Asia as long as sixty or a hundred thousand years ago.

Neanderthal Man had ancestors, human ones. Before him in time was a less advanced type: *Homo erectus.* Put him on the subway and people would probably take a suspicious look at him. Before *Homo erectus* was a really primitive type, *Homo habilis*; put him on the subway and people would probably move to the other end of the car. Before *Homo habilis* the human line may run out entirely. The next stop in the past, back of *Homo habilis,* might be something like Lucy.

All of the above are hominids. They are all erect walkers. Some were human, even though they were of exceedingly primitive types. Others were not human. Lucy was not. No matter what kind of clothes were put on Lucy, she would not look like a human being. She was too far back, out of the human range entirely. That is what happens going back along an evolutionary line. If one goes back far enough, one finds oneself dealing with a different kind of creature. On the hominid line the earliest ones are too primitive to be called humans. They must be given another name. Lucy is in that category.

For five years I kept Lucy in a safe in my office in the Cleveland Museum of Natural History. I had filled a wide shallow box with yellow foam padding, and had cut depressions in the foam so that each of her bones fitted into its own tailor-made nest. *Everybody* who came to the Museum—it seemed to me—wanted to see Lucy. What surprised people most was her small size.

Her head, on the evidence of the bits of her skull that had been recovered, was not much larger than a softball. Lucy herself stood only three and one-half feet tall, although she was fully grown. That could be deduced from her wisdom teeth, which were fully erupted and had been exposed to several years of wear. My best guess was that she was between twenty-five and thirty years old when she died. She had already begun to show the onset of arthritis or some other bone ailment, on the evidence of deformation of her vertebrae. If she had lived much longer, it probably would have begun to bother her.

Her surprisingly good condition—her completeness—came from the fact that she had died quietly. There were no tooth marks on her bones. They had not been crunched and splintered, as they would have been if she had been killed by a lion or a saber-toothed cat. Her head had not been carried off in one direction and her legs in another, as hyenas might have done with her. She had simply settled down in one piece right where she was, in the sand of a long-vanished lake or stream—and died. Whether from illness or accidentally drowning, it was impossible to say. The important thing was that she had not been found by a predator just after death and eaten. Her carcass had remained inviolate, slowly covered by sand or mud, buried deeper and deeper, the sand hardening into rock under the weight of subsequent depositions. She had lain silently in her adamantine grave for millennium after millennium until the rains at Hadar had brought her to light again.

That was where I was unbelievably lucky. If I had not followed a hunch that morning with Tom Gray,

*In this book the general term "man" is used to include both males and females of the genus *Homo.*

Lucy might never had been found. Why the other people who looked there did not see her, I do not know. Perhaps they were looking in another direction. Perhaps the light was different. Sometimes one person sees things that another misses, even though he may be looking directly at them. If I had not gone to Locality 162 that morning, nobody might have bothered to go back for a year, maybe five years. Hadar is a big place, and there is a tremendous amount to do. If I had waited another few years, the next rains might have washed many of her bones down the gully. They would have been lost, or at least badly scattered; it would not have been possible to establish that they belonged together. What was utterly fantastic was that she had come to the surface so recently, probably in the last year or two. Five years earlier, she still would have been buried. Five years later, she would have been gone. As it was, the front of her skull was already gone, washed away somewhere. We never did find it. Consequently, the one thing we really cannot measure accurately is the size of her brain.

Lucy always managed to look interesting in her little yellow nest—but to a nonprofessional, not overly impressive. There were other bones all around her in the Cleveland Museum. She was dwarfed by them, by drawer after drawer of fossils, hundreds of them from Hadar alone. There were casts of hominid specimens from East Africa, from South Africa and Asia. There were antelope and pig skulls, extinct rodents, rabbits and monkeys, as well as apes. There was one of the largest collections of gorilla skulls in the world. In that stupefying array of bones, I kept being asked, What was so special about Lucy? Why had she, as another member of the expedition put it, "blown us out of our little anthropological minds for months"?

"Three things," I always answered. "First: what she is—or isn't. She is different from anything that has been discovered and named before. She doesn't fit anywhere. She is just a very old, very primitive, very small hominid. Somehow we are going to have to fit her in, find a name for her.

"Second," I would say, "is her completeness. Until Lucy was found, there just weren't any very old skeletons. The oldest was one of those Neanderthalers I spoke of a little while ago. It is about seventy-five thousand years old. Yes, there *are* older hominid fossils, but they are all fragments. Everything that has been reconstructed from them has had to be done by matching up those little pieces—a tooth here, a bit of jaw there,

maybe a complete skull from somewhere else, plus a leg bone from some other place. The fitting together has been done by scientists who know those bones as well as I know my own hand. And yet, when you consider that such a reconstruction may consist of pieces from a couple of dozen individuals who may have lived hundreds of miles apart and may have been separated from each other by a hundred thousand years in time—well, when you look at the complete individual you've just put together you have to say to yourself, 'Just how real is he?' With Lucy you know. It's all there. You don't have to guess. You don't have to imagine an arm bone you haven't got. You *see* it. You see it for the first time from something older than a Neanderthaler."

"How much older?"

"That's point number three. The Neanderthaler is seventy-five thousand years old. Lucy is approximately 3.5 million years old. She is the oldest, most complete, best-preserved skeleton of any erect-walking human ancestor that has ever been found."

That is the significance of Lucy: her completeness and her great age. They make her unique in the history of hominid fossil collecting. She is easy to describe, and—as will be seen—she makes a number of anthropological problems easier to work out. But exactly what is she?

The rest of this book will be devoted to answering that question. Unique Lucy may be, but she is incomprehensible outside the context of other fossils. She becomes meaningless unless she is fitted into a scheme of hominid evolution and scientific logic that has been laboriously pieced together over more than a century by hundreds of specialists from four continents. Their fossil finds, their insights—sometimes inspired, sometimes silly—their application of techniques from such faraway disciplines as botany, nuclear physics and microbiology have combined to produce an increasingly clear and rich picture of man's emergence from the apes—a story that is finally, in the ninth decade of this century, beginning to make some sense. That story could not even begin to be told, of course, until Charles Darwin suggested in 1857 that we *were* descended from apes and not divinely created in 4004 B.C., as the Church insisted. But not even Darwin could have suspected some of the odd turns the hominid story would take. Nor could he have guessed which apes we are descended from. Indeed, we are not entirely sure about that even today.

2

Monkey Business in Bali:
Fieldwork and Teaching
Among the Temple Macaques

Agustín Fuentes

Agustín Fuentes is an associate professor of anthropology at the University of Notre Dame. He is the author most recently of Core Concepts in Biological Anthropology *(2007, McGraw-Hill) and co-editor of* Primates in Perspective *(2007, Oxford).*

Monkeys of genus *Macaca* are among the most widespread, numerous, and successful of primate groups. Field studies of these monkeys have provided us with invaluable data about primate behavior and thus about our own evolution. They have also given us important and interesting information about the interaction of humans with other species and about the human impact on our close relatives. Finally, of course, doing primatology in the field not only introduces us to the animals we study but also is an opportunity to immerse ourselves in an environment and culture often very different from our own. In this selection, Agustín Fuentes describes his experiences conducting research and leading primatology field schools in Bali and, in the process, provides a classic example of anthropology's holistic approach and multidimensional value.

As you read, consider the following questions:

1. Anthropologists use studies of nonhuman primates to shed light on human behavior. How much can we learn about our own behavior in this regard? For example, do the contrasting behaviors of "Teardrop" (F16) and "Stubby" (F3) bring to mind any human responses?

2. How do the behaviors of male and female long-tailed macaques differ? What might be the adaptive values of some of these behaviors? How are such questions being addressed in this series of field studies?

3. How has the close contact between these monkeys and humans affected the monkeys' behavior?

4. What have these researchers learned about the interaction of humans and nonhuman primates?

5. Beyond learning about our close relatives, what other benefits can students derive from participation in such studies?

In long-tailed macaque monkeys (*Macaca fascicularis*), young males leave the group they were born in and try to migrate into another. The young male I was following this day, M9, didn't seem to want to participate in this particular aspect of his species' heritage. Because of this he had spent the past few months receiving a hearty dose of aggression from most of the adults in

Prepared for publication in this work.

the group. M9 seemed to be a bit taken aback by all of the threats and was getting pretty jittery. As I approached the group, I saw M9 quickly jump down from the temple wall and, nervously glancing at the alpha male, M5, sprint across the ground toward the Banyan tree. The old female with the crippled leg, F2, let out an alarm bark and all 50 members of the group stopped what they were doing and stared at M9. Spock (M5 is called "Spock" because of his uncanny resemblance to Leonard Nimoy) and the other males cough-grunted to one another and sped off in pursuit of M9. As the chase moved off into the trees along the ravine, I sat down next to one of the large demon statues near the Pura Dalem (the main temple) and began the process of writing down the sequence of events leading up to the chase. It was going to be a busy morning among the macaques of the Padangtegal Sacred Monkey Forest.

The temple complex at Padangtegal, Ubud, in central Bali, Indonesia, is in a small patch of forest surrounded by rice fields, villages, and increasingly more tourist shops and hotels. Three groups of macaques totaling about 151 individuals currently live here. The first temples in the forest were built sometime in the fourteenth century A.D. and have been in constant use ever since. Legend has it that the macaques once roamed across much of the area, but over the years have come to favor residing in the protected forest surrounding the temple complex. Inside the forest they are safe from hunting and irate farmers, and are provided with some food by the temple staff and the growing number of tourists who come to see the famous monkeys of Ubud.

My area of interest in anthropology is behavior. Specifically, as a biological anthropologist I am interested in the evolution and biological basis of the wide range of social behaviors that relate to group living and relations between males and females. A major component in our attempt to understand human behavioral patterns is the utilization of a comparative approach via the study of other primates. That is what I do: I am an anthropologist who studies human and nonhuman primate behavior.

In 1989, as a young graduate student, I first came to Bali on a break from chasing leaf monkeys through the forests of Borneo and Sumatra. I thought a few weeks of rest would do me good, so I headed up to the beautiful central Balinese village of Ubud. Famous for its arts, museums, and fabulous rice terrace views, the area of Ubud is also home to one of the better-known monkey forests in the world. I ended up spending over a month in Ubud and most of that time in the forest watching the monkeys. I returned in 1990, 1992, and 1994, vowing that someday I'd undertake a serious long-term project on these amazing animals and their fascinating relationships with humans.

Building on Dr. Bruce Wheatley's work from the late 1980s and early 1990s, I formulated a plan to conduct a comparative study across the many monkey forests of Bali. In 1997 I proposed research on the Padangtegal (Ubud) monkey forest as part of a Bali-wide research project between myself and the Universitas Udayana Primate Research Center in Denpasar. Drs. I. D. K. Harya Putra and Komang Gde Suaryana agreed to the collaboration and we are currently into our fourth year of the project.

Why does a biological anthropologist want to look at a group of monkeys that spend their time around a bunch of temples and humans? There are three aspects to this type of project and they address each of my professional passions: primatology, human behavior, and teaching.

By observing groups of macaques over long periods of time you are able to get a good idea of not only their daily lives, but also the complex and dynamic ways that individuals deal with the challenges of getting food, mates, and social partners. Documenting variations in primate behavior allows us to examine what behavior is unique to humans and what is common among specific groups of primate species. We look for both primate-wide trends and species-specific behavior patterns. If we can understand the distribution of behaviors across related species, we can then attempt to model when, where, and how these behavior patterns evolved within groups of primates. Primatological studies can give us insight into our close relatives' behavior and, thus, help us to construct comparative models for the evolution of our own societies.

Male macaques group themselves into hierarchies by creating alliances, or partnerships, with other males and competing for status. Over the past few years, I have seen males rise up in the hierarchy through mischievous behavior, overt fighting, and, in at least one case, by continuously mating with nearly all the females in the group. M17 ("Mr. T") migrated into the central group (group 2) in 1998 and was subject to attacks from the resident group males. His strategy to work his way into the group came as a bit of a surprise to me: rather than fight, M17 avoided the males and sought out the females of the group. M17 courted the females nonstop (as many as 17 times in one day!) and by 2000, with the females' assistance, had become the highest-ranking male in the group.

Males are nearly twice the size of females in this species, and there are about five adult females to every one adult male in a group. Male-female relationships take on a number of different forms, and I have even observed males sometimes attacking females. However, male-female relaxed social interactions are also very common. In fact, some males and females seem to prefer one another and spend a great deal of time together, away from the rest of the group. Many anthropologists and psychologists propose that male violence toward females is an evolutionary pattern in primates (including ourselves). While this is a popular hypothesis, it hasn't been fully tested in most primates. Science, as a methodology, is based on testing and retesting hypotheses. It is important that a robust set of tests be conducted before any hypothesis is elevated into the powerful realm of theory. My concerns about the assumptions underlying the male aggression hypothesis pushed me to investigate the relationships between aggression and reproductive success for these macaques. Over the past four years we have documented a great deal of variation in the mating strategies of males at Padangtegal. Do aggressive males have more offspring? Knowing all of the males and watching them over many years, combined with genetic tests for paternity, will enable me to attempt to answer this question. This answer might add a piece to the search for the understanding of male aggression in primates.

There are many more females than males in the group, and it can be much harder to observe their social behavior as there is so much of it. Female macaques group themselves into clusters of related females (called matrilines). There are usually a number of matrilines in each macaque group. Females seem to have differential relationships based on the number of female relatives they have. Female relatives almost always support one another in conflicts, and having more relatives increases a female's chances of winning a conflict. These macaques also show a fascinating relationship wherein the younger daughters of females always outrank their older sisters. This "rank-reversal" might function to allow greater access to food by the infants over their older siblings.

An example of the importance of relatives is F16 (named "Teardrop" for the birthmark below her right eye). This female in group 3 has never been observed to reproduce. Without daughters to support her, she is socially outside of most of the group's interactions. F16 spends most of her time alone, occasionally grooming others and seldom being groomed herself. At times, when I am collecting behavioral observation data, F16 will come up and sit next to me and we'll both watch the other monkeys, as passive, external observers.

Sometimes personality drives a female's role in the group. F3 ("Stubby"), the highest-ranking female in group 2, has a domineering personality and frequently wins conflicts with not only the females but also most of the males. She spends a lot of time with high-ranking males, and other females always seem to be lining up to groom her. It probably doesn't hurt that she seems to have an infant nearly every year. Watching her swagger through the group can be an awe-inspiring sight, especially as she was born with what most would consider a serious handicap: she has no tail!

One of the most surprising behaviors in these macaques is that of infant taking. Females within a matriline frequently pass their infants around. Infants are a great source of interest to the females (and males) and most try to hold a new infant for at least a short while. Sometimes higher-ranking females will take infants from lower-ranking ones and hold them for up to a day. It is very difficult to watch a low-ranking female follow another female who is holding her squealing infant for hours on end. Especially because in a few cases this has resulted in injury to the infant and, occasionally, even death. Some males also hold infants and seem to spend more time around infants when they are trying to avoid fights.

The macaques of Padangtegal are an interesting study population in that they are "semi–free ranging;" that is, they are provisioned with some food and interact regularly with humans. Therefore, these groups differ in some respects from other groups of both captive and fully free ranging long-tailed macaques. At Padangtegal, the macaques are larger than their counterparts at non-provisioned sites. Also, their overall health is better, and nearly 50 percent of the young that are born survive past the first few years of life. The Padangtegal macaques rest a bit more and spend a little less time searching for food. Interestingly, they also play and manipulate non-food objects more than free ranging groups do. Overall, however, their behavior profiles are similar to long-tailed macaques at many sites across Southeast Asia. Currently, we are monitoring a number of macaque sites in Bali where there is a range of human interaction (from a lot to none) to get an idea of what specific, and subtle, behavioral differences there are across such groups.

As an anthropologist I enjoy watching both human and nonhuman primates interact. In Balinese culture, monkeys play an important role in myth, dance, and many aspects of folklore. At Padangtegal Monkey Forest there is a great deal of interaction between the macaques, local villagers, and tourists. The monkeys seem to know the villagers well, avoiding some and ignoring others. The macaques treat the temple staff very differently than they do all other humans. Some of the younger males, as they are pushed out of their groups, spend a great deal of time around the male human temple staff. A few even follow researchers or use researchers for a game of hide-and-seek. The macaques become very excited during temple ceremonies because by the end there are hundreds of edible offerings left for the gods and demons, which the macaques are more than happy to consume. I am always amazed at the incredible sight during a temple ceremony when the main temple (Pura Dalem) is packed with villagers and expectant macaques hover above on statues, altars, and the temple walls.

The Balinese are very tolerant of the macaques in and around the temples, and this has an economic benefit. Tourists come from around the world to see, and interact with, these monkeys. In 1999 nearly 50,000 tourists visited the forest and each paid an entry fee. These fees go toward village ceremonies, building and road construction, the maintenance of the temples and forests, and even some food for the monkeys. The village council appoints a manager for the monkey forest who supervises a group of fourteen men and women to keep the forest and temple area in shape and assist the priests. To me, the relationship between macaques, tourist dollars, and the local economy and culture is a fascinating one.

Since 1998 we have also been watching and interviewing the tourists. We are seeing that nationality, age, and sex seem to affect how humans behave around monkeys. While many try to feed the monkeys, and in turn have monkeys climbing on them, more adult humans are bitten than children, and more women are bitten than men. Bites are very rare and nearly all bites result from some sort of human teasing. Tourists from countries where monkeys occur naturally are seldom bitten. Most people talk to the monkeys and become frustrated when the monkeys do not seem to respond correctly. Frequently, a tourist will hold one banana in one hand and a bunch in the other and then scold the adult male macaque when he takes the bunch instead of the one. I have also seen tourists punch macaques and in one case even try to take a baby monkey from its mother. Our ongoing study is producing a very interesting glimpse into the way humans see "nature" and macaques, and the impact being a tourist has on the type of behavior one exhibits.

Finally, the monkey forest at Padangtegal is a wonderful place to teach. Since 1998 I have directed a field school run by Central Washington University, Universitas Udayana, and the University of Guam. Each summer, for five to six weeks, we bring between twelve and twenty undergraduate and graduate students to the villages of Ubud and Padangtegal and the monkey forest, our classroom without walls. During their stay in Bali, the students interact with many Balinese locals and researchers, and learn what different people from many cultures think about monkeys, conservation, and research. This cross-cultural experience is an important part of an anthropological field school. Although we have a nice homestay (a converted Balinese family house compound), a field site within walking distance, and even access to e-mail (an Internet café in the middle of a large rice field), the students still undergo culture shock. Being thousands of miles away from home surrounded by new sites, sounds, smells, and (unfortunately) intestinal parasites, can be stressful, even in such a wonderful place as Bali. The food, although amazingly delicious, is very different from what most Americans are accustomed to; the hot, humid, weather takes its toll, and the mosquitoes and spiders seem to prefer American college students over all other humans. Being challenged to learn and effectively work in conditions that are unfamiliar, and sometimes fatiguing, is an important part of the field school experience.

Learning about the scientific method, primate behavior, and data-collection methodologies in the classroom is important, but there is no substitute for actual experience and firsthand learning. I begin by teaching the students how to identify the macaques, conduct surveys and census groups, and identify behaviors. I then direct the students through a focus on data collection and focal follows (the following of one monkey for a set amount of time and recording its behavior). Over the first three to four weeks the students acquire the skills to observe behavior and accurately record it. During this time the students get to know the macaques and start to realize they have individual personalities and complex social lives. Over the past few years, the students have enjoyed coming up with nicknames for most of the adult macaques (I still receive e-mails from past students checking up on their favorite monkeys). For the last two weeks of the field school, each student proposes a hypothesis, collects data to test it, and, a month after the field school is over, turns in a research report. Of course, each student collects only a relatively small amount of actual data during this time period. However, the main goal of the field school is to provide these students with the skills to conduct behavioral observation and to lay a solid foundation for future research endeavors. Over the past few years, a number of former students have returned to participate in the larger, ongoing Balinese Macaque Project and conduct specific research mini-projects. As a behavioral scientist, it always gives me great pleasure to provide the opportunity for students to enter the fascinating world of data collection and start to learn how important, and difficult, it is to do good science.

As humans continue to change the planet, forests are shrinking and more species are being forced to coexist or perish. By studying the macaques of Padangtegal, I am looking at the effects of long-term coexistence and trying to understand what has enabled the macaques and humans to share this space for so long. By observing a population accustomed to human presence, we are able to get inside the world of the macaques and collect high-quality data in our quest to understand primate societies. As an anthropologist this research has enabled me to integrate many of my interests and introduce students to the wonderful world of research. Above all, the macaques of Padangtegal continue to force me to remember that behavior, in all of its forms, is a complex and fascinating thing.

3

The Homegoing

Michael Alan Park

I am a professor of anthropology at Central Connecticut State University. My professional focus is on anthropology education through teaching, writing, and public speaking. But now and then I get the opportunity to put some of my other skills into practice, as in the experience related here.

Forensic anthropology is the application of anthropological knowledge of human anatomy, in particular the human skeleton, to legal and historical matters, most commonly the identification of skeletal remains and, sometimes, determination of cause and time of death. On occasion, the bones may be those of the famous or the infamous. Sometimes, however, the remains examined may be those of "regular" folks, in need of identification, justice, and, as in the case here, of a long overdue "homegoing."

As you read, consider the following questions:

1. Why was a biological anthropologist required for the identification of Henry's bones when he was buried beneath a marked tombstone?

2. What evidence indicated that the bones recovered were indeed those of Henry?

3. What were the abnormal features found on Henry's bones?

On a hot July afternoon in 1993, I found myself standing over an open grave in a peaceful hillside cemetery in the small Connecticut town of Cornwall—waiting for a colleague to unearth the remains of a native Hawaiian who had lain interred there for 175 years.

A few weeks before, Nick Bellantoni, the Connecticut state archaeologist, had phoned me with a fascinating story, one I had never heard, although I had lived in the state for twenty years. In 1808, a sixteen-year-old Hawaiian named Opukahaia (Oh-poo-kah-hah-EE-ah) escaped the tribal warfare that had killed his parents and younger brother—reportedly before his eyes—by becoming the cabin boy aboard a Yankee sailing ship, the *Triumph*. Two years later, sailing by way of China and the West Indies, he landed in Connecticut, where he was taken under the care of the president of Yale University. He learned English, took the name Henry, and converted to Christianity, becoming a Congregationalist. He is said to be the first Christian Hawaiian. In 1817 he helped build a missionary school in Cornwall. His dream was to return to Hawaii (then known as the Sandwich Islands) and bring his new faith to his people.

Henry's dream was never realized. On February 17, 1818, at the age of twenty-six, he died during a typhoid fever epidemic that swept through Connecticut. His vision, however, helped inspire the missionary movement that would profoundly change the history of the Hawaiian Islands—including a role in their annexation by the United States in 1898. Henry's grave in Cornwall became a shrine both for the people of his adopted town and for visiting Hawaiians, who would leave offerings on his headstone. The inscription on the stone, reads: "Oh, how I want to see Hawaii! But I think I never shall—God will do right. He knows what is best."

Then, in the fall of 1992, Deborah Liikapeka Lee, a descendant of Henry's family, awoke from a dream convinced that Henry wanted to return to his homeland. A family association garnered the necessary funds and legal documents, and the next summer Henry's "homegoing" took place. And this is where anthropology comes in.

Old New England cemeteries vary in the precise placement of headstones relative to the bodies beneath them. Moreover, the acidic, often wet New England soil is unkind to organic remains. The recovery, removal, and accurate identification of whatever

Published here with permission of the author.

remained of Henry Opukahaia required the method-ologies of archaeology and forensic anthropology. Nick wanted my help with the latter—making sure anything recovered was indeed Henry. He also wanted my help, it turned out, in moving several tons of stone.

First in 1818, and then with modifications later, Henry's tomb had been carefully and lovingly assem-bled by the people of Cornwall's Congregational Church. They had placed a large horizontal headstone or ledger (the only one of its kind in the cemetery) on a pedestal of fieldstones and mortar several feet high. When we arrived, the headstone was covered by offerings—shells, flowers, candy, and coins. We removed and boxed these and then carefully sepa-rated the stone from the pedestal, locking it away in the cemetery sexton's tool shed. We dismantled the pedestal, carefully labeling and diagramming the posi-tion of each stone because the portion of the tomb above ground was to be rebuilt by a stone mason. Under the pedestal, and going down about 3 feet into the ground, we uncovered, as we dug, three more lay-ers of fieldstones that acted as a foundation for the monument above and as protection for the coffin and remains we hoped were still below. All the stones were removed, labeled, and set aside. When we were into a layer of sandy soil about 52 inches down, Nick worked alone in the excavated pit, delicately scraping away the dirt inch by inch with a trowel and a brush.

Late on the second day of our excavation, a dark stain became visible in the soil. The wooden coffin it-self had long since decayed, but the dark shadow of its six-sided outline could be seen. At that point we began to despair of finding much else. Indeed, the Hartford funeral home that was to prepare the remains for reburial had provided us only with a metal container about the size of a single file cabinet drawer. The fam-ily had been cautioned not to expect much.

But then something truly exciting came to light. It was a small portion of the wooden coffin lid, preserved (even to the inclusion of some black paint) possibly by the action of metals from the brass tacks that had been driven into it in the shape of a heart. This was not an uncommon practice for that time period in New Eng-land. Inside the heart shape, more tacks spelled out "H.O.," "ae" (from a Latin phrase for "age at the com-pletion of life"), and the numerals "26"—Henry's ini-tials and age at death. After another hour of careful scraping and brushing, Nick's trowel grazed some-thing hard, and within a few minutes the apparent remains of Henry Opukahaia saw the light of day for the first time in 175 years.

To our surprise, the skeleton was virtually com-plete. The elaborately constructed tomb and the sandy soil with good drainage had kept the bones dry enough for excellent preservation. Apparently, a regular coffin

FIGURE 1 Biological anthropologist Michael Park is handed one of Henry Opukahaia's bones by forensic archaeologist Nick Bellantoni. Together, the work of biological anthropology and forensic archaeology helped in the task of bringing Henry Opukahaia home. (Courtesy William F. Keegan)

was going to be needed for Henry's eventual reburial after all.

Nick carefully freed each bone from the soil and identified it as he handed it up to me (Figure 1). I con-firmed the identification, and the bone was checked off by one of our colleagues from a list of the 206 bones of the normal adult human skeleton. Each bone was wrapped in acid-free paper to prevent any surface damage and then placed in the metal box, which barely managed to accommodate all the bones. We all worked with surgical gloves because harmful pathogens have been known to persist even in old remains, and Henry had died of an infectious disease. (Later in our investigation we ran out of gloves and ignored the caution, but with no ill effects.)

Everything to this point clearly indicated we had recovered Henry's bones, but verification was still nec-essary. As we identified, recorded, and wrapped each bone, we compared important diagnostic bones with what we knew of Henry from written descriptions and a single drawn portrait. The skeleton was clearly that of a male and, at least at my brief first glance, seemed to conform to that of a person in his late twenties. Henry had been described as being "a little under six feet." We did not have precision measuring instruments with us in the field, but using my own six-foot-one stature as a gauge, I held several of the arm and leg bones up to my limbs and guessed that they belonged to someone a few inches shorter.

As Nick brushed the dirt away from the skull (saving it for last), the face of Henry Opukahaia emerged—the very image of his portrait. The skeleton is more than just a bony foundation for the body's soft tissues. The bones themselves are living tissue, connected in many ways to muscles, blood vessels, nerves, and skin. The shape of the outer body is reflected in the skeleton, and vice versa. With training, one can "see" the face of a person in the bony visage of the skull. The skull in the grave, with its prominent nose, high forehead, and heavy, squared jaw was clearly that of the man in the portrait.

We spent two more days with Henry, this time in the garage of the Hartford funeral home. With the bones laid out in anatomical orientation on a gurney, we were able to conduct a more thorough scientific analysis, cleaning, photographing, measuring, and describing the bones. The family graciously gave us their blessing to do this.

Henry's skeleton was indeed surprisingly complete. The only bones missing were the hyoid, a horseshoe-shaped bone in the throat, and five finger bones. The coccyx (tail bone) and xyphoid process (the pointy bone at the bottom of the breastbone) were badly decomposed and identifiable only by the place in which we found them relative to the other bones. Other than that, the only damage was some deterioration of the back and underside of the skull and to some of the cervical (neck) vertebrae. We hypothesized that Henry's head may have been laid on a pillow, which retained moisture that speeded decomposition.

The size and robusticity of the bones (as well as the perfect match with the portrait) all identified the skeleton as that of a male. The cranium had the typical male traits of brow ridges, a sloped forehead, a protruding, square chin, and rounded upper borders on the eye sockets. The angle at the back of the jaw (the gonial angle) was about 120 degrees—relatively large for males, who more typically have angles close to 90 degrees—and the mastoids (the bony humps behind the ears) were small for a male.

The pelvis, however, was unequivocally male. Essentially, everything about a female pelvis is wide and broad (an obvious adaptation to pregnancy and childbirth), whereas corresponding features of a male pelvis are narrow. The pelvis before us was as good and as typical an example of a male pelvis as any of us had seen.

There are several skeletal traits used to determine age at death. They are all based on changes that take place with regularity in the development of portions of the bones. The latest change that has *already* taken place, and the next change in the chronological order that has *yet* to take place, mark the minimum and maximum age at which the individual died. In Henry's case, the ends of all the long bones, which initially develop separately from the shafts, were almost all completely fused to form a single bone. The exceptions were the crest of the pelvis and the end of the collar bone where it meets the breastbone. Fusion was still taking place at these sites. This indicated an age at death of between eighteen and thirty.

The internal surfaces of the pubic bones (where the pelvic bones meet in front) change appearance at different ages. Henry's matched the standard for an average age of twenty-eight. Similarly, the front ends of the ribs undergo regular changes, and Henry's indicated an age range of nineteen to thirty-three, with a mean of 25.9. All these data coincided well with his documented age at death of twenty-six.

Traditionally, the closure of the cranial sutures has been used as a common method of determining age at death. It is based on the fact that the cranial vault begins as four separate bones that fuse, along suture lines, at certain ages. The method, however, has fallen from favor because there is too much individual variation. Henry's sutures were a case in point. At twenty-six all his major suture lines should have been open or in the process of fusing. In fact, they had all prematurely closed. Some sites were completely obliterated, a condition only seen in the very elderly. There is no indication why this occurred in Henry, nor is there any evidence that it caused any problems sometimes related to premature closure, such as cranial deformation.

There are a number of formulas for estimating overall stature from the measurement of one of the major long bones. Applying four of these to Henry's skeleton gave us an average stature estimate of five-foot-eight—a bit shorter than "a little under six feet"—but these estimates do not take into complete account differences in individual proportions. Henry could have been a bit taller than these calculations indicate.

Henry's skeleton displayed only a few abnormalities. The joint where his jaw met his cranium (the temporomandibular joint) was oddly shaped and noticeably worn. He may well have had some discomfort at this joint during his life. Both hip joints, where the femur articulates with the pelvis, were also oddly shaped, but here there was no indication that this condition caused him any pain or malfunction. Both joints were similarly shaped, and there were no other abnormalities of the bones involved.

Henry's right ribs, numbers 3 through 10, however, showed a striking condition. On the inside surface between the head of the ribs, where they attach to the vertebral column, and at the angle where they curve toward the front of the body, we observed an ashy, porous texture. On rib 7, this abnormal texture was 44 mm long. This condition is called osteomyelitis, which can be associated with various infectious diseases. In the midst of our scientific investigation, this observation served to remind us of the nature of the subject of our study—another human being whom we had come, in only a few days, to know very well indeed.

Toward the end of our analysis, a coffin arrived from Hawaii. It was a fairly plain wooden box but was covered in a layer of koa wood, which is native to the islands. The family requested that we lay out Henry's bones in the coffin in correct anatomical orientation. To do this we lined the bottom of the coffin with heavy foam rubber into which we cut spaces to hold each bone. The family kindly agreed to let us place the wrist, finger, ankle, and toe bones together in four bundles at the ends of the arms and legs. Cutting individual spaces for all those bones would have been quite time consuming.

The following Sunday about 200 people, including those of us who had helped exhume Henry's remains, gathered at the Congregational Church in Cornwall for a "homegoing" celebration. A local Congregational minister, himself a native Hawaiian, spoke over Henry's coffin, which was surrounded by ti leaves, flower and yarn leis, and bouquets of anthuriums. Henry's portrait faced the congregation. The next day Henry Opukahaia was flown home to Hawaii, taken by canoe to Kealakekua Bay on the "Big Island" where he had first boarded the *Triumph* in 1808, and, finally, buried in a cemetery overlooking the bay.

Except for two days of labor under the hot summer sun (and perhaps cutting those spaces in the foam rubber), this was not a particularly difficult endeavor. The archaeological and forensic applications and analyses were fairly straightforward. But in the Cornwall church that Sunday, as we lined up in front of Henry's coffin for photos and the family warmly thanked us for our help, I knew this was one of the most rewarding bits of anthropology I would ever participate in.

Note: Thanks to Nick Bellantoni for including me in the project, and for jogging my memory on some of the details for this article.

4

Bad Breath, Gangrene, and God's Angels

Katherine A. Dettwyler

Katherine A. Dettwyler is affiliated with Texas A&M University. The book from which this selection is taken won the Margaret Mead Award from the American Anthropological Association. Dettwyler is also co-editor with Patricia Stuart-Macadam of Breastfeeding: Biocultural Perspectives *(1995, Aldine). Her website on breastfeeding is www.kathydettwyler.org.*

Dealing with nonhuman primates or the remains of the dead (see Selections 1, 2, and 3) can be emotional enough, but when one's subjects are living people, even a scientist conducting research can have very personal responses. Your scientific objectivity is challenged and you are often presented with ethical dilemmas. In the process, however, you can learn a lot about yourself as well as your subjects. In this selection, Katherine Dettwyler recounts several emotionally charged experiences she had while conducting what started out to be rather routine research on human dentition. In this chapter from her book, she refers to Miranda, the daughter whom she had taken to Mali with her, and her son Peter, back home. It is relevant to her story to know that Peter has Down syndrome.

As you read, consider the following questions:

1. What was Dettwyler hoping to find out by examining the mouths and teeth of her subjects?
2. Why was the condition of the teeth of her subjects so poor compared with those of other people in Mali?
3. Why did the man Bakary object to Dettwyler's giving her daughter chicken to eat?
4. What are the problems encountered by Dettwyler's subjects with regard to self-administered medication?
5. Why are children with Down syndrome rare in societies like the one Dettwyler was studying?

There is more than one kind of freedom. Freedom to and freedom from. In the days of anarchy, it was freedom to. Now you are being given freedom from. Don't underrate it.
—Margaret Atwood

I stood in the doorway, gasping for air, propping my arms against the door frame on either side to hold me up. I sucked in great breaths of cool, clean air and rested my gaze on the distant hills, trying to compose myself. Ominous black thunderclouds were massed on the horizon and moved rapidly toward the schoolhouse. They rolled down the hills like wads of dark cotton, like the fog blankets that regularly obliterate the hills around San Francisco Bay. Thunder growled; the smell of ozone permeated the air. Rain pounded the

iron roof overhead, drowning out all thought, while great rivers of water streamed off the corners of the building. Gusts of wind whipped through the trees, blowing the rain into my face. I turned and plunged back inside, back into the fray.

The morning had begun pleasantly enough, with villagers waiting patiently under the huge mango tree in the center of the village. But before long, the approaching storm made it clear that we would have to move inside. The only building large enough to hold the crowd was the one-room schoolhouse, located on the outskirts of the village. Here adults learned to read and write the newly alphabetized written Bambara. General education for children was still a foreign concept.

Inside the schoolhouse, chaos reigned. It was 20 degrees hotter, ten times as noisy, and as dark as gloom. What little light there was from outside entered through the open doorway and two small windows. The entire population of the village crowded onto the rows of benches, or stood three deep around the periphery of the room. Babies cried until their mothers pulled them around front where they could nurse, children chattered, and adults seized the opportunity to converse with friends and neighbors. It was one big party, a day off from working in the fields, with a cooling rain thrown in for good measure. I had to shout the measurements out to Heather, to make myself heard over the cacophony of noise.

The stench in the room was incredible: hundreds of unwashed, sweaty bodies mingled with the ever-present undertones of wood smoke, tobacco, and spices. It was so dark inside the schoolroom that I had to shine a flashlight inside people's mouths, and peer closely, my face right in theirs, in order to count their teeth. Being this up close and personal made people understandably uncomfortable. They guffawed with embarrassment when I looked in their mouths, overwhelming me with the odor of rotting teeth. I had to keep retreating to the door of the schoolroom to compose myself and get some fresh air, to keep from throwing up. Halfway through the morning I gagged once again and turned to Heather in disgust. "I can't stand this anymore. I am absolutely giving up on looking for third molars in adults' mouths."

I was interested in third molar eruption as evidence that rural Malian adults had faces and jaws large enough to comfortably accommodate third molars (wisdom teeth). My hidden agenda was to argue that current understandings of human evolution were skewed, because they took modern Europeans, with their relatively small faces, as the epitome of what "modern humans" looked like. Arguments over interpretations of the fossil record and the date of the first appearance of "modern humans" with "small faces" became irrelevant when the full range of modern humans was appreciated, including particularly West Africans with their large, projecting lower faces and fully operational sets of third molars.

I knew from studies in Magnambougou that most urban adults had beautiful, healthy teeth, including all four third molars, fully erupted and in perfect occlusion. The lack of refined sugar, and the use of traditional tooth-cleaning sticks in many parts of Mali, resulted in few cavities. Every morning, adults walked around with the stub of a tooth-brushing stick protruding from one corner of their mouth. Only particular trees provided "tooth brushes"—sticks that were chewed to a frazzle at one end, then used to scrub and polish the teeth. Chemical analysis of these twigs showed that they had antibiotic and anticavity properties.

Apparently, the knowledge of this traditional mode of dental hygiene never made it to Merediela, and I found myself face-to-face with incredible dental wear, multiple cavities, exposed roots, and draining abscesses. I was familiar with all of these dental conditions from working with prehistoric Native American skeletal material, but I had never really pondered what they would be like in the flesh—what it meant for the living people who had to cope with teeth like that. Now I knew firsthand, and it was not a pretty sight, nor a pleasant smell. "It's no wonder kissing isn't big around here," I quipped, trying to find some humor in the situation. "From now on, I'm only looking in little kids' mouths. Next!"

A middle-aged man dressed in a threadbare pair of Levis shoved a crying child forward. I knelt down to encourage the little boy to step up onto the scales and saw that his leg was wrapped in dirty bandages. He hesitated before lifting his foot and whimpered as he put his weight onto it. "How old is this child?" I asked Heather. She consulted his birth certificate. "Four years old," she answered. By that time, he was crying loudly.

"What's the matter with his leg?" I asked his father.

"He hurt it in a bicycle accident," he said.

I rolled my eyes at Heather. "Let me guess. He was riding on the back fender, without wearing long pants, or shoes, and he got his leg tangled in the spokes." Moussa translated this aside into Bambara, and the man acknowledged that that was exactly what had happened.

Bicycle injuries of this kind were frequent, and they would often result in devastating wounds to children's legs and feet. In the country, children wear few or no clothes, and no shoes. They straddle the backs of rickety bicycles, hanging on behind their father or older brother. A moment's inattention, and they get caught. Bicycle spokes can do nasty things to children's limbs.

The father set the little boy up on the table we were using as a desk, gently unwrapping the filthy dressings. The last few layers were crusted over and had to be teased away, exposing the wound. One glance and I had to turn my head away in horror and dismay. The room suddenly seemed hotter, the air thicker than ever.

The festering wound encompassed the boy's ankle and part of his foot, deep enough to see bone at the bottom. His entire lower leg and foot were swollen and putrid; it was obvious that gangrene had a firm hold.

"When did this happen?" I asked the father.

"About five days ago," he replied.

"How did you treat the wound?"

"We just covered it with this cloth."

"Why didn't you take him to a doctor?"

"We thought it would get better by itself," he said, turning to look pleadingly at the boy's mother.

"You have to take him to the hospital in Sikasso immediately," I explained.

"But we can't afford to," he balked.

"You can't afford not to," I cried in exasperation, turning to Moussa. "He doesn't understand," I said to Moussa. "Please explain to him that the boy is certain to die of gangrene poisoning if he doesn't get to a doctor right away. It may be too late already, but I don't think so. He may just lose his leg." Moussa's eyes widened with alarm. Even he hadn't realized how serious the boy's wounds were. As the father took in what Moussa was saying, his face crumpled.

While the boy's father ran to get his cache of carefully horded coins and bills, I dressed the wound with antibiotic cream and a clean gauze bandage. I gave the boy some chewable children's aspirin, as though it would help. I had to do something constructive. The little boy cringed when I touched him, but he no longer cried. Father and son were last seen leaving Merediela, the boy perched precariously on the back of a worn-out donkey hastily borrowed from a neighbor, while the father trotted alongside, shoulders drooping, urging the donkey to greater speed.

Lunch back at the animatrice's compound provided another opportunity for learning about infant feeding beliefs in rural Mali, through criticism of my own child feeding practices. This time it was a chicken that had given its life for our culinary benefit. As we ate, without even thinking, I reached into the center pile of chicken meat and pulled pieces of meat off the bone. Then I placed them over in Miranda's section of the communal food bowl and encouraged her to eat.

"Why are you giving her chicken?" Bakary asked.

"I want to make sure she gets enough to eat," I replied. "She didn't eat very much porridge for breakfast, because she doesn't like millet."

"But she's just a child. She doesn't need good food. You've been working hard all morning, and she's just been lying around. Besides, if she wanted to eat, she would," he argued.

"It's true that I've been working hard," I admitted, "but she's still growing. Growing children need much more food, proportionately, than adults. And if I didn't encourage her to eat, she might not eat until we get back to Bamako."

Bakary shook his head. "In Dogo," he explained, "people believe that good food is wasted on children. They don't appreciate its good taste or the way it makes you feel. Also, they haven't worked hard to produce the food. They have their whole lives to work for good food for themselves, when they get older. Old people deserve the best food, because they're going to die soon."

"Well, I applaud your respect and honor for the elderly, but health-wise, that's completely wrong. How do you expect children to grow up to be functioning adults if they only get millet or rice to eat?" Of course,

many children don't grow up at all, on this diet. They die from malnutrition, or from diseases such as measles that wouldn't kill a well-nourished child. Studies of the long-term consequences of childhood malnutrition have shown that adults who have survived are functionally impaired when it comes to sustained work effort. They cannot work as long as adults who were not malnourished as children.

In Magnambougou, the prevailing idea in child nutrition was that children alone should decide when, what, and how much they wanted to eat, but they were usually offered whatever was available, including some of the meat and vegetables in the sauce. In rural southern Mali, "good food" (which included all the high protein/high calorie foods) was reserved for elders and other adults. Children subsisted almost entirely on the carbohydrate staples, flavored with a little sauce. My actions in giving Miranda my share of the chicken were viewed as bizarre and misguided—I was wasting good food on a mere child, and depriving myself.

Villagers' reactions to my behaviors were often very enlightening. This conversation was no exception, and I would have liked it to continue. However, it was interrupted by the arrival of a string of children with miscellaneous cuts and scrapes, coming for first aid. I quickly finished eating and went to attend to them. I did what I could with soap and water, antibiotic ointment and Band-Aids. One little boy sat straddling his mother's hip, his arms draped across her shoulders. She showed me an open sore on the back of one of his buttocks.

"What happened here?" I asked his mother.

"He had malaria, so I gave him an injection of Quinimax. Now the malaria is gone, but his leg is sore," she answered.

"But he can walk on it all right?" I asked, taking the boy's hand and leading him around to see if he could still use the leg.

"Oh yes, he can walk fine."

"Where did you get the needle for the shot?" I pressed, as I held the boy down and administered to the sore.

"From a neighbor," she answered.

In Mali, as in many medically underdeveloped places, injections are thought to be more effective than oral medicines. In many cases, the doctor merely prescribes the medicine to be purchased at the pharmacy; it is up to the patient to find a way to have the medicine injected. This often means tracking down a "neighborhood needle" and paying a small fee to borrow the needle. For a little extra, you can get someone to inject the medicine, or you can do it yourself. The needle may be rinsed in water between uses, but it certainly isn't sterilized. The multiple use of needles leads, not uncommonly, to minor infections at the injection site. As AIDS becomes more common in Mali, it will become even more dangerous. But as unsanitary as this method is, it may be better than having the injection done by the doctor at the clinic, as my friend from Magnambougou, Agnes, can attest.

During the rainy season of 1982, Agnes took her one-year-old daughter to the local maternal-child health clinic because she had a bad case of malaria. The doctor gave the infant an injection of Quinimax, a viscous oil-based chloroquine mixture, one of the strongest means of combating malaria. Oral chloroquine tablets probably would have done the job, but injections have that special cachet.

Unfortunately, the doctor, a Malian trained in France, had little understanding of anatomy. Instead of giving the shot into the fat and muscle tissue of the buttocks, or the front of the thigh, he administered it in the back of the thigh, directly into her sciatic nerve. This nerve, as thick as a finger, runs the length of the leg and provides communication between the brain and the leg muscles. Damage to the nerve by the needle had left the little girl crippled.

At one year of age, she had just learned how to walk, but she was immediately reduced to crawling again, dragging her useless leg behind her. Agnes fought back, though, taking her to Kati every month for acupuncture treatments and working with her for long hours every day, trying to strengthen her leg. It took more than a year, but eventually she was able to walk again. As horrible as her experience was, it had worse repercussions beyond her own family.

A few months after the Quinimax crippling episode, the little boy next door to Agnes came down with malaria. His mother faced a choice on her little boy's behalf: malaria or paralysis. He had already survived several bouts of malaria. From her perspective, a trip to the doctor carried a more certain risk of being crippled by an inept injection. She gambled, and kept him at home. She gambled, and lost. This time, he died of malaria.

In N'tenkoni the next morning, we were given use of the men's sacred meeting hut for our measuring session. A round hut about twenty feet in diameter, it had a huge center pole made from the trunk of a tree that held up the thatched roof. Because it had two large doorways, it was light and airy and would provide protection in the event of another thunderstorm.

The roof poles were hung with a variety of objects—a bundle of cow bones above one door, a bundle of corncobs above the other. Numerous boys' circumcision toys were wedged into the rafters. Known as *sistrums*, these wooden toys are made from tree branches and strung with serrated discs made from calabashes. Newly circumcised boys wear special clothing and are allowed to parade through the village shaking the toys. The calabash discs make a loud clacking sound, alerting everyone to the impending arrival of the boys, and people come out to give them small presents in honor of their new status as circumcised boys. I had never seen so many in one place.

There was some initial confusion caused by the fact that people outside couldn't really see what we were doing, and everyone tried to crowd in at once. That was straightened out by the chief, however, and measuring proceeded apace, men, women, children, men, women, children. One family at a time filed into the hut through one door, had their measurements taken, and departed through the other door. It was cool and pleasant inside the hut, in contrast to the hot sun and glare outside. Miranda sat off to one side, reading a book, glancing up from time to time, but generally bored by the whole thing.

"Mommy, look!" she exclaimed in mid-morning. "Isn't that an *angel*?" she asked, using our family's code word for a child with Down syndrome. Down syndrome children are often (though not always!) sweet, happy, and affectionate kids, and many families of children with Down syndrome consider them to be special gifts from God, and refer to them as angels. I turned and followed the direction of Miranda's gaze. A little girl had just entered the hut, part of a large family with many children. She had a small round head, and all the facial characteristics of a child with Down syndrome—"Oriental"-shaped eyes with epicanthic folds, a small flat nose, and small ears. There was no mistaking the diagnosis. Her name was Abi, and she was about four years old, the same age as Peter.

I knelt in front of the little girl. "Hi there, sweetie," I said in English. "Can I have a hug?" I held out my arms, and she willingly stepped forward and gave me a big hug.

I looked up at her mother. "Do you know that there's something 'different' about this child?" I asked, choosing my words carefully.

"Well, she doesn't talk," said her mother, hesitantly, looking at her husband for confirmation. "That's right," he said. "She's never said a word."

"But she's been healthy?" I asked.

"Yes," the father replied. "She's like the other kids, except she doesn't talk. She's always happy. She never cries. We know she can hear, because she does what we tell her to. Why are you so interested in her?"

"Because I know what's the matter with her. I have a son like this." Excitedly, I pulled a picture of Peter out of my bag and showed it to them. They couldn't see the resemblance, though. The difference in skin color swamped the similarities in facial features. But then, Malians think all white people look alike. And it's not true that all kids with Down syndrome look the same. They're "different in the same way," but they look most like their parents and siblings.

"Have you ever met any other children like this?" I inquired, bursting with curiosity about how rural Malian culture dealt with a condition as infrequent as Down syndrome. Children with Down syndrome are rare to begin with, occurring about once in every 700 births. In a community where 30 or 40 children are born each year at the most, a child with Down syndrome might be born only once in twenty years. And many of them would not survive long enough for anyone to be able to tell that they were different. Physical defects along the midline of the body (heart, trachea, intestines) are common among kids with Down syndrome; without immediate surgery and neonatal intensive care, many would not survive. Such surgery is routine in American children's hospitals, but nonexistent in rural Mali. For the child without any major physical defects, there are still the perils of rural Malian life to survive: malaria, measles, diarrhea, diphtheria, and polio. Some, like Peter, have poor immune systems, making them even more susceptible to childhood diseases. The odds against finding a child with Down syndrome, surviving and healthy in a rural Malian village, are overwhelming.

Not surprisingly, the parents knew of no other children like Abi. They asked if I knew of any medicine that could cure her. "No," I explained, "this condition can't be cured. But she will learn to talk, just give her time. Talk to her a lot. Try to get her to repeat things you say. And give her lots of love and attention. It may take her longer to learn some things, but keep trying. In my country, some people say these children are special gifts from God." There was no way I could explain cells and chromosomes and nondisjunction to them, even with Moussa's help. And how, I thought to myself, would that have helped them anyway? They just accepted her as she was.

We chatted for a few more minutes, and I measured the whole family, including Abi, who was, of course, short for her age. I gave her one last hug and a balloon and sent her out the door after her siblings. I turned to Moussa and Heather and said, "Guys, I need a break. I'll be right back."

I walked out of the hut, past the long line of villagers waiting patiently for their turn to be measured. They turned to stare as I passed. I went behind the animatrice's compound and sat down on a fallen log. I took several deep breaths, trying to get my emotions under control. Finally I gave in, hugged my knees close to my chest, and sobbed. I cried for Abi—what a courageous heart she must have; just think what she might have achieved given all the modern infant stimulation programs available in the West. I cried for Peter—another courageous heart; just think of what he might achieve given the chance to live in a culture that simply accepted him, rather than stereotyping and pigeonholing him, constraining him because people didn't think he was capable of more. I cried for myself—not very courageous at all; my heart felt as though it would burst with longing for Peter, my own sweet angel.

There was clearly some truth to the old adage that ignorance is bliss. Maybe pregnant women in Mali had to worry about evil spirits lurking in the latrine at night, but they didn't spend their pregnancies worrying about chromosomal abnormalities, the moral implications of amniocentesis, or the heart-wrenching exercise of trying to evaluate handicaps, deciding which ones made life not worth living. Women in the United States might have the freedom to choose not to give birth to children with handicaps, but women in Mali had freedom from worrying about it. Children in the United States had the freedom to attend special programs to help them overcome their handicaps, but children in Mali had freedom from the biggest handicap of all—other people's prejudice.

I had cried myself dry. I splashed my face with cool water from the bucket inside the kitchen and returned to the task at hand.

PART 2

The Nature of Science

An important part of bioanthropology's identity is the fact that it is a scientific study of the human species. Science is that method of inquiry that requires the generation, testing, and acceptance or rejection of hypotheses. The goal is to produce answers to questions about the world around us (and within us) and to describe that world. A hypothesis that is thought to accurately describe and account for some set of natural phenomena is called a theory.

In "Sex, Drugs, Disasters, and the Extinction of Dinosaurs," Stephen Jay Gould describes the scientific method by applying it to three hypotheses offered to explain the dinosaurs' demise. The application of the scientific method to a famous problem within bioanthropology is covered by archaeologist Kenneth L. Feder in "Piltdown, Paradigms, and the Paranormal." In "Science as a Way of Knowing," John A. Moore contrasts science with other methods of inquiry and places science in its context as a cultural endeavor.

SUGGESTED WEBSITES FOR FURTHER STUDY

http://home.tiac.net/~cri_a/piltdown/piltdown.html
http://www.csicop.org
http://highered.mcgraw-hill.com/sites/076742722x

5

Sex, Drugs, Disasters, and the Extinction of Dinosaurs

Stephen Jay Gould

Until his death in 2002, Stephen Jay Gould was the Alexander Agassiz Professor of zoology and professor of geology at Harvard and an honorary curator in invertebrates at the American Museum of Natural History in New York. For over twenty years, he wrote a monthly column for Natural History *magazine (never missing a month). In addition to nine books of collections of these columns (with a few from other journals), Gould authored, edited, or contributed to numerous others. Gould was generally considered one of the finest minds in evolutionary science and was certainly one of the best contemporary science essayists. Three pieces by him appear in this book; for many topics in evolution, nobody says it better.*

Many ideas quite seriously proposed to explain some phenomenon of nature seem at first so logically sound that we might easily consider them reasonable scientific hypotheses. But for a hypothesis to be scientific, it must be testable—it must be *possible* to obtain evidence both in support of and in refutation of it. Otherwise, no testing is possible and the idea is simply speculation, having no value in real scientific endeavors. Among the great scientific mysteries for which both reasonable and speculative explanations have been proposed is the extinction of the dinosaurs (and many other organisms) 65 million years ago. In this selection, Stephen Jay Gould examines three such explanations, showing that two can only be speculation, while the third, whether it eventually proves to be supported or not, is scientifically testable. It should be noted that since Gould first wrote this essay, sufficient evidence has accumulated for the "disaster" explanation that it is now well accepted.

As you read, consider the following questions:

1. What is the difference between a scientific hypothesis and a speculation? How do the concepts of truth and falsity relate to this difference?

2. Why are the "sex" and "drugs" explanations not scientific? What, on the other hand, is the evidence for the "disaster" account?

Science, in its most fundamental definition, is a fruitful mode of inquiry, not a list of enticing conclusions. The conclusions are the consequence, not the essence.

My greatest unhappiness with most popular presentations of science concerns their failure to separate fascinating claims from the methods that scientists use to establish the facts of nature. Journalists, and the public, thrive on controversial and stunning statements. But science is, basically, a way of knowing—in P. B. Medawar's apt words, "the art of the soluble." If the growing corps of popular science writers would focus on *how* scientists develop and defend those fascinating claims, they would make their greatest possible contribution to public understanding.

Consider three ideas, proposed in perfect seriousness to explain that greatest of all titillating puzzles—the extinction of dinosaurs. Since these three notions invoke the primally fascinating themes of our culture—sex, drugs, and violence—they surely reside in the category of fascinating claims. I want to show why two of them rank as silly speculation, while the other represents science at its grandest and most useful.

Science works with testable proposals. If, after much compilation and scrutiny of data, new information continues to affirm a hypothesis, we may accept it provisionally and gain confidence as further evidence mounts. We can never be completely sure that a hypothesis is right, though we may be able to show with confidence that it is wrong. The best scientific hypotheses are also generous and expansive: they suggest extensions and implications that enlighten related, and even far distant, subjects. Simply consider how the idea of evolution has influenced virtually every intellectual field.

Useless speculation, on the other hand, is restrictive. It generates no testable hypothesis, and offers no way to obtain potentially refuting evidence. Please note that I am not speaking of truth or falsity. The speculation may well be true; still, if it provides, in principle, no material for affirmation or rejection, we can make nothing of it. It must simply stand forever as an intriguing idea. Useless speculation turns in on itself and leads nowhere; good science, containing both seeds for its potential refutation and implications for more and different testable knowledge, reaches out. But, enough preaching. Let's move on to dinosaurs, and the three proposals for their extinction.

1. Sex: Testes function only in a narrow range of temperature (those of mammals hang externally in a scrotal sac because internal body temperatures are too high for their proper function). A worldwide rise in temperature at the close of the Cretaceous period caused the testes of dinosaurs to stop functioning and led to their extinction by sterilization of males.

2. Drugs: Angiosperms (flowering plants) first evolved toward the end of the dinosaurs' reign. Many of these plants contain psychoactive agents, avoided by mammals today as a result of their bitter taste. Dinosaurs had neither means to taste the bitterness nor livers effective enough to detoxify the substances. They died of massive overdoses.

3. Disasters: A large comet or asteroid struck the earth some 65 million years ago, lofting a cloud of dust into the sky and blocking sunlight, thereby suppressing photosynthesis and so drastically lowering world temperatures that dinosaurs and hosts of other creatures became extinct.

Before analyzing these three tantalizing statements, we must establish a basic ground rule often violated in proposals for the dinosaurs' demise. *There is no separate problem of the extinction of dinosaurs.* Too often we divorce specific events from their wider contexts and systems of cause and effect. The fundamental fact of dinosaur extinction is its synchrony with the demise of so many other groups across a wide range of habitats, from terrestrial to marine.

The history of life has been punctuated by brief episodes of mass extinction. [An] analysis by University of Chicago paleontologists Jack Sepkoski and Dave Raup, based on the best and most exhaustive tabulation of data ever assembled, shows clearly that five episodes of mass dying stand well above the "background" extinctions of normal times (when we consider all mass extinctions, large and small, they seem to fall in a regular 26-million-year cycle). The Cretaceous debacle, occurring 65 million years ago and separating the Mesozoic and Cenozoic eras of our geological time scale, ranks prominently among the five. Nearly all the marine plankton (single-celled floating creatures) died with geological suddenness; among marine invertebrates, nearly 15 percent of all families perished, including many previously dominant groups, especially the ammonites (relatives of squids in coiled shells). On land, the dinosaurs disappeared after more than 100 million years of unchallenged domination.

In this context, speculations limited to dinosaurs alone ignore the larger phenomenon. We need a coordinated explanation for a system of events that includes the extinction of dinosaurs as one component. Thus it makes little sense, though it may fuel our desire to view mammals as inevitable inheritors of the earth, to guess that dinosaurs died because small mammals ate their eggs (a perennial favorite among untestable speculations). It seems most unlikely that some disaster peculiar to dinosaurs befell these massive beasts—and that the debacle happened to strike just when one of history's five great dyings had enveloped the earth for completely different reasons.

The testicular theory, an old favorite from the 1940s, had its root in an interesting and thoroughly respectable study of temperature tolerances in the American alligator, published in the staid *Bulletin of the American Museum of Natural History* in 1946 by three experts on living and fossil reptiles—E. H. Colbert, my own first teacher in paleontology; R. B. Cowles; and C. M. Bogert.

The first sentence of their summary reveals a purpose beyond alligators: "This report describes an attempt to infer the reactions of extinct reptiles, especially the dinosaurs, to high temperatures as based upon reactions observed in the modern alligator." They studied, by rectal thermometry, the body temperatures of alligators under changing conditions of heating and cooling. (Well, let's face it, you wouldn't want to try sticking a thermometer under a 'gator's tongue.) The predictions under test go way back to an old theory first stated by Galileo in the 1630s—the unequal scaling of surfaces and volumes. As an animal, or any object, grows (provided its shape doesn't change), surface areas must increase more slowly than volumes—since surfaces get larger as length squared, while volumes increase much more rapidly, as length cubed. Therefore, small animals have high ratios of surface to volume, while large animals cover themselves with relatively little surface.

Among cold-blooded animals lacking a physiological mechanism for keeping their temperatures constant, small creatures have a hell of a time keeping warm—because they lose so much heat through their relatively large surfaces. On the other hand, large animals, with their relatively small surfaces, may lose heat so slowly that, once warm, they may maintain effectively constant temperatures against ordinary fluctuations of climate. (In fact, the resolution of the "hot-blooded dinosaur" controversy that burned so brightly a few years back may simply be that, while large dinosaurs possessed no physiological mechanism for constant temperature, and were not therefore warm-blooded in the technical sense, their large size and relatively small surface area kept them warm.)

Colbert, Cowles, and Bogert compared the warming rates of small and large alligators. As predicted, the small fellows heated up (and cooled down) more quickly. When exposed to a warm sun, a tiny 50-gram (1.76-ounce) alligator heated up one degree Celsius every minute and a half, while a large alligator, 260 times bigger at 13,000 grams (28.7 pounds), took seven and a half minutes to gain a degree. Extrapolating up to an adult 10-ton dinosaur, they concluded that a one-degree rise in body temperature would take eighty-six hours. If large animals absorb heat so slowly (through their relatively small surfaces), they will also be unable to shed any excess heat gained when temperatures rise above a favorable level.

The authors then guessed that large dinosaurs lived at or near their optimum temperatures; Cowles suggested that a rise in global temperatures just before the Cretaceous extinction caused the dinosaurs to heat up beyond their optimal tolerance—and, being so large, they couldn't shed the unwanted heat. (In a most unusual statement within a scientific paper, Colbert and Bogert then explicitly disavowed this speculative extension of their empirical work on alligators.) Cowles conceded that this excess heat probably wasn't enough to kill or even to enervate the great beasts, but since testes often function only within a narrow range of temperature, he proposed that this global rise might have sterilized all the males, causing extinction by natural contraception.

The overdose theory has recently been supported by UCLA psychiatrist Ronald K. Siegel. Siegel has gathered, he claims, more than 2,000 records of animals who, when given access, administer various drugs to themselves—from a mere swig of alcohol to massive doses of the big H. Elephants will swill the equivalent of twenty beers at a time, but do not like alcohol in concentrations greater than 7 percent. In a silly bit of anthropocentric speculation, Siegel states that "elephants drink, perhaps, to forget . . . the anxiety produced by shrinking rangeland and the competition for food."

Since fertile imaginations can apply almost any hot idea to the extinction of dinosaurs, Siegel found a way. Flowering plants did not evolve until late in the dinosaurs' reign. These plants also produced an array of aromatic, amino-acid-based alkaloids—the major group of psychoactive agents. Most mammals are "smart" enough to avoid these potential poisons. The alkaloids simply don't taste good (they are bitter); in any case, we mammals have livers happily supplied with the capacity to detoxify them. But, Siegel speculates, perhaps dinosaurs could neither taste the bitterness nor detoxify the substances once ingested. He recently told members of the American Psychological Association: "I'm not suggesting that all dinosaurs OD'd on plant drugs, but it certainly was a factor." He also argued that death by overdose may help explain why so many dinosaur fossils are found in contorted positions. (Do not go gentle into that good night.)

Extraterrestrial catastrophes have long pedigrees in the popular literature of extinction, but the subject exploded again in 1979, after a long lull, when the father-son, physicist-geologist team of Luis and Walter Alvarez proposed that an asteroid, some 10 km in diameter, struck the earth 65 million years ago (comets, rather than asteroids, have since gained favor. . . . Good science is self-corrective).

The force of such a collision would be immense, greater by far than the megatonnage of all the world's nuclear weapons. In trying to reconstruct a scenario that would explain the simultaneous dying of dinosaurs on land and so many creatures in the sea, the Alvarezes proposed that a gigantic dust cloud, generated by particles blown aloft in the impact, would so darken the earth that photosynthesis would cease and temperatures drop precipitously. (Rage, rage against the dying of the light.) The single-celled photosynthetic oceanic plankton, with life cycles measured in weeks, would perish outright, but land plants might survive through the dormancy of their seeds (land plants were not much affected by the Cretaceous extinction, and any adequate theory must account for the curious pattern of differential survival). Dinosaurs would die by starvation and freezing; small, warm-blooded mammals, with more modest requirements for food and better regulation of body temperature, would squeak through. "Let the bastards freeze in the dark," as bumper stickers of our chauvinistic neighbors in sun-belt states proclaimed several years ago during the Northeast's winter oil crisis.

All three theories, testicular malfunction, psychoactive overdosing, and asteroidal zapping, grab our attention mightily. As pure phenomenology, they rank about equally high on any hit parade of primal fascination. Yet one represents expansive science, the others restrictive and untestable speculation. The proper criterion lies in evidence and methodology; we must probe behind the superficial fascination of particular claims.

How could we possibly decide whether the hypothesis of testicular frying is right or wrong? We would have to know things that the fossil record cannot provide. What temperatures were optimal for dinosaurs? Could they avoid the absorption of excess heat by staying in the shade, or in caves? At what temperatures did their testicles cease to function? Were late Cretaceous climates ever warm enough to drive the internal temperatures of dinosaurs close to this ceiling? Testicles simply don't fossilize, and how could we infer their temperature tolerances even if they did? In short, Cowles's hypothesis is only an intriguing speculation leading nowhere. The most damning statement against it appeared right in the conclusion of Colbert, Cowles, and Bogert's paper, when they admitted: "It is difficult to advance any definite arguments against this hypothesis." My statement may seem paradoxical—isn't a hypothesis really good if you can't devise any arguments against it? Quite the contrary. It is simply untestable and unusable.

Siegel's overdosing has even less going for it. At least Cowles extrapolated his conclusion from some good data on alligators. And he didn't completely violate the primary guideline of siting dinosaur extinction in the context of a general mass dying—for rise in temperature could be the root cause of a general catastrophe, zapping dinosaurs by testicular malfunction and different groups for other reasons. But Siegel's speculation cannot touch the extinction of ammonites or oceanic plankton (diatoms make their own food with good sweet sunlight; they don't OD on the chemicals of terrestrial plants). It is simply a gratuitous, attention-grabbing guess. It cannot be tested, for how can we know what dinosaurs tasted and what their livers could do? Livers don't fossilize any better than testicles.

The hypothesis doesn't even make any sense in its own context. Angiosperms were in full flower ten million years before dinosaurs went the way of all flesh. Why did it take so long? As for the pains of a chemical death recorded in contortions of fossils, I regret to say (or rather I'm pleased to note for the dinosaurs' sake) that Siegel's knowledge of geology must be a bit

deficient: muscles contract after death and geological strata rise and fall with motions of the earth's crust after burial—more than enough reason to distort a fossil's pristine appearance.

The impact story, on the other hand, has a sound basis in evidence. It can be tested, extended, refined and, if wrong, disproved. The Alvarezes did not just construct an arresting guess for public consumption. They proposed their hypothesis after laborious geochemical studies with Frank Asaro and Helen Michael had revealed a massive increase of iridium in rocks deposited right at the time of extinction. Iridium, a rare metal of the platinum group, is virtually absent from indigenous rocks of the earth's crust; most of our iridium arrives on extraterrestrial objects that strike the earth.

The Alvarez hypothesis bore immediate fruit. Based originally on evidence from two European localities, it led geochemists throughout the world to examine other sediments of the same age. They found abnormally high amounts of iridium everywhere—from continental rocks of the western United States to deep sea cores from the South Atlantic.

Cowles proposed his testicular hypothesis in the mid-1940s. Where has it gone since then? Absolutely nowhere, because scientists can do nothing with it. The hypothesis must stand as a curious appendage to a solid study of alligators. Siegel's overdose scenario will also win a few press notices and fade into oblivion. The Alvarezes' asteroid falls into a different category altogether, and much of the popular commentary has missed this essential distinction by focusing on the impact and its attendant results, and forgetting what really matters to a scientist—the iridium. If you talk just about asteroids, dust, and darkness, you tell stories no better and no more entertaining than fried testicles or terminal trips. It is the iridium—the source of testable evidence—that counts and forges the crucial distinction between speculation and science.

The proof, to twist a phrase, lies in the doing. Cowles's hypothesis has generated nothing in thirty-five years. Since its proposal in 1979, the Alvarez hypothesis has spawned hundreds of studies, a major conference, and attendant publications. Geologists are fired up. They are looking for iridium at all other extinction boundaries. Every week exposes a new wrinkle in the scientific press. Further evidence that the Cretaceous iridium represents extraterrestrial impact and not indigenous volcanism continues to accumulate. As I revise this essay in November 1984 (this paragraph will be out of date when the book is published), new data include chemical "signatures" of other isotopes indicating unearthly provenance, glass spherules of a size and sort produced by impact and not by volcanic eruptions, and high-pressure varieties of silica formed (so far as we know) only under the tremendous shock of impact.

My point is simply this: Whatever the eventual outcome (I suspect it will be positive), the Alvarez hypothesis is exciting, fruitful science because it generates tests, provides us with things to do, and expands outward. We are having fun, battling back and forth, moving toward a resolution, and extending the hypothesis beyond its original scope.

As just one example of the unexpected, distant cross-fertilization that good science engenders, the Alvarez hypothesis made a major contribution to a theme that has riveted public attention in the past few months—so-called nuclear winter. In a speech delivered in April 1982, Luis Alvarez calculated the energy that a ten-kilometer asteroid would release on impact. He compared such an explosion with a full nuclear exchange and implied that all-out atomic war might unleash similar consequences.

This theme of impact leading to massive dust clouds and falling temperatures formed an important input to the decision of Carl Sagan and a group of colleagues to model the climatic consequences of nuclear holocaust. Full nuclear exchange would probably generate the same kind of dust cloud and darkening that may have wiped out the dinosaurs. Temperatures would drop precipitously and agriculture might become impossible. Avoidance of nuclear war is fundamentally an ethical and political imperative, but we must know the factual consequences to make firm judgments. I am heartened by a final link across disciplines and deep concerns—another criterion, by the way, of science at its best*: A recognition of the very phenomenon that made our evolution possible by exterminating the previously dominant dinosaurs and clearing a way for the evolution of large mammals, including us, might actually help to save us from joining those magnificent beasts in contorted poses among the strata of the earth.

---

*This quirky connection so tickles my fancy that I break my own strict rule about eliminating redundancies from these essays and end . . . this . . . piece with this prod to thought and action.

6

Piltdown, Paradigms, and the Paranormal

Kenneth L. Feder

Kenneth L. Feder is professor of anthropology at Central Connecticut State University. He is director of the Farmington River Archaeological Project and the author of six anthropology textbooks and numerous articles. Among his interests is the nature and application of scientific inquiry, especially with regard to matters in anthropology. He is a recognized authority on pseudoscientific claims within the subfield of archaeology. Ken Feder and I have coauthored one text and several articles.

Science, as Stephen Jay Gould pointed out in Selection 5, might search for objective reality, but science is, at the same time, conducted within a cultural environment. Expectations and, especially, the fulfillment of those expectations can color scientific judgment. Scientists, in other words, can make mistakes. They can even be fooled. And yet, in the end, the self-testing, questioning, skeptical, critical nature of science wins out. Wrong ideas are replaced; frauds are unmasked. In this selection, Ken Feder tells the story of the Piltdown fraud—often used as evidence of the fallibility of science and the gullibility of scientists, but really a tale of the triumph of science over preconceptions and even conscious deception.

As you read, consider the following questions:

1. On what preconceptions were the concoction of the Piltdown "fossil" and its acceptance based?
2. What was the paradigm, based on increasing evidence, that Piltdown contradicted?

"Piltdown, Paradigms, and the Paranormal" by Kenneth Feder, *Skeptical Inquirer*, Summer 1990, Vol. 14. Used by permission of the Skeptical Enquirer magazine. (text and illustrations)

Pseudoscience is a polymorphous enterprise; the range of pseudoscientific claims is enormous. The world would be far different from what orthodox science supposes if there were substantive validity to the assertions of psychics, astrologers, clairvoyants, past-life therapists, UFOlogists, ancient-astronaut enthusiasts, dowsers, creationists, pyramidologists, crystal boosters, faith healers, and the holders of myriad other beliefs in the paranormal, occult, and supernatural.

The claims made by the proponents of these various phenomena or perspectives are more than merely extreme. They, to varying degrees, fundamentally challenge existing paradigms—the ways we view the world around us or some specific aspect of the universe or reality. Within the framework of scientific discourse, however, it cannot be said that the claims made by parapsychologists and occultists are impossible simply because they sound improbable or because acceptance would alter the way we view reality. Certainly concerned scientists need to assess individual cases. The pages of this journal have seen many successful attempts to show specifically *why* some of these claims are pseudoscientific.

As Al Seckel (1989) has pointed out, however, refuting or debunking individual claims, though important, is simply not enough. There are always other claims. Refuting the myth of the Bermuda Triangle, for example, does not necessarily lead to a recognition of the pseudoscience in UFOlogy or claims of ancient astronauts.

Perhaps it is just as important, for those of us committed to skeptical inquiry, to show how science works, how it handles new, revolutionary claims, paranormal or otherwise. We need to ask: On what basis do our paradigms in science stand or fall? In so doing, we can show that scientists handle the claims made in pseudoscience no differently from the way they treat other claims that challenge current understanding of the universe.

On this topic, the early history of human evolutionary theory provides an excellent model for how science deals with claims that purport to topple our existing paradigms. I present it in the hope that others might find it useful in their discussions of the nature of scientific reasoning, especially when scientists are faced with emotional adherence to particular views, wishful thinking, or outright deception.

UPRIGHT APES OR FOUR-LEGGED HUMANS?

After the publication of Darwin's *Origin of Species* in 1859, many thinkers applied the idea of natural selection to a species that Darwin did not focus on in that work; they applied Darwin's theory to human beings. With very little fossil evidence to go on, they constructed a plausible scenario.

Biological taxonomists had long recognized the physical similarity between humans and other primates, in particular the apes. What most differentiates humans from other primates is our intelligence, made possible by large and very complex brains. The human brain was the aspect of our species that appeared to be the most changed—the most highly evolved—when compared with some hypothetical species ancestral to us and the apes. Our intelligence, it was argued, must therefore have begun to evolve before other of our uniquely human traits. So, fossil ancestors of our species were expected to show development of a humanlike brain first, with an apelike body lagging behind evolutionarily. As writer Charles Blinderman points out, such researchers as English anatomist Grafton Elliot Smith were quite explicit in predicting the discovery of human ancestors with large brains and primitive bodies (1986:36). Later, Smith went so far as to characterize early man as "merely an Ape with an overgrown brain" (1927:105–106). The paradigm of brain-centered evolution suited the sensibilities of the late nineteenth and early twentieth centuries: if we were indeed cousin to the ape, at least it had been our brains that first distinguished us from our common ancestor.

The fossil record, however, was not sympathetic to this scenario. The Neandertal finds in the second half of the nineteenth century and the discovery of Java Man in 1891 both showed a fossil ancestor virtually modern from the neck *down* and primitive from the neck up—the reverse of the expectation. Needless to say, this caused some confusion among researchers.

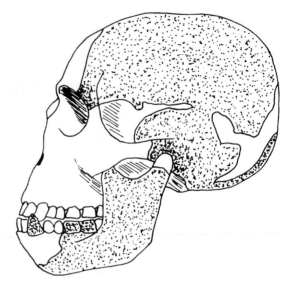

FIGURE 1 Reconstruction of the Piltdown skull. Stippled areas represent fossil fragments actually recovered. The cranium is large, with a round profile and steep forehead, as in modern *Homo sapiens*. The jaw, on the other hand, is quite apelike, with no chin and a shape that required a prognathic (forward thrust), apelike face.

Some initially tried to explain away these inconvenient data. For a time, Neandertal reconstructions were fudged to make them appear more apelike. As evidence mounted, however, and as committed as some were to the paradigm of brain-centered evolution, many adopted a paradigm in which upright posture significantly predated development of the modern human brain. They didn't like it, but they had little choice; it was what the evidence showed. The view that humanity began its evolutionary history as an upright ape rather than a four-legged human became increasingly popular at the end of the nineteenth and beginning of the twentieth centuries as more and more fossil evidence seemed to confirm this perspective.

Thus was the stage set for the announcement published in the British journal *Nature* on December 5, 1912, of the discovery of an important human fossil in Sussex at a place called Piltdown, in southern England. (See Weiner 1955, Millar 1972, and Blinderman 1986 for detailed treatments of the Piltdown story; see also Feder 2002.) The discovery consisted of a skull and lower jaw that seemed to confirm, not the prevailing, but the original paradigm; the cranium itself seemed indistinguishable from that of a modern human but the jaw was quite primitive and apelike (Figure 1). This fossil appeared to date from a geological period earlier than that ascribed to Neandertal, and at least as old as that of Java Man.

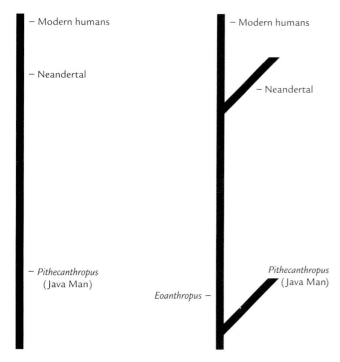

FIGURE 2 Without *Eoanthropus* (Piltdown Man), some placed *Pithecanthropus* (Java Man) and Neandertal in an evolutionary sequence leading directly to modern humanity (*left*). With *Eoanthropus*, many viewed *Pithecanthropus* and *Neandertal* as evolutionary dead ends (*right*). In this view, only *Eoanthropus* was directly ancestral to modern human beings.

Many researchers, some quite well known, seized upon the discovery at Piltdown. They saw Piltdown Man—which was called *Eoanthropus dawsoni*, or Dawson's Dawn Man, after its discoverer, Charles Dawson—as the true human ancestor. The Java and Neandertal specimens with their more primitive brains were viewed, therefore, as extinct offshoots of the main line of human evolution in which *Eoanthropus* stood at the base (Figure 2). Thus, at least for some, the older and preferred paradigm seemed reestablished; in human evolution it had been the brain, after all, that evolved into the modern form first, with the body, virtually from the lower jaw down, playing evolutionary catchup later on.

Clearly, *Eoanthropus* would overturn the existing paradigm that had seemed to be so well supported by fossil evidence accumulated over about 50 years, but only if subsequent research provided additional support for the notion of a brain-centered focus for early human evolution. One bit of enigmatic data, no matter how apparently compelling, cannot cause us to abandon well-supported views of human evolution—or, I might add, cosmogeny or human perception.

The years following Dawson's discovery saw many looking for additional evidence in the form of fossils similar to *Eoanthropus*. The famous excavations at the Chinese cave at Zhoukoudian, in which some 40 individuals of "Peking Man" were discovered, were, at least in part, an attempt to validate the discovery at Piltdown (Shapiro 1974). Anatomist Davidson Black, of the Peking Union Medical College, who for a time led the excavations, apparently had been inspired to dig at Zhoukoudian by a visit to the lab of Grafton Elliot Smith, a well-known supporter of *Eoanthropus*. The Jesuit priest and paleontologist Teilhard de Chardin, who had excavated at Piltdown after its initial discovery, also worked at Zhoukoudian. So, when they started excavation there in the 1920s they were looking for the Chinese equivalent of Piltdown Man. They got, instead, fossils with humanlike bodies and brains just two-thirds the mean size of the modern human brain.

Interestingly, with so many looking for confirming evidence, only one researcher was able to find a fossil that seemed to mirror the Piltdown discovery and, therefore, support its interpretation. That researcher was Charles Dawson, the discoverer of the original. It did little to validate the initial discovery. It only raised questions at the same time his apparent incredible luck raised eyebrows.

As the search for anything vaguely resembling *Eoanthropus* progressed, data continued to accumulate supporting the existing paradigm. More Neandertal discoveries were made and more fossils resembling Java Man and Peking Man (now called *Homo erectus*) were found. Beginning in the late 1920s an even older, more primitive and smaller-brained hominid species was discovered in Africa. Called *Australopithecus*, it provided rather forceful, further validation of the existing paradigm; this oldest of ancestral human fossils, then thought to be a million years old and now known to have varieties dating to more than 3.5 million years ago, possessed a brain less than one-third the modern human mean, but was fully upright. Even the earliest members of the genus are quite similar to modern humans from the neck down.

After the third decade of the twentieth century, *Eoanthropus* went from being a major concern of those interested in human evolutionary history to a cautionary footnote in evolution texts, where it went as an unexplained, enigmatic, anomalistic, and contradictory piece of data. This remained the case until a reexamination of the Piltdown fossil in the late 1940s and early 1950s showed that the modern-looking cranium and the apelike mandible were of entirely different ages, neither was particularly old, and the apelike quality of the lower jaw had a very simple explanation; it was, in fact, that of a modern ape and had been cleverly crafted to appear to fit the skull. Piltdown Man could overturn no paradigms. It was a fraud.

THE MEANING OF PILTDOWN

Many perceive the Piltdown story as a black mark against science. In fact, it shows how well science eventually sorts out frauds, mistakes, and wishful thinking. It clearly shows how science does react and must react when existing, well-supported paradigms are challenged by new data.

While lending apparent support for a cherished view of how human evolution had proceeded, Piltdown contradicted notions of human evolution based on a substantial body of data. Nevertheless, it could have been a valid discovery and could have served to overturn the existing, seemingly well-supported paradigm. But, as others have said before, extreme claims require extreme levels of proof or validation.

In the case of Piltdown, the claim challenged merely the existing paradigm of human evolution. This was significant enough and required an extreme level of validation—though, of course, none was forthcoming. In the case of, for example, parapsychology, existing paradigms in human psychology, neurology, anthropology, biology, and even physics are being challenged. So be it. Our paradigms indeed may be wrong, and the parapsychologists and the rest may be right, though it is significant that research conducted over the past hundred years has not shown this to the satisfaction of many scientists.

Moreover, the Piltdown story should put to rest the notion that science is inflexible and scientists closed-minded. Concepts concerning the pathways taken in human evolution changed and continue to change as evidence is collected. The changes in our views are not cyclical or random, but progressive. Though individual scientists may be swayed by personal biases, wishful thinking, or peer pressure, data cannot be explained away for very long. By and large, evolutionary scientists did not want to abandon a brain-centered view of evolution, but they did when evidence indicated that upright posture was much older than brain expansion. Some may have been fooled by Piltdown and returned to the brain-centered view of human evolution. However, with so much subsequent evidence supporting the view that humanity evolved, in a sense, from the ground up, Piltdown became trivial, even before it was finally proved fraudulent.

Paleontological skeptics in the early years of the twentieth century were certainly justified in asking for more than a single, seemingly inexplicable piece of evidence before evolutionary paradigms were rewritten. The scientific skeptics among us are similarly justified in asking for something more than has been provided before we overturn our view of reality. Until then, claimed evidence for ESP, telekinesis, clairvoyance, and the rest will remain the equivalent of *Eoanthropus dawsoni*.

ACKNOWLEDGMENTS

A preliminary version of this paper was presented at the Tenth Annual Griffiths Memorial Lecture at Drexel University in Philadelphia. I am grateful to my colleagues there for their comments. I also thank Michael Alan Park of the Department of Anthropology, Central Connecticut State University, for his suggestions.

REFERENCES

Blinderman, Charles. 1986. *The Piltdown Inquest*. Buffalo, N.Y.: Prometheus Books.

Feder, Kenneth L. 2002. *Frauds, Myths, and Mysteries: Science and Pseudoscience in Archaeology*, 4th ed. New York: McGraw-Hill.

Millar, Ronald. 1972. *The Piltdown Men*. New York: Ballantine Books.

Seckel, Al. 1989. Rather Than Just Debunking, Encourage People to Think. SKEPTICAL INQUIRER, 13:300–304.

Shapiro, Harry. 1974. *Peking Man*. New York: Simon and Schuster.

Smith, Grafton Elliot. 1927. *Essays on the Evolution of Man*. London: Oxford University Press.

Weiner, J. S. 1955. *The Piltdown Forgery*. London: Oxford University Press.

7

Science as a Way of Knowing

John A. Moore

John A. Moore (1915–2002) was professor emeritus of biology at the University of California, Riverside. He was a specialist in genetics and development and author of several textbooks.

"Science," says John A. Moore, "is the most powerful mechanism we have for obtaining confirmable information about the natural world." And yet, science is not the only method of inquiry, not the only way of knowing. Moreover, science is not something separate from the people who practice it and the society and culture within which they do so. In this selection, Moore discusses how science is contrasted with, yet related to, other ways of knowing and how the "state of society" influences and limits scientific inquiry.

As you read, consider the following questions:

1. What is the basic assumption of the sciences about the natural world?
2. What are essential processes in the scientific method?
3. How does science deal with the supernatural in its explanations of the natural world?
4. How are the investigations of scientific problems related to a social context?
5. In what ways is science "self-correcting"?

As the twentieth century stands down, we have a depth of understanding of that most distinctive and puzzling feature of life—its ability to self-replicate—that is satisfying to almost everyone, scientist and non-scientist alike. The answer to that puzzle is fairly simple: the basic units of life are cells, and self-replication involves the production of new cells. We have general answers not only for how cells can replicate but also how cells differentiate in the development of individuals and how the basis of evolution is built into the mechanisms for cell reproduction through errors in the replication of DNA.

Is the science of biology finished? Hardly. The concepts that inform our understanding, now mainly at the level of populations, whole organisms, and cells—holistic biology, if you will—are being revolutionized by discoveries at the molecular level. Events within cells, once a veritable black box, are now being explained in terms of specific chemical reactions. The

contributions of molecular biology to evolution are to be found in the ability to make detailed comparisons of the genetic makeup of individuals of different species and, therefore, to better understand relationships and phylogenies. It is even proving possible to extract DNA from the fossil remains of organisms that lived many millions of years ago and compare it with the DNA of living creatures. And for genetics itself, molecular probes are providing details about the architecture of genes and increasingly exact data about how the information built into the structure of genes is used to produce the substances, and to control the activities, within cells. This knowledge is providing a far better understanding of development. Now it is possible to specify when genes are turned on and off and thus to relate gene products to developmental events.

Some look upon this new knowledge from molecular biology with dread because soon we will be able to manipulate life in ways never before possible. Already genes can be transferred from one individual to another, and this raises profound ethical problems that many might prefer not to consider. But knowledge in itself cannot be bad: it has the potential for being either threat or opportunity. Which it becomes depends on who uses it and for what purpose. In short, human beings remain in control.

The answers to the fundamental questions of biology are so extraordinary that it is of interest to consider the methods by which they were obtained. In the last century these methods have given us a world dominated by science and its operational companion, technology. It is important, therefore, to inquire why science has become so powerful and pervasive in our lives. What is unique about science as a way of knowing compared with other ways of knowing?

Science is both knowledge of the natural world expressed in naturalistic terms and the procedures for obtaining that knowledge. The scientific way of knowing is not the only way of knowing and, for most of human history, it has not been the dominant mode. What it is can be best understood by first describing what it is not. From the earliest of times the dominant mode has been to "explain" natural things and processes as consequences of supernatural forces: sickness is due to divine wrath; all animals and plants were created by a deity; drought and sickness can be ended by prayer; lightning is a thunderbolt of Zeus; the sun is Apollo and his fiery chariot. That is, the events of the natural world are controlled by a putative supernatural world that is formless, unknowable, immune from discovery, and, in the view of many, nonexistent. The relationships of the natural and supernatural worlds need be neither constant nor predictable. The gods may have their own reasons and behave as they wish. Thus, if the cause of a natural event is the whim of a deity, the event is neither predictable nor fully understandable.

Science deals not with the gods above but with the worlds below. It does not refute the gods; it merely ignores them in its explanations of the natural world. The basic assumption of the sciences is that nature is, in principle, knowable and its phenomena are assumed to have constant cause–effect relationships. If oxygen and hydrogen unite today to form water, it is assumed that they will tomorrow. In discovering these cause–effect relationships, scientists strive to admit only those data obtained through observation and experimentation.

Explanations in science consist of relating natural phenomena one to another. A mountain is more than a pile of dirt. It is a consequence of an uplifting of the earth's crust and its wearing down by erosion. It may be composed of rocks formed from molten lava or sedimentary rocks formed at the bottom of some ancient sea. Usually it will have a thin skin of soil, formed by life itself, that supports many species of plants and animals. If the mountain is high, the climate will vary with the altitude and this will be reflected in differences in the species present.

To take another example, chromosomes became of interest when their behavior in cell division and their relationship to inheritance were discovered and established beyond all reasonable doubt. That phrase "beyond all reasonable doubt" is the goal of any scientific statement. It suggests a tentativeness because experience has shown that the science of today will be replaced by a better science tomorrow. Darwin's understanding of inheritance was full of doubt, Mendel's was much improved, and Sutton's was much better than that of any of his predecessors. Nevertheless, it was far less adequate than is ours today.

Science is a way of knowing by accumulating data from observations and experiments, seeking relationships of the data with other natural phenomena, and excluding supernatural explanations and personal wishes. It has proved a powerful procedure for understanding nature.

But why did it take so long to discover that cell replication is the basis of all self-replication? The answer to that question is that the scientific problems that can be solved depend on the state of society at the time. There was no way that Aristotle, in the fourth century B.C., could have answered these questions. The answer was hidden in an invisible world not to be revealed until microscopes were invented in the late sixteenth century A.D. But of even greater importance, how would Aristotle have begun an investigation? He could not have known how to ask a question—pose a hypothesis—that could be tested.

In fact, the clues that eventually led to an answer seemed totally unrelated to inheritance. The discovery and early studies of cells were not theory driven—they were just isolated descriptions of aspects of the natural world. Mendel's experiments, on the other hand, *were* theory driven, and they sought to provide a clearer picture of what happens in inheritance. He did not seek the physical basis of inheritance, but Mendel's laws made predictions for what the physical basis must be. It remained for Sutton to show that the behavior of chromosomes met those demands.

So science can tell us much about the natural world. Its methods are simple. They require disciplined minds capable of accurately recording observations, using the data from those observations to develop a tentative explanation (a hypothesis), testing the necessary deductions from that hypothesis, and relating the conclusions that are true beyond all reasonable doubt to the existing body of scientific information. Not only does the testing of hypotheses make science a self-correcting enterprise but so does the practice of one scientist testing the conclusions of another. The result is that science is the most powerful mechanism we have for obtaining confirmable information about the natural world.

But powerful as it is, we must never forget that decisions affecting human beings must be made by human beings; they do not emerge from science. Nevertheless, when human beings select some goal, not infrequently the data and procedures of science can help to achieve that goal. Alternatively, science might suggest that the goal is not obtainable—human beings are part of nature, after all, so human life will always be constrained by the basic laws of nature, which the gods cannot annul.

PART 3

The Evolution of Evolution

Biological evolution is not an easy concept to grasp, and, even when you understand it, it continues to challenge you with its nuances, controversies, and new data and interpretations. I found it helpful when I was first learning about evolution, and I have found it helpful in teaching the concept, to look at evolution's own evolution—the development of the science of evolution over the past several centuries. Understanding how the major players in the drama got it right and got it wrong lets you, in a way, evolve your own understanding of the ideas involved.

One of the failings of using this approach (and I'm guilty of it too) is that the words of the important contributors to the theory of evolution are usually paraphrased. This makes sense in one respect—the writing style of the nineteenth century and before is often, to the modern reader, awkward at best and, at worst, nearly incomprehensible because of now-archaic word usage, punctuation, and sentence structure.

Still, it's worth the effort. Going back to the original (or a good English translation) shows you just how insightful, careful, and logical were the likes of Darwin and Mendel, and even Lamarck, who is usually so denigrated for the parts of his proposal that turned out to be wrong. I have excerpted important sections from Lamarck's *Philosophie zoologique*, Darwin and Wallace's *Linnean Society Papers*, and Mendel's "Experiments on Plant Hybridization." These excerpts should show you what these scientists had to say and should also convey a bit of the flavor of how they said it.

Modern evolutionary theory is, as you can imagine, broad and multifaceted. We'll look at some of its details in Part 4. For now, however, we need some sense of the nature of evolutionary theory as a science and of its place in the domain of human knowledge. One way to begin to appreciate these is to compare modern evolutionary theory with a nonscientific explanation for the origin of species and for the evidence for the past found in the fossil and geological records. A modern example of such an explanation is called "scientific creationism." Stephen Jay Gould's "Evolution as Fact and Theory" explains how "scientific creationism" is not at all scientific and how the strength of modern evolutionary theory has been provided by the use of real science. Then, in "Darwin's Rib," Robert S.

Root-Bernstein shows how he explains the difference between science and nonscience in evolution in a real classroom situation. Finally, H. Allen Orr discusses so-called intelligent design, a current challenge to evolution, explaining why it does not fulfill the criteria of science.

SUGGESTED WEBSITES FOR FURTHER STUDY

http://www.pbs.org/wgbh/evolution
http://www.evolutionhappens.net
http://web.mit.edu/esgbio/www/mg/mgdir.html
http://www.literature.org/authors/darwin-charles/the-origin-of-species/index.html
http://anthro.palomar.edu/evolve/evolve_2.htm
http://www.natcenscied.org

8

The Inheritance of Acquired Characteristics (1809)

Jean Baptiste Pierre Antoine de Monet de Lamarck

Jean de Lamarck (1744–1829) studied medicine and botany in Paris. During the French Revolution he managed to be appointed "professor of insects and worms" at the Museum d'Histoire Naturelle—not a particularly prestigious position, but at least he kept his head while some scientists of the time were literally losing theirs. Despite poor acceptance of some of his work, he remained an enthusiastic scientist. He coined the term biology *and used the name* invertebrate *for the insects and worms he was in charge of. His major work on evolution, published as a text for his students in 1809 (the year of Darwin's birth), was* Philosophie zoologique. *His view of evolution in that book, although parts remained influential (even to Darwin), was criticized during Lamarck's lifetime, and he was never credited while alive with his noteworthy scientific accomplishments. He died in poverty in 1829.*

Perhaps because of his reluctance to accept the idea that any species becomes extinct, Lamarck adopted a view of evolution that precluded extinction. It was an idea that already existed, but Lamarck formalized it and, indeed, examined it using the principles of scientific inquiry (although some of the parts of his idea are pretty much beyond testing). There are three basic parts to Lamarck's idea, one of them essentially correct, the other two wrong. Lamarck said:

a. Organisms are adapted to their environments, and since environments are constantly changing, organisms have to change to remain adapted. This, as a general idea, is correct. But then he said:

b. Nature works toward producing animals "in succession [from] most imperfect or simplest, and ending her work with the most perfect, so as to create a gradually increasing complexity." In other words, evolution is progressive, each change being in the same direction—namely, toward more complex (read "more humanlike") organisms. This evolution occurs for the following reason:

c. An organism's "will" guides the animal to the necessary adaptive actions, and the organs that carry out those actions are stimulated by a "subtle fluid." Repetitions of these actions then can

"strengthen, stretch, develop and *even create*" [emphasis mine] the necessary organs. These modified or new organs are then preserved by reproduction and passed on intact to offspring. This model is called the inheritance of acquired characteristics. Because this process always works, thought Lamarck, there is no extinction. Organisms that *seem* to not be around anymore, like the dinosaurs, are simply organisms that have changed a great deal.

Lamarck was correct that a key to evolution is the adaptation of organisms to their environments, but he had it backward that organisms' traits are a "pure result of the environment" and "not the result of a shape which existed from the beginning." Read the following excerpts from Lamarck and then compare them with Darwin and Wallace's model of natural selection in the next selection.

At the same time, however, note Lamarck's use of the scientific method. In comparing what he calls "conclusion adopted hitherto" with "my individual conclusion," he lists the data that would support or refute each idea. This is how hypotheses are tested.

As you read, consider the following questions:

1. According to Lamarck, what is the relationship among the following factors of adaptation: environment, a species' habits, and a species' physical characteristics?

From *Zoological Philosophy*, Part I, Ch. 7. Translated by Hugh Elliot. Macmillan, 1914.

2.   What major piece of evidence does Lamarck cite for rejecting the idea that species are "fixed" and "invariable"?

3.   How did Lamarck think the traits of domesticated animals arose?

4.   What evidence does Lamarck cite that would show his model of evolutionary change to be false?

I shall show . . . that when the will guides an animal to any action, the organs which have to carry out that action are immediately stimulated to it by the influx of subtle fluids (the nervous fluid), which become the determining factor of the movements required. This fact is verified by many observations, and cannot now be called in question.

Hence it follows that numerous repetitions of these organised activities strengthen, stretch, develop and even create the organs necessary to them. We have only to watch attentively what is happening all around us, to be convinced that this is the true cause of organic development and changes.

Now every change that is wrought in an organ through a habit of frequently using it is subsequently preserved by reproduction, if it is common to the individuals who unite together in fertilisation for the propagation of their species. Such a change is thus handed on to all succeeding individuals in the same environment, without their having to acquire it in the same way that it was actually created. . . .

If I intended here to pass in review all the classes, orders, genera and species of existing animals, I should be able to show that the conformation and structure of individuals, their organs, faculties, etc., etc., are everywhere a pure result of the environment to which each species is exposed by its nature, and by the habits that the individuals composing it have been compelled to acquire: I should be able to show that they are not the result of a shape which existed from the beginning, and has driven animals into the habits they are known to possess. . . .

It is a fact that all animals have special habits corresponding to their genus and species, and always possess an organisation that is completely in harmony with those habits.

It seems from the study of this fact that we may adopt one or other of the two following conclusions, and that neither of them can be verified.

Conclusion adopted hitherto: Nature (or her Author) in creating animals, foresaw all the possible kinds of environment in which they would have to live, and endowed each species with a fixed organisation and with a definite and invariable shape, which compel each species to live in the places and climates where we actually find them, and there to maintain the habits which we know in them.

My individual conclusion: Nature has produced all the species of animals in succession, beginning with the most imperfect or simplest, and ending her work with the most perfect, so as to create a gradually increasing complexity in their organisation; these animals have spread at large throughout all the habitable regions of the globe, and every species has derived from its environment the habits that we find in it and the structural modifications which observation shows us.

The former of these two conclusions is that which has been drawn hitherto, at least by nearly everyone: it attributes to every animal a fixed organisation and structure which never have varied and never do vary; it assumes, moreover, that none of the localities inhabited by animals ever vary; for if they were to vary, the same animals could no longer survive, and the possibility of finding other localities and transporting themselves thither would not be open to them.

The second conclusion is my own: it assumes that by the influence of environment on habit, and thereafter by that of habit on the state of the parts and even on organisation, the structure and organisation of any animal may undergo modifications, possibly very great, and capable of accounting for the actual condition in which all animals are found.

In order to show that this second conclusion is baseless, it must first be proved that no point on the surface of the earth ever undergoes variation as to its nature, exposure, high or low situation, climate, etc., etc.; it must then be proved that no part of animals undergoes even after long periods of time any modifications due to a change of environment or to the necessity which forces them into a different kind of life and activity from what has been customary to them.

Now if a single case is sufficient to prove that an animal which has long been in domestication differs from the wild species whence it sprang, and if in any such domesticated species, great differences of conformation are found between the individuals exposed to such a habit and those which are forced into different habits, it will then be certain that the first conclusion is not consistent with the laws of nature, while the second, on the contrary, is entirely in accordance with them.

Everything then combines to prove my statement, namely: that it is not the shape either of the body or its parts which gives rise to the habits of animals and their mode of life; but that it is, on the contrary, the habits, mode of life and all the other influences of the environment which have in course of time built up the shape of the body and of the parts of animals. With new shapes, new faculties have been acquired, and little by little nature has succeeded in fashioning animals such as we actually see them.

9

Natural Selection (1858)

Charles R. Darwin and Alfred Russel Wallace

Charles R. Darwin (1809–1882) was born into a wealthy and well-known English family. His grandfather, Erasmus Darwin (1731–1802), a physician, amateur scientist, and poet, had a special influence on Charles's life, even though Charles never knew him. Among the elder Darwin's interests was evolution; he even devised a model that was similar to Lamarck's later idea. Charles studied medicine at Edinburgh University and, when that failed to interest him, moved to Cambridge University to study for a life as a country clergyman. At Cambridge he began to formalize his interest in natural history, and in 1831 he had the rare opportunity to observe nature as few others had by embarking upon a round-the-world voyage of discovery aboard the H.M.S. Beagle. *He left England on that journey as a Lamarckian, but shortly after his return he formulated his own idea to explain the evolution of species. As confident as Darwin may have been in his new model, however, he was unsure of its reception by his colleagues and by the public, and so he moved on to other scientific topics and left his evolutionary innovation unpublished—until, that is, he received a paper in 1858 from young Alfred Russel Wallace in which Wallace described his new model of evolution, which turned out to be exactly like Darwin's. Darwin's hand was called, and the next year he published* The Origin of Species by Means of Natural Selection or the Preservation of Favoured Races in the Struggle for Life. *Possibly to Darwin's surprise, the book sold out in a single day and was, for the most part, well received. Darwin went on to write about numerous other subjects in natural history, including the application of his model to human evolution in* The Descent of Man *(1871). Darwin died in 1882 and was buried, along with many of the most famous figures of British intelligentsia, in London's Westminster Abbey.*

Alfred Russel Wallace (1823–1913), also English, lived a very different life from Darwin's. Not born into privilege, Wallace dropped out of school at thirteen to work in his brother's surveying and architecture business. He continued his education on his own and later went into teaching. He had acquired an interest in aspects of natural history and was so inspired by stories of scientific journeys of discovery—including Darwin's account of the voyage of the Beagle—*that he embarked on a career of travel and observation, earning a living by selling specimens to scientific institutions back home. In 1858, while in Malaysia and suffering from a malaria-induced fever, Wallace devised ("in a flash of light," he said) an idea that explained, better than had Lamarck, how species change through time. He wrote a brief paper on the subject and sent it to Darwin for comment. This was the paper that forced Darwin to finally make public his idea, for their ideas were identical. "I never saw a more striking coincidence," said Darwin in a letter to famed geologist Charles Lyell. Although it is Darwin who is remembered for the idea of natural selection, Wallace went on to achieve his own reputation in science, particularly for his ideas on the geographic distribution of animals, although his reputation suffered at the same time because of his belief in spiritualism. Never a man of means, he ended up being supported by a government pension for which Darwin had petitioned the prime minister. Wallace died in 1913, living, unlike Darwin, long enough to see the gaps in their theory filled in by the "rediscovery" of the genetics of Gregor Mendel (see Selection 10).*

Lamarck thought that evolutionary variations occur as direct responses of organisms to their environments. Darwin and Wallace observed that variations *already exist* within species. Those variations that confer adaptive traits are passed on to more offspring than are variations for less-well-adapted or poorly adapted traits. Thus, adaptive traits accumulate through time, while maladaptive traits decrease in frequency. This process, which Darwin dubbed natural selection, maintains a species' adaptation to its environment. If environments change (which they always do), natural selection will still operate, although, under the new circumstances, the adaptive fitness of certain traits may change. Thus, Darwin and Wallace agreed with Lamarck that environmental change and the resultant adaptive changes within species are what explain evolution. They disagreed with Lamarck, however, in terms of the process of change and in the overall direction of that change. Darwin and Wallace said:

a. Natural selection operates to make each species as well adapted to its environment as possible. Evolutionary change has no particular direction. Species may become more complex over time, or they may become less complex. What works is, well, what works.

b. Adaptive traits do not arise when they are needed. Traits are already there in the variation within each species (although Darwin and Wallace, not knowing about genetics, did not understand where the variation came from). Nature "selects" adaptive traits in that those individuals within a species that possess such traits are more reproductively successful and so pass those traits on to more offspring. Note that this model relies on the luck of existing variation; thus, it isn't always successful, as is Lamarck's model. Extinction is possible under Darwin and Wallace's model, and they both realized that, in fact, it is quite common.

c. This process, acting constantly and over long periods of time, will eventually cause varieties within a species (Wallace also uses the term "race") to diverge so much from the original species that they would themselves become separate species. It is really the diversity of species that Darwin and Wallace are trying to explain. Recall the title of Darwin's famous book *The Origin of Species*.

The following excerpts are from the so-called Linnean Society Papers. They were short papers, one by each scientist, presented by the geologist Charles Lyell and the botanist Joseph Hooker, before the Linnean Society of London on July 1, 1858, "while," in Lyell's and Hooker's words, "the scientific world is waiting for the appearance of Mr. Darwin's complete work . . . as well as those of his able correspondent." I have added a few clarifying comments as notes.

As you read, consider the following questions:

1. How does Darwin and Wallace's mechanism for evolution differ from Lamarck's?

2. What facts about the populations of animals led Darwin to his conclusion?

3. Wallace directly addresses Lamarck's model. What does he say in argument against Lamarck?

On the Tendency of Species to form Varieties; and on the Perpetuation of Varieties and Species by Natural Means of Selection. By CHARLES DARWIN, Esq., F.R.S., F.L.S., & F.G.S., and ALFRED WALLACE, Esq. Communicated by Sir CHARLES LYELL, F.R.S., F.L.S., and J.D. HOOKER, Esq., M.D., V.P.R.S., F.L.S., &c.

—[Read July 1st, 1858]

I. *Extract from an unpublished work on Species, by C. Darwin Esq., consisting of a portion of a Chapter entitled "On the variation of Organic Beings in a state of Nature; on the Natural Means of Selection; on the Comparison of Domestic Races and true Species."*

From *The Linnean Society Papers*, 1859.

. . . **B**ut for animals without artificial means, the amount of food for each species must, *on an average*, be constant, whereas the increase of all organisms tends to be geometrical, and in a vast majority of cases at an enormous ratio. Suppose in a certain spot there are eight pairs of birds, and that only four pairs of them annually (including double hatches) rear *only* four young, and that these go on rearing their young at the same rate, then at the end of seven years (a short life, excluding violent deaths, for any bird) there will be 2048 birds, instead of the original sixteen. As this increase is quite impossible, we must conclude either that birds do not rear nearly half their young, or that the average life of a bird is, from accident, not nearly seven years. Both checks probably concur. The same kind of calculation applied to all plants and animals affords results more or less striking. . . .

. . . Reflect on the enormous multiplying power *inherent and annually in action* in all animals; reflect on the countless seeds scattered by a hundred ingenious contrivances, year after year, over the whole face of the land; and yet we have every reason to suppose that the average percentage of each of the inhabitants of a country usually remains constant. Finally, let it be borne in mind that this average number of individuals (the external conditions remaining the same) in each country is kept up by recurrent struggles against other species or against external nature (as on the borders of the arctic regions, where the cold checks life), and that ordinarily each individual of every species holds its place, either by its own struggle and capacity of acquiring nourishment in some period of its life, from the egg upwards; or by the struggle of its parents (in short-lived organisms, when the main check occurs at longer intervals) with other individuals of the *same* or *different* species.

But let the external conditions of a country alter. If in a small degree, the relative proportions of the inhabitants will in most cases simply be slightly changed; but let the number of inhabitants be small, as on an island, and free access to it from other countries be circumscribed, and let the change of conditions continue progressing (forming new stations), in such a case the original inhabitants must cease to be as perfectly adapted to the changed conditions as they were originally. It has been shown in a former part of this work, that such changes of external conditions would, from their acting on the reproductive system, probably cause the organization of those beings which were most affected to become, as under domestication, plastic.[1] Now, can it be doubted, from the struggle each individual has to obtain subsistence, that any minute variation in structure, habits, or instincts, adapting that individual better to the new conditions, would tell upon its vigour and health? In the struggle it would have a better *chance* of surviving; and those of its offspring which inherited the variation, be it ever so slight, would also have a better *chance*. Yearly more are bred than can survive; the smallest grain in the balance, in the long run, must tell on which death shall fall and which shall survive. Let this work of selection on the one hand, and death on the other, go on for a thousand generations, who will pretend to affirm that it would produce no effect, when we remember what, in a few years, Bakewell effected in cattle, and Western in sheep, by this identical principle of selection?

To give an imaginary example from changes in progress on an island:—let the organization of a canine animal which preyed chiefly on rabbits, but sometimes on hares, become slightly plastic; let these same changes cause the number of rabbits very slowly to decrease, and the number of hares to increase: the effect of this would be that the fox or dog would be driven to try to catch more hares: his organization, however, being slightly plastic, those individuals with the lightest forms, longest limbs, and best eyesight, let the difference be ever so small, would be slightly favoured, and would tend to live longer, and to survive during that time of the year when food was scarcest; they would also rear more young, which would tend to inherit these slight peculiarities. The less fleet ones would be rigidly destroyed. I can see no more reason to doubt that these causes in a thousand generations would produce a marked effect, and adapt the form of the fox or dog to the catching of hares instead of rabbits, than that greyhounds can be improved by selection and careful breeding. So would it be with plants under similar circumstances. If the number of individuals of a species with plumed seeds could be increased by greater powers of dissemination within its own area (that is if the check to increase fell chiefly on the seeds), those seeds which were provided with ever so little more down, would in the long run be most disseminated; hence a greater number of seeds thus formed would germinate, and would tend to produce plants inheriting the slightly better-adapted down.

III. *On the Tendency of Varieties to Depart Indefinitely from the Original Type. By* ALFRED RUSSEL WALLACE *(1823–1913).*

The life of wild animals is a struggle for existence. The full exertion of all faculties and all their energies is required to preserve their own existence and provide for that of their infant offspring. The possibility of procuring food during the least favourable seasons, and of escaping the attacks of their most dangerous enemies, are the primary conditions which determine the existence both of individuals and of entire species. These conditions will also determine the population of a species; and by a careful consideration of all the circumstances we may be enabled to comprehend, and in some degree to explain, what at first sight appears so inexplicable—the excessive abundance of some species while others closely allied to them are very rare. . . .

. . . It appears evident, therefore, that so long as a country remains physically unchanged, the numbers of its animal population cannot materially increase. If one species does so, some others requiring the same kind of food must diminish in proportion. The numbers that die annually must be immense; and as the individual existence of each animal depends upon itself, those that die must be the weakest—the very young, the aged, and the diseased—while those that prolong their existence can only be the most perfect in health and vigour—those who are best able to obtain food regularly, and avoid their numerous enemies. It is, as we commenced by remarking, a "struggle for existence," in which the weakest and least perfectly organized must always succumb. . . .

Most or perhaps all the variations from the typical form of a species must have some definite effect, however slight, on the habits or capacities of the individuals. Even a change of colour might, by rendering them more or less distinguishable, affect their safety; a greater or less development of hair might modify their habits. More important changes, such as an increase in the power or dimensions of the limbs or any of the external organs, would more or less affect their mode of procuring food or the range of country which they inhabit. It is also evident that most changes would affect, either favourably or adversely, the powers of prolonging existence. An antelope with shorter or weaker legs must necessarily suffer more from the attacks of the feline carnivora; the passenger pigeon with less powerful wings would sooner or later be affected in its powers of procuring a regular supply of food; and in both cases the result must necessarily be a diminution of the population of the modified species. If, on the other hand, any species should produce a variety having slightly increased powers of preserving existence, that variety must inevitably in time acquire a superiority in numbers. These results must follow as surely as old age, intemperance, or scarcity of food produce an increased mortality. In both cases there may be many individual exceptions; but on the average the rule will invariably be found to hold good. All varieties will therefore fall into two classes—those which under the same conditions would never reach the population of the parent species, and those which would in time obtain and keep a numerical superiority. Now, let some alteration of physical conditions occur in the district—a long period of drought, a destruction of vegetation by locusts, the irruption of some new carnivorous animal seeking "pastures new"—any change in fact tending to render existence more difficult to the species in question, and tasking its utmost powers to avoid complete extermination; it is evident that, of all the individuals composing the species, those forming the least numerous and most feebly organized variety would suffer first, and, were the pressure severe, must soon become extinct. The same causes continuing in action, the parent species would next suffer, would gradually diminish in numbers, and with a recurrence of similar unfavourable conditions might also become extinct. The superior variety would then alone remain, and on a return to favourable circumstances would rapidly increase in numbers and occupy the place of the extinct species and variety.

The *variety* would now have replaced the *species*, of which it would be a more perfectly developed and more highly organized form. It would be in all respects better adapted to secure its safety, and to prolong its individual existence and that of the race. . . . But this new, improved, and populous race might itself, in course of time, give rise to new varieties, exhibiting several diverging modifications of form, any of which, tending to increase the facilities for preserving existence, must, by the same general law, in their turn become predominant. Here, then, we have *progression and continued divergence* deduced from the general laws which regulate the existence of animals in a state of nature, and from the undisputed fact that varieties do frequently occur. . . .[2]

The hypothesis of Lamarck—that progressive changes in species have been produced by the attempts of animals to increase the development of their own organs, and thus modify their structure and habits—has been repeatedly and easily refuted by all writers on the subject of varieties and species, and it seems to have been considered that when this was done the whole question has been finally settled; but the view here developed renders such an hypothesis quite unnecessary, by showing that similar results must be produced by the action of principles constantly at work in nature. The powerful retractile talons of the falcon- and the cat-tribes have not been produced or increased by the volition of those animals; but among the different varieties which occurred in the earlier and less highly organized forms of these groups, *those always survived longest which had the greatest facilities for seizing their prey.* Neither did the giraffe acquire its long neck by desiring to reach the foliage of the more lofty shrubs, and constantly stretching its neck for the purpose, but because any varieties which occurred among its antitypes with a longer neck than usual *at once secured a fresh range of pasture over the same ground as their shorter-necked companions, and on the first scarcity of food were thereby enabled to outlive them.* Even the peculiar colors of many animals, especially insects, so closely resembling the soil or the leaves or the trunks on which they habitually reside, are explained on the same principle; for though in the course of ages varieties of many tints may have occurred, *yet those races having colours best adapted to concealment from their enemies would inevitably survive the longest. . . .*

. . . This progression, by minute steps, in various directions, but always checked and balanced by the necessary conditions, subject to which alone existence can be preserved, may, it is believed, be followed out so as to agree with all the phenomena presented by organized beings, their extinction and succession in past ages, and all the extraordinary modifications of form, instinct, and habits which they exhibit.

NOTES

1. By "plastic" Darwin means "variable." Although this sentence may seem Lamarckian at first, Darwin is trying to say that he believes some external force acts on the mechanism of inheritance to produce heritable variation within a species. In modern terms, we would say that there are a number of forces that produce mutations, which are the origin of all genetic variation.

2. Wallace uses the phrases "more perfectly developed" and "progression" (which also appears in the last sentence of the excerpt). He doesn't seem to mean this in the same sense that Lamarck did—that is, continual change in the particular direction of increasing complexity. Rather, by "more perfectly developed," he means better adapted to existing conditions, and by "progression, " he simply means change. Note that in the last sentence of the excerpt he specifically acknowledges extinction.

10

The Laws of Inheritance (1866)

Johann Gregor Mendel

Johann Mendel (1822–1884) studied math and physics as a teen before becoming an Augustinian monk at a monastery in Brno (now in the Czech Republic) in his mid-twenties. There he took the name Gregor, by which he is most commonly known today. He taught high school math for a time, and then, because his knowledge of biology was so poor that he failed a teacher's qualifying exam, he spent two years at the University of Vienna making up for his deficiencies. In 1856, back in Brno, Mendel began the series of experiments on pea plants for which he has become famous. After eight years, he described his research in the paper excerpted below. It made little or no impression on anyone. This may have been because of the mathematical nature of Mendel's analysis and perhaps because the implications of his work for organisms beyond the pea plant escaped his few readers. In 1868, Mendel became abbot of his monastery, and his new duties, along with his poor health (he was overweight and a smoker), prevented any further research in biology. Upon Mendel's death, many of his papers documenting his work were burned (his experiments were not popular with all his monastic colleagues), so we actually know little about the history of his thinking. In 1900 three scientists independently "rediscovered" Mendel's work and by that time understood its implications not only for the study of heredity but for the theory of evolution as well.

The basic laws of inheritance, called Mendelian genetics in honor of their discoverer, are well known. The excerpts below are included to show how Mendel went about discovering those laws and how he described them. If it all sounds familiar (even if in somewhat difficult language), that's because little in our understanding of these basic ideas has changed since Mendel's time. As you read, look for his descriptions of the particulate rather than the blending nature of inheritance, of dominant and recessive alleles, the law of segregation, and the law of independent assortment. The importance of Mendel's work to the theory of evolution is that his genetics fills in two important areas that Darwin acknowledged were missing from his model:

a. *The workings of inheritance.* Darwin thought inheritance was a blending of the traits of the parents. Mendel showed that inheritance involved individual factors, what we now call genes.

b. *The source of variation.* Although Mendel didn't know about mutations, the ultimate source of biological variation, he did discover the variation inherent in the reproductive process itself—the recombination of the individual factors of heredity into all their possible combinations.

This selection is from a paper Mendel published with the Natural History Society of Brünn (Brno).

As you read, consider the following questions:

1. What observation regarding hybrid plants was central to Mendel's model of inheritance?

2. What do the terms *dominant* and *recessive* mean to Mendel?

3. How does Mendel's genetics help us understand the origin of some of the biological variation within a species?

From "Experiments in Plant Hybridization" by Johann Gregor Mendel, translation by William Bateson, *The Garden, Journal of the Royal Horticultural Society*, 1901.

Experience of artificial fertilisation, such as is effected with ornamental plants in order to obtain new variations in colour, has led to the experiments which will here be discussed. The striking regularity with which the same hybrid forms always reappeared whenever fertilisation took place between the same species induced further experiments to be undertaken, the object of which was to follow up the developments of the hybrids in their progeny. . . .

. . . That, so far, no generally applicable law governing the formation and development of hybrids has been successfully formulated can hardly be wondered at by anyone who is acquainted with the extent of the task, and can appreciate the difficulties with which the experiments of this class have to contend. A final decision can only be arrived at when we shall have before us the results of detailed experiments made on plants belonging to the most diverse orders.

Those who survey the work in this department will arrive at the conviction that among all the numerous experiments made, not one has been carried out to such an extent and in such a way as to make it possible to determine the number of different forms under which the offspring of hybrids appear, or to arrange these forms with certainty according to their separate generations, or definitely to ascertain their statistical relations.

It requires indeed some courage to undertake a labour of such far-reaching extent; this appears, however, to be the only right way by which we can finally reach the solution of a question the importance of which cannot be overestimated in connection with the history of the evolution of organic forms.

The paper now presented records the results of such a detailed experiment. This experiment was practically confined to a small plant group, and is now, after eight years' pursuit, concluded in all essentials. Whether the plan upon which the separate experiments were conducted and carried out was the best suited to attain the desired end is left to the friendly decision of the reader. . . .

At the very outset special attention was devoted to the *Leguminosae* on account of their peculiar floral structure. Experiments which were made with several members of this family led to the result that the genus *Pisum* was found to possess the necessary qualifications. . . .

[*F₁*] THE FORMS OF THE HYBRIDS

Experiments which in previous years were made with ornamental plants have already afforded evidence that hybrids, as a rule, are not exactly intermediate between the parental species. With some of the more striking characters, those, for instance, which relate to the form and size of the leaves, the pubescence of the several parts, &c., the intermediate, indeed, is nearly always to be seen; in other cases, however, one of the two parental characters is so preponderant that it is difficult, or quite impossible, to detect the other in the hybrid.

This is precisely the case with the Pea hybrids. In the case of each of the seven crosses the hybrid-character resembles that of one of the parental forms so closely that the other either escapes observation completely or cannot be detected with certainty. This circumstance is of great importance in the determination and classification of the forms under which the offspring of the hybrids appear. Henceforth in this paper those characters which are transmitted entire, or almost unchanged in the hybridisation, and therefore in themselves constitute the characters of the hybrid, are termed the *dominant*, and those which become latent in the process *recessive*. The expression "recessive" has been chosen because the characters thereby designated withdraw or entirely disappear unchanged in their progeny, as will be demonstrated later on.

It was furthermore shown by the whole of the experiments that it is perfectly immaterial whether the dominant character belongs to the seedbearer or to the pollen-parent; the form of the hybrid remains identical in both cases. . . .

In [the *F₂*] generation there reappear, together with the dominant characters, also the recessive ones with their peculiarities fully developed, and this occurs in the definitely expressed proportion of three to one, so that among each four plants of this generation three display the dominant character and one the recessive. This relates without exception to all the characters which were investigated in the experiments. . . . *Transitional forms were not observed in any experiment.*

If *A* be taken as denoting one of the two constant characters, for instance the dominant, and *a* the recessive, and *Aa* the hybrid form in which both are conjoined, the expression

$$A + 2Aa + a$$

shows the terms in the series for the progeny of the hybrids of two differentiating characters. . . .

. . . There is therefore no doubt that for the whole of the characters involved in the experiments the principle applies that *the offspring of the hybrids in which several essentially different characters are combined exhibit the terms of a series of combinations, in which the developmental series for each pair of differentiating characters are united.* It is demonstrated at the same time that *the relation of each pair of different characters in hybrid union is independent of the other differences in the two original parental stocks. . . .*

. . . Thereby is simultaneously given the practical proof *that the constant characters which appear in the several varieties of a group of plants may be obtained in all the associations which are possible according to the [mathematical] laws of combination, by means of repeated artificial fertilisation. . . .*

THE REPRODUCTIVE CELLS OF THE HYBRIDS

The results of the previously described experiments led to further experiments, the results of which appear fitted to afford some conclusions as regards the composition of the egg and pollen cells of hybrids. An important clue is afforded in *Pisum* by the circumstance that among the progeny of the hybrids constant forms appear, and that this occurs, too, in respect of all combinations of the associated characters. So far as experience goes, we find it in every case confirmed that constant progeny can only be formed when the egg cells and the fertilising pollen are of like character, so that both are provided with the material for creating quite similar individuals, as is the case with the normal fertilisation of pure species. We must therefore regard it as certain that exactly similar factors must be at work also in the production of the constant forms in the hybrid plants. Since the various constant forms are produced in *one* plant, or even in *one* flower of a plant, the conclusion appears logical that in the ovaries of the hybrids there are formed as many sorts of egg cells, and in the anthers as many sorts of pollen cells, as there are possible constant combination forms, and that these egg and pollen cells agree in their internal composition with those of the separate forms.

In point of fact it is possible to demonstrate theoretically that this hypothesis would fully suffice to account for the development of the hybrids in the separate generations, if we might at the same time assume that the various kinds of egg and pollen cells were formed in the hybrids on the average in equal numbers. . . .

The result of the fertilisation may be made clear by putting the signs of the conjoined egg and pollen cells in the form of fractions, those for the pollen cells above and those for the egg cells below the line. We then have

$$\frac{A}{A} + \frac{A}{a} + \frac{a}{A} + \frac{a}{a}.$$

In the first and fourth term the egg and pollen cells are of like kind, consequently the product of their union must be constant, viz. A and a; in the second and third, on the other hand, there again results a union of the two differentiating characters of the stocks, consequently the forms resulting from these fertilisations are identical with those of the hybrid from which they sprang. *There occurs accordingly a repeated hybridisation.* This explains the striking fact that the hybrids are able to produce, besides the two parental forms, offspring which are like themselves; $\frac{A}{a}$ and $\frac{a}{A}$ both give the same union Aa, since, as already remarked above, it makes no difference in the result of fertilisation to which of the two characters the pollen or egg cells belong. We may write then

$$\frac{A}{A} + \frac{A}{a} + \frac{a}{A} + \frac{a}{a} = A + 2Aa + a.$$

This represents the average result of the self-fertilisation of the hybrids when two differentiating characters are united in them.

11

Evolution as Fact and Theory

Stephen Jay Gould

As one of the leading theorists in evolution and as one of the best-known science writers in the popular press, Stephen Jay Gould (see also Selection 5) was also one of the major targets of the scientific creationists. He was thus one of their most vocal and articulate opponents.

Creationism is any conviction that a higher power had a hand in the origin of the universe, the earth, and, most important, its living beings. Many evolutionary scientists might therefore consider themselves creationists. Scientific creationism, on the other hand, is an explicit belief in the following:

a. The universe and everything in it were created by a higher power, using supernatural processes.

b. These creations took place simultaneously around ten thousand years ago.

c. The universe today is virtually unchanged since the creation.

d. Living forms may undergo limited change within "kinds" of organisms (breeds of dog, for example, or different members of the horse family), but no "kinds" give rise to other "kinds"; they were all created separately. There has been, in other words, no evolution of new species.

e. The data from the geological and fossil records document events that have taken place over about ten thousand years. How so much change could have occurred over such a short period of time is accounted for by the claim that those records are largely the results of a single major worldwide catastrophe, a "primeval watery cataclysm"—in other words, Noah's flood.

These ideas stand in stark contrast to the model of mainstream evolutionary science, but the scientific creationists go further in asserting:

f. There is scientific evidence in support of their model and, at the same time, there are serious scientific problems with the model proposed by standard evolutionary science. Evolution, they sometimes say, is not a "fact" but is "just a theory."

In fact, however, when they are subjected to the stringent methodology of science (see Part 2), *not one shred* of evidence can be found in support of items b, c, d, and e of the scientific-creation model. Item a, of course, is not scientific at all, since it cannot be tested, or, put another way, it cannot be disproved. Thus, the model proposed by the scientific creationists is not scientific. It is a pseudoscience. The evolution model is scientific. In this selection, Gould elaborates on these points and explains how evolution is, indeed, both fact *and* theory and that these are very positive and well-supported scientific statements.

As you read, consider the following questions:

1. What is the popular definition of the word *theory*? What is its scientific definition?

2. What does Gould mean when he says evolution is a "fact"?

3. In what way is scientific creationism *not* scientific?

4. What are the three arguments for the fact of evolution?

5. How has Gould and Eldredge's theory of punctuated equilibrium been used against them by the scientific creationists?

Kirtley Mather, who died [in 1978] at age ninety, was a pillar of both science and Christian religion in America and one of my dearest friends. The difference of a half-century in our ages evaporated before our common interests. The most curious thing we shared was a battle we fought at the same age. For Kirtley had gone to Tennessee with Clarence Darrow to testify for evolution at the Scopes trial of 1925. When I think that we are enmeshed again in the same struggle for one of the best documented, most compelling and exciting concepts in all of science, I don't know whether to laugh or cry.

According to idealized principles of scientific discourse, the arousal of dormant issues should reflect fresh data that give renewed life to abandoned notions. Those outside the current debate may therefore be excused for suspecting that creationists have come up with something new, or that evolutionists have generated some serious internal trouble. But nothing has changed; the creationists have presented not a single new fact or argument. Darrow and Bryan were at least more entertaining than we lesser antagonists today. The rise of creationism is politics, pure and simple; it represents one issue (and by no means the major concern) of the resurgent evangelical right. Arguments that seemed kooky just a decade ago have reentered the mainstream.

The basic attack of modern creationists falls apart on two general counts before we even reach the supposed factual details of their assault against evolution. First, they play upon a vernacular misunderstanding of the word "theory" to convey the false impression that we evolutionists are covering up the rotten core of our edifice. Second, they misuse a popular philosophy of science to argue that they are behaving scientifically in attacking evolution. Yet the same philosophy demonstrates that their own belief is not science, and that "scientific creationism" is a meaningless and self-contradictory phrase, an example of what Orwell called "newspeak."

In the American vernacular, "theory" often means "imperfect fact"—part of a hierarchy of confidence running downhill from fact to theory to hypothesis to guess. Thus, creationists can (and do) argue: evolution is "only" a theory, and intense debate now rages about many aspects of the theory. If evolution is less than a fact, and scientists can't even make up their minds about the theory, then what confidence can we have in it? Indeed, President Reagan echoed this argument before an evangelical group in Dallas when he said (in what I devoutly hope was campaign rhetoric): "Well, it is a theory. It is a scientific theory only, and it has in recent years been challenged in the world of science—that is, not believed in the scientific community to be as infallible as it once was."

Well, evolution *is* a theory. It is also a fact. And facts and theories are different things, not rungs in a hierarchy of increasing certainty. Facts are the world's data. Theories are structures of ideas that explain and interpret facts. Facts do not go away while scientists debate rival theories for explaining them. Einstein's theory of gravitation replaced Newton's, but apples did not suspend themselves in mid-air pending the outcome. And human beings evolved from apelike ancestors whether they did so by Darwin's proposed mechanism or by some other, yet to be discovered.

Moreover, "fact" does not mean "absolute certainty." The final proofs of logic and mathematics flow deductively from stated premises and achieve certainty only because they are *not* about the empirical world. Evolutionists make no claim for perpetual truth, though creationists often do (and then attack us for a style of argument that they themselves favor). In science, "fact" can only mean "confirmed to such a degree that it would be perverse to withhold provisional assent." I suppose that apples might start to rise tomorrow, but the possibility does not merit equal time in physics classrooms.

Evolutionists have been clear about this distinction between fact and theory from the very beginning, if only because we have always acknowledged how far we are from completely understanding the mechanisms (theory) by which evolution (fact) occurred. Darwin continually emphasized the difference between his two great and separate accomplishments: establishing the fact of evolution, and proposing a theory—natural selection—to explain the mechanism of evolution. He wrote in *The Descent of Man*: "I had two distinct objects in view; firstly, to show that species had not been separately created, and secondly, that natural selection had been the chief agent of change... Hence if I have erred in... having exaggerated its [natural selection's] power... I have at least, as I hope, done good service in aiding to overthrow the dogma of separate creations."

Thus Darwin acknowledged the provisional nature of natural selection while affirming the fact of evolution. The fruitful theoretical debate that Darwin initiated has never ceased. From the 1940s through the 1960s, Darwin's own theory of natural selection did achieve a temporary hegemony that it never enjoyed in his lifetime. But renewed debate characterizes our decade, and, while no biologist questions the importance of natural selection, many now doubt its ubiquity. In particular, many evolutionists argue that substantial amounts of genetic change may not be subject to natural selection and may spread through populations at random. Others are challenging Darwin's linking of natural selection with gradual, imperceptible change through all intermediary degrees; they are arguing that most evolutionary events may occur far more rapidly than Darwin envisioned.

Scientists regard debates on fundamental issues of theory as a sign of intellectual health and a source of excitement. Science is—and how else can I say it?—most fun when it plays with interesting ideas, examines their implications, and recognizes that old information may be explained in surprisingly new ways. Evolutionary theory is now enjoying this uncommon vigor. Yet amidst all this turmoil no biologist has been led to doubt the fact that evolution occurred; we are debating *how* it happened. We are all trying to explain the same thing: the tree of evolutionary descent linking all organisms by ties of genealogy. Creationists pervert and caricature this debate by conveniently neglecting the common conviction that underlies it, and by falsely suggesting that we now doubt the very phenomenon we are struggling to understand.

Secondly, creationists claim that "the dogma of separate creations," as Darwin characterized it a century ago, is a scientific theory meriting equal time with evolution in high school biology curricula. But a popular viewpoint among philosophers of science belies this creationist argument. Philosopher Karl Popper has argued for decades that the primary criterion of science is the falsifiability of its theories. We can never prove absolutely, but we can falsify. A set of ideas that cannot, in principle, be falsified is not science.

The entire creationist program includes little more than a rhetorical attempt to falsify evolution by presenting supposed contradictions among its supporters. Their brand of creationism, they claim, is "scientific" because it follows the Popperian model in trying to demolish evolution. Yet Popper's argument must apply in both directions. One does not become a scientist by the simple act of trying to falsify a rival and truly scientific system; one has to present an alternative system that also meets Popper's criterion—it too must be falsifiable in principle.

"Scientific creationism" is a self-contradictory, nonsense phrase precisely because it cannot be falsified. I can envision observations and experiments that would disprove any evolutionary theory I know, but I cannot imagine what potential data could lead creationists to abandon their beliefs. Unbeatable systems are dogma, not science. Lest I seem harsh or rhetorical, I quote creationism's leading intellectual, Duane Gish, Ph.D., from his [1978] book, *Evolution? The Fossils Say No!* "By creation we mean the bringing into being by a supernatural Creator of the basic kinds of plants and animals by the process of sudden, or fiat, creation. We do not know how the Creator created, what processes He used, *for He used processes which are not now operating anywhere in the natural universe* [Gish's italics]. This is

why we refer to creation as special creation. We cannot discover by scientific investigations anything about the creative processes used by the Creator." Pray tell, Dr. Gish, in the light of your last sentence, what then is "scientific" creationism?

Our confidence that evolution occurred centers upon three general arguments. First, we have abundant, direct, observational evidence of evolution in action, from both field and laboratory. This evidence ranges from countless experiments on change in nearly everything about fruit flies subjected to artificial selection in the laboratory to the famous populations of British moths that became black when industrial soot darkened the trees upon which the moths rest. (Moths gain protection from sharp-sighted bird predators by blending into the background.) Creationists do not deny these observations; how could they? Creationists have tightened their act. They now argue that God only created "basic kinds," and allowed for limited evolutionary meandering within them. Thus toy poodles and Great Danes come from the dog kind and moths can change color, but nature cannot convert a dog to a cat or a monkey to a man.

The second and third arguments for evolution—the case for major changes—do not involve direct observation of evolution in action. They rest upon inference, but are no less secure for that reason. Major evolutionary change requires too much time for direct observation on the scale of recorded human history. All historical sciences rest upon inference, and evolution is no different from geology, cosmology, or human history in this respect. In principle, we cannot observe processes that operated in the past. We must infer them from results that still surround us: living and fossil organisms for evolution, documents and artifacts for human history, strata and topography for geology.

The second argument—that the imperfection of nature reveals evolution—strikes many people as ironic, for they feel that evolution should be most elegantly displayed in the nearly perfect adaptation expressed by some organisms—the camber of a gull's wing, or butterflies that cannot be seen in ground litter because they mimic leaves so precisely. But perfection could be imposed by a wise creator or evolved by natural selection. Perfection covers the tracks of past history. And past history—the evidence of descent—is the mark of evolution.

Evolution lies exposed in the *imperfections* that record a history of descent. Why should a rat run, a bat fly, a porpoise swim, and I type this essay with structures built of the same bones unless we all inherited them from a common ancestor? An engineer, starting from scratch, could design better limbs in each case. Why should all the large native mammals of Australia be marsupials, unless they descended from a common ancestor isolated on this island continent? Marsupials are not "better," or ideally suited for Australia; many have been wiped out by placental mammals imported by man from other continents. This principle of imperfection extends to all historical sciences. When we recognize the etymology of September, October, November, and December (seventh, eighth, ninth, and tenth), we know that the year once started in March, or that two additional months must have been added to an original calendar of ten months.

The third argument is more direct: transitions are often found in the fossil record. Preserved transitions are not common—and should not be, according to our understanding of evolution—but they are not entirely wanting, as creationists often claim. The lower jaw of reptiles contains several bones, that of mammals only one. The non-mammalian jawbones are reduced, step by step, in mammalian ancestors until they become tiny nubbins located at the back of the jaw. The "hammer" and "anvil" bones of the mammalian ear are descendants of these nubbins. How could such a transition be accomplished? the creationists ask. Surely a bone is either entirely in the jaw or in the ear. Yet paleontologists have discovered two transitional lineages of therapsids (the so-called mammal-like reptiles) with a double jaw joint—one composed of the old quadrate and articular bones (soon to become the hammer and anvil), the other of the squamosal and dentary bones (as in modern mammals). For that matter, what better transitional form could we expect to find than the oldest human, *Australopithecus afarensis*, with its apelike palate, its human upright stance, and a cranial capacity larger than any ape's of the same body size but a full 1,000 cubic centimeters below ours? If God made each of the half-dozen human species discovered in ancient rocks, why did he create in an unbroken temporal sequence of progressively more modern features—increasing cranial capacity, reduced face and teeth, larger body size? Did he create to mimic evolution and test our faith thereby?

Faced with these facts of evolution and the philosophical bankruptcy of their own position, creationists rely upon distortion and innuendo to buttress their rhetorical claim. If I sound sharp or bitter, indeed I am—for I have become a major target of these practices.

I count myself among the evolutionists who argue for a jerky, or episodic, rather than a smoothly gradual, pace of change. In 1972 my colleague Niles Eldredge and I developed the theory of punctuated equilibrium. We argued that two outstanding facts of the fossil record—geologically "sudden" origin of new species and failure to change thereafter (stasis)—reflect the predictions of evolutionary theory, not the imperfections of the fossil record. In most theories, small isolated populations are the source of new species, and the process of speciation takes thousands or tens of thousands of years. This amount of time, so long when measured against our lives, is a geological microsecond. It represents much less than 1 percent of the average life-span for a fossil invertebrate species—more than ten million years. Large, widespread, and well-established species, on the other hand, are not expected to change very much. We believe that the inertia of large populations explains the stasis of most fossil species over millions of years.

We proposed the theory of punctuated equilibrium largely to provide a different explanation for pervasive trends in the fossil record. Trends, we argued, cannot be attributed to gradual transformation within lineages, but must arise from the differential success of certain kinds of species. A trend, we argued, is more like climbing a flight of stairs (punctuation and stasis) than rolling up an inclined plane.

Since we proposed punctuated equilibria to explain trends, it is infuriating to be quoted again and again by creationists—whether through design or stupidity, I do not know—as admitting that the fossil record includes no transitional forms. Transitional forms are generally lacking at the species level, but they are abundant between larger groups. Yet a pamphlet entitled "Harvard Scientists Agree Evolution Is a Hoax" states: "The facts of punctuated equilibrium which Gould and Eldredge . . . are forcing Darwinists to swallow fit the picture that Bryan insisted on, and which God has revealed to us in the Bible."

Continuing the distortion, several creationists have equated the theory of punctuated equilibrium with a caricature of the beliefs of Richard Goldschmidt, a great early geneticist. Goldschmidt argued, in a famous book published in 1940, that new groups can arise all at once through major mutations. He referred to these suddenly transformed creatures as "hopeful monsters." (I am attracted to some aspects of the non-caricatured version, but Goldschmidt's theory still has nothing to do with punctuated equilibrium.) Creationist Luther Sunderland talks of the "punctuated equilibrium hopeful monster theory" and tells his hopeful readers that "it amounts to tacit admission that anti-evolutionists are correct in asserting there is no fossil evidence supporting the theory that all life is connected to a common ancestor." Duane Gish writes, "According to Goldschmidt, and now apparently according to Gould, a reptile laid an egg from which the first bird, feathers and all, was produced." Any evolutionist who believed such nonsense would rightly be laughed off the intellectual stage; yet the only theory that could ever envision such a scenario for the origin of birds is creationism—with God acting in the egg.

I am both angry at and amused by the creationists; but mostly I am deeply sad. Sad for many reasons. Sad because so many people who respond to creationist appeals are troubled for the right reason, but venting their anger at the wrong target. It is true that scientists have often been dogmatic and elitist. It is true that we have often allowed the white-coated, advertising image to represent us—"Scientists say that Brand X cures bunions ten times faster than . . ." We have not fought it adequately because we derive benefits from appearing as a new priesthood. It is also true that faceless and bureaucratic state power intrudes more and more into our lives and removes choices that should belong to individuals and communities. I can understand that school curricula, imposed from above and without local input, might be seen as one more insult on all these grounds. But the culprit is not, and cannot be, evolution or any other fact of the natural world. Identify and fight your legitimate enemies by all means, but we are not among them.

I am sad because the practical result of this brouhaha will not be expanded coverage to include creationism (that would also make me sad), but the reduction or excision of evolution from high school curricula. Evolution is one of the half dozen "great ideas" developed by science. It speaks to the profound issues of genealogy that fascinate all of us—the "roots" phenomenon writ large. Where did we come from? Where did life arise? How did it develop? How are organisms related? It forces us to think, ponder, and wonder. Shall we deprive millions of this knowledge and once again teach biology as a set of dull and unconnected facts, without the thread that weaves diverse material into a supple unity?

But most of all I am saddened by a trend I am just beginning to discern among my colleagues. I sense that some now wish to mute the healthy debate about theory that has brought new life to evolutionary biology. It provides grist for creationist mills, they say, even if only by distortion. Perhaps we should lie low and rally round the flag of strict Darwinism, at least for the moment—a kind of old-time religion on our part.

But we should borrow another metaphor and recognize that we too have to tread a straight and narrow path, surrounded by roads to perdition. For if we ever begin to suppress our search to understand nature, to quench our own intellectual excitement in a misguided effort to present a united front where it does not and should not exist, then we are truly lost.

12

Darwin's Rib

Robert S. Root-Bernstein

Robert S. Root-Bernstein is a professor of physiology at Michigan State University. He is author of Rethinking AIDS: The Tragic Cost of Premature Consensus *(1999, Free Press) and, with Michele M. Root-Bernstein,* Sparks of Genius: The Thirteen Thinking Tools of the World's Most Creative People *(2001, Mariner).*

Considering the nature of science, belief systems, and pseudosciences (such as "scientific" creationism) in abstract, theoretical terms is one thing. Applying these concepts in more concrete, down-to-earth situations is another—and often more difficult—matter. In this selection, Robert Root-Bernstein tells how he dealt with a student's confusion over one particular question and turned it into a lesson on the differences, and the relationships, among types of knowledge.

As you read, consider the following questions:

1. What types of evidence does Root-Bernstein cite in support of the fact of biological evolution?

2. How does Root-Bernstein show his student that the actual number of ribs in men and women can both support evolution theory and, at the same time, not necessarily contradict her particular religious beliefs?

As all good teachers know, students will work much harder for extra-credit points than at the assigned task. I like to take advantage of this convenient trait in my introductory course on evolution. Once my students—nonscience majors at a midwestern land-grant university—understand the basic terms, I offer additional points for answering the questions I really want them to investigate. Find a dozen differences between the skeletons of a chimpanzee and a human being, I challenge them; tell me how a human female skeleton differs anatomically from a male. The male and female skeletons I display are exemplary in their difference, and since most students should be able to guess what that difference is if they don't already know, I usually feel confident that the final answer is a giveaway. I say "usually" because seven years ago, the first time I taught the course, I got a surprising answer that still crops up with alarming regularity. Five minutes into the lab period, a young woman announced that she could answer the question without even examining the human skeletons.

I waited silently for her to explain that the female pelvis is shaped slightly differently from the male's,

with a larger opening for childbearing. That part was the giveaway. The real purpose of the exercise was to make her prove her conjecture with measurements—to translate the theory to practice. I also wanted her to explain why this sexual dimorphism—that is, this sexually determined physical difference—is not nearly so pronounced in nonhuman primates, such as chimpanzees.

She spoke: "Males have one fewer pair of ribs than females."

I was totally unprepared for her answer. My mandible dropped. After a moment's reflection, I realized she must be referring to the biblical story in which God creates Eve from one of Adam's ribs. My student was someone who believed in the literal truth of the Bible, and it was her religious belief, not her previous knowledge of human anatomy, that made her so sure of her answer. This was going to be a challenge.

I believe just as firmly in religious freedom as I do in the scientific search for understanding. Thus, while I adhere rigorously to teaching the best science and showing how scientists recognize it as the best, I never insist that students believe scientific results. On the contrary, I encourage them to be skeptical—as long as their skepticism is based on logic and evidence. Scientific results, in my view, should be compelling because the collected observations and experiments leave room for only one possible rational explanation. To insist that students accept my word (or the word of any scientist) about any fact would undermine the one thing that makes science different from all other belief systems. The acid test of science is the personal one of convincing yourself that you perceive what everyone else perceives, whatever reservations you may start with. The evidence should be so compelling that it convinces even the most serious skeptic—as long as that skeptic retains an open mind. Even more important, science must admit what it does not or cannot know. Questions are what drive science, not answers. A teacher who insists on blind faith might well crush some budding Darwin who sees a higher and more compelling truth about nature than the current dogma admits.

But in this instance, I was dealing with a pretty bare-bones case. The skeletons stood there as mute models of reality. Pedagogical ideals notwithstanding, I saw little hope of enlightening my young friend without attacking her religion outright.

I stalled for time. "Have you actually counted the ribs?" I asked. She admitted that she had not. "Well, since this is a science class," I admonished, "let's treat your statement as a hypothesis. Now you need to test it." So off she went to the back of the room, full of confidence that God would not let her down. The breather gave me a chance to plot out what I hoped would be an enlightened, and enlightening, approach to the crisis her assumption had precipitated.

I began by reviewing my lesson plans to see where I had gone wrong. After all, comparative anatomy lab exercises should be fairly straightforward stuff. The body of the work consists in finding and describing the usual anatomic features essential to understanding basic evolutionary theory. We look for homologies (body parts that spring from the same embryological parts but may have different functions, such as a whale's flipper, a human hand, and a bat's wing) and analogies (body parts that serve the same function but have very different developmental origins, such as the wings of birds and insects).

We go on to examine the evidence for transitional forms, using casts of the series of modifications that begins with the four-toed *Hyracotherium* and ends with the modern one-toed horse. The students generally get a few surprises while learning about divergent evolution—how living things become more and more different through geologic time. Imagine the ribs of a reptile broadening and fusing to become the bony back-plate of a tortoise. If you turn the skeleton over and look at the inside, you can even figure out how the shell evolved.

Convergent evolution is usually an eye-opener, too, since the notion that random mutations might lead to similar outcomes is anything but obvious. We study the point by examining a wonderful display of creatures that eat ants—spiny anteaters, silky anteaters, pangolins, and armadillos—each of which evolved from a different class of animals. Despite their disparate origins, they look generally similar: they all have the same long snouts; long, sticky tongues; and long, sharp claws for prying ants from their nests and eating them, and they all have little eyes and thick fur, spines, or scales to protect them from the bites of their tiny prey. Such examples of convergent evolution are among the best evidence for natural selection, because any animal that is going to eat ants, regardless of its anatomic origins, needs certain adaptations and will therefore end up looking similar to all the other animals that live in the same way.

Finally, we study vestigial traits—leftover parts that seem to serve no present function, such as the useless wings of flightless birds like ostriches and our apparently pointless appendix.

The students are required to understand these terms and be able to use their attendant principles to compare many amphibian, reptile, and mammalian skeletons, as well as a few fossil replicas. Was it really possible to learn all that and still think God created Eve from one of Adam's ribs?

"Are you sure those are male and female skeletons?" My cocksure friend was back, looking a little puzzled.

"They're the bona fide item," I answered. "Not only did they come so labeled from the company from which they were bought, but certain anatomic features that I have verified myself lead me to conclude that the labels are correct. But I'm glad you asked. Skepticism is a very useful scientific tool, and scientists do sometimes make mistakes. Not this time, though."

"Yes, but the skeletons have the same number of ribs," objected my student.

I agreed. "Why did you expect otherwise?" Best to get the argument out in the open. As I had guessed, her information came from the Bible, via Sunday school.

I had a sudden vision of whole classes being taught anatomic nonsense as truth. In my imagination, simple skeletons rose with a clamorous rattle to take on new lives as bones of contention. Wherever they appeared, dozens of Bible-toting students followed, egged on by ossified Sunday school teachers clustering around my desk to demand how I dare question Scripture. I knew my department chair would back me up, but the dean? The board of trustees? Weren't a few of them fundamentalists themselves? The problem was getting more difficult by the minute.

"But what does the Bible actually say?" I asked. Surely there had to be some way out of this mess.

"That God took a rib from Adam to create Eve."

"One rib or two?"

"One," she replied without hesitation.

"Don't forget that ribs come in pairs," I prompted her.

"Oh!" I could almost hear her mind whirring. "So men should be missing only one rib, not a pair—is that what you're saying?"

"I don't know." I shook my head. "Why should they be missing any?"

"Well, if God took a rib from Adam, wouldn't his children also be missing a rib?"

"All his children?" I countered. "Boys and girls?"

My young friend thought for a moment. "Oh, I see," she said. "Why should only males inherit the missing rib—why not females, too? That's a good question."

"I have a better one," I pressed on, a full plan of evolutionary enlightenment now formulated in my mind. "What kind of inheritance would this missing rib represent?"

In class we had discussed the differences between Lamarckian evolution by transmission of inherited somatic modifications and Mendelian inheritance through genes carried in the germ line of reproductive cells, but my student missed the point of my question. I explained. "Essentially, Lamarck maintained that anything that affects your body could affect your offspring. Lift weights regularly, and your daughter could inherit a bigger and stronger body than she would if you never stirred from the sofa. Chop off the tails of generation after generation of mice, and eventually you should end up with tailless mice. Make an antelope put its neck out for high-growing leaves, and its distant descendants will be giraffes.

"The problem is that generations of Jewish and Muslim males have been circumcised, without any effect on the presence or absence of the penile foreskin of later generations. Certain breeds of dogs have had their ears and tails cropped for hundreds of years without affecting the length or shape of the ears and tails of their offspring. In other words, Lamarck was wrong.

"In fact, if you recall from lectures, he couldn't have been right. Lamarckian types of inheritance aren't possible in higher animals. Remember: your egg cells are formed prior to birth and, mutations aside, contain essentially unalterable genetic information. Nothing you do to change your personal physiognomy, from lifting weights to having a nose job, will affect the genetic makeup of your offspring." As I reexplained these basic points, I realized that, lacking a problem to apply the information to, my student had not yet understood the important differences between Lamarck's and Mendel's theories. Information without a problem to which it can be applied is like a body without bones: a shapeless mass of muscle with nothing to work against. With Lamarck and Mendel in their fortuitous, Bible-generated problem context, I tried again.

"Look at it this way. Suppose you had an accident, and your right thumb had to be amputated. Would you expect all your children, assuming you have any, to be born lacking a right thumb?"

"Of course not," said my student. Then, after a pause, "Oh, I see. You mean that for the same reason my children would have thumbs even if I didn't, Adam's children would have the normal number of ribs even though God took one of his. Otherwise, it would be Lamarckian inheritance."

"Right!" I said. "And there is no creditable evidence to support Lamarckian inheritance. So you've actually got several problems here. First, Lamarckian inheritance doesn't work. Why should Adam's loss of a rib affect his children? Second, everyone has ribs, men and women alike. Ribs certainly aren't a sex-linked trait like excessive facial hair or a scrotum. So there's no reason I can think of that Adam's male offspring but not his female ones should be missing a rib. If the sons were missing a rib, wouldn't the daughters be missing one, too?

"Third, there is nothing in the Bible that says exactly how many ribs Adam started out with, or how many ribs we should have, is there? So you have no compelling reason to believe that in taking a rib from Adam, God left all his male offspring one short. That's an inference—and a particularly poor one since it relies on an outdated theory of evolutionary change. You don't really want to use a discarded evolutionary theory to prop up the Bible, do you?"

I was pleased to see that my ploy had worked. My student accepted this rebuff of accepted wisdom with good grace and an active intellect. Her religion was intact, but she was learning to think about her assumptions and to reason a bit more like a scientist. She was soon back at the human skeletons counting and measuring other bones. With some help, and a few broad hints ("How can you tell the difference between a man and a woman from behind, if they are the same height and have equal-length hair?"), she finally realized that the reason she wore a different cut of jeans from the men in the class was because she is built slightly differently. *Vive la différence!*

Most human females have a relatively wider pelvis than males because the human brain (even in a newborn) is too large to pass through a narrow birth canal. Thus, one of the reasons sexual dimorphism is so much more pronounced in humans than in most other primates is relative brain size. ("Don't trust me," I told her, "check it—the skeletons are there!") Bigger brains require bigger hips.

By the end of the course, five more students had reported to me that they too knew without having to look at the skeletons that women have more ribs than men. Some of them trotted off to count the ribs and came back to report that they had verified their preconceived notion. I had to stand beside them and count the ribs two or three times before they would believe that there really are the same number in the two skeletons.

These days I'm better prepared than I was that first year. Sometimes I bring in an extra pair of skeletons or a medical textbook with X-ray photographs of the chest, so that the students can count ribs to their hearts' content. I've come to expect at least 10 percent of the students in each class to tell me that men and women differ in rib count. I have conducted surveys of nearly a thousand first-year college students who either are nonscience majors or have not yet declared a major. More than 25 percent report believing that God created the Earth within the last 10,000 years and that man was formed in God's image exactly as described in the Bible. Another 50 percent report being undecided as to whether evolution is a valid scientific theory or a hoax. Only about 20 percent enter my university having learned enough about science and the evidence for evolution to consider it a valid scientific theory.

My college classroom numbers follow fairly closely those reported in recent national polls. A 1991 Gallup poll, for example, found that 47 percent of the respondents believed that God created man within the last 10,000 years. Forty percent believed that man evolved over millions of years but that God had a direct hand in guiding that process. Only 9 percent said man evolved without God's direct intervention. In many communities, such as mine, there are ongoing, active attempts to exclude evolution from the public school curriculum. Lecturing on evolution is an interesting challenge under these circumstances.

But I always have the last laugh. I share it with my classes after they have counted ribs for themselves and know for themselves the correct answer. You see, I really do have one fewer pair of ribs than my mother.

Don't get me wrong: I'm perfectly normal. I have 12 pairs of ribs, just like almost every other human being, male or female. So, as far as we know, do my father and brother. My mother is the unusual one. She has 13 pairs of ribs.

Oh yes, and that 5,300-year-old man they found frozen in a glacier in the Alps a few years back? He's got only 11 pairs of ribs. It happens. Still, imagine what might happen if the creation "scientists" get hold of a replica of the 5,300-year-old man's skeleton and try to pawn it off as proof of the Bible. Or consider the havoc my mother might wreak if her bones find their way into some science class to be compared with a typical male skeleton.

I chuckle at the thought, but I also check my skeletons twice. You can never be too careful. For example, there's a condition known as polydactyly—literally, "many digits"—in which people have extra fingers or toes. In one town in Spain, there has been so much inbreeding that almost everyone has six or seven fingers on each hand. I don't want any of my students unexpectedly claiming that a significant difference between chimps and us is the number of fingers or toes.

On the other hand, I wouldn't say no to a seven-fingered skeleton with 13 pairs of ribs. What a wonderful extra-credit assignment that would make, and what a wonderful example of how nature evades every generalization we try to impose on it. Take nothing for granted, I counsel my students: that is what makes a scientist. But don't ignore the exceptions, either. I'll make no bones about it: anatomic differences are what drive evolution—and its teaching.

13

Devolution

H. Allen Orr

H. Allen Orr is a professor of biology at the University of Rochester. His research focuses on population genetics, the genetics of speciation, and the genetics of adaptation. He is a frequent contributor to the New Yorker *and other magazines, writing about evolution.*

A current threat to the accurate, scientific teaching of evolutionary theory is the philosophical idea of intelligent design (I.D.). It seems to have enjoyed a wide acceptance among the general public (including politicians) in large measure because its proponents give it the veneer of a legitimate scientific model, with arguments from molecular biology and statistics. In this selection, biologist H. Allen Orr describes the premises of I.D. and then addresses these from the perspective of mainstream science, showing why I.D. is clearly not in that category.

As you read, consider the following questions:

1. What are the main claims of I.D. and what is the claimed evidence for these ideas?
2. How and to what extent does I.D. incorporate the concept of biological evolution?
3. What is the concept of "irreducible complexity" and what role does it play in the claims of I.D.?
4. How do mainstream biology and evolutionary biology answer the claims of I.D.?
5. What does Orr feel is the real motivation behind the I.D. movement?

If you are in ninth grade and live in Dover, Pennsylvania, you are learning things in your biology class that differ considerably from what your peers just a few miles away are learning. In particular, you are learning that Darwin's theory of evolution provides just one possible explanation of life, and that another is provided by something called intelligent design. You are being taught this not because of a recent breakthrough in some scientist's laboratory but because the Dover Area School District's board mandates it. In October, 2004, the board decreed that "students will be made aware of gaps/problems in Darwin's theory and of other theories of evolution including, but not limited to, intelligent design."

While the events in Dover have received a good deal of attention as a sign of the political times, there has been surprisingly little discussion of the science that's said to underlie the theory of intelligent design, often called I.D. Many scientists avoid discussing I.D.

for strategic reasons. If a scientific claim can be loosely defined as one that scientists take seriously enough to debate, then engaging the intelligent-design movement on scientific grounds, they worry, cedes what it most desires: recognition that its claims are legitimate scientific ones.

Meanwhile, proposals hostile to evolution are being considered in more than twenty states; earlier this month, a bill was introduced into the New York State Assembly calling for instruction in intelligent design for all public-school students. The Kansas State Board of Education is weighing new standards, drafted by supporters of intelligent design, that would encourage schoolteachers to challenge Darwinism. Senator Rick Santorum, a Pennsylvania Republican, has argued that "intelligent design is a legitimate scientific theory that should be taught in science classes." An I.D.-friendly amendment that he sponsored to the No Child Left Behind Act—requiring public schools to help students understand why evolution "generates so much continuing controversy"—was overwhelmingly approved in the Senate. (The amendment was not included in the version of the bill that was signed into law, but similar language did appear in a conference report that accompanied it.) In the past few years, college students across the country have formed Intelligent Design and Evolution Awareness chapters. Clearly, a policy of limited scientific engagement has failed. So just what is this movement?

First of all, intelligent design is not what people often assume it is. For one thing, I.D. is not Biblical literalism. Unlike earlier generations of creationists—the so-called Young Earthers and scientific creationists—proponents of intelligent design do not believe that the universe was created in six days, that Earth is ten thousand years old, or that the fossil record was deposited during Noah's flood. (Indeed, they shun the label "creationism" altogether.) Nor does I.D. flatly reject evolution: adherents freely admit that some evolutionary change occurred during the history of life on Earth. Although the movement is loosely allied with, and heavily funded by, various conservative Christian groups—and although I.D. plainly maintains that life was created—it is generally silent about the identity of the creator.

The movement's main positive claim is that there are things in the world, most notably life, that cannot be accounted for by known natural causes and show features that, in any other context, we would attribute to intelligence. Living organisms are too complex to be explained by any natural—or, more precisely, by any mindless—process. Instead, the design inherent in organisms can be accounted for only by invoking a designer, and one who is very, very smart.

All of which puts I.D. squarely at odds with Darwin. Darwin's theory of evolution was meant to show how the fantastically complex features of organisms—eyes, beaks, brains—could arise without the intervention of a designing mind. According to Darwinism, evolution largely reflects the combined action of random mutation and natural selection. A random mutation in an organism, like a random change in any finely tuned machine, is almost always bad. That's why you don't, screwdriver in hand, make arbitrary changes to the insides of your television. But, once in a great while, a random mutation in the DNA that makes up an organism's genes slightly improves the function of some organ and thus the survival of the organism. In a species whose eye amounts to nothing more than a primitive patch of light-sensitive cells, a mutation that causes this patch to fold into a cup shape might have a survival advantage. While the old type of organism can tell only if the lights are on, the new type can detect the *direction* of any source of light or shadow. Since shadows sometimes mean predators, that can be valuable information. The new, improved type of organism will, therefore, be more common in the next generation. That's natural selection. Repeated over billions of years, this process of incremental improvement should

allow for the gradual emergence of organisms that are exquisitely adapted to their environments and that look for all the world as though they were designed. By 1870, about a decade after "The Origin of Species" was published, nearly all biologists agreed that life had evolved, and by 1940 or so most agreed that natural selection was a key force driving this evolution.

Advocates of intelligent design point to two developments that in their view undermine Darwinism. The first is the molecular revolution in biology. Beginning in the nineteen-fifties, molecular biologists revealed a staggering and unsuspected degree of complexity within the cells that make up all life. This complexity, I.D.'s defenders argue, lies beyond the abilities of Darwinism to explain. Second, they claim that new mathematical findings cast doubt on the power of natural selection. Selection may play a role in evolution, but it cannot accomplish what biologists suppose it can.

These claims have been championed by a tireless group of writers, most of them associated with the Center for Science and Culture at the Discovery Institute, a Seattle-based think tank that sponsors projects in science, religion, and national defense, among other areas. The center's fellows and advisers—including the emeritus law professor Phillip E. Johnson, the philosopher Stephen C. Meyer, and the biologist Jonathan Wells—have published an astonishing number of articles and books that decry the ostensibly sad state of Darwinism and extol the virtues of the design alternative. But Johnson, Meyer, and Wells, while highly visible, are mainly strategists and popularizers. The scientific leaders of the design movement are two scholars, one a biochemist and the other a mathematician. To assess intelligent design is to assess their arguments.

Michael J. Behe, a professor of biological sciences at Lehigh University (and a senior fellow at the Discovery Institute), is a biochemist who writes technical papers on the structure of DNA. He is the most prominent of the small circle of scientists working on intelligent design, and his arguments are by far the best known. His book "Darwin's Black Box" (1996) was a surprise best-seller and was named by *National Review* as one of the hundred best nonfiction books of the twentieth century. (A little calibration may be useful here; "The Starr Report" also made the list.)

Not surprisingly, Behe's doubts about Darwinism begin with biochemistry. Fifty years ago, he says, any biologist could tell stories like the one about the eye's evolution. But such stories, Behe notes, invariably began with cells, whose own evolutionary origins were essentially left unexplained. This was harmless enough as long as cells weren't qualitatively more complex than the larger, more visible aspects of the eye. Yet when biochemists began to dissect the inner workings of the cell, what they found floored them. A cell is packed full of exceedingly complex structures— hundreds of microscopic machines, each performing a specific job. The "Give me a cell and I'll give you an eye" story told by Darwinists, he says, began to seem suspect: starting with a cell was starting ninety per cent of the way to the finish line.

Behe's main claim is that cells are complex not just in degree but in kind. Cells contain structures that are "irreducibly complex." This means that if you remove any single part from such a structure, the structure no longer functions. Behe offers a simple, nonbiological example of an irreducibly complex object: the mousetrap. A mousetrap has several parts—platform, spring, catch, hammer, and hold-down bar—and all of them have to be in place for the trap to work. If you remove the spring from a mousetrap, it isn't slightly worse at killing mice; it doesn't kill them at all. So, too, with the bacterial flagellum, Behe argues. This flagellum is a tiny propeller attached to the back of some bacteria. Spinning at more than twenty thousand r.p.m.s, it motors the bacterium through its aquatic world. The flagellum comprises roughly thirty different proteins, all precisely arranged, and if any one of them is removed the flagellum stops spinning.

In "Darwin's Black Box," Behe maintained that irreducible complexity presents Darwinism with "unbridgeable chasms." How, after all, could a gradual process of incremental improvement build something like a flagellum, which needs *all* its parts in order to work? Scientists, he argued, must face up to the fact that "many biochemical systems cannot be built by natural selection working on mutations." In the end, Behe concluded that irreducibly complex cells arise the same way as irreducibly complex mousetraps— someone designs them. As he put it in a recent *Times* Op-Ed piece: "If it looks, walks, and quacks like a duck, then, absent compelling evidence to the contrary, we have warrant to conclude it's a duck. Design should not be overlooked simply because it's so obvious." In "Darwin's Black Box," Behe speculated that the designer might have assembled the first cell, essentially solving the problem of irreducible complexity, after which evolution might well have proceeded by more or less conventional means. Under Behe's brand of creationism, you might still be an ape that evolved on the African savanna; it's just that your cells harbor micro-machines engineered by an unnamed intelligence some four billion years ago.

But Behe's principal argument soon ran into trouble. As biologists pointed out, there are several different ways that Darwinian evolution can build irreducibly complex systems. In one, elaborate structures may evolve for one reason and then get co-opted for some entirely different, irreducibly complex function. Who says those thirty flagellar proteins weren't present in bacteria long before bacteria sported flagella? They may have been performing other jobs in the cell and only later got drafted into flagellum-building. Indeed, there's now strong evidence that several flagellar proteins once played roles in a type of molecular pump found in the membranes of bacterial cells.

Behe doesn't consider this sort of "indirect" path to irreducible complexity—in which parts perform one function and then switch to another—terribly plausible. And he essentially rules out the alternative possibility of a direct Darwinian path: a path, that is, in which Darwinism builds an irreducibly complex structure while selecting all along for the same biological function. But biologists have shown that direct paths to irreducible complexity are possible, too. Suppose a part gets added to a system merely because the part improves the system's performance; the part is not, at this stage, essential for function. But, because subsequent evolution builds on this addition, a part that was at first just advantageous might *become* essential. As this process is repeated through evolutionary time, more and more parts that were once merely beneficial become necessary. This idea was first set forth by H. J. Muller, the Nobel Prize–winning geneticist, in 1939, but it's a familiar process in the development of human technologies. We add new parts like global-positioning systems to cars not because they're necessary but because they're nice. But no one would be surprised if, in fifty years, computers that rely on G.P.S. actually drove our cars. At that point, G.P.S. would no longer be an attractive option; it would be an essential piece of automotive technology. It's important to see that this process is thoroughly Darwinian: each change might well be small and each represents an improvement.

Design theorists have made some concessions to these criticisms. Behe has confessed to "sloppy prose" and said he hadn't meant to imply that irreducibly complex systems "by definition" cannot evolve gradually. "I quite agree that my argument against Darwinism does not add up to a logical proof," he says—though he continues to believe that Darwinian paths to irreducible complexity are exceedingly unlikely. Behe and his followers now emphasize that, while irreducibly complex systems can in principle evolve, biologists can't reconstruct in convincing detail just how any such system did evolve.

What counts as a sufficiently detailed historical narrative, though, is altogether subjective. Biologists actually know a great deal about the evolution of biochemical systems, irreducibly complex or not. It's significant, for instance, that the proteins that typically make up the parts of these systems are often similar to one another. (Blood clotting—another of Behe's examples of irreducible complexity—involves at least twenty proteins, several of which are similar, and all of which are needed to make clots, to localize or remove clots, or to prevent the runaway clotting of all blood.) And biologists understand why these proteins are so similar. Each gene in an organism's genome encodes a particular protein. Occasionally, the stretch of DNA that makes up a particular gene will get accidentally copied, yielding a genome that includes two versions of the gene. Over many generations, one version of the gene will often keep its original function while the other one slowly changes by mutation and natural selection, picking up a new, though usually related, function. This process of "gene duplication" has given rise to entire families of proteins that have similar functions; they often act in the same biochemical pathway or sit in the same cellular structure. There's no doubt that gene duplication plays an extremely important role in the evolution of biological complexity.

It's true that when you confront biologists with a particular complex structure like the flagellum they sometimes have a hard time saying which part appeared before which other parts. But then it can be hard, with any complex historical process, to reconstruct the exact order in which events occurred, especially when, as in evolution, the addition of new parts encourages the modification of old ones. When you're looking at a bustling urban street, for example, you probably can't tell which shop went into business first. This is partly because many businesses now depend on each other and partly because new shops trigger changes in old ones (the new sushi place draws twenty-somethings who demand wireless Internet at the café next door). But it would be a little rash to conclude that all the shops must have begun business on the same day or that some Unseen Urban Planner had carefully determined just which business went where.

The other leading theorist of the new creationism, William A. Dembski, holds a Ph.D. in mathematics, another in philosophy, and a master of divinity in theology. He has been a research professor in the conceptual foundations of science at Baylor University, and was recently appointed to the new Center for Science and Theology at Southern Baptist Theological Seminary. (He is a longtime senior fellow at the Discovery Institute as well.) Dembski publishes at a staggering pace. His books—including "The Design Inference," "Intelligent Design," "No Free Lunch," and "The Design Revolution"—are generally well written and packed with provocative ideas.

According to Dembski, a complex object must be the result of intelligence if it was the product neither of chance nor of necessity. The novel "Moby Dick," for example, didn't arise by chance (Melville didn't scribble random letters), and it wasn't the necessary consequence of a physical law (unlike, say, the fall of an apple). It was, instead, the result of Melville's intelligence. Dembski argues that there is a reliable way to recognize such products of intelligence in the natural world. We can conclude that an object was intelligently designed, he says, if it shows "specified complexity"—complexity that matches an "independently given pattern." The sequence of letters "JKXVCJUDOPLVM" is certainly complex: if you randomly type thirteen letters, you are very unlikely to arrive at this particular sequence. But it isn't *specified:* it doesn't match any independently given sequence of letters. If, on the other hand, I ask you for the first sentence of "Moby Dick" and you type the letters "CALLMEISHMAEL," you have produced something that is both complex and specified. The sequence you typed is unlikely to arise by chance alone, and it matches an independent target sequence (the one written by Melville). Dembski argues that specified complexity, when expressed mathematically, provides an unmistakable signature of intelligence. Things like "CALLMEISHMAEL," he points out, just don't arise in the real world without acts of intelligence. If organisms show specified complexity, therefore, we conclude that they are the handiwork of an intelligent agent.

For Dembski, it's telling that the sophisticated machines we find in organisms match up in astonishingly precise ways with recognizable human technologies. The eye, for example, has a familiar, cameralike design, with recognizable parts—a pinhole opening for light, a lens, and a surface on which to project an image—all arranged just as a human engineer would arrange them. And the flagellum has a motor design, one that features recognizable O-rings, a rotor, and a drive shaft. Specified complexity, he says, is there for all to see.

Dembski's second major claim is that certain mathematical results cast doubt on Darwinism at the most basic conceptual level. In 2002, he focussed on so-called No Free Lunch, or N.F.L., theorems, which were derived in the late nineties by the physicists David H. Wolpert and William G. Macready. These theorems relate to the efficiency of different "search algorithms." Consider a search for high ground on some unfamiliar, hilly terrain. You're on foot and it's a moonless night; you've got two hours to reach the highest place you can. How to proceed? One sensible search algorithm might say, "Walk uphill in the steepest possible direction; if no direction uphill is available, take a couple of steps to the left and try again." This algorithm insures that you're generally moving upward. Another search algorithm—a so-called blind search algorithm—might say, "Walk in a random direction." This would sometimes take you uphill but sometimes down. Roughly, the N.F.L. theorems prove the surprising fact that, averaged over all possible terrains, no search algorithm is better than any other. In some landscapes, moving uphill gets you to higher ground in the allotted time, while in other landscapes moving randomly does, but on average neither outperforms the other.

Now, Darwinism can be thought of as a search algorithm. Given a problem—adapting to a new disease, for instance—a population uses the Darwinian algorithm of random mutation plus natural selection to search for a solution (in this case, disease resistance). But, according to Dembski, the N.F.L. theorems prove that this Darwinian algorithm is no better than any other when confronting all possible problems. It follows that, over all, Darwinism is no better than blind search, a process of utterly random change unaided by any guiding force like natural selection. Since we don't expect blind change to build elaborate machines showing an exquisite coördination of parts, we have no right to expect Darwinism to do so, either. Attempts to sidestep this problem by, say, carefully constraining the class of challenges faced by organisms inevitably involve sneaking in the very kind of order that we're trying to explain—something Dembski calls the displacement problem. In the end, he argues, the N.F.L. theorems and the displacement problem mean that there's only one plausible source for the design we find in organisms: intelligence. Although Dembski is somewhat noncommittal, he seems to favor a design theory in which an intelligent agent programmed design into early life, or even into the early universe. This design then unfolded through the long course of evolutionary time, as microbes slowly morphed into man.

Dembski's arguments have been met with tremendous enthusiasm in the I.D. movement. In part, that's because an innumerate public is easily impressed by a bit of mathematics. Also, when Dembski is wielding his equations, he gets to play the part of the hard scientist busily correcting the errors of those soft-headed biologists. (Evolutionary biology actually features an extraordinarily sophisticated body of mathematical theory, a fact not widely known because neither of evolution's great popularizers—Richard Dawkins and the late Stephen Jay Gould—did much math.) Despite all the attention, Dembski's mathematical claims about design and Darwin are almost entirely beside the point.

The most serious problem in Dembski's account involves specified complexity. Organisms aren't trying to match any "independently given pattern": evolution has no goal, and the history of life isn't trying to get anywhere. If building a sophisticated structure like an eye increases the number of children produced, evolution may well build an eye. But if destroying a sophisticated structure like the eye increases the number of children produced, evolution will just as happily destroy the eye. Species of fish and crustaceans that have moved into the total darkness of caves, where eyes are both unnecessary and costly, often have degenerate eyes, or eyes that begin to form only to be covered by skin—crazy contraptions that no intelligent agent would design. Despite all the loose talk about design and machines, organisms aren't striving to realize some engineer's blueprint; they're striving (if they can be said to strive at all) only to have more offspring than the next fellow.

Another problem with Dembski's arguments concerns the N.F.L. theorems. Recent work shows that these theorems don't hold in the case of co-evolution, when two or more species evolve in response to one another. And most evolution is surely co-evolution. Organisms do not spend most of their time adapting to rocks; they are perpetually challenged by, and adapting to, a rapidly changing suite of viruses, parasites, predators, and prey. A theorem that doesn't apply to these situations is a theorem whose relevance to biology is unclear. As it happens, David Wolpert, one of the authors of the N.F.L. theorems, recently denounced Dembski's use of those theorems as "fatally informal and imprecise." Dembski's apparent response has been a tactical retreat. In 2002, Dembski triumphantly proclaimed, "The No Free Lunch theorems dash any hope of generating specified complexity via evolutionary algorithms." Now he says, "I certainly never argued that the N.F.L. theorems provide a direct refutation of Darwinism."

Those of us who have argued with I.D. in the past are used to such shifts of emphasis. But it's striking that Dembski's views on the history of life contradict Behe's. Dembski believes that Darwinism is incapable of building anything interesting; Behe seems to believe that, given a cell, Darwinism might well have built you and me. Although proponents of I.D. routinely inflate the significance of minor squabbles among evolutionary biologists (did the peppered moth evolve dark color as a defense against birds or for other reasons?), they seldom acknowledge their own, often major differences of opinion. In the end, it's hard to view intelligent design as a coherent movement in any but a political sense.

It's also hard to view it as a real research program. Though people often picture science as a collection of clever theories, scientists are generally staunch pragmatists: to scientists, a good theory is one that inspires new experiments and provides unexpected insights into familiar phenomena. By this standard, Darwinism is one of the best theories in the history of science: it has produced countless important experiments (let's re-create a natural species in the lab—yes, that's been done) and sudden insight into once puzzling patterns (*that's* why there are no native land mammals on oceanic islands). In the nearly ten years since the publication of Behe's book, by contrast, I.D. has inspired no nontrivial experiments and has provided no surprising insights into biology. As the years pass, intelligent design looks less and less like the science it claimed to be and more and more like an extended exercise in polemics.

In 1999, a document from the Discovery Institute was posted, anonymously, on the Internet. This Wedge Document, as it came to be called, described not only the institute's long-term goals but its strategies for accomplishing them. The document begins by labelling the idea that human beings are created in the image of God "one of the bedrock principles on which Western civilization was built." It goes on to decry the catastrophic legacy of Darwin, Marx, and Freud—the alleged fathers of a "materialistic conception of reality" that eventually "infected virtually every area of our culture." The mission of the Discovery Institute's scientific wing is then spelled out: "nothing less than the overthrow of materialism and its cultural legacies." It seems fair to conclude that the Discovery Institute has set its sights a bit higher than, say, reconstructing the origins of the bacterial flagellum.

The intelligent-design community is usually far more circumspect in its pronouncements. This is not to say that it eschews discussion of religion; indeed, the intelligent-design literature regularly insists that Darwinism represents a thinly veiled attempt to foist a secular religion—godless materialism—on Western culture. As it happens, the idea that Darwinism is yoked to atheism, though popular, is also wrong. Of the five founding fathers of twentieth-century evolutionary biology—Ronald Fisher, Sewall Wright, J. B. S. Haldane, Ernst Mayr, and Theodosius Dobzhansky—one was a devout Anglican who preached sermons and published articles in church magazines, one a practicing Unitarian, one a dabbler in Eastern mysticism, one an apparent atheist, and one a member of the Russian Orthodox Church and the author of a book on religion and science. Pope John Paul II himself acknowledged, in a 1996 address to the Pontifical Academy of Sciences, that new research "leads to the recognition of the theory of evolution as more than a hypothesis." Whatever larger conclusions one thinks *should* follow from Darwinism, the historical fact is that evolution and religion have often coexisted. As the philosopher Michael Ruse observes, "It is simply not the case that people take up evolution in the morning, and become atheists as an encore in the afternoon."

Biologists aren't alarmed by intelligent design's arrival in Dover and elsewhere because they have all sworn allegiance to atheistic materialism; they're alarmed because intelligent design is junk science. Meanwhile, more than eighty per cent of Americans say that God either created human beings in their present form or guided their development. As a succession of intelligent-design proponents appeared before the Kansas State Board of Education earlier this month, it was possible to wonder whether the movement's scientific coherence was beside the point. Intelligent design has come this far by faith.

PART 4

The Processes of Evolution

The processes of evolution and their results—changes within species and the origin of new species—are complex. As scientific principles, they naturally need to be described and examined in broad, often abstract theoretical terms. But these processes affect *real* living organisms and the *real* world in which we live. Full understanding can be achieved only by looking at them from various perspectives, including examples of evolution in action.

We recognize four basic processes of biological evolution:

1. *Mutation*—mistakes in the genetic mechanism that add new variation to a species' gene pool

2. *Natural selection*—the differential reproduction of individuals based on the adaptive value of their traits within local environments

3. *Gene flow*—the mixing of genes as populations within a species move about and interbreed

4. *Genetic drift*—the splitting of populations to found new populations with new sets of gene frequencies (*fission* and the *founder effect*) and the nonrepresentative sampling of parental genes as each new generation is produced (*gamete sampling*)

New species arise when a population within an existing species becomes isolated. Isolation is often ecological—a species is literally split into isolated parts by movement into different and isolated geographic areas, or by some environmental change that divides portions of a species (a river changing its course, to cite just one obvious example). Isolation can also be genetic, when a macromutation (a mutation with extensive phenotypic results) within a subpopulation of a species makes that subpopulation different enough from the rest of the original species to set it off on a new evolutionary pathway. In isolation, then, such new populations experience the processes of genetic variations and phenotypic adaptation separate from the parent species. One result of differentiating traits may be characters that act as reproductive isolating mechanisms, meaning that even if the populations once again have the opportunity to interbreed, they will not be able to do so. They are separate species.

In "Curse and Blessing of the Ghetto," evolutionary biologist Jared Diamond provides an intriguing example of the possible action of natural selection in a living human population. He seeks to explain the unexpectedly high incidence of a fatal genetic disease, Tay-Sachs, among Ashkenazic Jews of Eastern Europe. His story is also a classic example of the holistic nature of anthropological investigations.

Josie Glausiusz, in "Unfortunate Drift," looks at other genetic diseases that are also common among the Ashkenazim and offers an explanation based not on natural selection but rather on another evolutionary process, genetic drift. Indeed, she takes issue with Diamond's explanation for the high frequency of Tay-Sachs disease in this group. The two articles make for a nice contrast and a perfect example of the questioning, self-critical character of science.

We turn again to Stephen Jay Gould for a discussion called "What Is a Species?" Gould not only discusses the definition of a species but also describes how species evolve and what the shape of the evolutionary "family tree" looks like.

SUGGESTED WEBSITES FOR FURTHER STUDY

http://www.emory.edu/Living_Links
http://users.rcn.com/jkimball.ma.ultranet/BiologyPages/S/Speciation.html
http://www.ntsad.org/pages/t-sachs.htm

14

Curse and Blessing of the Ghetto

Jared Diamond

Jared Diamond is a professor of physiology at the UCLA School of Medicine and research associate in ornithology at the American Museum of Natural History in New York. His early research on the bird life of New Guinea has led to an interest in evolutionary biology, and he now writes extensively on many areas within that subject. He is a contributing editor to Discover *magazine. Along with Stephen Jay Gould, he has become one of our best-known contemporary science essayists. His book* Guns, Germs, and Steel: The Fates of Human Societies *(1997, Norton) won a Pulitzer Prize in 1998. His latest book is* Collapse: How Societies Choose to Fail or Succeed *(2005, Viking).*

Some of our most striking examples of the processes of evolution in action come from understanding seemingly anomalous, hard-to-explain phenomena—such as unusually high frequencies of potentially fatal genetic diseases among certain populations. The classic example, of course, is sickle-cell anemia, a fatal condition that occurs in frequencies as high as 20 percent in some African populations. The explanation is that although being homozygous for sickle cell usually results in death, being heterozygous results in less severe cases of anemia and also confers an immunity to malaria. Thus, in areas where malaria is common, heterozygotes for sickle cell are at a selective advantage—they are the most reproductively successful, and every time two of them reproduce, they stand a one-in-four chance of producing a child who will have full-blown sickle-cell anemia. They also have a one-in-two chance of producing heterozygotes like themselves, each of whom carries one gene for the disease. In this selection, Jared Diamond turns his attention to another possible example of such a selective advantage inherent in a fatal genetic disease. (Compare Diamond's analysis with that presented in Selection 15.)

As you read, consider the following questions:

1. What are the four possible explanations for the high frequency of Tay-Sachs disease among Ashkenazic Jews?

2. What are Diamond's arguments against genetic drift and the founder effect as explanations?

3. What is Diamond's hypothesis regarding the relationship between Tay-Sachs and tuberculosis?

4. What are the questions that remain to be answered in testing this hypothesis?

5. What is genetic screening, and how can it help decrease the frequency of certain genetically based diseases? How has it helped in the case of Tay-Sachs? What are some of the ethical problems that might be related to genetic screening?

6. In what way is this article an example of the holistic nature of anthropological analysis?

M arie and I hated her at first sight, even though she was trying hard to be helpful. As our obstetrician's genetics counselor, she was just doing her job, explaining to us the unpleasant results that might come out of the

genetic tests we were about to have performed. As a scientist, though, I already knew all I wanted to know about Tay-Sachs disease, and I didn't need to be reminded that the baby sentenced to death by it could be my own.

Fortunately, the tests would reveal that my wife and I were not carriers of the Tay-Sachs gene, and our preparenthood fears on that matter at least could be put to rest. But at the time I didn't yet know that. As I glared angrily at the poor genetics counselor, so strong was my anxiety that now, four years later, I can still clearly remember what was going through my mind: If I were an evil deity, I thought, trying to devise exquisite tortures for babies and their parents, I would be proud to have designed Tay-Sachs disease.

Tay-Sachs is completely incurable, unpreventable, and preprogrammed in the genes. A Tay-Sachs infant usually appears normal for the first few months after birth, just long enough for the parents to grow to love him. An exaggerated "startle reaction" to sounds is the first ominous sign. At about six months the baby starts to lose control of his head and can't roll over or sit without support. Later he begins to drool, breaks out into unmotivated bouts of laughter, and suffers convulsions. Then his head grows abnormally large, and he becomes blind. Perhaps what's most frightening for the parents is that their baby loses all contact with his environment and becomes virtually a vegetable. By the child's third birthday, if he's still alive, his skin will turn yellow and his hands pudgy. Most likely he will die before he's four years old.

My wife and I were tested for the Tay-Sachs gene because at the time we rated as high-risk candidates, for two reasons. First, Marie was carrying twins, so we had double the usual chance to bear a Tay-Sachs baby. Second, both she and I are of Eastern European Jewish ancestry, the population with by far the world's highest Tay-Sachs frequency.

In peoples around the world Tay-Sachs appears once in every 400,000 births. But it appears a hundred times more frequently—about once in 3,600 births— among descendants of Eastern European Jews, people known as Ashkenazim. For descendants of most other groups of Jews—Oriental Jews, chiefly from the Middle East, or Sephardic Jews, from Spain and other Mediterranean countries—the frequency of Tay-Sachs disease is no higher than in non-Jews. Faced with such a clear correlation, one cannot help but wonder: What is it about this one group of people that produces such an extraordinarily high risk of this disease?

Finding the answer to this question concerns all of us, regardless of our ancestry. Every human population is especially susceptible to certain diseases, not only because of its lifestyle but also because of its genetic inheritance. For example, genes put European whites at high risk for cystic fibrosis, African blacks for sickle-cell disease, Pacific Islanders for diabetes—and Eastern European Jews for ten different diseases, including Tay-Sachs. It's not that Jews are notably susceptible to genetic diseases in general; but a combination of historical factors has led to Jews' being intensively studied, and so their susceptibilities are far better known than those of, say, Pacific Islanders.

Tay-Sachs exemplifies how we can deal with such diseases; it has been the object of the most successful screening program to date. Moreover, Tay-Sachs is helping us understand how ethnic diseases evolve. Within the past couple of years, discoveries by molecular biologists have provided tantalizing clues to precisely how a deadly gene can persist and spread over the centuries. Tay-Sachs may be primarily a disease of Eastern European Jews, but through this affliction of one group of people, we gain a window on how our genes simultaneously curse and bless us all.

The disease's hyphenated name comes from the two physicians—British ophthalmologist W. Tay and New York neurologist B. Sachs—who independently first recognized the disease, in 1881 and 1887, respectively. By 1896 Sachs had seen enough cases to realize that the disease was most common among Jewish children.

Not until 1962, however, were researchers able to trace the cause of the affliction to a single biochemical abnormality: the excessive accumulation in nerve cells of a fatty substance called G_{M2} ganglioside. Normally G_{M2} ganglioside is present at only modest levels in cell membranes, because it is constantly being broken down as well as synthesized. The breakdown depends on the enzyme hexosaminidase A, which is found in the tiny structures within our cells known as lysosomes. In the unfortunate Tay-Sachs victims this enzyme is lacking, and without it the ganglioside piles up and produces all the symptoms of the disease.

We have two copies of the gene that programs our supply of hexosaminidase A, one inherited from our father, the other from our mother; each of our parents, in turn, has two copies derived from their own parents. As long as we have one good copy of the gene, we can produce enough hexosaminidase A to prevent a buildup of G_{M2} ganglioside and we won't get Tay-Sachs. This genetic disease is of the sort termed recessive rather than dominant—meaning that to get it, a child must inherit a defective gene not just from one parent but from both of them. Clearly each parent must have had one good copy of the gene along with the defective copy—if either had had two defective genes, he or she would have died of the disease long before reaching the age of reproduction. In genetic terms the diseased child is homozygous for the defective gene and both parents are heterozygous for it.

None of this yet gives any hint as to why the Tay-Sachs gene should be the most common among Eastern European Jews. To come to grips with that question, we must take a short detour into history.

From their biblical home of ancient Israel, Jews spread peacefully to other Mediterranean lands, Yemen, and India. They were also dispersed violently through conquest by Assyrians, Babylonians, and

Romans. Under the Carolingian kings of the eighth and ninth centuries, Jews were invited to settle in France and Germany as traders and financiers. In subsequent centuries, however, persecutions triggered by the Crusades gradually drove Jews out of Western Europe; the process culminated in their total expulsion from Spain in 1492. Those Spanish Jews—called Sephardim—fled to other lands around the Mediterranean. Jews of France and Germany—the Ashkenazim—fled east to Poland and from there to Lithuania and western Russia, where they settled mostly in towns, as businessmen engaged in whatever pursuit they were allowed.

There the Jews stayed for centuries, through periods of both tolerance and oppression. But toward the end of the nineteenth century and the beginning of the twentieth, waves of murderous anti-Semitic attacks drove millions of Jews out of Eastern Europe, with most of them heading for the United States. My mother's parents, for example, fled to New York from the Lithuanian pogroms of the 1880s, while my father's parents fled from the Ukrainian pogroms of 1903–6. The more modern history of Jewish migration is probably well known to you all: most Jews who remained in Eastern Europe were exterminated during World War II, while most of the survivors immigrated to the United States and Israel. Of the 13 million Jews alive today, more than three-quarters are Ashkenazim, the descendants of the Eastern European Jews and the people most at risk for Tay-Sachs.

Have these Jews maintained their genetic distinctness through the thousands of years of wandering? Some scholars claim that there has been so much intermarriage and conversion that Ashkenazic Jews are now just Eastern Europeans who adopted Jewish culture. However, modern genetic studies refute that speculation.

First of all, there are those ten genetic diseases that the Ashkenazim have somehow acquired, by which they differ both from other Jews and from Eastern European non-Jews. In addition, many Ashkenazic genes turn out to be ones typical of Palestinian Arabs and other peoples of the eastern Mediterranean areas where Jews originated. (In fact, by genetic standards the current Arab-Israeli conflict is an internecine civil war.) Other Ashkenazic genes have indeed diverged from Mediterranean ones (including genes of Sephardic and Oriental Jews) and have evolved to converge on genes of Eastern European non-Jews subject to the same local forces of natural selection. But the degree to which Ashkenazim prove to differ genetically from Eastern European non-Jews implies an intermarriage rate of only about 15 percent.

Can history help explain why the Tay-Sachs gene in particular is so much more common in Ashkenazim

than in their non-Jewish neighbors or in other Jews? At the risk of spoiling a mystery, I'll tell you now that the answer is yes, but to appreciate it, you'll have to understand the four possible explanations for the persistence of the Tay-Sachs gene.

First, new copies of the gene might be arising by mutation as fast as existing copies disappear with the death of Tay-Sachs children. That's the most likely explanation for the gene's persistence in most of the world, where the disease frequency is only one in 400,000 births—that frequency reflects a typical human mutation rate. But for this explanation to apply to the Ashkenazim would require a mutation rate of at least one per 3,600 births—far above the frequency observed for any human gene. Furthermore, there would be no precedent for one particular gene mutating so much more often in one human population than in others.

As a second possibility, the Ashkenazim might have acquired the Tay-Sachs gene from some other people who already had the gene at high frequency. Arthur Koestler's controversial book *The Thirteenth Tribe*, for example, popularized the view that the Ashkenazim are really not a Semitic people but are instead descended from the Khazar, a Turkic tribe whose rulers converted to Judaism in the eighth century. Could the Khazar have brought the Tay-Sachs gene to Eastern Europe? This speculation makes good romantic reading, but there is no good evidence to support it. Moreover, it fails to explain why deaths of Tay-Sachs children didn't eliminate the gene by natural selection in the past 1,200 years, nor how the Khazar acquired high frequencies of the gene in the first place.

The third hypothesis was the one preferred by a good many geneticists until recently. It invokes two genetic processes, termed the founder effect and genetic drift, that may operate in small populations. To understand these concepts, imagine that 100 couples settle in a new land and found a population that then increases. Imagine further that one parent among those original 100 couples happens to have some rare gene, one, say, that normally occurs at a frequency of one in a million. The gene's frequency in the new population will now be one in 200 as a result of the accidental presence of that rare founder.

Or suppose again that 100 couples found a population, but that one of the 100 men happens to have lots of kids by his wife or that he is exceptionally popular with other women, while the other 99 men are childless or have few kids or are simply less popular. That one man may thereby father 10 percent rather than a more representative one percent of the next generation's babies, and their genes will disproportionately reflect that man's genes. In other words, gene frequencies will have drifted between the first and second generation.

Through these two types of genetic accidents a rare gene may occur with an unusually high frequency in a small expanding population. Eventually, if the gene is harmful, natural selection will bring its frequency back to normal by killing off gene bearers. But if the resultant disease is recessive—if heterozygous individuals don't get the disease and only the rare, homozygous individuals die of it—the gene's high frequency may persist for many generations.

These accidents do in fact account for the astonishingly high Tay-Sachs gene frequency found in one group of Pennsylvania Dutch: out of the 333 people in this group, 98 proved to carry the Tay-Sachs gene. Those 333 are all descended from one couple who settled in the United States in the eighteenth century and had 13 children. Clearly, one of that founding couple must have carried the gene. A similar accident may explain why Tay-Sachs is also relatively common among French Canadians, who number 5 million today but are descended from fewer than 6,000 French immigrants who arrived in the New World between 1638 and 1759. In the two or three centuries since both these founding events, the high Tay-Sachs gene frequency among Pennsylvania Dutch and French Canadians has not yet had enough time to decline to normal levels.

The same mechanisms were once proposed to explain the high rate of Tay-Sachs disease among the Ashkenazim. Perhaps, the reasoning went, the gene just happened to be overrepresented in the founding Jewish population that settled in Germany or Eastern Europe. Perhaps the gene just happened to drift up in frequency in the Jewish populations scattered among the isolated towns of Eastern Europe.

But geneticists have long questioned whether the Ashkenazim population's history was really suitable for these genetic accidents to have been significant. Remember, the founder effect and genetic drift become significant only in small populations, and the founding populations of Ashkenazim may have been quite large. Moreover, Ashkenazic communities were considerably widespread; drift would have sent gene frequencies up in some towns but down in others. And, finally, natural selection has by now had a thousand years to restore gene frequencies to normal.

Granted, those doubts are based on historical data, which are not always as precise or reliable as one might want. But within the past several years the case against those accidental explanations for Tay-Sachs disease in the Ashkenazim has been bolstered by discoveries by molecular biologists.

Like all proteins, the enzyme absent in Tay-Sachs children is coded for by a piece of our DNA. Along that particular stretch of DNA there are thousands of different sites where a mutation could occur that would result in no enzyme and hence in the same set of symptoms. If molecular biologists had discovered that all cases of Tay-Sachs in Ashkenazim involved damage to DNA at the same site, that would have been strong evidence that in Ashkenazim the disease stems from a single mutation that has been multiplied by the founder effect or genetic drift—in other words, the high incidence of Tay-Sachs among Eastern European Jews is accidental.

In reality, though, several different mutations along this stretch of DNA have been identified in Ashkenazim, and two of them occur much more frequently than in non-Ashkenazim populations. It seems unlikely that genetic accidents would have pumped up the frequency of the same gene not once but twice in the same population.

And that's not the sole unlikely coincidence arguing against accidental explanations. Recall that Tay-Sachs is caused by the excessive accumulation of one fatty substance, G_{M2} ganglioside, from a defect in one enzyme, hexosaminidase A. But Tay-Sachs is one of ten genetic diseases characteristic of Ashkenazim. Among those other nine, two—Gaucher's disease and Niemann-Pick disease—result from the accumulation of two other fatty substances similar to G_{M2} ganglioside, as a result of defects in two other enzymes similar to hexosaminidase A. Yet our bodies contain thousands of different enzymes. It would have been an incredible roll of the genetic dice if, by nothing more than chance, Ashkenazim had independently acquired mutations in three closely related enzymes—and had acquired mutations in one of those enzymes twice.

All these facts bring us to the fourth possible explanation of why the Tay-Sachs gene is so prevalent among Ashkenazim: namely, that something about them favored accumulation of G_{M2} ganglioside and related fats.

For comparison, suppose that a friend doubles her money on one stock while you are getting wiped out with your investments. Taken alone, that could just mean she was lucky on that one occasion. But suppose that she doubles her money on each of two different stocks and at the same time rings up big profits in real estate while also making a killing in bonds. That implies more than lady luck; it suggests that something about your friend—like shrewd judgment—favors financial success.

What could be the blessings of fat accumulation in Eastern European Jews? At first this question sounds weird. After all, that fat accumulation was noticed only because of the curses it bestows: Tay-Sachs, Gaucher's, or Niemann-Pick disease. But many of our common genetic diseases may persist because they bring both blessings and curses. . . . They kill or impair individuals who inherit two copies of the faulty gene, but they help those who receive only one defective gene by protecting them against other diseases. The best understood example is the sickle-cell gene of African blacks, which often kills homozygotes but protects heterozygotes against malaria. Natural selection sustains such genes because more heterozygotes than normal individuals survive to pass on their genes, and those extra gene copies offset the copies lost through the deaths of homozygotes.

So let us refine our question and ask, What blessing could the Tay-Sachs gene bring to those individuals who are heterozygous for it? A clue first emerged back in 1972, with the publication of the results of a questionnaire that had asked U.S. Ashkenazic parents of Tay-Sachs children what their own Eastern European–born parents had died of. Keep in mind that since these unfortunate children had to be homozygotes, with two copies of the Tay-Sachs gene, all their parents had to be heterozygotes, with one copy, and half of the parents' parents also had to be heterozygotes.

As it turned out, most of those Tay-Sachs grandparents had died of the usual causes: heart disease, stroke, cancer, and diabetes. But, strikingly, only one of the 306 grandparents had died of tuberculosis, even though TB was generally one of the big killers in these grandparents' time. Indeed, among the general population of large Eastern European cities in the early twentieth century, TB caused up to 20 percent of all deaths.

This big discrepancy suggested that Tay-Sachs heterozygotes might somehow have been protected against TB. Interestingly, it was already well known that Ashkenazim in general had some such protection: even when Jews and non-Jews were compared within the same European city, class, and occupational group (for example, Warsaw garment workers), Jews had only half the TB death rate of non-Jews, despite their being equally susceptible to infection. Perhaps, one could reason, the Tay-Sachs gene furnished part of that well-established Jewish resistance.

A second clue to a heterozygote advantage conveyed by the Tay-Sachs gene emerged in 1983, with a fresh look at the data concerning the distributions of TB and the Tay-Sachs gene within Europe. The statistics showed that the Tay-Sachs gene was nearly three times more frequent among Jews originating from Austria, Hungary, and Czechoslovakia—areas where an amazing 9 or 10 percent of the population were heterozygotes—than among Jews from Poland, Russia, and Germany. At the same time, records from an old Jewish TB sanatorium in Denver in 1904 showed that among patients born in Europe between 1860 and 1910, Jews from Austria and Hungary were overrepresented.

Initially, in putting together these two pieces of information, you might be tempted to conclude that because the highest frequency of the Tay-Sachs gene appeared in the same geographic region that produced the most cases of TB, the gene in fact offers no protection whatsoever. Indeed, this was precisely the mistaken conclusion of many researchers who had looked at these data before. But you have to pay careful attention to the numbers here: even at its highest frequency the Tay-Sachs gene was carried by far fewer people than would be infected by TB. What the statistics really indicate is that where TB is the biggest threat, natural selection produces the biggest response.

Think of it this way: You arrive at an island where you find that all the inhabitants of the north end wear suits of armor, while all the inhabitants of the south end wear only cloth shirts. You'd be pretty safe in assuming that warfare is more prevalent in the north—and that war-related injuries account for far more deaths there than in the south. Thus, if the Tay-Sachs gene does indeed lend heterozygotes some protection against TB, you would expect to find the gene most often precisely where you find TB most often. Similarly, the sickle-cell gene reaches its highest frequencies in those parts of Africa where malaria is the biggest risk.

But you may believe there's still a hole in the argument: If Tay-Sachs heterozygotes are protected against TB, you may be asking, why is the gene common just in the Ashkenazim? Why did it not become common in the non-Jewish populations also exposed to TB in Austria, Hungary, and Czechoslovakia?

At this point we must recall the peculiar circumstances in which the Jews of Eastern Europe were forced to live. They were unique among the world's ethnic groups in having been virtually confined to towns for most of the past 2,000 years. Being forbidden to own land, Eastern European Jews were not peasant farmers living in the countryside, but businesspeople forced to live in crowded ghettos, in an environment where tuberculosis thrived.

Of course, until recent improvements in sanitation, these towns were not very healthy places for non-Jews either. Indeed, their populations couldn't sustain themselves: deaths exceeded births, and the number of dead had to be balanced by continued emigration from the countryside. For non-Jews, therefore, there was no genetically distinct urban population. For ghetto-bound Jews, however, there could be no emigration from the countryside; thus the Jewish population was under the strongest selection to evolve genetic resistance to TB.

These are the conditions that probably led to Jewish TB resistance, whatever particular genetic factors prove to underlie it. I'd speculate that G_{M2} and related fats accumulate at slightly higher-than-normal levels in heterozygotes, although not at the lethal levels seen in homozygotes. (The fat accumulation in heterozygotes probably takes place in the cell membrane, the cell's "armor.") I'd also speculate that the accumulation provides heterozygotes with some protection against TB, and that that's why the genes for Tay-Sachs, Gaucher's, and Niemann-Pick disease reached high frequencies in the Ashkenazim.

Having thus stated the case, let me make clear that I don't want to overstate it. The evidence is still speculative. Depending on how you do the calculation, the low frequency of TB deaths in Tay-Sachs grandparents either barely reaches or doesn't quite reach the level of proof that statisticians require to accept an effect as real rather than as one that's arisen by chance. Moreover, we have no idea of the biochemical mechanism by which fat accumulation might confer resistance against TB. For the moment, I'd say that the evidence points to some selective advantage of Tay-Sachs heterozygotes among the Ashkenazim, and that TB resistance is the only plausible hypothesis yet proposed.

For now Tay-Sachs remains a speculative model for the evolution of ethnic diseases. But it's already a proven model of what to do about them. Twenty years ago a test was developed to identify Tay-Sachs heterozygotes, based on their lower-than-normal levels of hexosaminidase A. The test is simple, cheap, and accurate: all I did was to donate a small sample of my blood, pay $35, and wait a few days to receive the results.

If that test shows that at least one member of a couple is not a Tay-Sachs heterozygote, then any child of theirs can't be a Tay-Sachs homozygote. If both parents prove to be heterozygotes, there's a one-in-four chance of their child being a homozygote; that can then be determined by other tests performed on the mother early in pregnancy. If the results are positive, it's early enough for her to abort, should she choose to. That critical bit of knowledge has enabled parents who had gone through the agony of bearing a Tay-Sachs baby and watching him die to find the courage to try again.

The Tay-Sachs screening program launched in the United States in 1971 was targeted at the high-risk population: Ashkenazic Jewish couples of childbearing age. So successful has this approach been that the number of Tay-Sachs babies born each year in this country has declined tenfold. Today, in fact, more Tay-Sachs cases appear here in non-Jews than in Jews, because only the latter couples are routinely tested. Thus, what used to be the classic genetic disease of Jews is so no longer.

There's also a broader message to the Tay-Sachs story. We commonly refer to the United States as a melting pot, and in many ways that metaphor is apt. But in other ways we're not a melting pot, and we won't be for a long time. Each ethnic group has some characteristic genes of its own, a legacy of its distinct history. Tuberculosis and malaria are not major causes of death in the United States, but the genes that some of us evolved to protect ourselves against them are still frequent. Those genes are frequent only in certain ethnic groups, though, and they'll be slow to melt through the population.

With modern advances in molecular genetics, we can expect to see more, not less, ethnically targeted practice of medicine. Genetic screening for cystic fibrosis in European whites, for example, is one program that has been much discussed recently; when it comes, it will surely be based on the Tay-Sachs experience. Of course, what that may mean someday is more anxiety-ridden parents-to-be glowering at more dedicated genetics counselors. It will also mean fewer babies doomed to the agonies of diseases we may understand but that we'll never be able to accept.

15

Unfortunate Drift

Josie Glausiusz

Josie Glausiusz is an associate editor of Discover *magazine.*

A process of evolution other than natural selection appears to account for ITD (idiopathic torsion dystonia), another of the ten diseases found in unusually high frequencies among the Ashkenazim. In this selection, Josie Glausiusz describes the evidence for attributing the high frequency of ITD to genetic drift and the founder effect. In fact, she presents a different interpretation from Diamond's (see Selection 14) for the high frequency of Tay-Sachs among the same people. Contrasting these two articles provides a good example of the self-critical, self-testing, ever-questioning nature of science.

As you read, consider the following questions:

1. How does Glausiusz account for the high frequency of ITD among the Ashkenazim?

2. In contrast to Jared Diamond, what are Glausiusz's arguments *for* the importance of genetic drift and the founder effect in accounting for the high frequencies of certain diseases in this population? How does this article differently interpret the same data—for example, the frequency of Tay-Sachs among French Canadians?

3. How did geneticist Neil Risch reconstruct the date of origin of ITD among the Askenazic Jews?

Ashkenazi Jews—those of Central and Eastern European origin, which includes most American Jews—are prey to a unique set of genetic diseases. The best known is Tay-Sachs, which kills in early infancy, but there are at least nine other inherited disorders that are especially prevalent among Ashkenazim. Why? The pattern of inheritance offers a clue: most of the diseases are caused by recessive genes, meaning that symptoms appear only if two copies of the mutant gene are inherited, one from each parent. One copy does no harm and might even do some good—which would cause natural selection to spread the mutation through a human population instead of weeding it out. Many researchers believe the Ashkenazi burden has this sort of flip side; they argue, for instance, that the Tay-Sachs gene protects its carriers against tuberculosis, a disease that was endemic in the crowded ghettos of Eastern Europe.

But there has always been an alternative theory, says Stanford population geneticist Neil Risch: mutant genes may have become concentrated in the Ashkenazi population purely by chance or historical

accident. Now Risch and his colleagues have found evidence that such "genetic drift" does indeed underlie the high incidence among Ashkenazim of idiopathic torsion dystonia (ITD), a disease that causes involuntary muscle contractions. The researchers think drift may explain or help explain the other Ashkenazi diseases as well. The mutant genes may have achieved their high frequency, says Risch, not so much because they confer a selective advantage but because they happened to arise among a relatively small number of Jews who produced a large number of descendants.

ITD, however, is a special case—as Risch and his colleagues discovered when they started analyzing its pattern of inheritance in their study group of 59 Ashkenazi families in the United States. Unlike all the other Ashkenazi diseases, they found, ITD isn't recessive—it's dominant, meaning that a single copy of the gene is enough to transmit the disease. For reasons unknown, though, it usually doesn't. Between one in 1,000 and one in 3,000 Ashkenazim carry the ITD gene, Risch estimates, but only 30 percent of them show symptoms—muscles that cramp and twist a part of the body into contorted positions—and only 10 percent have incapacitating ones. The low incidence of disease allows the gene to survive in the population; most of

From *Discover*, June 1995. Copyright © 1995 by Josie Glausiusz. Reprinted by permission of the author.

its carriers can still have children. On the other hand, the gene doesn't seem to confer any type of advantage that would explain why it became so common among Ashkenazi Jews.

Another clue that genetic drift rather than natural selection might explain the spread of ITD is the history of the Ashkenazim. *Ashkenazi* is a Hebrew term for "German." Beginning in the fourteenth century, a wave of German Jews fleeing east to escape persecution established new homes in Eastern Europe. The immigrant Jews generally didn't marry members of the surrounding communities, and although historical evidence from the period is sketchy, there is some evidence that their initial population was small. If so, it was an ideal candidate for a type of genetic drift known as the founder effect: when a small group of immigrants founds a new population, isolated from others, whatever mutations the founders happen to have, good or bad, will necessarily be more concentrated in that new, smaller population than they were in the old, larger one the founders came from.

That's just what happened with ITD, says Risch. He and his colleagues have found that a single genetic mutation is responsible for most cases of the disease, and they have traced it to its source. They did so by showing that 90 percent of the families in their study had an identical pattern of genetic markers—recognizable bits of noncoding DNA—flanking the ITD gene on chromosome 9. Since chromosomes swap pieces of DNA each time a sex cell is formed by meiosis, marker patterns tend to get scrambled over time. That 90 percent of the families still had identical markers showed they had all inherited the same mutation—and also that the mutation had arisen in a single individual fairly recently.

Knowing the rate at which chromosomes swap DNA, Risch could estimate when the original ITD mutation occurred: around 1650, plus or minus a century or two—but probably after the Ashkenazi Jews migrated to Eastern Europe. When Risch started asking the people in his study about their grandparents and great-grandparents, he found that more than two-thirds of the oldest ITD carriers who could be traced hailed from Lithuania and Belorussia. The most likely scenario, Risch concludes, is that the progenitor of the ITD mutation lived in one of those two places some 350 years ago. That person's descendants spread the mutation to other parts of what came to be known as the Jewish Pale of Settlement—a region that included Poland, the Ukraine, and parts of Russia. (From the late eighteenth century on, Jews living under the Russian czar were confined to the Pale.) In the late nineteenth century, Jews fleeing pogroms in Eastern Europe carried the mutation to other parts of the world, including the United States.

By 1900 there were 5 million Jews living in the Pale of Settlement; in spite of repeated persecutions, the population had grown explosively since at least 1765, when the earliest reliable census put it at 560,000. Extrapolating that growth rate backward in time, Risch estimates that in the mid-seventeenth century, when the ITD mutation most likely appeared, the Ashkenazi population in the Pale was around 100,000. The mutation's initial frequency, then, would have been around one in 100,000. How could the frequency have risen to at least one in 3,000 among today's Ashkenazim?

The answer, Risch thinks, is a second type of genetic drift. In the seventeenth century and later, he says, not all Ashkenazi Jews left equal numbers of children. Family genealogies suggest that the more affluent classes—business and community leaders as well as scholars and rabbis, who were considered desirable marriage partners—had between four and nine children who reached adulthood. In contrast, poorer Jewish families, who were more subject to overcrowding and thus more at risk from epidemics, left fewer surviving descendants. Risch thinks the original ITD mutation just happened to arise in an affluent family, and that it spread rapidly because the affluent Jews tended to marry one another and to have many children. ITD is so common among the Ashkenazim today, he argues, because most of the world's 11 million Ashkenazim are descended from just a few thousand people who lived in the Pale of Settlement in the seventeenth century.

What about the other Ashkenazi diseases? They are all recessive, which means natural selection could more easily have influenced their frequency. Typically only 1 percent or so of the carriers of a rare recessive mutation get sick (because they have two copies of the mutated gene), compared with 30 percent of the carriers of ITD. As a result, even a small selective advantage might be enough to spread a recessive mutation through the population. Risch points out that natural selection and genetic drift could have worked together to spread the Ashkenazi diseases; the two are not mutually exclusive. But he also thinks further studies will show that most or all of the diseases are, like ITD, of recent origin—too recent for the slow grind of evolution to be the main reason they have achieved such high frequency.

There is another population, Risch points out, whose history makes for an instructive comparison with the Ashkenazim. "The French Canadians have Tay-Sachs also—a different mutation, but almost at the same frequency as the Ashkenazim," he says. "I've never heard anybody arguing that Tay-Sachs gives them an advantage against tuberculosis in crowded ghettos! In fact, the French Canadians are well known for having their own, unique genetic diseases. Their demography is remarkably similar to that of the Ashkenazi Jews—there are currently about 5 million French Canadians who are descended from a relatively small founder population, in the thousands or tens of thousands, dating to 300 or 400 years ago.

"And in Eastern Europe, tuberculosis was quite common in non-Jews also, and you don't see them with these genetic diseases. But our study confirms that the conditions for the operation of genetic drift existed there. You would expect it to apply not just to the ITD gene but to others also." If Risch turns out to be right, the diseases that plague the Ashkenazim will no longer be seen as an example of the cruel beauty of evolution. They'll just be an example of bad luck.

16

What Is a Species?

Stephen Jay Gould

Stephen Gould was perhaps most famous for formulating, along with paleontologist Niles Eldredge, the model of evolution called punctuated equilibrium (see Selection 11), a model that describes the pace and tempo of macroevolution, the origin of new species from existing species. In this capacity, Gould was interested not only in how species evolve but also in the problem of identifying and distinguishing species. Shortly before his death in 2002, he published his magnum opus, the 1,433-page Structure of Evolutionary Theory *(2002, Belknap Press).*

The products of the evolutionary processes are species—reproductively isolated natural units. How species evolve from other species was the ultimate problem that Darwin's great book addressed. In this selection, Gould defines the term *species* and tells just how the process of speciation works. He describes the overall pace of evolution—the "shape" of the evolutionary family tree—showing that species generally remain unchanged over most of their time on earth and that new species arise "relatively quickly" when a small population within an existing species becomes isolated and subsequently undergoes all the evolutionary processes to become sufficiently different to be a separate species. What I've just described is, indeed, Gould and Eldredge's punctuated equilibrium. Gould then shows how other units of classification—phyla, families, genera, subspecies, and so on—are human constructs, names we apply to try to organize all the trunks and branches of the evolutionary tree (or "bush," as Gould calls it). Finally, Gould shows how the definition of species and understanding of

speciation can affect our concerns about preserving the earth's biodiversity.

As you read, consider the following questions:

1. What does Gould mean when he says that evolution is a "bush" and not a "ladder" or a "salami"?

2. How, and how fast, according to Gould, do new species emerge from existing species?

3. What is the functional definition of a species—that is, how do we know two organisms belong to the same species, or that two populations are actually different species?

4. How do we organize species into higher (larger) categories, such as genera, families, and phyla? What is our rationale for naming subspecies?

5. How are the nature and definition of species related to our concerns for preserving the diversity of life on earth?

Ihad visited every state but Idaho. A few months ago, I finally got my opportunity to complete the roster of 50 by driving east from Spokane, Washington, into western Idaho. As I crossed the state line, I made the same feeble attempt at humor that so many of us try in similar situations: "Gee, it doesn't look a bit different from easternmost Washington." We make such comments because we feel the discomfort of discord

between our mental needs and the world's reality. Much of nature (including terrestrial real estate) is continuous, but both our mental and political structures require divisions and categories. We need to break large and continuous items into manageable units.

Many people feel the same way about species as I do about Idaho—but this feeling is wrong. Many people suppose that species must be arbitrary divisions of an evolutionary continuum in the same way that state boundaries are conventional divisions of unbroken land. Moreover, this is not merely an abstract issue of scientific theory but a pressing concern of political reality. The Endangered Species Act, for example, sets policy (with substantial teeth) for the preservation of species. But if species are only arbitrary divisions in nature's continuity, then what are we trying to preserve and how shall we define it? I write this article to argue that such a reading of evolutionary theory is wrong and that species are almost always objective entities in nature.

Let us start with something uncontroversial: the bugs in your backyard. If you go out to make a complete collection of all the kinds of insects living in this small discrete space, you will collect easily definable "packages," not intergrading continua. You might find a kind of bee, three kinds of ants, a butterfly or two, several beetles, and a cicada. You have simply validated the commonsense notion known to all: in any small space during any given moment, the animals we see belong to separate and definable groups—and we call these groups species.

In the eighteenth century this commonsense observation was translated, improperly as we now know, into the creationist taxonomy of Linnaeus. The great Swedish naturalist regarded species as God's created entities, and he gathered them together into genera, genera into orders, and orders into classes, to form the taxonomic hierarchy that we all learned in high school (several more categories, families and phyla, for example, have been added since Linnaeus's time). The creationist version reached its apogee in the writings of America's greatest nineteenth-century naturalist (and last truly great scientific creationist), Louis Agassiz. Agassiz argued that species are incarnations of separate ideas in God's mind, and that higher categories (genera, orders, and so forth) are therefore maps of the interrelationships among divine thoughts. Therefore, taxonomy is the most important of all sciences because it gives us direct insight into the structure of God's mind.

Darwin changed this reverie forever by proving that species are related by the physical connection of genealogical descent. But this immensely satisfying resolution for the great puzzle of nature's order engendered a subsidiary problem that Darwin never fully resolved: If all life is interconnected as a genealogical continuum, then what reality can species have? Are they not just arbitrary divisions of evolving lineages? And if so, how can the bugs in my backyard be ordered in separate units? In fact, the two greatest evolutionists of the nineteenth century, Lamarck and Darwin, both questioned the reality of species on the basis of their evolutionary convictions. Lamarck wrote, "In vain do naturalists consume their time in describing new species," while Darwin lamented: "we shall have to treat species as . . . merely artificial combinations made for convenience. This may not be a cheering prospect; but we shall at least be freed from the vain search for

the undiscovered and undiscoverable essence of the term *species*" (from the *Origin of Species*).

But when we examine the technical writings of both Lamarck and Darwin, our sense of paradox is heightened. Darwin produced four long volumes on the taxonomy of barnacles, using conventional species for his divisions. Lamarck spent seven years (1815–1822) publishing his generation's standard, multivolume compendium on the diversity of animal life—*Histoire naturelle des animaux sans vertèbres*, or *Natural History of Invertebrate Animals*—all divided into species, many of which he named for the first time himself. How can these two great evolutionists have denied a concept in theory and then used it so centrally and extensively in practice? To ask the question more generally: If the species is still a useful and necessary concept, how can we define and justify it as evolutionists?

The solution to this question requires a preamble and two steps. For the preamble, let us acknowledge that the conceptual problem arises when we extend the "bugs in my backyard" example into time and space. A momentary slice of any continuum looks tolerably discrete; a slice of salami or a cross section of a tree trunk freezes a complexly changing structure into an apparently stable entity. Modern horses are discrete and separate from all other existing species, but how can we call the horse (*Equus caballus*) a real and definable entity if we can trace an unbroken genealogical series back through time to a dog-size creature with several toes on each foot? Where did this "dawn horse," or "eohippus," stop and the next stage begin; at what moment did the penultimate stage become *Equus caballus*? I now come to the two steps of an answer.

First, if each evolutionary line were like a long salami, then species would not be real and definable in time and space. But in almost all cases large-scale evolution is a story of branching, not of transformation in a single line—bushes, not ladders, in my usual formulation. A branch on a bush is an objective division. One species rarely turns into another by total transformation over its entire geographic range. Rather, a small population becomes geographically isolated from the rest of the species—and this fragment changes to become a new species while the bulk of the parental population does not alter. "Dawn horse" is a misnomer because rhinoceroses evolved from the same parental lineage. The lineage split at an objective branching point into two lines that became (after further events of splitting) the great modern groups of horses (eight species, including asses and zebras) and rhinos (a sadly depleted group of formerly successful species).

Failure to recognize that evolution is a bush and not a ladder leads to one of the most common vernacular misconceptions about human biology. People often challenge me: "If humans evolved from apes, why are

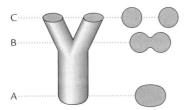

FIGURE 1 Species go through a period of ambiguity while a new branch is forming (B), and then become clearly separate (C). (Copyright © 1992 Alan E. Cober. Adapted by permission of *Discover* magazine)

FIGURE 2 The time of ambiguity at the origin of the new species (B) from a parental line (A) is relatively short. (Copyright © 1992 Alan E. Cober. Adapted by permission of *Discover* magazine)

apes still around?" To anyone who understands the principle of bushes, there simply is no problem: the human lineage emerged as a branch, while the rest of the trunk continued as apes (and branched several more times to yield modern chimps, gorillas, and so on). But if you think that evolution is a ladder or a salami, then an emergence of humans from apes should mean the elimination of apes by transformation.

Second, you might grasp the principle of bushes and branching but still say: Yes, the ultimate products of a branch become objectively separate, but early on, while the branch is forming, no clear division can be made, and the precursors of the two species that will emerge must blend indefinably (Figure 1). And if evolution is gradual and continuous, and if most of a species' duration is spent in this state of incipient formation, then species will not be objectively definable during most of their geologic lifetimes.

Fair enough as an argument, but the premise is wrong. New species do (and must) have this period of initial ambiguity. But species emerge relatively quickly, compared with their period of later stability, and then live for long periods—often millions of years—with minimal change (Figure 2). Now, suppose that on average (and this is probably a fair estimate), species spend one percent of their geologic lifetimes in this initial state of imperfect separation. Then, on average, about one species in a hundred will encounter problems in definition, while the other 99 will be discrete and objectively separate—cross sections of branches showing no confluence with others (C, Figure 1). Thus, the principle of bushes, and the speed of branching, resolve the supposed paradox: continuous evolution can and does yield a world in which the vast majority of species are separate from all others and clearly definable at any moment in time. Species are nature's objective packages.

I have given a historical definition of species—as unique and separate branches on nature's bush. We also need a functional definition, if only because historical evidence (in the form of a complete fossil record) is usually unavailable. The standard criterion,

in use at least since the days of the great French naturalist Georges de Buffon (a contemporary of Linnaeus), invokes the capacity for interbreeding. Members of a species can breed with others in the same species but not with individuals belonging to different species.

This functional criterion is a consequence of the historical definition: distinct separateness of a branch emerges only with the attainment of sufficient evolutionary distance to preclude interbreeding, for otherwise the branch is not an irrevocably separate entity and can amalgamate with the parental population. Exceptions exist, but the reproductive criterion generally works well and gives rise to the standard one-liner for a textbook definition of a species: "a population of actually or potentially reproducing organisms sharing a common gene pool."

Much of the ordinary activity of evolutionary biologists is devoted to learning whether or not the groups they study are separate species by this criterion of "reproductive isolation." Such separateness can be based on a variety of factors, collectively termed "isolating mechanisms": for example, genetic programs so different that an embryo cannot form even if egg and sperm unite, behaviors that lead members of one species to shun individuals from other populations; even something so mundane as breeding at different times of the year, or in different parts of the habitat—say, for example, on apple trees rather than on plum trees—so that contact can never take place. (We exclude simple geographic separation—living on different continents, for example—because an isolating mechanism must work when actively challenged by a potential for interbreeding through spatial contact. I do not belong to a separate species from my brethren in Brazil just because I have never been there. Similarly, reproductive isolation must be assessed by ordinary behavior in a state of nature. Some truly separate species can be induced to interbreed in zoos and laboratories. The fact that zoos can make tiglons—tiger-lion hybrids—does not challenge the separate status of the two populations as species in nature.)

Modern humans (species *Homo sapiens*) fit these criteria admirably. We are now spread all over the world in great numbers, but we began as a little twig in Africa (the historical criterion). We may look quite different from one another in a few superficially striking aspects of size, skin color, and hair form, but there is astonishingly little overall genetic difference among our so-called races. Above all (the functional criterion), we can all interbreed with one another (and do so with avidity, always, and all over the world), but not with any member of another species (movies about flies notwithstanding). We are often reminded, quite correctly, that we are very similar in overall genetic program to our nearest cousin, the chimpanzee—but no one would mistake a single individual of either species, and we do not hybridize (again, various science fictions notwithstanding).

I do not say that these criteria are free from exceptions; nature is nothing if not a domain of exceptions, where an example against any clean generality can always be found. Some distinct populations of plants, for example, can and frequently do interbreed with others that ought to be separate species by all other standards. (This is why the classification of certain groups—the rhododendrons, for example—is such a mess.) But the criteria work in the vast majority of cases, including humans. Species are not arbitrary units, constructed for human convenience, in dividing continua. Species are the real and objective items of nature's morphology. They are "out there" in the world as historically distinct and functionally separate populations "with their own historical role and tendency" (as the other textbook one-liner proclaims).

Species are unique in the Linnaean hierarchy as the only category with such objectivity. All higher units—genera, families, phyla, et cetera—are human conventions in the following important respect. The evolutionary tree itself is objective; the branches (species) emerge, grow, and form clusters by subsequent branching. The clusters (Figure 3) are clearly discernible. But the status we award to these so-called higher taxa (clusters of branches with a single root of common evolutionary ancestry) is partly a matter of human decision. Clusters A and B in the figure are groups of species with a common parent. Each branch in each cluster is an objective species. But what are the clusters themselves? Are they two genera or two families? Our decision on this question is partly a matter of human preference constrained by the rules of logic and the facts of nature. (For example, we cannot take one species from cluster A and one from cluster B and put them together as a single genus—for this would violate the rule that all members of a higher taxon must share a common ancestor without excluding other species that are more closely related to the common

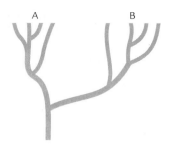

FIGURE 3 Branches are objective species. But the clusters they form (A and B) are classified partly according to human conventions. (Copyright © 1992 Alan E. Cober. Adapted by permission of *Discover* magazine)

ancestor. We cannot put domestic cats and dogs in one family while classifying lions and wolves in another.)

The taxonomic hierarchy recognizes only one unit below species—the subspecies. Like higher taxa, subspecies are also partly objective but partly based on human decision. Subspecies are defined as distinctive subpopulations that live in a definite geographic subsection of the entire range of the species. I cannot, for example, pluck out all tall members of a species, or all red individuals, wherever they occur over the full geographic range, and establish them as subspecies. A subspecies must be a distinct geographic subpopulation—not yet evolved far enough to become a separate species in its own right but different enough from other subpopulations (in terms of anatomy, genetic structure, physiology, or behavior) that a taxonomist chooses to memorialize the distinction with a name. Yet subspecies cannot be irrevocably unique natural populations (like full species) for two reasons: First, the decision to name them rests with human taxonomists and isn't solely dictated by nature. Second, they are, by definition, still capable of interbreeding with other subpopulations of the species and are, therefore, impermanent and subject to reamalgamation.

This difference between species and subspecies becomes important in practice because our Endangered Species Act currently mandates the protection of subspecies as well. I do not dispute the act's intention or its teeth, for many subspecies do manifest distinctly evolved properties of great value and wonder (even if these properties do not render them reproductively isolated from other populations of the species). We would not, after all, condone the genocide of all Caucasian human beings because members of other races would still exist; human races, if formally recognized at all, are subspecies based on our original geographic separations. But since subspecies do not have the same objective status as species (and since not all distinct local populations bear separate names), argument over what does and does not merit protection is inevitable.

Most of the major ecological wrangles of recent years—rows over the Mount Graham red squirrel or the Northern spotted owl—involve subspecies, not species.

These taxonomic issues were once abstract, however important. They are now immediate and vital—and all educated people must understand them in the midst of our current crisis in biodiversity and extinction. I therefore close with two observations.

By grasping the objective status of species as real units in nature (and by understanding why they are not arbitrary divisions for human convenience), we may better comprehend the moral rationale for their preservation. You can expunge an arbitrary idea by rearranging your conceptual world. But when a species dies, an item of natural uniqueness is gone forever. Each species is a remarkably complex product of evolution—a branch on a tree that is billions of years old. All the king's horses and men faced an easy problem compared with what we would encounter if we tried to reconstitute a lost species. Reassembling Humpty-Dumpty is just an exceedingly complex jigsaw puzzle, for the pieces lie at the base of the wall. There are no pieces left when the last dodo dies.

But all species eventually die in the fullness of geologic time, so why should we worry? In the words of Tennyson (who died exactly 100 years ago, so the fact is no secret):

From scarped cliff and quarried stone
She cries, "A thousand types are gone:
I care for nothing. All shall go."
                    —(From *In Memoriam*.)

The argument is true, but the time scale is wrong for our ethical concerns. We live our lives within geologic instants, and we should make our moral decisions at this proper scale—not at the micromoment of thoughtless exploitation for personal profit and public harm; but not at Earth's time scale of billions of years either (a grand irrelevancy for our species' potential tenure of thousands or, at most, a few million years).

We do not let children succumb to easily curable infections just because we know that all people must die eventually. Neither should we condone our current massive wipeout of species because all eventually become extinct. The mass extinctions of our geologic past may have cleared space and created new evolutionary opportunity—but it takes up to 10 million years to reestablish an interesting new world, and what can such an interval mean to us? Mass extinctions may have geologically distant benefits, but life in the midst of such an event is maximally unpleasant—and that, friends, is where we now reside, I fear.

Species are living, breathing items of nature. We lose a bit of our collective soul when we drive species (and their entire lineages with them), prematurely and in large numbers, to oblivion. Tennyson, paraphrasing Goethe, hoped that we could transcend such errors when he wrote, in the same poem:

I held it truth, with him who sings
To one clear harp in divers tones
That men may rise on stepping-stones
Of their dead selves to higher things.

PART 5

The Primates and Primate Behavior

An important aspect of biological anthropology is *primatology*—the study of the taxonomic order that includes humans and about two hundred other living species. Primates, of course, are interesting in their own right, but our focus in bioanthropology is on what the nonhuman primates can tell us about ourselves—about our relative place in the world of living things and about our biological and behavioral evolution.

As we look to the other primates for insights into our species, we must exercise an important caution. We must remember that evolution works by the branching of new species from existing species, which then go off on their own unique evolutionary paths (see Selection 16). Two living species may exhibit similarities in anatomy or behavior, but those similarities may be the results of very different evolutionary paths. Such similarities are called analogies. The wings of a bat and those of a butterfly are analogous: although they serve the same purpose, they are anatomically, developmentally, and thus evolutionarily unrelated. The only similarities that are of value to us in the use of one species to shed light on the evolution of another are those similarities that have the same evolutionary ancestor. These are called homologies. The wings of a bat and the arms of a human are homologous; although they serve different functions, they are both variations on the same theme—the forelimbs of mammals.

Thus, for our purposes, we must assess the evolutionary closeness of the species with which we are comparing ourselves. It is likely that any similarities between humans and chimpanzees are homologues because chimps are our closest relatives, separated from us by a mere 1.5 percent of our genetic makeups and by a short (in evolutionary terms) 5 million years. We are on less secure ground using monkeys as models for our evolution. Although they too are primates, our common ancestor with the monkeys is around 36 million years in the past. Similarities between what we do and what they do may be based on the same *general* primate behavioral themes, but they may not be the *same* behaviors. Put another way, when we look at our primate relatives, we are *not* looking at representatives of our evolutionary past. We are looking at living, modern creatures who are the results of their own evolutionary histories. Closely related species, however, like humans and chimpanzees, may have evolutionary histories that share a starting point in the recent past.

We begin with Jonathan Marks's "98% Alike?" in which he points out that the meaning of the small genetic difference between humans and apes depends on one's point of reference and that the common reaction to the 98 percent figure is very much a function of how our culture views the science of genetics.

Moving to field studies of nonhuman primates, Sharon Pochron and Patricia Wright show, in "Dance of the Sexes," how complex the behavioral adaptations of some Madagascar lemurs can be in response to varied and unpredictable environments.

In "Close Encounters," Craig Stanford examines the relationship between the chimps and gorillas that inhabit one forest in Uganda and discovers some things that might shed light on the behaviors of early hominids. In "Chimps in the Wild Show Stirrings of Culture," Gretchen Vogel describes some studies that provide compelling evidence that chimps also have behavioral variations and traditions that could fall under the rubric of culture.

Finally, Robert W. Sussman, in "Exploring Our Basic Human Nature: Are Humans Inherently Violent?" shows what light can and cannot be shed on this important question by comparing the behavior of humans with that of nonhuman primates.

SUGGESTED WEBSITES FOR FURTHER STUDY

http://chimp.st-and.ac.uk/cultures3/default.htm
http://www.discoverchimpanzees.org
http://www.primate.wisc.edu/pin
http://www.indiana.edu/~primate/primates.html
http://www.emory.edu/Living_Links

17

98% Alike?
(What Our Similarity to Apes Tells Us About Our Understanding of Genetics)

Jonathan Marks

Jonathan Marks is a professor of anthropology at the University of North Carolina at Charlotte. He specializes in molecular anthropology, looking into genetic changes that have been part of human evolution. For a longer treatment of the topic of this selection, and much else, see Marks's What It Means to be 98% Chimpanzee: Apes, People, and Their Genes *(2002, University of California Press).*

Humans and chimps are said to differ by a mere 2 percent of our DNA. This figure, however, as amazing as it seems at first, must be interpreted. Moreover, we need to put the figure into perspective. What are the implications for our kinship as indicated by taxonomic classification; are humans, indeed, apes, or apes hominids? And just *how* different is 2 percent? Does it mean that our phenotypes—our bodies and behaviors—are also just 2 percent different? In this selection, Jon Marks addresses these questions and shows the importance of considering the cultural context and interpretation of our scientific data. (See also Selection 34 for more detail on the chimpanzee genome.)

As you read, consider the following questions:

1. What is the "apparent paradox" to which Marks refers in the second paragraph?

2. In a comparison of any two species, how different are two random sequences of their DNA likely to be? Why is this?

3. Does the more than 98 percent genetic similarity between humans and chimps reflect a 98 percent similarity in their phenotypes? In what important ways are our genes different?

4. Marks says that humans are apes in the same way that humans are fish. What does he mean by this?

5. What is it about genetics that, according to Marks, can mislead us as we draw conclusions from genetic data?

It's not too hard to tell Jane Goodall from a chimpanzee. Goodall is the one with long legs and short arms, a prominent forehead, and whites in her eyes. She's the one with a significant amount of hair only on her head, not all over her body. She's the one who walks, talks, and wears clothing.

A few decades ago, however, the nascent field of molecular genetics recognized an apparent paradox: However easy it may be to tell Jane Goodall from a chimpanzee on the basis of physical characteristics, it

is considerably harder to tell them apart according to their genes.

More recently, geneticists have been able to determine with precision that humans and chimpanzees are over 98 percent identical genetically, and that figure has become one of the most well-known factoids in the popular scientific literature. It has been invoked to argue that we are simply a third kind of chimpanzee, together with the common ·chimp and the rarer bonobo; to claim human rights for nonhuman apes; and to explain the roots of male aggression.

Using the figure in those ways, however, ignores the context necessary to make sense of it. Actually, our amazing genetic similarity to chimpanzees is a scientific fact constructed from two rather more mundane

From *The Chronicle of Higher Education*, May 12, 2000. Reprinted with permission from the author.

facts: our familiarity with the apes and our unfamiliarity with genetic comparisons.

To begin with, it is unfair to juxtapose the differences between the bodies of people and apes with the similarities in their genes. After all, we have been comparing the bodies of humans and chimpanzees for 300 years, and we have been comparing DNA sequences for less than 20 years.

Now that we are familiar with chimpanzees, we quickly see how different they look from us. But when the chimpanzee was a novelty, in the 18th century, scholars were struck by the overwhelming similarity of human and ape bodies. And why not? Bone for bone, muscle for muscle, organ for organ, the bodies of humans and apes differ only in subtle ways. And yet, it is impossible to say just how physically similar they are. Forty percent? Sixty percent? Ninety-eight percent? Three-dimensional beings that develop over their lifetimes don't lend themselves to a simple scale of similarity.

Genetics brings something different to the comparison. A DNA sequence is a one-dimensional entity, a long series of A, G, C, and T subunits. Align two sequences from different species and you can simply tabulate their similarities; if they match 98 out of 100 times, then the species are 98 percent genetically identical.

But is that more or less than their bodies match? We have no easy way to tell, for making sense of the question "How similar are a human and a chimp?" requires a frame of reference. In other words, we should be asking: "How similar are a human and a chimp, compared to what?"

Let's try and answer the question. How similar are a human and a chimp, compared to, say, a sea urchin? The human and chimpanzee have limbs, skeletons, bilateral symmetry, a central nervous system; each bone, muscle, and organ matches. For all intents and purposes, the human and chimpanzee aren't 98 percent identical, they're 100 percent identical.

On the other hand, when we compare the DNA of humans and chimps, what does the percentage of similarity mean? We conceptualize it on a linear scale, on which 100 percent is perfectly identical and 0 percent is totally different. But the structure of DNA gives the scale a statistical idiosyncrasy.

Because DNA is a linear array of those four bases—A, G, C, and T—only four possibilities exist at any specific point in a DNA sequence. The laws of chance tell us that two random sequences from species that have no ancestry in common will match at about one in every four sites.

Thus even two unrelated DNA sequences will be 25 percent identical, not 0 percent identical. (You can, of course, generate sequences more different than that, but greater differences would not occur randomly.) The most different two DNA sequences can be, then, is 75 percent different.

Now consider that all multicellular life on earth is related. A human, a chimpanzee, and the banana the chimpanzee is eating share a remote common ancestry, but a common ancestry nevertheless. Therefore, if we compare any particular DNA sequence in a human and a banana, the sequence would have to be more than 25 percent identical. For the sake of argument, let's say 35 percent. In other words, your DNA is over one-third the same as a banana's. Yet, of course, there are few ways other than genetically in which a human could be shown to be one-third identical to a banana.

That context may help us to assess the 98 percent DNA similarity of humans and chimpanzees. The fact that our DNA is 98 percent identical to that of a chimp is not a transcendent statement about our natures, but merely a decontextualized and culturally interpreted datum.

Moreover, the genetic comparison is misleading because it ignores qualitative differences among genomes. Genetic evolution involves much more than simply replacing one base with another. Thus, even among such close relatives as human and chimpanzee, we find that the chimp's genome is estimated to be about 10 percent larger than the human's; that one human chromosome contains a fusion of two small chimpanzee chromosomes; and that the tips of each chimpanzee chromosome contain a DNA sequence that is not present in humans.

In other words, the pattern we encounter genetically is actually quite close to the pattern we encounter anatomically. In spite of the shock the figure of 98 percent may give us, humans are obviously identifiably different from, as well as very similar to, chimpanzees. The apparent paradox is simply a result of how mundane the apes have become and how exotic DNA still is.

Another way in which humans and apes are frequently conflated is phylogenetically. Humans, the argument runs, fall within a group that comprises chimpanzees, gorillas, and orangutans—the great apes. We are genetically more closely related to chimpanzees than they are to orangutans. Because we fall within the ape group, we are ourselves apes.

True, but again we need to look at the context.

Traditional zoological classifications incorporate two evolutionary processes: descent and divergence. The category of great apes is marked by the divergence of humans from it. It is, in taxonomic parlance, paraphyletic: The group is missing some close relatives that fall within it and is an artificial amalgam of the species left behind.

Two other famous paraphyletic categories are invertebrates, a motley assortment of things that didn't evolve a backbone; and reptiles, the diverse scaly creatures that the birds left behind.

More to the point, consider the coelacanth, which by virtue of its limb structure is more closely related to tetrapods—animals with four limbs—than to other fish, such as trout. Therefore, fish are also a paraphyletic category, an assemblage of vertebrates that didn't evolve four limbs. Tetrapods are a phylogenetic subset of fish, although they have diverged extensively from their aquatic relatives.

Humans, of course, are tetrapods. Because of that fact, and because tetrapods share an ancestry with fish—including both the closely related coelacanth and the distant trout—the conclusion should be obvious: Humans are indeed apes, but only in precisely the same way that humans are fish. We simply fall within a diverse group of creatures with broad, general similarities to one another, from whom our ancestors radically diverged.

Our apeness, like our fishness, is not a profound revelation about human nature, but merely an artifact of the way we classify things.

Genetics has the power to make a familiar fact seem unfamiliar and to give biases and opinions the ring of scientific authority. Social and political activists have invoked genetics over the full course of the last century and will undoubtedly continue to do so over the course of this one. It is thus of the utmost importance that we regard genetic data in a cultural and critical framework and place them intellectually where the study of heredity intersects the study of human systems of meaning.

In a [1999] issue of *Anthropology Today*, Gisli Palsson and Paul Rabinow analyzed the Iceland genome project and called for "a molecular anthropology that includes scientific, technological, political, cultural, and ethical dimensions." I agree that we need such a molecular anthropology, which should be informed by genetics and which should, at the same time, approach genetics with a critical, analytical, and ethnographic eye.

The time is ripe for such an interdisciplinary endeavor. Our place in nature is not determined by genetic data alone; it is a contested site on the boundary of godliness and animalness, between beast and angel. To make sense of the data requires both anthropological and biological knowledge.

18

Dance of the Sexes

Sharon T. Pochron and Patricia C. Wright

Sharon T. Pochron is an assistant research professor at the Institute for the Conservation of Tropical Environments (ICTE) at Stony Brook University in New York. Patricia C. Wright, a professor of anthropology at Stony Brook University, is ICTE's executive director and the international coordinator for the Ranomafana National Park Project in Madagascar.

Behavior patterns are highly variable among primate species and even within primate species, and at times it can be difficult to interpret the behaviors of the primates in terms of Darwinian fitness. Among the most complex behaviors are those between females and males of a species, as each is adapted to maximize its contribution to future generations. In this selection, Sharon Pochron and Patricia White describe their ongoing research into the seemingly odd and variable behavior of female and male sifakas, lemurs of Madagascar. It is an interesting example, too, of science in action.

As you read, consider the following questions:

1. Why do the primates of Madagascar exhibit traits not typical of primates of other locations?

2. Why are male sifakas the same size as females, given that larger size in males is typical of groups structured like theirs?

3. What can you say about the group structure of the sifaka?

4. How do the authors reconcile the sifakas' high infant mortality with their slow reproductive rate? How are life span and environment tied in with the answer to this question?

The group of lemurs, known as Milne-Edwards's* sifakas, was small—an adult male, an adult female, and two large offspring. With only four animals, distinguishing them should have been easy. "That's the male," said Georges Rakotonirina, pointing. Rakotonirina was the lead field technician, a native of Madagascar who had been studying the sifakas with one of us (Wright) since 1986. "And that's the female." The novice among us (Pochron), new to the study in 2000, stared at the dark forms up in the tree and blinked. They all looked the same.

"Look," said Rakotonirina. "They're eating *vahiabanikondro*."

"What?" Pochron thought to herself. "How can he tell from down here what they're eating? And can I

possibly learn to pronounce and spell . . . whatever it is?" Hearing chattering in the forest canopy, Pochron then asked aloud, "What bird is that?"

Rakotonirina laughed. "That's the sifaka," he said. "It means he wants to stop fighting." Pochron knew then and there she had some catching up to do, notwithstanding her previous experience studying baboons in Tanzania. But like Wright and many others whose first encounter with lemurs was life-changing, she was hooked.

The lemurs of Madagascar are the surviving members of a lineage that has been genetically isolated from the rest of the primate family for at least 65 million years. The island became separated from the African mainland 160 million years ago, and from the Indian landmass 80 million years ago. The ancestors of lemurs probably colonized the island by rafting there on drifting vegetation. Until relatively recently, lemurs lived in a separate world. Meanwhile, primates elsewhere evolved into monkeys, apes, and humans.

That ancient genetic split is surely one reason lemurs often boast such unusual traits, compared with

---

*Milne-Edwards's sifaka, one of the lemur species of Madagascar, lives in trees, mainly on a diet of fruits, leaves, and seeds. The species has been the subject of a long-term study by the authors.

humanity's closer primate relatives. For example, dwarf lemurs store up fat in their tails and then draw on it while hibernating; in contrast, no monkey or ape hibernates. Members of one lemur family, the indriids, maintain an upright, kangaroolike posture as they leap from one tree trunk and cling to another; monkeys, however, are quadrupedal, like squirrels. All lemurs have toothcombs—a set of teeth ideally shaped for grooming; monkey and ape teeth are shaped for biting and chewing.

Especially surprising to evolutionary biologists, in most groups of lemurs, females are dominant over

Variation in group composition

Single pair   Polyandrous   Polygynous   Multiple adults of each sex

Conflict when an outsider joins a group

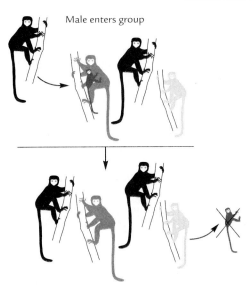

Male enters group

Incoming male may kill dependent young; males can coexist peaceably in the same group.

Female enters group

Incoming female fights with resident female and may kill dependent young; newcomer drives off resident female.

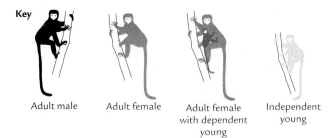

Key

Adult male   Adult female   Adult female with dependent young   Independent young

Composition of groups of Milne-Edwards's sifakas varies widely, and may shift from year to year within a single group, as shown in this schematic diagram. Groups range in size from two to nine individuals; as juveniles mature, many leave to join other groups. When an outsider tries to join a group, fighting may ensue, particularly between adult females.

males. In some lemur species female dominance becomes manifest only in conflicts over food; in other species it emerges in all social settings. Yet in monkeys and apes—indeed, in mammals generally—female dominance is rare. What has led to such an unusual social characteristic among lemurs, with its far-reaching implications?

Female mammals that do dominate males are usually well equipped physically to do so. Female spotted hyenas are often bigger than males. Female reindeer rule over males during the short season when males have shed their antlers prior to growing new ones and the females have not yet shed theirs. Female golden hamsters call the shots when they are fatter than males.

But female lemurs are not usually larger than males, nor do they have any special weapons for enforcing dominance, such as bigger teeth. Members of the two sexes are virtually monomorphic, or similar, when it comes to physical strength. How do females manage to get their way without the brawn to back up a threat? We and our colleagues do not yet have a definitive answer to that question, but after eighteen years studying one indriid species, we have some inklings.

The center of our universe is the Milne-Edwards's sifaka (Propithecus edwardsi). Until recently it was considered a subspecies of the diademed sifaka, but geneticists have now determined that it is a separate species. Weighing in at about thirteen pounds and looking like something out of the Muppet studio, the animal lives throughout Ranomafana National Park, a 170-square-mile emerald forest set in cloud-covered mountains, and in adjacent regions . . . . It has orange eyes and woolly, water-resistant fur (a useful trait in a rainforest), which is colored dark brown to black except for two large, white patches on the animal's back. The females have a lemony, maple-syrupy smell; the males, which have more glands for scent marking, smell muskier.

Active by day, Milne-Edwards's sifakas prefer to hang out some forty feet up in the trees, and they travel, as do other indriids, by leaping from one tree trunk to the next. Adults are mainly leaf eaters, but they also rely heavily on fruits and seeds.

Females and males do not often come into conflict, but when they do, the females win about 95 percent of the time. Apparently males are letting females win such altercations. What are they giving up by submitting? The answer may be calories. Adult females, for instance, appear to eat more seeds than adult males do. The difference is most pronounced during the mating season. Seeds are generally high in fat, and storing up fat is good preparation for a female on her way to becoming reproductively active. When you see males and females fighting, you will probably find tempting seeds nearby.

If males are allowing females to enjoy more seeds, what are they getting in return? The answers that jump to mind are: sex and offspring. And that would make sense in evolutionary terms. Unfortunately for the theory, the annual estrus cycle of the female lasts only ten hours, and in that short period she may mate with several males. None of those mating males is likely to know whose baby the female is having. If he allows a female to take his food, and she uses it to raise another male's offspring, he has not helped himself at all. So why would he allow her to win extra calories? Nature is hardly known for its generosity. In our years of field observations seeking answers to this question, we

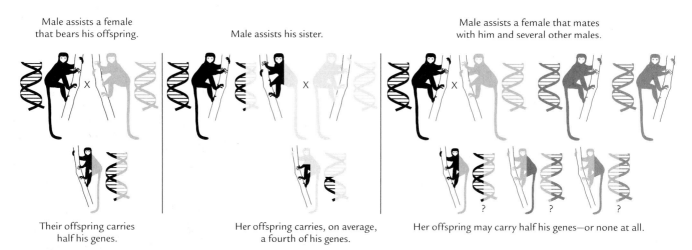

Male assists a female that bears his offspring.

Male assists his sister.

Male assists a female that mates with him and several other males.

Their offspring carries half his genes.

Her offspring carries, on average, a fourth of his genes.

Her offspring may carry half his genes—or none at all.

According to evolutionary theory, a male will assist a female—for example, by ceding disputed food to her—only if his action will increase the likelihood of perpetuating his own genes. At least one of the three social conditions outlined in the schematic diagram above must hold if males in future generations are to inherit his "altruistic" behavior. Males and females are represented by the shapes shown in the key in the [preceding diagram].

have found ourselves bumping into some other unusual and fascinating lemur traits. Our goal, then, is to find a coherent explanation that makes sense of it all: with apologies to the high-energy physicists, our holy grail is a kind of grand unified theory of the lemur.

Milne-Edwards's sifakas usually occur in small groups ranging from two to nine individuals. Typically, the groups include three adults (either two males and one female, or vice versa), infants, and older offspring. A female may come into her brief period of estrus at any time during the mating season, which runs from late November through mid-January. The babies are born in May, June, and July. A female gives birth to only one baby at a time, and nurses it attentively until the next mating season, if it survives until then. The cycle puts weaning at a propitious time, when food is most likely to be abundant. A mother that has nursed a baby that long is apt to skip a year before breeding again, most likely because it takes a while to store up enough fat.

Within a group of sifakas life is reasonably peaceful: members spend a lot more time grooming each other than they do squabbling. Males within a group get along most of the year. During the mating season, though, fights between males can be among the most aggressive in this species. There is little question that the fights are about sex, and the fact that fighters sometimes suffer injuries to their testicles may be no accident. You can tell that a threatening look, a swipe, or a bite has had an effect if you hear the intended target emit birdlike chatter, the equivalent of, "Stop picking on me! I'll leave now!"

Since the males are clearly competing with each other for access to fertile females, it is puzzling that males have not evolved to be larger than the females (or to have bigger teeth or other such endowments). According to classic behavioral ecology, when males compete, the larger or stronger males usually prevail. The larger males thus have more offspring, and those offspring carry the genes associated with being large. After several generations the repeated selection for large males should lead to males that are larger than the females. When the males and females of a species differ in such physical characteristics, the species is said to be sexually dimorphic.

Most large mammal species are sexually dimorphic. Monomorphism, where it is found, typically occurs in monogamous species, in which a single male and female pair up to raise their offspring together. To succeed evolutionarily, monogamy has to be a two-way street. The male has the genetic incentive to help feed, carry, and protect the young of a particular female only if the monogamous bond assures him the young are his. If the female needs a devoted mate to help raise her young, she has a genetic incentive of her own—to avoid mating with a male that beats up other males, because, despite winning the "right" to take many "wives," he cannot offer parental care to all his offspring. When male fighting is suppressed by such female preferences, so too is sexual dimorphism. Some lemurs such as indris (*Indri indri*) fit that pattern: they are monomorphic and monogamous [*for a comparison of the indri with the diademed sifaka, see "Scent Wars," by Joyce A. Powzyk, April 2002*].

Paradoxically, though, most lemur species do not behave like indris: they mate promiscuously, and males provide little or no care for infants, which may or may not be theirs. In short, they look like monogamous species, but they act like nonmonogamous ones. The Milne-Edwards's sifaka fits that pattern, too. But how can it be a stable arrangement?

Our observations offer part of the solution to the puzzle. First, no male, even if he is stronger than other males, can prevent a female from mating promiscuously. Nor does a larger male have the advantage of producing more sperm, because during the breeding season the testicles of all the males are roughly the same size. Thus the ejaculate of a heavy male cannot, as has been observed in some mammalian and avian species, overwhelm the ejaculate of a light male: if they both mate with a particular female, each has an equal chance to father her offspring.

Aside from the competition between males over females, serious fighting may also erupt when a new adult animal joins a group. Such transitions in group membership shed additional light on the roles of males and females—and, in particular, the dominance of females—within lemur groups.

Milne-Edwards's sifaka groups are far less predictable in composition than those of monkey and ape species. A baboon troop, for instance, characteristically includes many adult males and females. Gorilla groups are generally polygynous, consisting of one silverback male, his harem of several adult females, their young, and one or more subordinate males. By contrast, sifaka groups can be polyandrous (one female and two or more males) or polygynous (one male and two or more females). They can include multiple males and multiple females—or just one adult pair [see illustration on page 85].

Not only do all such combinations turn up with roughly equal frequency, but a group may change in composition from one year to the next. A new member is most likely to join a group from August until October, just before the mating season. If a new male seeks to join a group, all the animals may coexist peacefully. Sometimes, though, the resident male and the newcomer fight, and one is driven away. And sometimes a female prefers the new male, and she may help force the old male to leave.

For any dependent offspring in the group, an incoming male poses great danger: he is likely to kill them, a measure that is evolutionarily adaptive because it speeds up his chance to father offspring. Such behavior is well documented in primates.

When an adult female tries to join a group, friction with the resident female seems inevitable. The two sometimes bite, slap, and chase each other. The resident female generally leaves, probably an indication that the incoming female has shrewdly judged her chances before attempting to gain entry. Just as males do, an incoming female may kill any dependent young. In other primates, at least, it is less common—and less easily explained as adaptive behavior—for the female to kill the young than it is for the male. The murderous action of the incoming female seems to hasten the departure of the resident female. When two adult females live together peaceably in a group, we suspect that they are closely related. Genetic studies currently under way should clarify this.

To investigate why the sifaka's social arrangements vary so widely, we compared sifaka survivorship and fertility patterns with those of some other primates. For example, tamarins and marmosets, both New World monkeys, suffer high mortality in their early years; sensibly, then, they reach sexual maturity and begin reproducing at an early age. By contrast, many Old World monkeys, such as baboons and macaques, live longer, start to reproduce later, and have more time between babies.

The mortality pattern of the Milne-Edwards's sifaka closely resembles that of the tamarins and marmosets: many die in their first few years of life. In fertility, however, Milne-Edwards's sifakas resemble baboons and macaques: the sifakas that do survive reach sexual maturity fairly late (about three and a half years for females, and four and a half years for males), and they reproduce at a slow rate over a span approaching thirty years. It is almost as if sifakas have deliberately chosen the most difficult of all the primate patterns ever observed: high mortality coupled with slow reproduction. By the end of her life, a female tamarin or marmoset will have three or four daughters; a baboon or macaque will have two or three. But by the end of her lifespan, a female sifaka will rarely have more than one daughter that survives to reproduce. The constraints on reproduction may be responsible for encouraging the sifakas' highly flexible group structures.

The sifaka's lifespan is unusual for a mammal its size. On average, the larger the species, the longer it lives. As we noted earlier, Milne-Edwards's sifakas weigh about thirteen pounds, yet they live nearly thirty years in the wild. Such longevity may have evolved in response to unpredictable environmental conditions. After all, a longer life gives the animals a better chance of reproducing during the years when conditions are most favorable. It is hard to imagine that food could ever be scarce in a place such as Ranomafana National Park, where greenery covers every surface. Yet the availability of food varies seasonally, with the rain. Furthermore, Madagascar is prone to cyclones and droughts, which can also lead to shortages.

Perhaps here too is part of the solution to our original question about lemurs: why are females the dominant sex? The behavioral pattern, in which males cede food to females, appears essential for balancing female and male reproductive needs. For females, fertility, pregnancy, and nursing all depend on sufficient body weight. Weight is less important for males, because their reproductive role is limited to copulation and, as we mentioned earlier, during the breeding season, the testes of small-bodied males are the same size as those of larger-bodied males. If the males did grow larger overall, Madagascar's unpredictable environment might prove fatal to them. In sum, neither having a small body size nor relinquishing high-calorie foods to females seems to compromise the fertility of males.

In the past few years we have considered a number of ways to account for these observations. Because the females mate promiscuously, perhaps each male simply defers to all females, on the grounds that there is always some chance that one of them will bear his offspring. Or a male may yield food to a female only when he has some good reasons for thinking he will sire her offspring. Or a male may defer to a close female relative (mother, sister, daughter), whose offspring would indirectly share some of his genes. Or maybe the reality is some combination of all those factors [see illustration on page 86].

One way to learn more about what is going on is to test offspring for paternity. Toni Lyn Morelli, one of Wright's graduate students, has been sampling blood of these sifakas and analyzing it genetically. In a species where the average number of adults in a group is three, however, discerning a statistically significant pattern may take some time. And—who knows?—the results may lead us to some new lemur mystery.

19

Close Encounters

Craig Stanford

Craig Stanford is a professor of anthropology and biological sciences at the University of Southern California in Los Angeles and a codirector of L.A.'s Jane Goodall Research Center. He has conducted field studies of primates in India, Bangladesh, Peru, Tanzania, and Uganda, and is best known for his work on the meat-eating behavior of wild chimpanzees. See his book Significant Others: The Ape-Human Continuum and the Quest for Human Nature *(2001, Basic Books).*

....

We often think about species in isolation, but, of course, a species' environment includes other species, possibly even closely related ones. Of special interest to us, of course, are our close cousins, the apes. In this selection, Craig Stanford describes his study of chimps and gorillas in the wonderfully named Bwindi Impenetrable National Park in Uganda and shows how the two species can be ecologically separate while living in the same area. The study suggests some scenarios for some of our early hominid ancestors.

As you read, consider the following questions:

1. In what relevant ways do the gorillas and chimps in the Uganda forest differ from one another?

2. How do the chimps and gorillas in the study area differ from members of their species elsewhere?

3. In what ways are these chimps and gorillas "typical" of their species?

4. What does this study suggest about the behavior of some of our early hominid ancestors?

....

It's a rare sunny morning in the Bwindi Impenetrable National Park of southwestern Uganda, and a party of chimpanzees is feeding noisily in an enormous fig tree. My colleague John Bosco Nkurunungi and I sit fifty yards away on the other side of the small valley, surveying the scene at eye level through binoculars. The apes, which belong to a group Nkurunungi and I have been observing as part of our field studies, stand upright on thick branches as they stuff themselves with the little fruits. The group's alpha male—we call him Mboneire ("handsome" in Ruchiga, a local language)—eats next to a female we call Martha, and her daughter, May. Grizzled old Kushoto plucks fruit nimbly with his right hand (his left was damaged when it was caught in a poacher's wire snare).

Suddenly the branches in the forest understory begin to sway, and a large, black-haired figure pops partly into view from the green foliage.

"Who's that big guy?" I whisper, refocusing my binoculars. "That's not someone we've seen before." Judging from the size of the top of its head, the new arrival looks to be the biggest chimpanzee I've ever seen.

Peering through his binoculars, Nkurunungi straightens me out: "Craig," he says, "that's not a chimpanzee. It's a gorilla!"

Nkurunungi and I and our assistants in the Bwindi Impenetrable Great Ape Project are well aware that in this forest the ranges of the two ape species overlap. Yet this occasion, in the project's fifth year, is the first time we've ever witnessed an encounter between them. The newcomer, an adult female, emerges from the foliage and sits out in the open on a large branch only twenty feet below the chimpanzees. She's much larger than any of them, and displays the serene and confident demeanor that gorillas always seem to possess. As we watch, she climbs to within ten feet of the chimpanzees, casually plucking figs along the way. Then another gorilla shows up below her, this one a silverback, or mature male, that appears to weigh at least 400 pounds. He joins the female, and the two feed amicably side by side.

For the most part the two ape species pay no attention to each other, but after about twenty minutes the silverback notices us watching from across the way. As suddenly as they appeared, the two gorillas drop out of the tree and then disappear in the dense undergrowth.

As a biological anthropologist, I started the Bwindi Impenetrable Great Ape Project (or BIGAPE, as I like to call it) in 1996, and for seven years now, Nkurunungi, a doctoral student from Makerere University in Kampala, and I have worked together in Bwindi Impenetrable National Park (formerly, the Impenetrable Forest). Our goal is to understand the ecological relations between the chimpanzees (*Pantroglodytes schweinfurthii*) and the mountain gorillas (*Gorilla gorilla beringei*) that share this rugged habitat. Ecological theory predicts that in order for species to coexist over the long haul of evolution by natural selection, they must avoid head-to-head competition. So two closely related species living in the same habitat typically diverge in some key aspects of their anatomy, behavior, or ecology. Diet is often the main point of divergence, and to find out if that is the case among Bwindi's gorillas and chimpanzees, Nkurunungi and I have had to "walk the walk" of field observation.

Our interest, though, goes beyond the apes themselves. Anthropologists have long studied the behavior and ecology of the great apes—bonobo, chimpanzee, gorilla, and orangutan—to try to shed light on the lives of early hominids. Investigators have looked specifically at the relations between gorillas and chimpanzees for clues about how early hominid groups may have similarly shared a habitat. And, to be sure, at certain times and places in human prehistory, more than one species of hominid lived in the same habitat.

At Olduvai Gorge in northern Tanzania, for instance, *Australopithecus boisei* and *Homo habilis* (the latter an early member of our own genus) occupied the same territory about 1.8 million years ago. Still earlier, about 3.5 million years ago, both *Australopithecus afarensis*, of which the famed fossil Lucy was a member, and the recently discovered *Kenyanthropus platyops* lived in fairly close proximity in East Africa. Anthropologists are keen to determine what kinds of associations such closely related species forged with each other. Did they share their habitat amicably, coming into peaceful contact on a regular basis? Or did they compete—perhaps even aggressively—for food, shelter, and other resources?

The most important clues to the ecological competitions of the distant past are teeth. Often well preserved in fossil records, teeth, their anatomy, and their wear patterns reflect the diet of their former owner. For example, Olduvai's *H. habilis* possessed unimpressive molars in a modestly proportioned skull. We believe this hominid consumed fruit, leaves, and some meat. In contrast, *A. boisei* had massive molars and a skull with a large bony crest on top, along the midline—the attachment place for formidable jaw muscles. Those features indicate that *A. boisei* was adapted to a diet of either tough and fibrous or hard-shelled foods. Fossil investigators think those dietary differences made it possible for the two human relatives to survive alongside each other for hundreds of thousands of years. Had they instead competed for the same resources, one of them would probably have become quickly extinct.

Beginning with the pioneering studies of wild chimpanzees by the primatologist Jane Goodall and of mountain gorillas by the primatologist Dian Fossey, investigators have watched apes in their natural habitats for more than four decades. As the data accumulated, it began to seem as if the two species occupied quite different ecological niches. In fact, aside from living in tropical forests across equatorial Africa, the two apes were long thought to have little in common. Chimpanzees were portrayed as high-energy arboreal nomads, traveling miles each day to gather a high-carbohydrate diet of ripe fruit supplemented with leaves, insects, and mammalian prey. They ate and made their sleeping nests in tall trees.

Gorillas, in contrast, appeared to be groundbased foragers of wild celery and other fibrous, nutrient-poor foods. Fossey portrayed them as lumbering, sedentary, terrestrial beasts. The idea grew that, although their large brains were impressive, gorillas were the cows—the slow-moving herbivores—of the ape world.

In recent years, however, the general view that there is a wide ecological dichotomy between chimpanzees and gorillas has, to some extent, broken down. As other populations of gorillas have been studied across Africa, it has become clear that Fossey's gorillas, which inhabit the cold, mountainous forest cloaking Rwanda's Virunga volcanoes, lead quite different lives from those of gorilla populations elsewhere. Recent studies show that most gorillas, like chimpanzees, actually prefer fruit, and travel considerable distances to find it. To get other cherished foods, such as fungi and epiphytes, they climb tall trees, just as chimpanzees do. And sometimes they, too, nest in trees, even near the tree nests of chimpanzees. With all those parallels, how chimpanzees and gorillas can be ecologically separated while living in the same habitat is not immediately clear.

Bwindi Impenetrable National Park encompasses some 130 square miles of wet, rugged hills cut into steep ravines by cold rushing streams. The park is one of the last large tracts of montane wet forest in eastern or central Africa. It boasts an extraordinary biodiversity—at least ten primate species live there, as well as nearly 400 species of birds, including some that occur nowhere else in the region.

The population of Bwindi gorillas is about 300. That may seem so small that the population is at risk of vanishing, but apparently it is stable. The situation is more alarming in other parts of Africa, where gorillas are under much greater pressure from forest cutting, poaching, and, most recently, an outbreak of Ebola virus. In the past five or ten years alone, the total number of gorillas in Africa, believed to have been between 80,000 and 100,000, may have been cut in half. We know less about the Bwindi chimpanzee population, estimated at no more than 200, but across Africa the species faces the same perils.

Research in Bwindi, however, is not without its drawbacks. The area has suffered several periods of political instability in the past. In early 1999, Rwandan rebels killed a warden and kidnapped fourteen people from a tourist camp, and shortly thereafter they murdered eight of their captives. Since that tragedy, however, the Ugandan government has worked to ensure that the area is secure. Both ecotourism and research are thriving once again.

My colleagues and I are compiling a digital map, aided by Global Positioning System technology, which shows how the chimpanzees and gorillas use the Bwindi landscape. Carrying handheld GPS units, our research assistants plot the coordinates of every observation of the two ape species, noting if an observation is made at a sleeping nest or at a feeding tree. They also map sites where the animals have nested and the position and fruiting season of every major food tree—including the great fig trees that tend to fruit unpredictably. As the mapping has proceeded over a period of years, we have been able to build a digital portrait of how the two apes differ in their use of habitat from month to month. We can see whether the movements and feeding of one species influences those of the other, and record overlaps in their diets.

The Bwindi gorilla group we are following is quite a cohesive one, made up of thirteen individuals, including two silverbacks. The animals do not follow the lifestyle of their chimpanzee neighbors, and their behavior also differs in key ways from that of the gorillas in the Virunga mountains. In a break from the herbivore stereotype, from January until July, when fruit is most plentiful, our gorillas search for it far and wide. Most of the fruits they eat are the same ones eaten by the chimpanzees, but the gorillas in both Bwindi and in the neighboring forests of eastern Congo exploit a greater variety of fruits than do the chimpanzees in the same habitats.

From August until December, when the fruit supply in the forest is low, the gorillas turn to browsing leafy forest undergrowth, a salad that is low in calories as well as in most other nutrients, but is abundantly available. The consumption of this fallback staple is what seems to distinguish gorillas from chimpanzees everywhere. In the same months that gorillas rely on leafy matter, chimpanzees simply expand their search for the increasingly scarce trees with ripe fruit, traveling greater distances each day across Bwindi's hills and valleys.

Another *Gorillas in the Mist* stereotype pictures all gorillas plowing slowly through cold misty meadows of ferns, never bothering to seek the fruits readily available in the upper reaches of the trees. In fact, though, the Bwindi gorillas we observe climb with agility. To see a 400-pound silverback swaying from the uppermost tree branches as he picks figs or orchids and other epiphytic plants for his lunch is a truly impressive sight. Although some investigators have suggested that Bwindi mountain gorillas might possess some genetic adaptation to tree foraging, I prefer a far simpler, common-sense explanation.

The mountainous terrain in Bwindi park extends from 4,000 to 8,000 feet in elevation, whereas Rwanda's Virunga volcanoes, which lie just twenty-five miles to the south, rise as high as 14,700 feet. The lower altitude of Bwindi's mountains makes for a warmer habitat, one that is much more hospitable to fruit trees. In contrast, the habitat of the Virunga gorillas is so cold that few fruit trees (in fact, fewer trees of any kind) grow there. Virunga gorillas often have no choice but to stay on the ground and eat herbs. The difference in habitat may also explain why there are no chimpanzees living in the Virungas.

A third feature of gorilla behavior we expected to confirm turned out to be just as misleading a stereotype as leaf-eating and ground-foraging. We suspected at the outset of our study that the chimpanzees would always nest in trees and the gorillas would nest on the ground. Hence nighttime would find them ecologically separated. But at Bwindi, about one-fifth of all gorilla nests are built in small understory trees, which groan under the weight of such massive occupants. And unlike most other chimpanzees that have been studied, the ones in Bwindi occasionally build nests on the ground.

Our studies of Bwindi apes suggest that the striking behavioral and ecological differences between gorillas and chimpanzees stressed by earlier investigators were, in part, artifacts of the environments where those early studies were done. But our close observations still confirm important behavioral differences that others have noted between the two species of ape. Unlike the cohesive gorillas, for instance, the Bwindi chimpanzees live in the same fluid groups that characterize chimpanzees everywhere. The group we study, which ranges over at least eight square miles, is made up of at least twenty-five chimpanzees. It includes five adult males, plus females and their offspring. At any given moment, however, it is likely to break up into temporary subgroups, or parties.

I noted earlier that chimpanzees and gorillas diverge in their reliance on "fallback" foods, eaten in times of scarcity: the gorillas turn to fibrous plants, whereas the chimpanzees scour more territory for fruits. Another obvious dietary difference is the chimpanzees' love of meat. Virtually everywhere they have been studied—and Bwindi is no exception—chimpanzees avidly hunt and eat monkeys and forest antelope. Although the density of these mammals in our study area is fairly low, we have found that nearly 10 percent of chimpanzee fecal samples contain the bones or hair of prey. In contrast, gorillas do not eat meat at all, and have been only rarely observed in the wild consuming insects. Studies of gorillas in captivity show that their ability to metabolize the fats and cholesterol in meat is quite limited.

In our study area—the high elevation part of the park—the two ape species share roughly the same home range. But within that area the two apes use the forest differently. Chimpanzees are long-distance commuters, covering large parts of their range every week. The gorillas, meanwhile, range over only small portions of the area even in a given month, and it may take them a year or more to fully exploit the available resources. That difference may reduce the ecological overlap between the two species.

Measuring ecological overlap is one thing. But another goal of our study is to investigate whether there is competition between the two apes. That is much more difficult, because it requires showing that one species, through its behavior, is actually reducing the food intake of the other.

The most straightforward way to demonstrate such competition is to document encounters between chimpanzees and gorillas. We have now recorded four such encounters, in which members of both groups occupied the same tree. Three of them were quite amicable: the gorillas arrived at a tree in which chimpanzees were feeding, entered the tree themselves, fed near their cousins, and then departed.

But one encounter was not nearly so cordial. In April 2002, a party of nine chimpanzees was feeding in a tall *Chrysophyllum gorungosanum* tree (a species of star apple). The tree was laden with the fuzzy brown fruits with their milky-white pulp that both chimpanzees and gorillas relish. As the chimpanzees fed, our research assistants heard gorillas grunting and moving about in the undergrowth below the tree, apparently feeding on fallen fruits. Then a female gorilla, followed by one of the silverbacks, began to climb up the trunk. That prompted two of the male chimpanzees to stop feeding and descend to the first large fork of the trunk, where they obstructed the ascent of the two gorillas with a noisy, hair-bristling, branch-slapping display.

The standoff continued on and off for nearly an hour. All the while, the gorillas remained on the ground or lower branches, calmly watching their boisterous challengers. Finally, the arrival of other research assistants who had been tracking the gorillas startled the chimpanzees, which fled to an adjacent treetop. The gorillas immediately climbed into the *Chrysophyllum* tree and began to partake of the fruit.

This interaction may have been confrontational because *Chrysophyllum* fruit is more highly prized than the figs the apes were eating in the other encounters we witnessed. Although it is risky to generalize from this one observation, the outcome of the contest suggests that in Bwindi, chimpanzees are dominant to gorillas when it comes to competition over food.

It is tempting to imagine, too, that, millions of years ago, *H. habilis*, a direct human ancestor, played chimpanzee to *A. boisei*'s gorilla. Perhaps *H. habilis* was the more freely ranging hominid, less inclined to give in to foraging for salad when the going got tough. Perhaps *H. habilis* was the meat eater, smaller but more aggressive. We will never be certain. But we are certain that in African forests today, two of our closest kin are threatened with imminent extinction. They seek only to coexist—with each other, and with us.

20

Chimps in the Wild Show Stirrings of Culture

Gretchen Vogel

Gretchen Vogel is a news writer for the journal Science.

Culture has always been a central theme in anthropology. We define culture in a biological way as a nongenetic means of adaptation. More specifically, it is defined as ideas and behaviors that are learned and transmitted and as systems of these ideas and behaviors characteristic of particular societies. We have long considered culture the unique attribute of humans. But if we define and recognize culture as learned and shared traditions that differ from one society to the next, then some grooming, communication, and tool-use behaviors among our closest relatives might well fit the definition. In this selection, Gretchen Vogel describes new research that appears to point to that interpretation and discusses what it might mean for our understanding of the evolution of culture among the early hominids.

As you read, consider the following questions:

1. What is the traditional definition of culture among anthropologists? How have some biologists defined culture?

2. What general types of evidence are sought as indicators of the presence of culture among nonhumans?

3. What specific pieces of evidence support the presence of culture among chimpanzees? How were data from chimp studies analyzed to address this question?

4. What conditions among our early ancestors might have provided the impetus for the evolution of more complex cultural behaviors?

TAÏ NATIONAL FOREST, CÔTE D'IVOIRE, WEST AFRICA—At the foot of a buttress tree, in the dappled sunlight of the rainforest floor, a young chimpanzee named Lefkas is working hard for his lunch. He holds a rock with both hands and a foot and slams it down with a sharp crack on a round coula nut, a bit smaller than a golf ball, which is balanced on a flat rock on the ground. After a few tries the nut cracks. The chimp pops the meat in his mouth and scampers off.

The ground where Lefkas was sitting is strewn with coula nut shells, the leavings of other chimpanzees' meals. Indeed, from December through February, coula nut cracking is one of these chimps' main pastimes; primatologist Christophe Boesch, who has studied Lefkas's group at Taï for 20 years, says he watched another young chimp crack nuts nonstop for 5 hours.

But chimps from just a few hundred kilometers away would probably stroll right past Lefkas's dining site. In a survey of chimps throughout Côte d'Ivoire, Boesch found no evidence for nut cracking anywhere east of a river called the Sassandra-N'Zo, even though both nuts and rocks are readily available throughout the forest. To Boesch, who is director of the Max Planck Institute for Evolutionary Anthropology in Leipzig, Germany, such differences in customs are akin to the use of chopsticks in Japan and forks in France: signs of distinct cultures, in which groups develop their own sets of behaviors based on social ties and shared history.

Most people think of culture as encompassing such uniquely human skills as language, music, art, and clothing styles. But some biologists have a simpler definition: any behaviors common to a population that are learned from fellow group members rather than inherited through genes. By this generous definition, bird song dialects and the calls of whales might classify as animal "culture" (*Science*, 27 November 1998, p. 1616).

Most anthropologists stick to a narrower definition, requiring culture to include language and whole systems of behavior. But in the past decade, a growing number of primatologists and psychologists have sought to approach the question more rigorously, defining specific elements of culture that could potentially be observed in animals, then seeking these behaviors in the wild and in labs. They are turning up increasing evidence that nonhuman primates, in particular chimpanzees, may have a primitive type of culture that bridges the gap between the two definitions. Their argument rests on two main kinds of evidence: examples in which one chimp learns from another, and the results of such learning—the seemingly arbitrary differences in habits between chimpanzee groups at different sites. Although most examples of "culture" among animals involve just one or two behaviors, chimpanzees have dozens of learned behaviors involving tool use, social customs, and calls, says Andrew Whiten of the University of St. Andrews in Fife, Scotland.

Of course, no primate society can build a mud hut or do any number of other tasks that are relatively easy for humans to master. Some researchers argue that that is because our primate cousins do not learn as we do, by imitation and instruction. And most agree that primates don't seem to be able to build on previous inventions, an ability that "is the hallmark of human culture" and that allows us to develop complex technologies and rituals, notes psychologist Bennett Galef of McMaster University in Hamilton, Ontario. Even so, Boesch and others argue that the nascent cultural stirrings of our primate cousins may help uncover the roots of human culture, showing that, for example, gregariousness—hunting and foraging together rather than alone—may have spurred cultural development. To see the beginnings of culture in other species, says Boesch, "helps us to see what is unique about humans."

MULTICULTURAL CHIMPS

Some of the best evidence for primate culture has come from field studies comparing the repertoire of chimpanzee skills and behaviors in groups around Africa. For example, in 1974 William McGrew of Miami University in Oxford, Ohio, detailed how chimps at Jane Goodall's Gombe site in Tanzania used sticks to fish driver ants out of their nests. A decade later at Taï, Boesch and his colleagues noticed a slightly different technique. At Gombe, chimps use 60-centimeter-long sticks to probe an ant nest. They wait for the insects to swarm halfway up the stick, then withdraw the tool and sweep ants off with their free hand, gathering a crunchy mouthful of hundreds of ants. At Taï, chimps use sticks about half as long, wait only a few seconds, then use their lips to sweep about a dozen ants directly into their mouth. The Taï method, analogous to eating soup with a tiny sugar spoon, collects only one-fourth as many ants per minute, but in 2 decades of observation, no animals at Taï have ever eaten ants Gombe-style, presumably because no chimp there ever discovered it. "A Gombe chimp would laugh at [the Taï chimps]" for their "primitive" method of ant fishing, says McGrew.

Social interactions vary among groups, too. For example, McGrew, primatologist Linda Marchant, and their colleagues have recently documented a new behavior they call "social scratch" in which one chimp rakes its hand up and down another's back after grooming. The behavior is common at Mahale in Tanzania but never seen elsewhere. Like some human fads and fashions, the behavior isn't utilitarian, but a part of social etiquette that apparently caught on simply because it feels good. "It's unlikely to be related to functional significance of grooming," McGrew says, but rather helps to reinforce the social hierarchy. In preliminary studies, higher ranking chimpanzees received more social scratches per grooming session.

Such examples add up to an impressive list. In last week's issue of *Nature*, researchers from the seven longest established chimpanzee field studies combined observations and listed 39 behaviors, from tool design to grooming to mating displays, that are distinct to particular groups and not readily explained by ecological differences. "We now have, in a sense, an ethnographic record" of chimp populations, McGrew says. "We have enough data in enough populations that we can start doing the sorts of comparisons that cultural anthropologists do across human populations."

Such geographical differences suggest that a chimpanzee's specific behavior and skills are shaped by where it is raised. That idea "is the most exciting finding" in chimpanzee field research this decade, says primatologist Tetsuro Matsuzawa of the Primate Research Institute at Kyoto University in Japan. Yet simply noting these geographical differences begs the question of how they develop and how they are maintained.

DO APES APE?

A chimpanzee pant-hoot sounds like nothing else in the forest: who-ho-who-ho-who AH AH AH AH. Another voice usually responds, and soon the din drowns out even the copulation cries of monkeys and the screech of the hyrax. "Chimps are the loudest animals in the forest, except for humans," Boesch notes, when the din dies down. Researchers are now analyzing these hair-raising hoots for another proof of culture, one that helps explain the origin of geographical customs: that chimps learn from one another.

In 1992, primatologist John Mitani of the University of Michigan, Ann Arbor, reported that different chimpanzee groups had distinct pant-hoot patterns and pitch, suggesting the possibility of learned chimpanzee "dialects." But earlier this year he noted that those differences correlate with factors such as average body size and so might be genetic rather than "cultural" in origin. To find out, anthropologist Richard Wrangham of Harvard University and his colleagues studied calls in two captive groups where chimps from a mix of wild populations live together. In spite of the mixture of genetic backgrounds, each colony had a characteristic style of pant-hoot. "This is some of the best evidence for learning" of vocalizations, says Wrangham. "It's very difficult to think of an alternative hypothesis here."

Evidence that chimp behaviors can spread from one group to another would also strengthen the case that they are learned. Successful human practices tend to spread when people travel, and Matsuzawa has shown that in at least one case, a chimp skill spread the same way. He studies a community near the village of Bossou, Guinea, where the chimps are skilled tool users and frequently use rock hammers and anvils to crack the hard shells of oil palm nuts to get at the fatty meat inside; coula nuts do not grow here, although they are found on nearby Mount Nimba.

In a 1996 experiment, Matsuzawa and his colleagues left rocks, oil palm nuts, and the unfamiliar coula nuts in a clearing, then hid behind a grass screen and videotaped the chimps. Several chimps picked up the unfamiliar nuts, but only an adult female named Yo cracked and ate them. Although other adults ignored Yo's nutcracking, a few young chimps watched her intently and later picked up and cracked nuts themselves. Matsuzawa suspects that Yo, who joined the group as an adolescent and may have been raised in the coula-rich Mount Nimba area, remembered the skill from her childhood. The fact that she passed it on to other young chimps shows, he says, that chimpanzee behaviors can spread from one group to another throughout a region, just as human cultural behaviors do.

But the field is divided over whether monkeys and apes learn from one another the same way that humans do, and researchers interpret the same experimental results in very different ways. For example, in the very first evidence of possible primate culture, reported in 1958, primatologists Shunzo Kawamura and Masao Kawai of Kyoto University observed as a young female macaque living on the small island of Koshima discovered how to wash sandy sweet potatoes (provided by the researchers) in a nearby stream. Eventually most of her group was doing it too. Kawamura suggested that this was a "precultural" behavior, and the observations were touted in textbooks for decades as evidence for culture among animals.

But in the early 1990s McMaster's Galef and other animal behaviorists pointed out that the skill took several years to spread through the group and suggested that troop members, once they paid attention to the potatoes, discovered on their own how to wash them—essentially reinventing the wheel. In contrast, humans learning a new skill tend to carefully mimic the exact movements they see in an expert and are often deliberately taught by another person. Although reinvention might work for learning to crack nuts or fish for ants, says psychologist Celia Heyes of University College London, it wouldn't work for passing on more sophisticated cultural behaviors such as chipping arrowheads or weaving baskets.

Such critiques sparked a flurry of new work in both the field and lab to discern whether great apes do in fact imitate. St. Andrews's Whiten and his colleagues developed "artificial fruits," which required several steps to open, and found in 1996 that chimpanzees tended to complete the steps in the same order as the demonstrator. Primatologists such as McGrew say that the experiments have "nailed down" the point: "In the right sorts of circumstances, chimps imitate." The observations of the different ant-dipping methods offer an example in the wild, adds Whiten. "It's difficult to see how such consistent behaviors could come about with anything but imitation," he says.

But the animal behaviorists aren't so sure. Following the order of simple actions is not the same as humans' imitation of fine motor movements such as dance steps, says Heyes. And Matsuzawa cautions that chimp imitation is rare in the wild. "Imitation is much more difficult than we expected," he says. "Yes, there is imitation, but it is very, very difficult for the chimpanzee." He and others also note that active, deliberate teaching, which some claim is a prerequisite for culture, is rare among chimpanzees. Boesch has described two instances of mothers helping their offspring with the fine details of nutcracking, but as Galef points out, only two clear examples in 20 years of observation suggests that teaching is very rare. "The primatologists are pushing very hard for a rich interpretation of the data that are available," he says. "Given that imitation is rare in nonhuman primates and teaching is essentially nonexistent, it's hard to see how you're going to get the cumulative culture which is the hallmark of our culture."

THE BENEFITS OF TOLERANCE

Whether you call primate behaviors "culture" or not, researchers say that primate traditions may offer insight into the origins of human culture. Take orangutans,

LIFE—AND DEATH—IN THE FOREST

TAÏ NATIONAL FOREST, CÔTE D'IVOIRE—A day spent watching chimpanzees here begins before sunrise, with a headlong crash through tangled forest to the trees where researchers watched the 32-member group nest the night before. Later there may be another dash through the jungle, trying to keep up with a hunting party as they race through the treetops chasing their favorite prey, red colobus monkeys. There are quiet moments as well, of patient watching and waiting as the animals nap, notes veteran chimp watcher Christophe Boesch of the Max Planck Institute for Evolutionary Anthropology in Leipzig, Germany. But often the forest seems to be crawling with chimps—three or four juveniles swing in trees, adult females sit with young ones eating fruit, and an adolescent male doggedly follows his latest crush, a female currently in heat. Keeping track of who is doing what with whom sometimes seems like trying to keep track of a kindergarten class on a field trip.

It's an exhausting way to gather data. But for researchers seeking to test theories about chimpanzee behavior, including the idea that the animals have a sort of rudimentary culture (see main text), watching the animals in the wild is the only way. So scientists rearrange their work and lives to accommodate the chimpanzee rhythms, spending several months a year in remote jungles, largely out of contact with the rest of the world.

The first lesson for wannabe chimp observers is patience. Chimpanzees are wary creatures and flee the moment they spot an intruder. It can take as long as 5 years to accustom a group to the presence of note-taking humans, a process called habituation. When Boesch began to work here as part of his graduate studies back in 1979, he spent endless hours just chasing dark shadows in the forest. "In the first 2 months, we never saw a chimp. We only heard them running away," recalls Boesch, who worked with his wife, Hedwidge Boesch-Achermann, to habituate the chimps. "In the first 2 years, we spent full days in the forest and saw chimps only 1% of the time. In the third year, we had a dramatic increase—to 5%," he says. It was 5 years before a chimp first looked at a researcher without running away or otherwise changing its behavior.

In order to get his thesis done before his adviser and funders lost patience, Boesch studied nut-cracking behavior, in part because the sharp, rhythmic ring of rock on nut can be heard throughout a forest even when no chimps are in sight. By the time his thesis was done, the chimpanzees were nearly habituated, and he could move on to more firsthand studies.

After 20 years, the data-gathering is highly systematic. Boesch still takes notes by hand in a spiral notebook kept in a plastic bag in his breast pocket, but several of his students and assistants type three-letter codes for behaviors into handheld computers, then download that data directly to a laptop back at camp. Often a researcher will follow one animal for the whole day, noting its behavior and interactions and photographing and videotaping it.

Still, even after a group is habituated and has been studied for years, the entire research program is vulnerable to everything that threatens the chimps themselves, from poaching to disease. The group here has suffered two epidemics of Ebola, and last month, a suspected measles outbreak killed another eight chimpanzees, leaving the group's survival in question. Boesch and his colleagues have successfully habituated another group in the southern part of the forest and are working on a third, but studies of family relationships and social structures in the first group have been crippled. "It is the way of nature," Boesch says sadly, "but that does not make it easier."

—G.V.

which love to eat the high-fat seeds of the neesia fruit. "It's like chocolate; they eat it for hours," says Duke University biological anthropologist Carel van Schaik. Most orangs won't touch the fruit after it ripens, however, because the seeds are then surrounded by stinging hairs. But one population, in Sumatra, uses sticks to scrape out the hairs and get at the seeds. "The whole population knows the trick," van Schaik says. "It's very similar to what we see in some chimp populations." And it's the only case in which orangs—skilled tool users in captivity—have been spotted using tools in the wild.

Orangs that avoid ripe neesia have the same sticks available for tools, so lack of materials can't explain why their behavior differs, van Schaik says. The key difference, he and his colleagues found, is that whereas most orangs are solitary, the Sumatran tool-using animals travel and feed close together, perhaps because there is plenty of food to go around. In most environments, food is thinly distributed and the animals "can't afford" to forage together, says van Schaik. The extra interaction in Sumatra allows an invention by one animal to spread when its compatriots observe it, he adds.

The pattern also holds for chimpanzees, as van Schaik and his colleagues report in . . . the *Journal of Human Evolution*. In a survey of the behaviors reported at the five longest running chimp field studies, the researchers found that those with higher "social tolerance" (measured by the amount of meat sharing, female-female grooming, and similar indicators) have more varied tool use. The theory could help to explain why captive primates are better at using tools than wild ones, as animals in captivity have more chances to observe one another and have plenty of food, van Schaik says.

The correlation might help explain the rise of human tool use as well. The earliest tool-using hominids "didn't have a much bigger brain yet, so we shouldn't look for major cognitive advances," van Schaik says. "I hypothesize that there was a social change that made them tolerate each other," which led to increased opportunities to learn and build on each other's inventions.

The fossil record might support such a theory, says anthropologist John Fleagle of the State University of New York, Stony Brook. Ancient humans have small canine teeth and lots of tools compared to other apes, he notes, and "when you look at the fossil record, you see reduction of canines early and tools later." He thinks smaller teeth might be a sign of increased tolerance, as canines are often used in fighting among group members. "And once you have tolerance, you have bigger tool kits."

But the researchers attempting to learn the roots of culture by studying wild primates worry that they are running out of time. Habitat loss and increased hunting are pushing many great ape populations to the brink of extinction. Illegal loggers are threatening the Sumatran orangutans that van Schaik studies. And on a recent market day at the village of Taï, just outside the park where Boesch works, three chimpanzee heads were stashed in the game warden's office, confiscated from poachers. If Boesch and his colleagues are correct, says Whiten, such sights mean "we're not just losing chimpanzees; we're losing lots of different chimpanzee cultures." That, he says, would be a major loss for humans. "If we want to understand how humans came to have the minds we have and the cultures we have, then we're only going to learn about that by looking for similar characteristics in our close relatives"—close relatives who are fast disappearing.

21

Exploring Our Basic Human Nature: Are Humans Inherently Violent?

Robert W. Sussman

Robert W. Sussman is professor of anthropology at Washington University in St. Louis. He is editor-in-chief emeritus of American Anthropologist, *the journal of the American Anthropological Association. A recent work is a collection of articles titled* The Biological Basis of Human Behavior: A Critical Review *(1999, Prentice Hall).*

We humans have obviously inherited some of our basic anatomical features from our primate ancestors. We share with the other primates, for example, our stereoscopic color vision, our prehensile hands and opposable thumbs, our flexible forelimbs, and our relatively large, complex brains. Although we are unique among the primates in being habitually bipedal and terrestrial, while most other primates are arboreal quadrupeds, we can clearly see—even in our hairless, upright, large-headed bodies—the primate antecedents of our features.

It stands to reason, then, that we may also have inherited from our nonhuman primate ancestors some general behavioral themes. Although the immediate reasons for our specific behaviors are clearly cultural, those behaviors might be seen as cultural variations on biological themes. Thus, the close bonds seen between chimpanzee mother and offspring and between nonrelated friends become families and other units in humans, with all the variation in their cultural meanings and culturally defined rules of behavior. In this selection, Robert Sussman examines the more controversial question of whether or not we humans have inherited our seeming propensity for violent behavior from our nonhuman ancestors and to what extent we can address that question by observing our closest living kin, the chimpanzee and bonobo.

As you read, consider the following questions:

1. What is the hypothesis of Richard Wrangham and Dale Peterson as proposed in their book, *Demonic Males*?

2. What are the intellectual antecedents of Wrangham and Peterson's idea? How does their model differ from earlier ones? How do they support their argument with principles from evolutionary theory, especially the process of natural selection?

3. According to Sussman, what is the problem with using living species like the chimpanzee as models for our remote ancestors?

4. According to the evidence Sussman presents, what can we conclude about aggressive and violent behavior among chimpanzees?

Are human beings forever doomed to be violent? Is aggression fixed within our genetic code, an inborn action pattern that threatens to destroy us? Or, as asked by Richard Wrangham and Dale Peterson in their [1997] book, *Demonic Males: Apes and the Origins of*

From *AnthroNotes*, Fall 1997, Vol. 19, No. 3. Reprinted with permission from the National Museum of Natural History, Smithsonian Institution.

Human Violence, can we get beyond our genes, beyond our essential "human nature"?

Wrangham and Peterson's belief in the importance of violence in the evolution and nature of humans is based on new primate research that they assert demonstrates the continuity of aggression from our great ape ancestors. The authors argue that 20–25 years ago most scholars believed human aggression was unique. Research at that time had shown great apes to be basically non-aggressive gentle creatures. Furthermore, the separation of humans from our ape ancestors was thought to have occurred 15–20 million years ago (mya). Although Raymond Dart, Sherwood Washburn, Robert Ardrey, E. O. Wilson, and others had argued through much of the 20th century that hunting, killing, and extreme aggressive behaviors were biological traits inherited from our earliest hominid hunting ancestors, many anthropologists still believed that patterns of aggression were environmentally determined and culturally learned behaviors, not inherited characteristics.

Demonic Males discusses new evidence that killer instincts are not unique to humans, but rather shared with our nearest relative, the common chimpanzee. The authors argue that it is this inherited propensity for killing that allows hominids and chimps to be such good hunters.

According to Wrangham and Peterson, the split between humans and the common chimpanzee was only 6–8 mya. Furthermore, humans may have split from the chimpanzee-bonobo line after gorillas, with bonobos (pygmy chimps) separating from chimps only 2.5 mya. Because chimpanzees may be the modern ancestor of all these forms, and because the earliest australopithecines were quite chimpanzee-like, Wrangham speculates (in a separate article) that "chimpanzees are a conservative species and an amazingly good model for the ancestor of hominids" (1995, reprinted in Sussman 1997:106). If modern chimpanzees and modern humans share certain behavioral traits, these traits have "long evolutionary roots" and are likely to be fixed, biologically inherited parts of our basic human nature and not culturally determined.

Wrangham argues that chimpanzees are almost on the brink of humanness:

> Nut-smashing, root-eating, savannah-using chimpanzees, resembling our ancestors, and capable by the way of extensive bipedalism. Using ant-wands, and sandals, and bowls, meat-sharing, hunting cooperatively. Strange paradox . . . a species trembling on the verge of hominization, but so conservative that it has stayed on that edge. . . . (1997:107)

Wrangham and Peterson (1996:24) claim that only two animal species, chimpanzees and humans, live in patrilineal, male-bonded communities "with intense, male initiated territorial aggression, including lethal raiding into neighboring communities in search of vulnerable enemies to attack and kill." Wrangham asks:

> Does this mean chimpanzees are naturally violent? Ten years ago it wasn't clear. . . . In this cultural species, it may turn out that one of the least variable of all chimpanzee behaviors is the intense competition between males, the violent aggression they use against strangers, and their willingness to maim and kill those that

frustrate their goals. . . . As the picture of chimpanzee society settles into focus, it now includes infanticide, rape and regular battering of females by males. (1997:108)

Since humans and chimpanzees share these violent urges, the implication is that human violence has long evolutionary roots. "We are apes of nature, cursed over six million years or more with a rare inheritance, a Dostoyevskyan demon. . . . The coincidence of demonic aggression in ourselves and our closest kin bespeaks its antiquity" (1997:108–109).

INTELLECTUAL ANTECEDENTS

From the beginning of Western thought, the theme of human depravity runs deep, related to the idea of humankind's fall from grace and the emergence of original sin. This view continues to pervade modern "scientific" interpretations of the evolution of human behavior. Recognition of the close evolutionary relationship between humans and apes, from the time of Darwin's *Descent of Man* (1874) on, has encouraged theories that look to modern apes for evidence of parallel behaviors reflecting this relationship.

By the early 1950s, large numbers of australopithecine fossils and the discovery that the large-brained "fossil" ancestor from Piltdown, in England, was a fraud, led to the realization that our earliest ancestors were more like apes than like modern humans. Accordingly, our earliest ancestors must have behaved much like other nonhuman primates. This, in turn, led to a great interest in using primate behavior to understand human evolution and the evolutionary basis of human nature. The subdiscipline of primatology was born.

Raymond Dart, discoverer of the first australopithecine fossil some thirty years earlier, was also developing a different view of our earliest ancestors. At first Dart believed that australopithecines were scavengers barely eking out an existence in the harsh savanna environment. But from the fragmented and damaged bones found with the australopithecines, together with dents and holes in these early hominid skulls, Dart eventually concluded that this species had used bone, tooth and antler tools to kill, butcher and eat their prey, as well as to kill one another. This hunting hypothesis (Cartmill 1997:511) "was linked from the beginning with a bleak, pessimistic view of human beings and their ancestors as instinctively bloodthirsty and savage." To Dart, the australopithecines were

> confirmed killers: carnivorous creatures that seized living quarries by violence, battered them to death, tore apart their broken bodies, dismembered them limb from limb, slaking their ravenous thirst with the hot

blood of victims and greedily devouring livid writhing flesh. (1953:209)

Cartmill, in a recent book (1993), shows that this interpretation of early human morality is reminiscent of earlier Greek and Christian views. Dart's (1953) own treatise begins with a 17th-century quote from the Calvinist R. Baxter: "of all the beasts, the man-beast is the worst/to others and himself the cruellest foe."

Between 1961 and 1976, Dart's view was picked up and extensively popularized by the playwright Robert Ardrey (*The Territorial Imperative, African Genesis*). Ardrey believed it was the human competitive and killer instinct, acted out in warfare, that made humans what they are today. "It is war and the instinct for territory that has led to the great accomplishments of Western Man. Dreams may have inspired our love of freedom, but only war and weapons have made it ours" (1961:324).

MAN THE HUNTER

In the 1968 volume *Man the Hunter*, Sherwood Washburn and Chet Lancaster presented a theory of "The evolution of hunting," emphasizing that it is this behavior that shaped human nature and separated early humans from their primate relatives.

> To assert the biological unity of mankind is to affirm the importance of the hunting way of life. . . . However much conditions and customs may have varied locally, the main selection pressures that forged the species were the same. The biology, psychology and customs that separate us from the apes . . . we owe to the hunters of time past . . . for those who would understand the origins and nature of human behavior there is no choice but to try to understand "Man the Hunter." (1968:303)

Rather than amassing evidence from modern hunters and gatherers to prove their theory, Washburn and Lancaster (1968:299) use the 19th-century concept of cultural "survivals": behaviors that persist as evidence of an earlier time but are no longer useful in society.

> Men enjoy hunting and killing, and these activities are continued in sports even when they are no longer economically necessary. If a behavior is important to the survival of a species . . . then it must be both easily learned and pleasurable. (Washburn and Lancaster, p. 299)

MAN THE DANCER

Using similar logic for the survival of ancient "learned and pleasurable" behaviors, perhaps it could easily have been our propensity for dancing rather than our desire to hunt that can explain much of human behavior. After all, men and women love to dance; it is a behavior found in all cultures but has even less obvious function today than hunting. Our love of movement and dance might explain, for example, our propensity for face-to-face sex, and even the evolution of bipedalism and the movement of humans out of trees and onto the ground.

Could the first tool have been a stick to beat a dance drum, and the ancient Laetoli footprints evidence of two individuals going out to dance the "Afarensis shuffle"? Although it takes only two to tango, a variety of social interactions and systems might have been encouraged by the complex social dances known in human societies around the globe.

SOCIOBIOLOGY AND E. O. WILSON

In the mid-1970s, E. O. Wilson and others described a number of traits as genetically based and therefore human universals, including territoriality, male-female bonds, male dominance over females, and extended maternal care leading to matrilineality. Wilson argued that the genetic basis of these traits was indicated by their relative constancy among our primate relatives and by their persistence throughout human evolution and in human societies. Elsewhere, I have shown that these characteristics are neither general primate traits nor human universals (Sussman 1995). Wilson, however, argued that these were a product of our evolutionary hunting past.

> For at least a million years—probably more—Man engaged in a hunting way of life, giving up the practice a mere 10,000 years ago. . . . Our innate social responses have been fashioned through this life style. With caution, we can compare the most widespread hunter-gatherer qualities with similar behavior displayed by some of the nonhuman primates that are closely related to Man. Where the same pattern of traits occurs in . . . most or all of those primates—we can conclude that it has been subject to little evolution. (Wilson 1976, in Sussman 1997:65–66)

Wilson's theory of sociobiology, the evolution of social behavior, argued that

1. the goal of living organisms is to pass on one's genes at the expense of all others;
2. an organism should only cooperate with others if
   a. they carry some of his/her own genes (kin selection) or
   b. if at some later date the others might aid you (reciprocal altruism).

To sociobiologists, evolutionary morality is based on an unconscious need to multiply our own genes, to build group cohesion in order to win wars. We should not look down on our warlike, cruel nature but rather understand its success when coupled with "making nice" with some other individuals or groups. The genetically driven "making nice" is the basis of human ethics and morality.

> Throughout recorded history the conduct of war has been common . . . some of the noblest traits of mankind, including team play, altruism, patriotism, bravery . . . and so forth are the genetic product of warfare. (Wilson 1975:572–573)

The evidence for any of these universals or for the tenets of sociobiology is as weak as was the evidence for Dart's, Ardrey's, and Washburn and Lancaster's theories of innate aggression. Not only are modern gatherer-hunters and most apes remarkably non-aggressive, but in the 1970s and 1980s studies of fossil bones and artifacts have shown that early humans were not hunters and that weapons were a later addition to the human repertoire. In fact, C. K. Brain (1981) showed that the holes and dents in Dart's australopithecine skulls matched perfectly with fangs of leopards or with impressions of rocks pressing against the buried fossils. Australopithecines apparently were the hunted, not the hunters (Cartmill 1993, 1997).

BEYOND OUR GENES

Wrangham and Peterson's book goes beyond the assertion of human inborn aggression and propensity toward violence. The authors ask the critical question: Are we doomed to be violent forever because this pattern is fixed within our genetic code or can we go beyond our past?—get out of our genes, so to speak.

The authors believe that we can look to the bonobo or pygmy chimpanzee as one potential savior, metaphorically speaking.

Bonobos, although even more closely related to the common chimpanzee than humans, have become a peace-loving, love-making alternative to chimpanzee-human violence. How did this happen? In chimpanzees and humans, females of the species select partners that are violent. . . . "While men have evolved to be demonic males, it seems likely that women have evolved to prefer demonic males. . . . As long as demonic males are the most successful reproducers, any female who mates with them is provided with sons who themselves will likely be good reproducers" (Wrangham and Peterson 1996:239). However, among pygmy chimpanzees, females form alliances and have chosen to mate with less aggressive males. So, after all,

it is not violent males that have caused humans and chimpanzees to be their inborn, immoral, dehumanized selves; it is, rather, poor choices by human and chimpanzee females.

Like Dart, Washburn, and Wilson before them, Wrangham and Peterson believe that killing and violence is inherited from our ancient relatives of the past. However, unlike these earlier theorists, Wrangham and Peterson argue this is not a trait unique to hominids, nor is it a by-product of hunting. In fact, it is just this violent nature and a natural "blood lust" that makes both humans and chimpanzees such good hunters. It is the bonobos that help the authors come to this conclusion. Because bonobos have lost the desire to kill, they also have lost the desire to hunt.

> . . . do bonobos tell us that the suppression of personal violence carried with it the suppression of predatory aggression? The strongest hypothesis at the moment is that bonobos came from a chimpanzee-like ancestor that hunted monkeys and hunted one another. As they evolved into bonobos, males lost their demonism, becoming less aggressive to each other. In so doing they lost their lust for hunting monkeys, too. . . . Murder and hunting may be more closely tied together than we are used to thinking. (Wrangham and Peterson 1996:219)

THE SELFISH GENE THEORY

Like Ardrey, Wrangham and Peterson believe that blood lust ties killing and hunting tightly together but it is the killing that drives hunting in the latter's argument. This lust to kill is based upon the sociobiological tenet of the selfish gene. "The general principle that behavior evolves to serve selfish ends has been widely accepted; and the idea that humans might have been favored by natural selection to hate and to kill their enemies has become entirely, if tragically, reasonable" (Wrangham and Peterson 1996:23).

As with many of the new sociobiological or evolutionary anthropology theories, I find problems with both the theory itself and with the evidence used to support it. Two arguments that humans and chimpanzees share biologically fixed behaviors are: (1) they are more closely related to each other than chimpanzees are to gorillas; (2) chimpanzees are a good model for our earliest ancestor and retain conservative traits that should be shared by both.

The first of these statements is still hotly debated and, using various genetic evidence, the chimp-gorilla-human triad is so close that it is difficult to tell exact divergence time or pattern among the three. The second statement is just not true. Chimpanzees have been evolving for as long as humans and gorillas, and there is no reason to believe ancestral chimps were similar to present-day chimps. The fossil evidence for the last 5–8 million years is extremely sparse, and it is likely that many forms of apes have become extinct just as have many hominids.

Furthermore, even if the chimpanzee were a good model for the ancestral hominid, and was a conservative representative of this phylogenetic group, this would not mean that humans would necessarily share specific behavioral traits. As even Wrangham and Peterson emphasize, chimps, gorillas, and bonobos all behave very differently from one another in their social behavior and in their willingness to kill conspecifics.

EVIDENCE AGAINST "DEMONIC MALES"

The proof of the "Demonic Male" theory does not rest on any theoretical grounds but must rest solely on the evidence that violence and killing in chimpanzees and in humans are behaviors that are similar in pattern; have ancient, shared evolutionary roots; and are inherited. Besides killing of conspecifics, Wrangham "includes infanticide, rape, and regular battering of females by males" as a part of this inherited legacy of violent behaviors shared by humans and chimpanzees (1997:108).

Wrangham and Peterson state: "That chimpanzees and humans kill members of neighboring groups of their own species is . . . a startling exception to the normal rule for animals" (1996:63). "Fighting adults of almost all species normally stop at winning: They don't go on to kill" (1996:155). However, as Wrangham points out, there are exceptions, such as lions, wolves, spotted hyenas, and I would add a number of other predators. In fact, most species do not have the weapons to kill one another as adults.

Just how common is conspecific killing in chimpanzees? This is where the real controversy may lie. Jane Goodall described the chimpanzee as a peaceful, non-aggressive species during the first 24 years of study at Gombe (1950–1974). During one year of concentrated study, Goodall observed 284 agonistic encounters: of these 66% were due to competition for introduced bananas, and only 34% "could be regarded as attacks occurring in 'normal' aggressive contexts" (1968:278). Only 10 percent of the 284 attacks were classified as "violent," and "even attacks that appeared punishing to me often resulted in no discernable injury. . . . Other attacks consisted merely of brief pounding, hitting or rolling of the individual, after which the aggressor often touched or embraced the other immediately" (1968:277).

Chimpanzee aggression before 1974 was considered no different from patterns of aggression seen in many other primate species. In fact, Goodall explains in her 1986 monograph, *The Chimpanzees of Gombe*, that

she uses data mainly from after 1975 because the earlier years present a "very different picture of the Gombe chimpanzees" as being "far more peaceable than humans" (1986:3). Other early naturalists' descriptions of chimpanzee behavior were consistent with those of Goodall and confirmed her observations. Even different communities were observed to come together with peaceful, ritualized displays of greeting (Reynolds and Reynolds 1965; Suguyama 1972; Goodall 1968).

Then, between 1974 and 1977, five adult males from one subgroup were attacked and disappeared from the area, presumably dead. Why after 24 years did the patterns of aggression change? Was it because the stronger group saw the weakness of the other and decided to improve their genetic fitness? But surely there were stronger and weaker animals and subgroups before this time. Perhaps we can look to Goodall's own perturbations for an answer. In 1965, Goodall began to provide "restrictive human-controlled feeding." A few years later she realized that

> the constant feeding was having a marked effect on the behavior of the chimps. They were beginning to move about in large groups more often than they had ever done in the old days. Worst of all, the adult males were becoming increasingly aggressive. When we first offered the chimps bananas the males seldom fought over their food; . . . now . . . there was a great deal more fighting than ever before. . . . (Goodall 1971:143)

The possibility that human interference was a main cause of the unusual behavior of the Gombe chimps was the subject of an excellent, but generally ignored, book by Margaret Power (1991). Wrangham and Peterson (1996:19) footnote this book, but as with many other controversies, they essentially ignore its findings, stating that yes, chimpanzee violence might have been unnatural behavior if it weren't for the evidence of similar behavior occurring since 1977 and "elsewhere in Africa" (1996:19).

FURTHER EVIDENCE

What is this evidence from elsewhere in Africa? Wrangham and Peterson provide only four brief examples, none of which is very convincing:

1. Between 1979 and 1982, the Gombe group extended its range to the south and conflict with a southern group, Kalande, was suspected. In 1982, a "raiding" party of males reached Goodall's camp. The authors state: "Some of these raids may have been lethal" (1996:19). However, Goodall describes this "raid" as follows: One female "was chased by a Kalande male and

mildly attacked. . . . Her four-year-old son . . . encountered a second male—but was only sniffed" (1986:516). Although Wrangham and Peterson imply that these encounters were similar to those between 1974 and 1977, no violence was actually witnessed. The authors also refer to the discovery of the dead body of Humphrey; what they do not mention is Humphrey's age of 35 and that wild chimps rarely live past 33 years!

2. From 1970 to 1982, six adult males from one community in the Japanese study site of Mahale disappeared, one by one over this 12-year period. None of the animals were observed being attacked or killed, and one was sighted later roaming as a solitary male (Nishida et al., 1985:287–289).

3. In another site in West Africa, Wrangham and Peterson report that Boesch and Boesch believe "that violent aggression among the chimpanzees is as important as it is in Gombe" (1986:20). However, in the paper referred to, the Boesches simply state that encounters by neighboring chimpanzee communities are more common in their site than in Gombe (1 per month vs. 1 every 4 months). There is no mention of violence during these encounters.

4. At a site that Wrangham began studying in 1984, an adult male was found dead in 1991. Wrangham states: "In the second week of August, Ruizoni was killed. No human saw the big fight" (Wrangham and Peterson 1996:20). Wrangham gives us no indication of what has occurred at this site over the last 6 years.

In fact, this is the total amount of evidence of warfare and male-male killing among chimpanzees after 37 years of research! The data for infanticide and rape among chimpanzees is even less impressive. In fact, data are so sparse for these behaviors among chimps that Wrangham and Peterson are forced to use examples from the other great apes, gorillas and orangutans. However, just as for killing among chimpanzees, both the evidence and the interpretations are suspect and controversial.

CAN WE ESCAPE OUR GENES?

What if Wrangham and Peterson are correct and we and our chimp cousins are inherently sinners? Are we doomed to be violent forever because this pattern is fixed within our genetic code?

After 5 million years of human evolution and 120,000 or so years of *Homo sapiens* existence, is there a way to rid ourselves of our inborn evils?

What does it do for us, then, to know the behavior of our closest relatives? Chimpanzees and bonobos are an extraordinary pair. One, I suggest, shows us some of the worst aspects of our past and our present; the other shows an escape from it. . . . Denial of our demons won't make them go away. But even if we're driven to accepting the evidence of a grisly past, we're not forced into thinking it condemns us to an unchanged future. (Wrangham 1997:110)

In other words, we can learn how to behave by watching bonobos. But, if we can change our inherited behavior so simply, why haven't we been able to do this before *Demonic Males* enlightened us? Surely, there are variations in the amounts of violence in different human cultures and individuals. If we have the capacity and plasticity to change by learning from example, then our behavior is determined by socialization practices and by our cultural histories and not by our nature! This is true whether the examples come from benevolent bonobos or conscientious objectors.

CONCLUSION

The theory presented by Wrangham and Peterson, although it also includes chimpanzees as our murdering cousins, is very similar to "man the hunter" theories proposed in the past. It also does not differ greatly from early European and Christian beliefs about human ethics and morality. We are forced to ask: Are these theories generated by good scientific fact, or are they just "good to think" because they reflect, reinforce, and reiterate our traditional cultural beliefs, our morality and our ethics? Is the theory generated by the data, or are the data manipulated to fit preconceived notions of human morality and ethics?

Since the data in support of these theories have been weak, and yet the stories created have been extremely similar, I am forced to believe that "Man the Hunter" is a myth, that humans are not necessarily prone to violence and aggression, but that this belief will continue to reappear in future writings on human nature. Meanwhile, primatologists must continue their field research, marshaling the actual evidence needed to answer many of the questions raised in Wrangham and Peterson's volume.

REFERENCES

Ardrey, Robert. 1961. *African Genesis: A Personal Investigation into Animal Origins and Nature of Man*. Atheneum.

———. 1966. *The Territorial Imperative*. Atheneum.

Brain, C. K. 1981. *The Hunted or the Hunter? An Introduction to African Cave Taphonomy*. Univ. of Chicago.

Cartmill, Matt. 1997. "Hunting Hypothesis of Human Origins." In *History of Physical Anthropology: An Encyclopedia*, ed. F. Spencer, pp. 508–512. Garland.

———. 1993. *A View to a Death in the Morning: Hunting and Nature Through History*. Harvard Univ.

Dart, Raymond. 1953. "The Predatory Transition from Ape to Man." *International Anthropological and Linguistic Review* 1:201–217.

Darwin, Charles. 1874. *The Descent of Man and Selection in Relation to Sex*. 2nd ed. The Henneberry Co.

Goodall, Jane. 1986. *The Chimpanzees of Gombe: Patterns of Behavior*. Belknap.

———. 1971. *In the Shadow of Man*. Houghton Mifflin.

———. 1968. "The Behavior of Free-Living Chimpanzees in the Gombe Stream Reserve." *Animal Behavior Monographs* 1:165–311.

Nishida, T., Hiraiwa-Hasegawa, M., and Takahtat, Y. 1985. "Group Extinction and Female Transfer in Wild Chimpanzees in the Mahali National Park, Tanzania." *Zeitschrift für Tierpsychologie* 67:281–301.

Power, Margaret. 1991. *The Egalitarian Human and Chimpanzee: An Anthropological View of Social Organization*. Cambridge University.

Reynolds, V., and Reynolds, F. 1965. "Chimpanzees of Budongo Forest." In *Primate Behavior: Field Studies of Monkeys and Apes*, ed. I. DeVore, pp. 368–424. Holt, Rinehart, and Winston.

Suguyama, Y. 1972. "Social Characteristics and Socialization of Wild Chimpanzees." In *Primate Socialization*, ed. F. E. Poirier, pp. 145–163. Random House.

Sussman, R. W., ed. 1997. *The Biological Basis of Human Behavior*. Simon and Schuster.

Sussman, R. W. 1995. "The Nature of Human Universals." *Reviews in Anthropology* 24:1–11.

Washburn, S. L., and Lancaster, C. K. 1968. "The Evolution of Hunting." In *Man the Hunter*, eds. R. B. Lee and I. DeVore, pp. 293–303. Aldine.

Wilson, E. O. 1997. "Sociobiology: A New Approach to Understanding the Basis of Human Nature." *New Scientist* 70(1976):342–345. (Reprinted in R. W. Sussman, 1997.)

———. 1975. *Sociobiology: The New Synthesis*. Cambridge: Harvard University.

Wrangham, R. W. 1995. "Ape, Culture, and Missing Links." *Symbols* (Spring):2–9, 20. (Reprinted in R. W. Sussman, 1997.)

Wrangham, Richard, and Peterson, Dale. 1996. *Demonic Males: Apes and the Origins of Human Violence*. Houghton Mifflin.

FURTHER READING

Bock, Kenneth. 1980. *Human Nature and History: A Response to Sociobiology*. Columbia University.

Gould, Stephen J. 1996. *Mismeasure of Man*. W. W. Norton.

PART 6

Hominid Evolution

Nowhere in bioanthropology is the nature of the scientific method better exemplified than in the study of the human evolutionary past. In Part 5, we saw how data, even from the recent past, can be less than perfect and can present serious challenges to analysis. We also saw how conclusions from the same data can differ widely, depending on interpretation. These problems are amplified when our interest is in the more remote periods of our evolution—when we are trying to sort out the details of the origin of the hominids 5 million years ago, or even the origin of modern *Homo sapiens*, which may be as recent as 150,000 years ago. As a result, we see in such studies all the aspects of the scientific method come into play—the collecting of data, the fitting of the data into existing (and differing) models, the generation of hypotheses from those data, and, most important, the testing of hypotheses and their modification as new data, new techniques, and new ideas come to light.

It may at first seem strange that scientists would expend so much energy, and sometimes emotion, over a pile of bones from millennia ago. But by answering the kinds of questions addressed in the following selections, we are actually answering a question that should matter on some level to everyone—the question of just who we are and of where, when, and how we came to be.

In "Born to Run," Adam Summers describes a new idea that adds endurance running to the benefits of bipedalism, the evolutionary hallmark of the hominids.

William R. Leonard focuses on the importance of food in human evolution in "Food for Thought." He links diet and food acquisition to some of the major trends in our history, including bipedalism, big brains, and migrations. He also discusses the importance of diet in what he calls our "modern quandaries."

Kate Wong writes about "The Littlest Human," an account of a still-controversial set of diminutive hominid fossils from Indonesia that may show us that human evolution is more complex than we had thought. "How the Hobbit Shrugged" by Elizabeth Culotta presents a new analysis of the ancestry of these enigmatic bones.

Kate Wong again tackles a contentious issue in human evolution in "The Morning of the Modern Mind," addressing the question of how far back in our evolutionary history we can find behaviors that supposedly define modern humans as different from our archaic ancestors.

SUGGESTED WEBSITES FOR FURTHER STUDY

http://uk.dir.yahoo.com/science/biology/evolution/Human_Evolution
http://www.ifi.unizh.ch/~zolli/Neanderthals.htm
http://www.becominghuman.org

22

Born to Run

Adam Summers

Adam Summers is an assistant professor of bioengineering and ecology and evolutionary biology at the University of California, Irvine.

The proposed adaptive benefits of human bipedalism are well known by now. They all focus on making walking in open spaces more efficient and safe and, in the fossil record, are thought to mark the beginning of the hominids, going back through the australopithecines to the very earliest members of our lineage. In this selection, however, Adam Summers reports on new research that indicates bipedalism may also have evolved to benefit endurance running and that the *kind* of bipedalism we modern humans have is not shared by our earlier ancestors. Indeed, the australopithecines are more apelike in some of their features related to locomotion. This seems to make members of genus *Homo* even more distinct from the increasingly large array of possible early hominids.

As you read, consider the following questions:

1. What is endurance running and how does it differ from sprinting? What other animals are good endurance runners?

2. What is the physical evidence for our endurance running ability? How do our traits in this regard differ from those of apes and early hominids?

3. What might have been the benefit of endurance running to early members of genus *Homo*?

Paleoanthropologists, the paleontologists of the human lineage, have a tough task. Hominid fossils are scarce, and they're usually incomplete. Worse, the missing bits are often the ones investigators would most like to find—making it difficult to assemble an evolutionary tree of fossil hominids.

But if that's a tough job, imagine what life is like for anyone seeking to describe how bones and muscles functioned in ancient hominids. The scarcity and incompleteness of hominid fossils has often prolonged biomechanical debates concerning hominids. "Lucy" (*Australopithecus afarensis*) is a case in point. She was discovered more than thirty years ago, but a disagreement about whether those of her species walked more like a person or more like a chimpanzee was only recently decided in favor of the former.

That debate was important because a long-standing hypothesis holds that long-distance walking migrations played an important role in the evolution of our genus *Homo*. Many of the features that distinguish the various species of *Homo*, which lived in the open savanna, from Lucy and her kin, which were forest primates, are traits useful for walking: longer legs, narrower waists, shorter toes. Now Dennis M. Bramble, a biomechanist and vertebrate biologist at the University of Utah in Salt Lake City, and Daniel E. Lieberman, a biomechanist and anthropologist at Harvard University, have added a major new wrinkle to the story of human bipedalism. The two argue, in a review synthesizing several decades' worth of work by a large number of investigators, that running also played an important role in shaping our species.

If you've ever chased a cat that's trying to avoid a bath, you have every right to conclude that, for our size, we humans are pretty poor runners. But chasing a cat is sprinting. Where we excel is endurance running. Moreover, we run long distances at fast speeds: many joggers do a mile in seven-and-a-half minutes, and top male marathoners can string five-minute miles together for more than two hours. A quadruped of similar weight, about 150 pounds, prefers to run a mile at a trot, which takes nine-and-a-half minutes, and would have to break into a gallop to keep pace with a good recreational jogger. That same recreational jogger

Reprinted with permission from "Born to Run" by Adam Summers from *Natural History*, April 2005. Copyright © Natural History Magazine, Inc., 2005.

could keep up with the preferred trotting speed of a thousand-pound horse.

Good endurance runners are rare among animals. Although humans share the ability with some other groups, such as wolves and dogs, hyenas, wildebeest, and horses, we alone among primates can run long distances with ease.

But what evidence can support the idea that endurance running by itself gave early humans an evolutionary advantage, and that it wasn't just "piggybacking" on our ability to walk? Many traits, after all, are useful for both activities; long legs, for instance, and the long stride they enable, are helpful to walking as well as to running. But running and walking are mechanically different gaits. A walking person, aided by gravity, acts as an inverted pendulum: the hip swings over the planted foot [see "The Biomechanist Went Over the Mountain," by Adam Summers, November 2004]. In contrast, a runner bounces along, aided by tendons and ligaments that act as springs, which alternately store and release energy.

Bramble and Lieberman point to a number of features, preserved in fossils, that imply *Homo* adapted to a bouncy gait—whereas *Australopithecus* stuck with walking. . . . Fossils lack tendons and ligaments, of course, but traces of their attachment points are sometimes present, and the characteristics of the missing tissue can be inferred by comparing how the attachments fitted with the rest of the animal's anatomy. For example, the Achilles tendon, attached to the heel bone, is one of the most important elements in a human's bouncy gait. In *Australopithecus*, however, the attachment point of the tendon is distinctly chimpanzee-like. Another spring occurs in the foot itself: tendons in the sole of a human's foot keep it arched. The arch flattens and springs back with each step. In contrast, Lucy had only a partial arch. *Homo habilis* had a full arch. Chimpanzees have no arch at all.

In addition to springs, endurance running requires more stabilization of the trunk than walking does. Members of the genus *Homo* have substantial gluteus maximus (butt) muscles. Those muscles have numerous large attachments from the hip to the base of the spine. In *Australopithecus* fossils, though, the muscle has a much more limited area of attachment. If you've seen a chimpanzee in trousers, you know how baggy they look. Chimpanzees are gluteally challenged as well. Large butt muscles are not only better looking in

pants; they also make for efficient energy transfer during running by stabilizing each hip. But the muscles are not used for walking on level ground.

In contrast with the trunk, the shoulder of the chimpanzee is well stabilized, tied to the spine and the head by several strong muscles. Lucy retained the stabilized shoulder, but in humans those muscle connections are less robust—and for good reasons. When we walk, our shoulders don't move much, but when we run, because of the relatively loose attachment, the shoulders rotate strongly one way while the hips rotate the other. The counterrotations help keep us in balance. And because only one part of the trapezius muscle attaches to the head, we can swing the upper body without inadvertently rotating the head—which enables us to see where we're going.

In spite of the loose attachment between head and shoulders, running joggles the head more than walking does. *Homo* therefore has several "antibobblehead" adaptations that other apes and *Australopithecus* lack. The first is a modification of the semicircular canals, the organs in each inner ear that tell the brain which way is up. Three such canals sit at right angles to one another in each inner ear. Two are enlarged in *Homo*, and the size makes it easier to sense, and presumably to counteract, a nodding head. An elastic ligament that runs from a ridge at the base of the skull to the base of the neck, damps the bobbing effect. Analogous ridge structures, to which damping ligaments can be attached, occur in dogs and horses, the other long distance runners, but not in Lucy.

Bramble and Lieberman's wide-ranging analysis makes important corrections to the scientific picture of early humans. Our ancestors may have ranged across large distances in the heat of the African savanna in relatively short spurts of long-distance running, as well as by walking. They may have been trying to maximize the chance of encountering carrion before other scavengers did, or perhaps they were adapted to running down prey before spear throwers or bows were invented.

In any case, our current appetite for jogging is made possible by the early selective pressures that made humans one of the most accomplished endurance-running animals. For myself, though, I imagine another adaptation. The heat and the running must have been powerful motivators for our ancestors to sit in the shade and ponder how to affix a rock to a stick.

23

Food for Thought

William R. Leonard

William R. Leonard is a professor of anthropology at Northwestern University. He specializes in nutrition and energetics in contemporary and prehistoric populations and has studied human groups in Ecuador, Bolivia, Peru, and Siberia.

"The search for food," says William Leonard, "its consumption and, ultimately, how it is used for biological processes are all critical aspects of an organism's ecology." In this selection, Leonard addresses three of the ways in which humans differ from the "primate norm"—bipedalism, big brains, and our spread over the globe—and focuses on food and food-related factors to explain their evolution. He also looks at modern health concerns from a food-related perspective.

As you read, consider the following questions:

1. How does Leonard explain the importance of food to the evolution of each of the major topics— bipedalism, big brains, and migration?

2. What scientific evidence does he present for each of these analyses?

3. How is food related to some of what Leonard calls our "modern quandaries"?

We humans are strange primates. We walk on two legs, carry around enormous brains and have colonized every corner of the globe. Anthropologists and biologists have long sought to understand how our lineage came to differ so profoundly from the primate norm in these ways, and over the years all manner of hypotheses aimed at explaining each of these oddities have been put forth. But a growing body of evidence indicates that these miscellaneous quirks of humanity in fact have a common thread: they are largely the result of natural selection acting to maximize dietary quality and foraging efficiency. Changes in food availability over time, it seems, strongly influenced our hominid ancestors. Thus, in an evolutionary sense, we are very much what we ate.

Accordingly, what we eat is yet another way in which we differ from our primate kin. Contemporary human populations the world over have diets richer in calories and nutrients than those of our cousins, the great apes. So when and how did our ancestors' eating habits diverge from those of other primates? Further,

to what extent have modern humans departed from the ancestral dietary pattern?

Scientific interest in the evolution of human nutritional requirements has a long history. But relevant investigations started gaining momentum after 1985, when S. Boyd Eaton and Melvin J. Konner of Emory University published a seminal paper in the *New England Journal of Medicine* entitled "Paleolithic Nutrition." They argued that the prevalence in modern societies of many chronic diseases—obesity, hypertension, coronary heart disease and diabetes, among them—is the consequence of a mismatch between modern dietary patterns and the type of diet that our species evolved to eat as prehistoric hunter-gatherers. Since then, however, understanding of the evolution of human nutritional needs has advanced considerably—thanks in large part to new comparative analyses of traditionally living human populations and other primates—and a more nuanced picture has emerged. We now know that humans have evolved not to subsist on a single, Paleolithic diet but to be flexible eaters, an insight that has important implications for the current debate over what people today should eat in order to be healthy.

To appreciate the role of diet in human evolution, we must remember that the search for food, its consumption and, ultimately, how it is used for biological processes are all critical aspects of an organism's ecology. The energy dynamic between organisms and their environments—that is, energy expended in relation to energy acquired—has important adaptive consequences for survival and reproduction. These two components of Darwinian fitness are reflected in the way we divide up an animal's energy budget. Maintenance energy is what keeps an animal alive on a day-to-day basis. Productive energy, on the other hand, is associated with producing and raising offspring for the next generation. For mammals like ourselves, this must cover the increased costs that mothers incur during pregnancy and lactation.

The type of environment a creature inhabits will influence the distribution of energy between these components, with harsher conditions creating higher maintenance demands. Nevertheless, the goal of all organisms is the same: to devote sufficient funds to reproduction to ensure the long-term success of the species. Thus, by looking at the way animals go about obtaining and then allocating food energy, we can better discern how natural selection produces evolutionary change.

BECOMING BIPEDS

Without exception, living nonhuman primates habitually move around on all fours, or quadrupedally, when they are on the ground. Scientists generally assume therefore that the last common ancestor of humans and chimpanzees (our closest living relative) was also a quadruped. Exactly when the last common ancestor lived is unknown, but clear indications of bipedalism—the trait that distinguished ancient humans from other apes—are evident in the oldest known species of *Australopithecus*, which lived in Africa roughly four million years ago. Ideas about why bipedalism evolved abound in the paleoanthropological literature. C. Owen Lovejoy of Kent State University proposed in 1981 that two-legged locomotion freed the arms to carry children and foraged goods. More recently, Kevin D. Hunt of Indiana University has posited that bipedalism emerged as a feeding posture that enabled access to foods that had previously been out of reach. Peter Wheeler of Liverpool John Moores University submits that moving upright allowed early humans to better regulate their body temperature by exposing less surface area to the blazing African sun.

The list goes on. In reality, a number of factors probably selected for this type of locomotion. My own research, conducted in collaboration with my wife, Marcia L. Robertson, suggests that bipedalism evolved in our ancestors at least in part because it is less energetically expensive than quadrupedalism. Our analyses of the energy costs of movement in living animals of all sizes have shown that, in general, the strongest predictors of cost are the weight of the animal and the speed at which it travels. What is striking about human bipedal movement is that it is notably more economical than quadrupedal locomotion at walking rates.

Apes, in contrast, are not economical when moving on the ground. For instance, chimpanzees, which employ a peculiar form of quadrupedalism known as knuckle walking, spend some 35 percent more calories during locomotion than does a typical mammalian quadruped of the same size—a large dog, for example. Differences in the settings in which humans and apes evolved may help explain the variation in costs of movement. Chimps, gorillas, and orangutans evolved in and continue to occupy dense forests where only a mile or so of trekking over the course of the day is all that is needed to find enough to eat. Much of early hominid evolution, on the other hand, took place in more open woodland and grassland, where sustenance is harder to come by. Indeed, modern human hunter-gatherers living in these environments, who provide us with the best available model of early human subsistence patterns, often travel six to eight miles daily in search of food.

These differences in day range have important locomotor implications. Because apes travel only short distances each day, the potential energetic benefits of moving more efficiently are very small. For far-ranging foragers, however, cost-effective walking saves many calories in maintenance energy needs—calories that can instead go toward reproduction. Selection for energetically efficient locomotion is therefore likely to be more intense among far-ranging animals because they have the most to gain.

For hominids living between 5 million and 1.8 million years ago, during the Pliocene epoch, climate change spurred this morphological revolution. As the African continent grew drier, forests gave way to grasslands, leaving food resources patchily distributed. In this context, bipedalism can be viewed as one of the first strategies in human nutritional evolution, a pattern of movement that would have substantially reduced the number of calories spent in collecting increasingly dispersed food resources.

BIG BRAINS AND HUNGRY HOMINIDS

No sooner had humans perfected their stride than the next pivotal event in human evolution—the dramatic enlargement of the brain—began. According to the fossil record, the australopithecines never became much brainier than living apes, showing only a modest increase in brain size, from around 400 cubic centimeters four million years age to 500 cubic centimeters two million years later. *Homo* brain sizes, in contrast, ballooned from 600 cubic centimeters in *H. habilis* some two million years ago up to 900 cubic centimeters in early *H. erectus* just 300,000 years later. The *H. erectus* brain did not attain modern human proportions (1,350 cubic centimeters on average), but it exceeded that of living nonhuman primates.

From a nutritional perspective, what is extraordinary about our large brain is how much energy it consumes—roughly 16 times as much as muscle tissue per unit weight. Yet although humans have much bigger brains relative to body weight than do other primates (three times larger than expected), the total resting energy requirements of the human body are no greater than those of any other mammal of the same size. We therefore use a much greater share of our daily energy budget to feed our voracious brains. In fact, at rest brain metabolism accounts for a whopping 20 to 25 percent of an adult human's energy needs—far more than the 8 to 10 percent observed in nonhuman primates, and more still than the 3 to 5 percent allotted to the brain by other mammals.

By using estimates of hominid body size compiled by Henry M. McHenry of the University of California at Davis, Robertson and I have reconstructed the proportion of resting energy needs that would have been required to support the brains of our ancient ancestors. Our calculations suggest that a typical, 80- to 85-pound australopithecine with a brain size of 450 cubic centimeters would have devoted about 11 percent of its resting energy to the brain. For its part, *H. erectus*, which weighed in at 125 to 130 pounds and had a brain size of some 900 cubic centimeters, would have earmarked about 17 percent of its resting energy—that is, about 260 out of 1,500 kilocalories a day—for the organ.

How did such an energetically costly brain evolve? One theory, developed by Dean Falk of Florida State University, holds that bipedalism enabled hominids to cool their cranial blood, thereby freeing the heat-sensitive brain of the temperature constraints that had kept its size in check. I suspect that, as with bipedalism, a number of selective factors were probably at work. But brain expansion almost certainly could not have occurred until hominids adopted a diet sufficiently rich in calories and nutrients to meet the associated costs.

Comparative studies of living animals support that assertion. Across all primates, species with bigger brains dine on richer foods, and humans are the extreme example of this correlation, boasting the largest relative brain size and the choicest diet [see "Diet and Primate Evolution," by Katharine Milton; SCIENTIFIC AMERICAN, August 1993]. According to recent analyses by Loren Cordain of Colorado State University, contemporary hunter-gatherers derive, on average, 40 to 60 percent of their dietary energy from animal foods (meat, milk and other products). Modern chimps, in comparison, obtain only 5 to 7 percent of their calories from these comestibles. Animal foods are far denser in calories and nutrients than most plant foods. For example, 3.5 ounces of meat provides upward of 200 kilocalories. But the same amount of fruit provides only 50 to 100 kilocalories. And a comparable serving of foliage yields just 10 to 20 kilocalories. It stands to reason, then, that for early *Homo*, acquiring more gray matter meant seeking out more of the energy-dense fare.

Fossils, too, indicate that improvements to dietary quality accompanied evolutionary brain growth. All australopithecines had skeletal and dental features built for processing tough, low-quality plant foods. The later, robust australopithecines—a dead-end branch of the human family tree that lived alongside members of our own genus—had especially pronounced adaptations for grinding up fibrous plant foods, including massive, dish-shaped faces; heavily built mandibles; ridges, or sagittal crests, atop the skull for the attachment of powerful chewing muscles; and huge, thickly enameled molar teeth. (This is not to say that australopithecines never ate meat. They almost certainly did on occasion, just as chimps do today.) In contrast, early members of the genus *Homo*, which descended from the gracile australopithecines, had much smaller faces, more delicate jaws, smaller molars and no sagittal crests—despite being far larger in terms of overall body size than their predecessors. Together these features suggest that early *Homo* was consuming less plant material and more animal foods.

As to what prompted *Homo*'s initial shift toward the higher-quality diet necessary for brain growth, environmental change appears to have once more set the stage for evolutionary change. The continued desiccation of the African landscape limited the amount and variety of edible plant foods available to hominids. Those on the line leading to the robust australopithecines coped with this problem morphologically, evolving anatomical specializations that enabled them to subsist on more widely available, difficult-to-chew foods. *Homo* took a different path. As it turns out, the spread of grasslands also led to an increase in the relative abundance of grazing mammals such as antelope and gazelle, creating opportunities for hominids capable of exploiting them. *H. erectus* did just that, developing the first hunting-and-gathering economy in which game animals became a significant part of the diet and resources were shared among members of the foraging groups. Signs of this behavioral revolution are visible in the archaeological record, which shows an increase in animal bones at hominid sites during this period, along with evidence that the beasts were butchered using stone tools.

INTO THE FIRE

Eating more animal foods is one way of boosting the caloric and nutrient density of the diet, a shift that appears to have been critical in the evolution of the human lineage. But might our ancient forebears have improved dietary quality another way? Richard Wrangham of Harvard University and his colleagues recently examined the importance of cooking in human evolution. They showed that cooking not only makes plant foods softer and easier to chew, it substantially increases their available energy content, particularly for starchy tubers such as potatoes and manioc. In their raw form, starches are not readily broken down by the enzymes in the human body. When heated, however, these complex carbohydrates become more digestible, thereby yielding more calories.

The researchers propose that *Homo erectus* was probably the first hominid to apply fire to food, starting perhaps 1.8 million years ago. They argue that early cooking of plant foods (especially tubers) enabled this species to evolve smaller teeth and bigger brains than those of their predecessors. Additionally, the extra calories allowed *H. erectus* to start hunting—an energetically costly activity—more frequently.

From an energetics perspective, this is a logical enough line of reasoning. What makes the hypothesis difficult to swallow is the archaeological evidence Wrangham's team uses to make its case. The authors cite the East African sites of Koobi Fora and Chesowanja, which date to around 1.6 million and 1.4 million years ago, respectively, to indicate control of fire by *H. erectus*. These localities do indeed exhibit evidence of fires, but whether hominids were responsible for creating or harnessing the flames is a matter of some debate. The earliest unequivocal manifestations of fire use—stone hearths and burned animal bones from sites in Europe—are only some 200,000 years old.

Cooking was clearly an innovation that considerably improved the quality of the human diet. But it remains unclear when in our past this practice arose.

—W.R.L.

These changes in diet and foraging behavior did not turn our ancestors into strict carnivores; however, the addition of modest amounts of animal foods to the menu, combined with the sharing of resources that is typical of hunter-gatherer groups, would have significantly increased the quality and stability of hominid diets. Improved dietary quality alone cannot explain *why* hominid brains grew, but it appears to have played a critical role in enabling that change. After the initial spurt in brain growth, diet and brain expansion probably interacted synergistically: bigger brains produced more complex social behavior, which led to further shifts in foraging tactics and improved diet, which in turn fostered additional brain evolution.

A MOVABLE FEAST

The evolution of *H. erectus* in Africa 1.8 million years ago also marked a third turning point in human evolution: the initial movement of hominids out of Africa. Until recently, the locations and ages of known fossil sites suggested that early *Homo* stayed put for a few hundred thousand years before venturing out of the motherland and slowly fanning out into the rest of the Old World. Earlier work hinted that improvements in tool technology around 1.4 million years ago—namely, the advent of the Acheulean hand ax—allowed hominids to leave Africa. But new discoveries indicate that *H. erectus* hit the ground running, so to speak. Rutgers University geochronologist Carl Swisher III and his colleagues have shown that the earliest *H. erectus*

sites outside of Africa, which are in Indonesia and the Republic of Georgia, date to between 1.8 million and 1.7 million years ago. It seems that the first appearance of *H. erectus* and its initial spread from Africa were almost simultaneous.

The impetus behind this newfound wanderlust again appears to be food. What an animal eats dictates to a large extent how much territory it needs to survive. Carnivorous animals generally require far bigger home ranges than do herbivores of comparable size because they have fewer total calories available to them per unit area.

Large-bodied and increasingly dependent on animal foods, *H. erectus* most likely needed much more turf than the smaller, more vegetarian australopithecines did. Using data on contemporary primates and human hunter-gatherers as a guide, Robertson, Susan C. Antón of Rutgers University and I have estimated that the larger body size of *H. erectus*, combined with a moderate increase in meat consumption, would have necessitated an eightfold to 10-fold increase in home range size compared with that of the late australopithecines—enough, in fact, to account for the abrupt expansion of the species out of Africa. Exactly how far beyond the continent that shift would have taken *H. erectus* remains unclear, but migrating animal herds may have helped lead it to these distant lands.

As humans moved into more northern latitudes, they encountered new dietary challenges. The Neandertals, who lived during the last ice ages of Europe, were among the first humans to inhabit arctic environments, and they almost certainly would have needed

NEANDERTAL HUNTERS

To reconstruct what early humans ate, researchers have traditionally studied features on their fossilized teeth and skulls, archaeological remains of food-related activities, and the diets of living humans and apes. Increasingly, however, investigators have been tapping another source of data: the chemical composition of fossil bones. This approach has yielded some especially intriguing findings with regard to the Neandertals.

Michael Richards, now at the University of Bradford in England, and his colleagues recently examined isotopes of carbon (^{13}C) and nitrogen (^{15}N) in 29,000-year-old Neandertal bones from Vindija Cave in Croatia. The relative proportions of these isotopes in the protein part of human bone, known as collagen, directly reflect their proportions in the protein of the individual's diet. Thus, by comparing the isotopic "signatures" of the Neandertal bones to those of other animals living in the same environments, the authors were able to determine whether the Neandertals were deriving the bulk of their protein from plants or from animals.

The analyses show that the Vindija Neandertals had ^{15}N levels comparable to those seen in northern carnivores such as foxes and wolves, indicating that they obtained almost all their dietary protein from animal foods. Earlier work hinted that inefficient foraging might have been a factor in the subsequent demise of the Neandertals. But Richards and his collaborators argue that in order to consume as much animal food as they apparently did, the Neandertals had to have been skilled hunters. These findings are part of a growing body of literature that suggests Neandertal subsistence behavior was more complex than previously thought [see "Who Were the Neandertals?" by Kate Wong; SCIENTIFIC AMERICAN, April 2000].

—W.R.L.

ample calories to endure under those circumstances. Hints at what their energy requirements might have been come from data on traditional human populations that live in northern settings today. The Siberian reindeer-herding populations known as the Evenki, which I have studied with Peter Katzmarzyk of Queen's University in Ontario and Victoria A. Galloway of the University of Toronto, and the Inuit (Eskimo) populations of the Canadian Arctic have resting metabolic rates that are about 15 percent higher than those of people of similar size living in temperate environments. The energetically expensive activities associated with living in a northern climate ratchet their caloric cost of living up further still. Indeed, whereas a 160-pound American male with a typical urban way of life requires about 2,600 kilocalories a day, a diminutive, 125-pound Evenki man needs more than 3,000 kilocalories a day to sustain himself. Using these modern northern populations as benchmarks, Mark Sorensen of Northwestern University and I have estimated that Neandertals most likely would have required as many as 4,000 kilocalories a day to survive. That they were able to meet these demands for as long as they did speaks to their skills as foragers (see the accompanying box).

MODERN QUANDARIES

Just as pressures to improve dietary "quality" influenced early human evolution, so, too, have these factors played a crucial role in the more recent increases in population size. Innovations such as cooking, agriculture and even aspects of modern food technology can all be considered tactics for boosting the quality of the human diet. Cooking, for one, augmented the energy available in wild plant foods (see the box on p. [112]). With the advent of agriculture, humans began to manipulate marginal plant species to increase their productivity, digestibility and nutritional content—essentially making plants more like animal foods. This kind of tinkering continues today, with genetic modification of crop species to make "better" fruits, vegetables and grains. Similarly, the development of liquid nutritional supplements and meal replacement bars is a continuation of the trend that our ancient ancestors started: gaining as much nutritional return from our food in as little volume and with as little physical effort as possible.

Overall, that strategy has evidently worked: humans are here today and in record numbers to boot. But perhaps the strongest testament to the importance of energy- and nutrient-rich foods in human evolution lies in the observation that so many health concerns facing societies around the globe stem from deviations from the energy dynamic that our ancestors established. For children in rural populations of the developing world, low-quality diets lead to poor physical growth and high rates of mortality during early life. In these cases, the foods fed to youngsters during and after weaning are often not sufficiently dense in energy and nutrients to meet the high nutritional needs associated with this period of rapid growth and development. Although these children are typically similar in length and weight to their U.S. counterparts at birth, they are much shorter and lighter by the age of three, often resembling the smallest 2 to 3 percent of American children of the same age and sex.

Various diets can satisfy human nutritional requirements. Some populations subsist almost entirely on plant foods; others eat mostly animal foods. Although Americans consume less meat than do a number of the traditionally living people described here, they have on average higher cholesterol levels and higher levels of obesity (as indicated by body mass index) because they consume more energy than they expend and eat meat that is higher in fat.

Population	Energy Intake (kilocalories/ day)	Energy from Animal Foods (%)	Energy from Plant Foods (%)	Total Blood Cholesterol (milligrams/ deciliter)	Body Mass Index (weight/ height squared)
Hunter-Gatherers					
!Kung (Botswana)	2,100	33	67	121	19
Inuit (North America)	2,350	96	4	141	24
Pastoralists					
Turkana (Kenya)	1,411	80	20	186	18
Evenki (Russia)	2,820	41	59	142	22
Agriculturalists					
Quechua (Highland Peru)	2,002	5	95	150	21
Industrial Societies					
U.S.	2,250	23	77	204	26

Note: Energy intake figures reflect the adult average (males and females); blood cholesterol and body mass index (BMI) figures are given for males.
Healthy BMI = 18.5–24.9; overweight = 25.0–29.9; obese = 30 and higher.

In the industrial world, we are facing the opposite problem: rates of childhood and adult obesity are rising because the energy-rich foods we crave—notably these packed with fat and sugar—have become widely available and relatively inexpensive. According to recent estimates, more than half of adult Americans are overweight or obese. Obesity has also appeared in parts of the developing world where it was virtually unknown less than a generation ago. This seeming paradox has emerged as people who grew up malnourished move from rural areas to urban settings where food is more readily available. In some sense, obesity and other common diseases of the modern world are continuations of a tenor that started millions of years ago. We are victims of our own evolutionary success, having developed a calorie-packed diet while minimizing the amount of maintenance energy expended on physical activity.

The magnitude of this imbalance becomes clear when we look at traditionally living human populations. Studies of the Evenki reindeer herders that I have conducted in collaboration with Michael Crawford of the University of Kansas and Ludmila Osipova of the Russian Academy of Sciences in Novosibirsk indicate that the Evenki derive almost half their daily calories from meat, more than 2.5 times the amount consumed by the average American. Yet when we compare Evenki men with their U.S. peers,

they are 20 percent leaner and have cholesterol levels that are 30 percent lower.

These differences partly reflect the compositions of the diets. Although the Evenki diet is high in meat, it is relatively low in fat (about 20 percent of their dietary energy comes from fat, compared with 35 percent in the average U.S. diet), because free-ranging animals such as reindeer have less body fat than cattle and other feedlot animals do. The composition of the fat is also different in free-ranging animals, tending to be lower in saturated fats and higher in the polyunsaturated fatty acids that protect against heart disease. More important, however, the Evenki way of life necessitates a much higher level of energy expenditure.

Thus, it is not just changes in diet that have created many of our pervasive health problems but the interaction of shifting diets and changing lifestyles. Too often modern health problems are portrayed as the result of eating "bad" foods that are departures from *the* natural human diet—an oversimplification embodied by the current debate over the relative merits of a high-protein, high-fat Atkins-type diet or a low-fat one that emphasizes complex carbohydrates. This is a fundamentally flawed approach to assessing human nutritional needs. Our species was not designed to subsist on a single, optimal diet. What is remarkable about human beings is the extraordinary variety of what we eat. We have been able to thrive in almost

A DIVERSITY OF DIETS

The variety of successful dietary strategies employed by traditionally living populations provides an important perspective on the ongoing debate about how high-protein, low-carbohydrate regimens such as the Atkins diet compare with those that underscore complex carbohydrates and fat restriction. The fact that both these schemes produce weight loss is not surprising, because both help people shed pounds through the same basic mechanism: limiting major sources of calories. When you create an energy deficit—that is, when you consume fewer calories than you expend—your body begins burning its fat stores and you lose weight.

The larger question about healthy weight-loss or weight-maintenance diets is whether they create eating patterns that are sustainable over time. On this point it appears that diets that severely limit large categories of foods (carbohydrates, for example) are much more difficult to sustain than are moderately restrictive diets.

In the case of the Atkins-type regimen, there are also concerns about the potential long-term consequences of eating foods derived largely from feedlot animals, which tend to contain more fat in general and considerably more saturated fats than do their free-ranging counterparts.

In September the National Academy of Sciences's Institute of Medicine put forth new diet and exercise guidelines that mesh well with the ideas presented in this article. Not only did the institute set broader target ranges for the amounts of carbohydrates, fat, and protein that belong in a healthy diet—in essence, acknowledging that there are various ways to meet our nutritional needs—the organization also doubled the recommended amount of moderately intense physical activity to an hour a day. By following these guidelines and balancing what we eat with exercise, we can live more like the Evenki of Siberia and other traditional societies—and more like our hominid ancestors.

—W.R.L.

---

every ecosystem on the earth, consuming diets ranging from almost all animal foods among populations of the Arctic to primarily tubers and cereal grains among populations in the high Andes. Indeed, the hallmarks of human evolution have been the diversity of strategies that we have developed to create diets that meet our distinctive metabolic requirements and the ever increasing efficiency with which we extract energy and nutrients from the environment. The challenge our modern societies now face is balancing the calories we consume with the calories we burn.

MORE TO EXPLORE

Evolutionary Perspectives on Human Nutrition: The Influence of Brain and Body Size on Diet and Metabolism. William R. Leonard and Marcia L. Robertson in *American Journal of Human Biology*, Vol. 6, No. 1, pages 77–88; January 1994.

Rethinking the Energetics of Bipedality. William R. Leonard and Marcia L. Robertson in *Current Anthropology*, Vol. 38, No. 2, pages 304–309; April 1997.

Human Biology: An Evolutionary and Biocultural Approach. Edited by Sara Stinson, Barry Bogin, Rebecca Huss-Ashmore, and Dennis O'Rourke. Wiley-Liss, 2000.

Ecology, Health and Lifestyle Change among the Evenki Herders of Siberia. William R. Leonard, Victoria A. Galloway, Evgueni Ivakine, Ludmila Osipova, and Marina Kazakovtseva in *Human Biology of Pastoral Populations*. Edited by William R. Leonard and Michael H. Crawford. Cambridge University Press, 2002.

An Ecomorphological Model of the Initial Hominid Dispersal from Africa. Susan C. Antón, William R. Leonard, and Marcia L. Robertson in *Journal of Human Evolution* [2002].

24

"Hobbits" from Indonesia

Kate Wong and Elizabeth Culotta

Kate Wong is editorial director of Scientific American.com. Elizabeth Culotta is a contributing editor at Science.

In 2004, some potentially spectacular finds on the Indonesian island of Flores indicated that modern humans may have shared the earth with another species of hominid in fairly recent times and that our picture of human evolution may therefore be even more complex than we thought. But as more discoveries have been made and hypotheses generated, we also see that any definitive conclusions about these fossils and tools now are premature and that the process of scientific inquiry is alive and well in addressing these data and their implications. In the first selection, Kate Wong describes the finds and the possible interpretations. In the second selection, Elizabeth Culotta talks about some of the latest ideas, showing that the controversy is far from over.

As you read, consider the following questions:

1. What was found on Flores and why are the fossils so interesting? How do they differ from what has been discovered so far in the fossil record of human evolution?

2. What are the proposed explanations for the diminutive size of *Homo floresiensis* and what are the pros and cons of each?

3. What are the interpretations of the place in human evolution of *H. floresiensis*?

4. How have the latest new analyses and thinking added to the controversy?

The Littlest Human *by Kate Wong*

On the island of Flores in Indonesia, villagers have long told tales of a diminutive, upright-walking creature with a lopsided gait, a voracious appetite, and soft, murmuring speech. They call it *ebu gogo,* "the grandmother who eats anything." Scientists' best guess was that macaque monkeys inspired the *ebu gogo* lore. But last October, an alluring alternative came to light. A team of Australian and Indonesian researchers excavating a cave on Flores unveiled the remains of a lilliputian human—one that stood barely a meter tall—whose kind lived as recently as 13,000 years ago.

The announcement electrified the paleoanthropology community. *Homo sapiens* was supposed to have had the planet to itself for the past 25 millennia, free from the company of other humans following the

apparent demise of the Neandertals in Europe and *Homo erectus* in Asia. Furthermore, hominids this tiny were known only from fossils of australopithecines (Lucy and the like) that lived nearly three million years ago—long before the emergence of *H. sapiens.* No one would have predicted that our own species had a contemporary as small and primitive-looking as the little Floresian. Neither would anyone have guessed that a creature with a skull the size of a grapefruit might have possessed cognitive capabilities comparable to those of anatomically modern humans.

ISLE OF INTRIGUE

This is not the first time Flores has yielded surprises. In 1998 archaeologists led by Michael J. Morwood of the University of New England in Armidale, Australia, reported having discovered crude stone artifacts some 840,000 years old in the Soa Basin of central Flores. Although no human remains turned up with the tools, the implication was that *H. erectus,* the only hominid known to have lived in Southeast Asia during that time, had crossed the deep waters separating Flores from Java. To the team, the find showed *H. erectus* to be a seafarer, which was startling because elsewhere *H. erectus* had left behind little material culture to suggest that it was anywhere near capable of making watercraft. Indeed, the earliest accepted date for boat-building was 40,000 to 60,000 years ago, when modern humans colonized Australia. (The other early fauna on Flores probably got there by swimming or accidentally drifting over on flotsam. Humans are not strong enough swimmers to have managed that voyage, but skeptics say they may have drifted across on natural rafts.

Hoping to document subsequent chapters of human occupation of the island, Morwood and Radien P. Soejono of the Indonesian Center for Archaeology in Jakarta turned their attention to a large limestone cave called Liang Bua located in western Flores. Indonesian archaeologists had been excavating the cave intermittently since the 1970s, depending on funding availability, but workers had penetrated only the uppermost deposits. Morwood and Soejono set their sights on reaching bedrock and began digging in July 2001. Before long, their team's efforts turned up abundant stone tools and bones of a pygmy version of an extinct elephant relative known as *Stegodon*. But it was not until nearly the end of the third season of fieldwork that diagnostic hominid material in the form of an isolated tooth surfaced. Morwood brought a cast of the tooth back to Armidale to show to his department

---

MINI HUMANS

- Conventional wisdom holds that *Homo sapiens* has been the sole human species on the earth for the past 25,000 years. Remains discovered on the Indonesian island of Flores have upended that view.

- The bones are said to belong to a dwarf species of *Homo* that lived as recently as 13,000 years ago.

- Although the hominid is as small in body and brain as the earliest humans, it appears to have made sophisticated stone tools, raising questions about the relation between brain size and intelligence.

- The find is controversial, however—some experts wonder whether the discoverers have correctly diagnosed the bones and whether anatomically modern humans might have made those advanced artifacts.

---

colleague Peter Brown. "It was clear that while the premolar was broadly humanlike, it wasn't from a modern human," Brown recollects. Seven days later Morwood received word that the Indonesians had recovered a skeleton. The Australians boarded the next plane to Jakarta.

Peculiar though the premolar was, nothing could have prepared them for the skeleton, which apart from the missing arms was largely complete. The pelvis anatomy revealed that the individual was bipedal and probably a female, and the tooth eruption and wear indicated that it was an adult. Yet it was only as tall as a modern three-year-old, and its brain was as small as the smallest australopithecine brain known. There were other primitive traits as well, including the broad pelvis and the long neck of the femur. In other respects, however, the specimen looked familiar. Its small teeth and narrow nose, the overall shape of the braincase and the thickness of the cranial bones all evoked *Homo*.

Brown spent the next three months analyzing the enigmatic skeleton, catalogued as LB1 and affectionately nicknamed the Hobbit by some of the team members, after the tiny beings in J.R.R. Tolkien's *The Lord of the Rings* books. The decision about how to classify it did not come easily. Impressed with the characteristics LB1 shared with early hominids such as the australopithecines, he initially proposed that it represented a new genus of human. On further consideration, however, the similarities to *Homo* proved more persuasive. Based on the 18,000-year age of LB1, one might have reasonably expected the bones to belong to *H. sapiens*, albeit a very petite representative. But when Brown and his colleagues considered the morphological characteristics of small-bodied modern humans—including normal ones, such as pygmies, and abnormal ones, such as pituitary dwarfs—LB1 did not seem to fit any of those descriptions. Pygmies have small bodies and large brains—the result of delayed growth during puberty, when the brain has already attained its full size. And individuals with genetic disorders that produce short stature and small brains have a range of distinctive features not seen in LB1 and rarely reach adulthood, Brown says. Conversely, he notes, the Flores skeleton exhibits archaic traits that have never been documented for abnormal small-bodied *H. sapiens*.

What LB1 looks like most, the researchers concluded, is a miniature *H. erectus*. Describing the find in the journal *Nature*, they assigned LB1 as well as the isolated tooth and an arm bone from older deposits to a new species of human, *Homo floresiensis*. They further argued that it was a descendant of *H. erectus* that had become marooned on Flores and evolved in isolation into a dwarf species, much as the elephant-like *Stegodon* did.

Biologists have long recognized that mammals larger than rabbits tend to shrink on small islands, presumably as an adaptive response to the limited food supply. They have little to lose by doing so, because these environments harbor few predators. On Flores, the only sizable predators were the Komodo dragon and another, even larger monitor lizard. Animals smaller than rabbits, on the other hand, tend to attain brobdingnagian proportions—perhaps because bigger bodies are more energetically efficient than small ones. Liang Bua has yielded evidence of that as well, in the form of a rat as robust as a rabbit.

But attributing a hominid's bantam size to the so-called island rule was a first. Received paleoanthropological wisdom holds that culture has buffered us humans from many of the selective pressures that mold other creatures—we cope with cold, for example, by building fires and making clothes, rather than evolving a proper pelage. The discovery of a dwarf hominid species indicates that, under the right conditions, humans can in fact respond in the same, predictable way that other large mammals do when the going gets tough. Hints that *Homo* could deal with resource fluxes in this manner came earlier in 2004 from the discovery of a relatively petite *H. erectus* skull from Olorgesailie in Kenya, remarks Richard Potts of the Smithsonian Institution, whose team recovered the bones. "Getting small is one of the things *H. erectus* had in its biological tool kit," he says, and the Flores hominid seems to be an extreme instance of that.

CURIOUSER AND CURIOUSER

H. Floresiensis's teeny brain was perplexing. What the hominid reportedly managed to accomplish with such a modest organ was nothing less than astonishing. Big brains are a hallmark of human evolution. In the space of six million to seven million years, our ancestors more than tripled their cranial capacity, from some 360 cubic centimeters in *Sahelanthropus*, the earliest putative hominid, to a whopping 1,350 cubic centimeters on average in modern folks. Archaeological evidence indicates that behavioral complexity increased correspondingly. Experts were thus fairly certain that large brains are a prerequisite for advanced cultural practices. Yet whereas the pea-brained australopithecines left behind only crude stone tools at best (and most seem not to have done any stone working at all), the comparably gray-matter-impoverished *H. floresiensis* is said to have manufactured implements that exhibit a level of sophistication elsewhere associated exclusively with *H. sapiens*.

The bulk of the artifacts from Liang Bua are simple flake tools struck from volcanic rock and chert, no more advanced than the implements made by late australopithecines and early *Homo*. But mixed in among the pygmy *Stegodon* remains excavators found a fancier set of tools, one that included finely worked points, large blades, awls and small blades that may have been hafted for use as spears. To the team, this association suggests that *H. floresiensis* regularly hunted *Stegodon*. Many of the *Stegodon* bones are those of young individuals that one *H. floresiensis* might have been able to bring down alone. But some belonged to adults that weighed up to half a ton, the hunting and transport of which must have been a coordinated group activity—one that probably required language, surmises team member Richard G. ("Bert") Roberts of the University of Wollongong in Australia.

The discovery of charred animal remains in the cave suggests that cooking, too, was part of the cultural repertoire of *H. floresiensis.* That a hominid as cerebrally limited as this one might have had control of fire gives pause. Humans are not thought to have tamed flame until relatively late in our collective cognitive development: the earliest unequivocal evidence of fire use comes from 200,000-year-old hearths in Europe that were the handiwork of the large-brained Neandertals.

If the *H. floresiensis* discoverers are correct in their interpretation, theirs is one of the most important paleoanthropological finds in decades. Not only does it mean that another species of human coexisted with our ancestors just yesterday in geological terms, and that our genus is far more variable than expected, it raises all sorts of questions about brain size and intelligence. Perhaps it should come as no surprise, then, that controversy has accompanied their claims.

CLASSIFICATION CLASH

It did not take long for alternative theories to surface. In a letter that ran in the October 31 edition of Australia's *Sunday Mail*, just three days after the publication of the *Nature* issue containing the initial reports, paleoanthropologist Maciej Henneberg of the University of Adelaide countered that a pathological condition known as microcephaly (from the Greek for "small brain") could explain LB1's unusual features. Individuals afflicted with the most severe congenital form of microcephaly, primordial microcephalic dwarfism, die in childhood. But those with milder forms, though mentally retarded, can survive into adulthood. Statistically comparing the head and face dimensions of LB1 with those of a 4,000-year-old skull from Crete that is known to have belonged to a microcephalic, Henneberg found no significant differences between the two. Furthermore, he argued, the isolated forearm bone found deeper in the deposit corresponds to a height of 151 to 162 centimeters—the stature of many modern women and some men, not that of a dwarf—suggesting that larger-bodied people, too, lived at Liang Bua. In Henneberg's view, these findings indicate that LB1 is more likely a microcephalic *H. sapiens* than a new branch of *Homo.*

Susan C. Antón of New York University disagrees with that assessment. "The facial morphology is completely different in microcephalic [modern] humans," and their body size is normal, not small, she says. Antón questions whether LB1 warrants a new species, however. "There's little in the shape that differentiates it from *Homo erectus,*" she notes. One can argue that it's a new species, Antón allows, but the difference in shape between LB1 and *Homo erectus* is less striking than that between a Great Dane and a Chihuahua. The possibility exists that the LB1 specimen is a *H. erectus* individual with a pathological growth condition stemming from microcephaly or nutritional deprivation, she observes.

But some specialists say the Flores hominid's anatomy exhibits a more primitive pattern. According to Colin P. Groves of the Australian National University and David W. Cameron of the University of Sydney, the small brain, the long neck of the femur and other characteristics suggest an ancestor along the lines of *Homo habilis,* the earliest member of our genus, rather than the more advanced *H. erectus.* Milford H. Wolpoff of the University of Michigan at Ann Arbor wonders whether the Flores find might even represent an offshoot of *Australopithecus.* If LB1 is a descendant of *H. sapiens* or *H. erectus,* it is hard to imagine how natural selection left her with a brain that's even smaller than expected for her height, Wolpoff says. Granted, if she descended from *Australopithecus,* which had massive jaws and teeth, one has to account for her relatively delicate jaws and dainty dentition. That, however, is a lesser evolutionary conundrum than the one posed by her tiny brain, he asserts. After all, a shift in diet could explain the reduced chewing apparatus, but why would selection downsize intelligence?

Finding an australopithecine that lived outside of Africa—not to mention all the way over in Southeast Asia—18,000 years ago would be a first. Members of this group were thought to have died out in Africa one and a half million years ago, never having left their mother continent. Perhaps, researchers reasoned, hominids needed long, striding limbs, large brains and better technology before they could venture out into the rest of the Old World. But the recent discovery of 1.8-million-year-old *Homo* fossils at a site called Dmanisi in the Republic of Georgia refuted that explanation—the Georgian hominids were primitive and small and utilized tools like those australopithecines had made a million years before. Taking that into consideration, there is no a priori reason why australopithecines (or habilines, for that matter) could not have colonized other continents.

TROUBLING TOOLS

Yet if *Australopithecus* made it out of Africa and survived on Flores until quite recently, that would raise the question of why no other remains supporting that scenario have turned up in the region. According to Wolpoff, they may have: a handful of poorly studied Indonesian fossils discovered in the 1940s have been variously classified as *Australopithecus, Meganthropus* and, most recently, *H. erectus.* In light of the Flores find, he says, those remains deserve reexamination.

Many experts not involved in the discovery back Brown and Morwood's taxonomic decision, however. "Most of the differences [between the Flores hominid and known members of *Homo*], including apparent similarities to australopithecines, are almost certainly related to very small body mass," declares David R. Begun of the University of Toronto. That is, as the Flores people dwarfed from *H. erectus,* some of their anatomy simply converged on that of the likewise little australopithecines. Because LB1 shares some key derived features with *H. erectus* and some with other members of *Homo,* "the most straightforward option is to call it a new species of *Homo,*" he remarks. "It's a fair and reasonable interpretation," *H. erectus* expert G. Philip Rightmire of Binghamton University agrees. "That was quite a little experiment in Indonesia."

Even more controversial than the position of the half-pint human on the family tree is the notion that it made those advanced-looking tools. Stanford University paleoanthropologist Richard Klein notes that the artifacts found near LB1 appear to include few, if any, of the sophisticated types found elsewhere in the cave. This brings up the possibility that the modern-looking tools were produced by modern humans, who could have occupied the cave at a different time. Further excavations are necessary to determine the stratigraphic relation between the implements and the hominid remains, Klein opines. Such efforts may turn up modern humans like us. The question then, he says, will be whether there were two species at the site or whether modern humans alone occupied Liang Bua—in which case LB1 was simply a modern who experienced a growth anomaly.

Stratigraphic concerns aside, the tools are too advanced and too large to make manufacture by a primitive, diminutive hominid likely, Groves contends. Although the Liang Bua implements allegedly date back as far as 94,000 years ago, which the team argues makes them too early to be the handiwork of *H. sapiens,* Groves points out that 67,000-year-old tools have turned up in Liujiang, China, and older indications of a modern human presence in the Far East might yet emerge. "*H. sapiens,* once it was out of Africa, didn't take long to spread into eastern Asia," he comments.

"At the moment there isn't enough evidence" to establish that *H. floresiensis* created the advanced tools, concurs Bernard Wood of George Washington University. But as a thought experiment, he says, "let's pretend that they did." In that case, "I don't have a clue about brain size and ability," he confesses. If a hominid with no more gray matter than a chimp has can create a material culture like this one, Wood contemplates, "why did it take people such a bloody long time to make tools" in the first place?

"If *Homo floresiensis* was capable of producing sophisticated tools, we have to say that brain size doesn't add up to much," Rightmire concludes. Of course, humans today exhibit considerable variation in gray matter volume, and great thinkers exist at both ends of the spectrum. French writer Jacques Anatole François Thibault (also known as Anatole France), who won the 1921 Nobel Prize for Literature, had a cranial capacity of only about 1,000 cubic centimeters; England's General Oliver Cromwell had more than twice that. "What that means is that once you get the brain to a certain size, size no longer matters, it's the organization of the brain," Potts states. At some point, he adds, "the internal wiring of the brain may allow competence even if the brain seems small."

LB1's brain is long gone, so how it was wired will remain a mystery. Clues to its organization may reside on the interior of the braincase, however. Paleontologists can sometimes obtain latex molds of the insides of fossil skulls and then create plaster endocasts that reveal the morphology of the organ. Because LB1's bones are too fragile to withstand standard casting procedures, Brown is working on creating a virtual endocast based on CT scans of the skull that he can then use to generate a physical endocast via stereolithography, a rapid-prototyping technology.

"If it's a little miniature version of an adult human brain, I'll be really blown away," says paleoneurologist Dean Falk of the University of Florida. Then again, she muses, what happens if the convolutions look chimplike? Specialists have long wondered whether bigger brains fold differently simply because they are bigger or whether the reorganization reflects selection for increased cognition. "This specimen could conceivably answer that," Falk observes.

RETURN TO THE LOST WORLD

Since submitting their technical papers to *Nature,* the Liang Bua excavators have reportedly recovered the remains of another five or so individuals, all of which fit the *H. floresiensis* profile. None are nearly so complete as LB1, whose long arms turned up during the most recent field season. But they did unearth a second lower jaw that they say is identical in size and shape to LB1's. Such duplicate bones will be critical to their case that they have a population of these tiny humans (as opposed to a bunch of scattered bones from one person). That should in turn dispel concerns that LB1 was a diseased individual.

Additional evidence may come from DNA: hair samples possibly from *H. floresiensis* are undergoing analysis at the University of Oxford, and the hominid teeth and bones may contain viable DNA as well. "Tropical environments are not the best for long-term preservation of DNA, so we're not holding our breath," Roberts remarks, "but there's certainly no harm in looking."

The future of the bones (and any DNA they contain) is uncertain, however. In late November, Teuku Jacob of the Gadjah Mada University in Yogyakarta, Java, who was not involved in the discovery or the analyses, had the delicate specimens transported from their repository at the Indonesian Center for Archaeology to his own laboratory with Soejono's assistance. Jacob, the dean of Indonesian paleoanthropology, thinks LB1 was a microcephalic and allegedly ordered the transfer of it and the new, as yet undescribed finds for examination and safekeeping, despite strong objections from other staff members at the center. At the time this article was going to press, the team was waiting for Jacob to make good on his promise to return the remains to Jakarta by January 1 of this year, but his reputation for restricting scientific access to fossils has prompted pundits to predict that the bones will never be studied again.

Efforts to piece together the *H. floresiensis* puzzle will proceed, however. For his part, Brown is eager to find the tiny hominid's large-bodied forebears. The possibilities are threefold, he notes. Either the ancestor dwarfed on Flores (and was possibly the maker of the 840,000-year-old Soa Basin tools), or it dwindled on another island and later reached Flores, or the ancestor was small before it even arrived in Southeast Asia. In fact, in many ways, LB1 more closely resembles African *H. erectus* and the Georgian hominids than the geographically closer Javan *H. erectus,* he observes. But whether these similarities indicate that *H. floresiensis* arose from an earlier *H. erectus* foray into Southeast Asia than the one that produced Javan *H. erectus* or are merely coincidental results of the dwarfing process remains to be determined. Future excavations may connect the dots. The team plans to continue digging on Flores and Java and will next year begin work on other Indonesian islands, including Sulawesi to the north.

The hominid bones from Liang Bua now span the period from 95,000 to 13,000 years ago, suggesting to the team that the little Floresians perished along with the pygmy *Stegodon* because of a massive volcanic eruption in the area around 12,000 years ago, although they may have survived later farther east. If *H. erectus* persisted on nearby Java until 25,000 years ago, as some evidence suggests, and *H. sapiens* had arrived in the region by 40,000 years ago, three human species lived cheek by jowl in Southeast Asia for at least 15,000 years. And the discoverers of *H. floresiensis* predict that more will be found. The islands of Lombok and Sumbawa would have been natural stepping-stones for hominids traveling from Java or mainland Asia to Flores. Those that put down roots on these islands may well have set off on their own evolutionary trajectories.

Perhaps, it has been proposed, some of these offshoots of the *Homo* lineage survived until historic times. Maybe they still live in remote pockets of Southeast Asia's dense rain forests, awaiting (or avoiding) discovery. On Flores, oral histories hold that the *ebu gogo* was still in existence when Dutch colonists settled there in the 19th century. And Malay folklore describes another small, humanlike being known as the *orang pendek* that supposedly dwells on Sumatra to this day.

"Every country seems to have myths about these things," Brown reflects. "We've excavated a lot of sites around the world, and we've never found them. But then [in September 2003] we found LB1." Scientists may never know whether tales of the *ebu gogo* and *orang pendek* do in fact recount actual sightings of other hominid species, but the newfound possibility will no doubt spur efforts to find such creatures for generations to come.

MORE TO EXPLORE

Archaeology and Age of a New Hominin from Flores in Eastern Indonesia. M. J. Morwood et al. in *Nature,* Vol. 431, pages 1087–1091; October 28, 2004.

A New Small-Bodied Hominin from the Late Pleistocene of Flores, Indonesia. P. Brown et al. in *Nature,* Vol. 431, pages 1055–1061; October 28, 2004.

A Q&A with Peter Brown is at www.sciam.com/ontheweb

How the Hobbit Shrugged: Tiny Hominid's Story Takes New Turn *by Elizabeth Culotta*

SAN JUAN, PUERTO RICO—The strangest ancient humans may be Indonesia's "hobbits," the 1-meter-tall people who made stone tools and hunted dwarf elephants 18,000 years ago. When announced 2 years ago, the fossils from the island of Flores seemed almost too bizarre for fiction. Now, close-up looks at some of the bones have given the hobbits' saga even more odd twists.

At a recent meeting here,* two anatomists presented analyses suggesting that the original hobbit skeleton may not be female, as first described, and that its shoulders differ from those of modern people and hark back to an ancient human ancestor, *Homo erectus.* That detail and others bolster the notion that an *H. erectus* population on the island evolved into the dwarf form

"How the Hobbit Shrugged" by Elizabeth Culotta from *Science,* May 2006, pp. 983–984. Copyright © 2006 American Association for the Advancement of Science.

* Paleoanthropology Society, 24–26 April.

of *H. floresiensis,* anatomist Susan Larson of Stony Brook University in New York said in her talk at the meeting.

Other researchers' opinions about almost every aspect of the hobbits, however, continue to run the gamut. Many are impressed with Larson's analysis. "I support Larson's observations . . . [and see] evidence of a faint phylogenetic signal" connecting the finds with *H. erectus,* says paleoanthropologist Russell Ciochon of the University of Iowa in Iowa City, who calls the skeleton from Flores "a very important link to our past." But a few researchers still find the whole tale too tall to swallow. In a Technical Comment published online this week by *Science,* paleoanthropologist Robert D. Martin of the Field Museum in Chicago, Illinois, and colleagues argue that the single skull is that of a modern human suffering from microcephaly (see sidebar). And even some researchers who are reasonably convinced that the fossils do not represent diseased modern people caution that the sample size for the shoulder bones is one [N=1]. "It's always nicer to have more than one individual" to hang a hypothesis on, says Eric Delson of Lehman College, City University of New York.

At the meeting, a packed room listened intently as Larson described her work on the upper arm bone, or humerus, of the original skeleton, labeled LB1 as the first human from Liang Bua cave. The LB1 humerus is

BUT IS IT PATHOLOGICAL?

Even as some researchers draw inferences about the ancestry of *Homo floresiensis* (see main text), others remain convinced that the bizarre bones from the Indonesian island of Flores are nothing more than diseased modern humans. In a Technical Comment published online by *Science* this week (www.sciencemag.org/cgi/content/full/312/5776/999b), paleoanthropologist Robert D. Martin of the Field Museum of Natural History in Chicago, Illinois, and colleagues make that case.

Martin gathered scaling data on the brains and bodies of other mammals, including data on the proportions of elephants as they evolved into dwarf forms on islands. Using several possible scaling models, he argues that shrinking a *H. erectus* brain to roughly the size of the Liang Bua skull would yield a body size no greater than 11 kilograms—the size of a small monkey.

If the Liang Bua bones aren't a new species of human, what are they? Martin argues that the single tiny skull may be a modern human with microcephaly, or a pathologically small head. A previous *Science* paper by Dean Falk of Florida State University in Tallahassee and her colleagues argued that the Liang Bua skull did not show the extreme pathology seen in a microcephalic brain. But Martin counters that some microcephalic brains exhibit much less pathology, including one from a 32-year-old woman reported to have had the body size of a 12-year-old child. "I'm not saying I'm 100% certain it's microcephaly," says Martin. "I'm saying that that brain size is simply too small" to be normal.

Jean-Jacques Hublin of the Max Planck Institute for Evolutionary Anthropology in Leipzig, Germany, who has seen the original specimens, finds the scaling arguments "quite convincing." But Martin's arguments are provoking a sharp response. Falk calls Martin's claims "unsubstantiated assertions" and adds that her team is surveying microcephalics to learn more. And bones from several small individuals have now been recovered from Flores, notes William Jungers of Stony Brook University in New York. He says that Martin's explanation implies that the island was home to "a village of microcephalic idiots." He adds that "there are precious few 'scaling laws' out there" and that examples of unusual scaling are not unexpected.

Paleoanthropologist Ralph Holloway of Columbia University, who is also studying microcephalic brains, says that so far he sees some differences between the Liang Bua skull and what's called primary microcephaly. But he warns that it will take a substantial survey to be sure. "I am coming around to believing that it isn't primary microcephaly," he says. But "I certainly would not rule out pathology just yet."

—E.C.

peculiar—or, rather, it lacks a peculiarity shared by living people.

In modern humans, the top or head of the humerus is twisted with respect to the elbow joint by about 145 to 165 degrees. As a result, when you stand straight, the insides of your elbows face slightly forward, allowing you to bend your elbows and work with your hands in front of your body.

But in *H. floresiensis*, the humerus appeared only slightly twisted. Last fall, Michael Morwood of the University of New England in Armidale, Australia, co-discoverer of the Flores bones, asked Larson, known for her work on the upper arm, how this could work in a toolmaking hominid. "I told him I didn't know," says Larson. "It *wouldn't* work."

So at the invitation of Morwood and Tony Djubiantono of the Indonesian Centre for Archaeology in Jakarta, Larson flew to Jakarta last fall to study the bones with her Stony Brook colleague William Jungers, who was to work on the lower limbs. The pair are among the handful of researchers who have studied the original specimens.

Larson found that the LB1 humeral head was in fact rotated only about 110 degrees. (No rotation would be expressed as 90 degrees.) Curious, she examined LB1's broken collarbone plus a shoulder blade from another individual.

Larson concluded that the upper arm and shoulder were oriented slightly differently in *H. floresiensis* than in living people. The shoulder blade was shrugged slightly forward, changing its articulation with the humerus and allowing the small humans to bend their elbows and work with their hands as we do. This slightly hunched posture would not have hampered the little people, except when it came to making long overhand throws: They would have been bad baseball pitchers, says Larson.

When Larson looked at other human fossils for comparison, she found another surprise: The only *H. erectus* skeleton known, the 1.55-million-year-old "Nariokotome boy" from Kenya, also has a relatively untwisted humerus, a feature not previously noted. Larson concluded that the evolution of the modern shoulder was a two-stage process and that *H. erectus* and *H. floresiensis* preserved the first step.

H. erectus expert G. Philip Rightmire of Binghamton University in New York, who works on fossils from Dmanisi, Georgia, supports this view. Larson's and

Jungers's analyses "make it clearer and clearer that *Homo floresiensis* is not some sort of dwarf modern human. This is a different species from us," he says.

In a separate talk, Jungers reported more unexpected findings. He was able to reconstruct the pelvis, which had been broken when the bones were moved to a competing lab in Indonesia (*Science*, 25 March 2005, p. 1848). Although previous publications had described the pelvis as similar to those of the much more primitive australopithecines, Jungers found that the orientation of the pelvic blades is modern. The observation adds weight to the notion that hobbits had *H. erectus*, rather than australopithecine, ancestry.

The skeleton was first described as female, although the competing Indonesian-Australian team described it as male in press accounts. Now Jungers says he is "agnostic" about its sex. He notes that limb bones from other individuals from Liang Bua are even smaller— "they make LB1 look like the Hulk," he says—raising the possibility that males and females differed in size, with LB1 in the role of big male.

More surprises are still to come. Jungers said in his talk that LB1 includes an essentially complete foot, something not identified previously, and hinted that the foot is extremely large. Indonesia's hobbits, like J. R. R. Tolkien's fictional creatures, may have trekked about on big hairy feet.

25

The Morning of the Modern Mind

Kate Wong

Kate Wong is editorial director of Scientific American.com.

As you read, consider the following questions:

An ongoing debate in anthropology concerns the age and nature of *Homo sapiens,* the species to which all modern humans belong. How old is our species? Opinions vary from around 200,000 years to 2 million years. Key to this issue is the question of what *defines* a member of our species, a modern human. Because anatomical and genetic data are inconclusive so far, much of the debate has centered on behavior: When, where, and how did we start to have modern intellectual and cognitive abilities? Do those abilities define our species, or do we share them with other hominid species? If that's the case, *are* they actually different species? In this selection, Kate Wong looks at the most recent data from archaeology and describes the various ways in which it has been interpreted.

1. What does it mean to say that authorities view the emergence of modern human behavior as either *revolution* or *evolution*?

2. What kinds of archaeological evidence have recently been described that are relevant to this debate?

3. How can we find evidence of "symbolically organized behavior, including language"?

4. Is there any indication that groups of humans considered to be species other than *H. sapiens* may have had some symbolic behavior?

CAPE TOWN, SOUTH AFRICA—Christopher Henshilwood empties a tiny plastic bag and hands me a square of worn blue cardstock to which 19 snail shells no larger than kernels of corn have been affixed in three horizontal rows. To the casual onlooker, they might well appear unremarkable, a handful of discarded mollusk armor, dull and gray with age. In fact, they may be more precious than the glittering contents of any velvet-lined Cartier case.

The shells, discovered in a cave called Blombos located 200 miles east of here, are perfectly matched in size, and each bears a hole in the same spot opposite the mouth, notes Henshilwood, an archaeologist at the University of Bergen in Norway. He believes they were collected and perforated by humans nearly 75,000 years ago to create a strand of lustrous, pearllike beads. If he is correct, these modest shells are humanity's crown jewels—the oldest unequivocal evidence of personal adornment to date and proof that our ancestors were thinking like us far earlier than is widely accepted.

A BEHAVIORAL BIG BANG

By most accounts, the origin of anatomically modern *Homo sapiens* was a singularly African affair. In 2003 the unveiling of fossils found in Herto, Ethiopia, revealed that this emergence had occurred by 160,000 years ago. And this past February researchers announced that they had redated *H. sapiens* remains from another Ethiopian site, Omo Kibish, potentially pushing the origin of our species back to 195,000 years ago.

Far less clear is when our kind became modern of mind. For the past two decades, the prevailing view has been that humanity underwent a behavioral revolution around 40,000 years ago. Scholars based this assessment primarily on the well-known cultural remains of Ice Age Europeans. In Europe, the relevant archaeological record is divided into the Middle Paleolithic (prior to around 40,000 years ago) and the Upper Paleolithic (from roughly 40,000 years ago onward), and the difference between the two could not be more striking. Middle Paleolithic people seem to have made mostly the same relatively simple stone tools humans had been producing for tens of thousands of years and not much else. The Upper Paleolithic, in contrast, ushered in a suite of sophisticated practices. Within a geologic blink of an eye, humans from the Rhône Valley to the Russian plain were producing advanced weaponry, forming long-distance trade networks, expressing themselves through art and music, and generally engaging in all manner of activities that archaeologists typically associate with modernity. It was, by all appearances, the ultimate Great Leap Forward.

Perhaps not coincidentally, it is during this Middle to Upper Paleolithic transition that humans of modern appearance had begun staking their claim on Europe, which until this point was strictly Neandertal territory. Although the identity of the makers of the earliest Upper Paleolithic artifacts is not known with certainty, because of a lack of human remains at the sites, they are traditionally assumed to have been anatomically modern *H. sapiens* rather than Neandertals. Some researchers have thus surmised that confrontation between the two populations awakened in the invaders a creative ability that had heretofore lain dormant.

Other specialists argue that the cultural explosion evident in Europe grew out of a shift that occurred somewhat earlier in Africa. Richard G. Klein of Stanford University, for one, contends that the abrupt change from the Middle to the Upper Paleolithic mirrors a transition that took place 5,000 to 10,000 years beforehand in Africa, where the comparative culture periods are termed the Middle and Later Stone Age. The impetus for this change, he theorizes, was not an encounter with another hominid type (for by this time in Africa, *H. sapiens* was free of competition with other human species) but rather a genetic mutation some 50,000 years ago that altered neural processes and thereby unleashed our forebears' powers of innovation.

Key evidence for this model, Klein says, comes from a site in central Kenya called Enkapune Ya Muto, the "twilight cave," that places the origin of the Later Stone Age at 45,000 to 50,000 years ago. There Stanley H. Ambrose of the University of Illinois and his team have uncovered obsidian knives, thumbnail-size scrapers and—most notably—tiny disk-shaped beads fashioned from ostrich eggshell in Later Stone Age levels dating back some 43,000 years. Strands of similar beads are still exchanged as gifts today among the !Kung San hunter-gatherers of Botswana. Ambrose posits that the ancient bead makers at Enkapune Ya Muto created them for the same reason: to foster good relationships with other groups as a hedge against hard times. If so, according to Klein, a genetically conferred ability to communicate through symbols—in concert with the cognitive prowess to conceive of better hunting technology and resource use—may have been what enabled our species finally, nearly 150,000 years after it originated, to set forth from its mother continent and conquer the world.

EVOLVED THINKING

- Archaeologists have traditionally envisioned *Homo sapiens* becoming modern of mind quickly and recently—sometime in the past 50,000 years, more than 100,000 years after attaining anatomical modernity.
- New discoveries in Africa indicate that many of the elements of modern human behavior can be traced much farther back in time.
- The finds suggest that our species had a keen intellect at its inception and exploited that creativity in archaeologically visible ways only when it was advantageous to do so—when population size increased, for instance.
- *H. sapiens* may not have been the only hominid to possess such advanced cognition: some artifacts hint that Neandertals were comparably gifted.

SEEDS OF CHANGE

In recent years, however, a small but growing number of archaeologists have eschewed the big bang theories of the origin of culture in favor of a fundamentally different model. Proponents believe that there was no lag between body and brain. Rather, they contend, modern human behavior emerged over a long period in a process more aptly described as evolution than revolution. And some workers believe that cognitive modernity may have evolved in other species, such as the Neandertals, as well.

The notion that our species' peerless creativity might have primeval roots is not new. For years, scientists have known of a handful of objects that, taken at face value, suggest that humans were engaging in modern practices long before *H. sapiens* first painted a cave wall in France. They include three 400,000-year-old wooden throwing spears from Schöningen, Germany; a 233,000-year-old putative figurine from the site of Berekhat Ram in Israel; a 60,000-year-old piece of flint incised with concentric arcs from Quneitra, Israel; two 100,000-year-old fragments of notched bone from South Africa's Klasies River Mouth Cave; and a polished plate of mammoth tooth from Tata in Hungary, dated to between 50,000 and 100,000 years ago. Many archaeologists looked askance at these remains, however, noting that their age was uncertain or that their significance was unclear. Any sign of advanced intellect that did seem legitimately ancient was explained away as a one-off accomplishment, the work of a genius among average Joes.

That position has become harder to defend in the face of the growing body of evidence in Africa that our forebears' mental metamorphosis began well before the start of the Later Stone Age. In a paper entitled "The Revolution That Wasn't: A New Interpretation of the Origin of Modern Human Behavior," published in the *Journal of Human Evolution* in 2000, Sally McBrearty of the University of Connecticut and Alison S. Brooks of George Washington University laid out their case. Many of the components of modern human behavior said to emerge in lockstep between 40,000 and 50,000 years ago, they argued, are visible tens of thousands of years earlier at Middle Stone Age locales. Moreover, they appear not as a package but piecemeal, at sites far-flung in time and space.

At three sites in Katanda, Democratic Republic of the Congo, Brooks and John Yellen of the Smithsonian Institution have found elaborate barbed harpoons carved from bone that they say date to at least 80,000 years ago, which would place them firmly within the Middle Stone Age. These artifacts exhibit a level of sophistication comparable to that seen in 25,000-year-old harpoons from Europe, not only in terms of the complexity of the weapon design but the choice of raw material: the use of bone and ivory in tool manufacture was not thought to have occurred until the Later Stone Age and Upper Paleolithic. In addition, remains of giant Nile catfish have turned up with some of the Katanda harpoons, suggesting to the excavators that people were going there when the fish were spawning—the kind of seasonal mapping of resources previously thought to characterize only later humans.

Other Middle Stone Age sites, such as ≠Gi (the "≠" denotes a click sound) in Botswana's Kalahari Desert, which is dated to 77,000 years ago, have yielded butchered animal remains that have put paid to another oft-made claim, namely, that these ancient people were not as competent at hunting as Later Stone Age folks. The residents at ≠Gi appear to have regularly pursued such large and dangerous prey as zebra and Cape warthog. And Hilary J. Deacon of Stellenbosch University has suggested that at sites such as South Africa's Klasies River Mouth Cave humans

more than 60,000 years ago were deliberately burning grassland to encourage the growth of nutritious tubers, which are known to germinate after exposure to fire.

Some discoveries hint that certain alleged aspects of behavioral modernity arose even before the genesis of *H. sapiens*. Last summer excavations by McBrearty's team at a site near Lake Baringo in Kenya turned up stone blades—once a hallmark of the Upper Paleolithic material cultures—more than 510,000 years old. At a nearby locality, in levels dated to at least 285,000 years ago, her team has uncovered vast quantities of red ochre (a form of iron ore) and grindstones for processing it, signaling to McBrearty that the Middle Stone Age people at Baringo were using the pigment for symbolic purposes—to decorate their bodies, for instance—just as many humans do today. (Baringo is not the only site to furnish startlingly ancient evidence of ochre processing—Twin Rivers Cave in Zambia has yielded similar material dating back to more than 200,000 years ago.) And 130,000-year-old tool assemblages from Mumba Rock Shelter in Tanzania include flakes crafted from obsidian that came from a volcanic flow about 200 miles away—compelling evidence that the hominids who made the implements traded with other groups for the exotic raw material.

Critics, however, have dismissed these finds on the basis of uncertainties surrounding, in some cases, the dating and, in others, the intent of the makers. Ochre, for one, may have been used as mastic for attaching blades to wooden handles or as an antimicrobial agent for treating animal hides, skeptics note.

SMART FOR THEIR AGE

It is against this backdrop of long-standing controversy that the discoveries at Blombos have come to light. Henshilwood discovered the archaeological deposits at Blombos Cave in 1991 while looking for much younger coastal hunter-gatherer sites to excavate for his Ph.D. Located near the town of Still Bay in South Africa's southern Cape, on a bluff overlooking the Indian Ocean, the cave contained few of the Holocene artifacts he was looking for but appeared rich in Middle Stone Age material. As such, it was beyond the scope of his research at the time. In 1997, however, he raised the money to return to Blombos to begin excavating in earnest. Since then, Henshilwood and his team have unearthed an astonishing assemblage of sophisticated tools and symbolic objects and in so doing have sketched a portrait of a long-ago people who thought like us.

From levels dated by several methods to 75,000 years ago have come an array of advanced implements, including 40 bone tools, several of which are finely worked awls, and hundreds of bifacial points made of silcrete and other difficult-to-shape stones, which the Blombos people could have used to hunt the antelopes and other game that roamed the area. Some of the points are just an inch long, suggesting that they may have been employed as projectiles. And the bones of various species of deep-sea fish—the oldest of which may be more than 130,000 years old—reveal that the Blombos people had the equipment required to harvest creatures in excess of 80 pounds from the ocean.

Hearths for cooking indicate that the cave was a living site, and teeth representing both adults and children reveal that a family group dwelled there. But there are so many of the stone points, and such a range in their quality, that Henshilwood wonders whether the occupants may have also had a workshop in the tiny cave, wherein masters taught youngsters how to make the tools.

They may have passed along other traditions as well. The most spectacular material to emerge from Blombos is that which demonstrates that its occupants thought symbolically. To date, the team has recovered one piece of incised bone, nine slabs of potentially engraved red ochre and dozens of the tiny beads—all from the same 75,000-year-old layers that yielded the tools. In addition, sediments that may date back to more than 130,000 years ago contain vast quantities of processed ochre, some in crayon form.

Scientists may never know exactly what meaning the enigmatic etchings held for their makers. But it is clear that they were important to them. Painstaking analyses of two of the engraved ochres, led by Francesco d'Errico of the University of Bordeaux in France, reveal that the rust-colored rocks were hand-ground on one side to produce a facet that was then etched repeatedly with a stone point. On the largest ochre, bold lines frame and divide the crosshatched design.

Bead manufacture was likewise labor-intensive. Henshilwood believes the marine tick shells, which belong to the *Nassarius kraussianus* snail, were collected from either of two estuaries, located 12 miles from the cave, that still exist today. Writing in the January issue of the *Journal of Human Evolution*, Henshilwood, d'Errico and their colleagues report that experimental reconstruction of the process by which the shells were perforated indicates that the precocious jewelers used bone points to punch through the lip of the shell from the inside out—a technique that commonly broke the shells when attempted by team members. Once pierced, the beads appear to have been strung, as evidenced by the wear facets ringing the perforations, and traces of red ochre on the shells hint that they may have lain against skin painted with the pigment.

In the case for cognitive sophistication in the Middle Stone Age, "Blombos is the smoking gun," McBrearty declares. But Henshilwood has not convinced everyone of his interpretation. Doubts have come from Randall White of New York University, an expert on Upper Paleolithic body ornaments. He suspects that the perforations and apparent wear facets on the *Nassarius* shells are the result of natural processes, not human handiwork.

HERE TODAY, GONE TOMORROW

If read correctly, however, the remarkable discoveries at Blombos offer weighty evidence that at least one group of humans possessed a modern mind-set long before 50,000 years ago, which may in some ways make previous claims for early behavioral modernity easier to swallow. So, too, may recent finds from sites such as Diepkloof in South Africa's Western Cape, which has produced pieces of incised ostrich eggshell dated to around 60,000 years ago, and Loiyangalani in Tanzania, where workers have found ostrich eggshell beads estimated to be on the order of 70,000 years old.

Yet it remains the case that most Middle Stone Age sites show few or none of the traits researchers use to identify fully developed cognition in the archaeological record. Several other locales in South Africa, for example, have yielded the sophisticated bifacial points but no evidence of symbolic behavior. Of course, absence of evidence is not evidence of absence, as prehistorians are fond of saying. It is possible the people who lived at these sites did make art and decorate their bodies, but only their stone implements have survived.

Perhaps the pattern evident thus far in the African record—that of ephemeral glimpses of cognitive modernity before the start of the Later Stone Age and ubiquitous indications of it after that—is just an artifact of preservational bias or the relatively small number of African sites excavated so far. Then again, maybe these fits and starts are exactly what archaeologists should expect to see if anatomically modern *H. sapiens* possessed the capacity for modern human behavior from the get-go but tapped that potential only when it provided an advantage, as many gradualists believe.

The circumstances most likely to elicit advanced cultural behaviors, McBrearty and others hypothesize, were those related to increased population size. The presence of more people put more pressure on resources, forcing our ancestors to devise cleverer ways to obtain food and materials for toolmaking, she submits. More people also raised the chances of encounters among groups. Beads, body paint and even stylized tool manufacture may have functioned as indicators of an individual's membership and status in a clan, which would have been especially important when laying claim to resources in short supply. Symbolic objects may have also served as a social lubricant during stressful times, as has been argued for the beads from Enkapune Ya Muto.

"You have to make good with groups around you because that's how you're going to get partners," Henshilwood observes. "If a gift exchange system is going on, that's how you're maintaining good relations." Indeed, gift giving may explain why some of the tools at Blombos are so aesthetically refined. A beautiful tool is not going to be a better weapon, he remarks, it is going to function as a symbolic artifact, a keeper of the peace.

Conversely, when the population dwindled, these advanced practices subsided—perhaps because the people who engaged in them died out or because in the absence of competition they simply did not pay off and were therefore forgotten. The Tasmanians provide a recent example of this relationship: when Europeans arrived in the region in the 17th century, they encountered a people whose material culture was simpler than even those of the Middle Paleolithic, consisting of little more than basic stone flake tools. Indeed, from an archaeological standpoint, these remains would have failed nearly all tests of modernity that are commonly applied to prehistoric sites. Yet the record shows that several thousand years ago, the Tasmanians possessed a much more complex tool kit, one that included bone tools, fishing nets, and bows and arrows. It seems that early Tasmanians had all the latest gadgetry before rising sea levels cut the island off from the mainland 10,000 years ago but lost the technology over the course of their small group's separation from the much larger Aboriginal Australian population.

This might be why South African sites between 60,000 and 30,000 years old so rarely seem to bear the modern signature: demographic reconstructions suggest that the human population in Africa crashed around 60,000 years ago because of a precipitous drop in temperature. Inferring capacity from what people produced is inherently problematic, White observes. Medieval folks doubtless had the brainpower to go to the moon, he notes. Just because they did not does not mean they were not our cognitive equals. "At any given moment," White reflects, "people don't fulfill their entire potential."

SYMBOL-MINDED

The debate over when, where and how our ancestors became cognitively modern is complicated by the fact that experts disagree over what constitutes modern human behavior in the first place. In the strictest sense, the term encompasses every facet of culture evident today—from agriculture to the iPod. To winnow the definition into something more useful to archaeologists, many workers employ the list of behavioral traits that distinguish the Middle and Upper Paleolithic in Europe. Others use the material cultures of modern and recent hunter-gatherers as a guide. Ultimately, whether or not a set of remains is deemed evidence of modernity can hinge on the preferred definition of the evaluator.

Taking that into consideration, some experts instead advocate focusing on the origin and evolution of arguably the most important characteristic of modern human societies: symbolically organized behavior, including language. "The ability to store symbols externally, outside of the human brain, is the key to everything we do today," Henshilwood asserts. A symbol-based system of communication might not be a perfect proxy for behavioral modernity in the archaeological record, as the Tasmanian example illustrates, but at least researchers seem to accept it as a defining aspect of the human mind as we know it, if not *the* defining aspect.

It remains to be seen just how far back in time symbolic culture arose. And discoveries outside of Africa and Europe are helping to flesh out the story. Controversial evidence from the rock shelters of Malakunanja II and Nauwalabila I in Australia's Northern Territory, for instance, suggests that people had arrived there by 60,000 years ago. To reach the island continent, emigrants traveling from southeastern Asia would have to have built sturdy watercraft and navigated a minimum of 50 miles of open water, depending on the sea level. Scholars mostly agree that any human capable of managing this feat must have been fully modern. And in Israel's Qafzeh Cave, Erella Hovers of the Hebrew University of Jerusalem and her team have recovered dozens of pieces of red ochre near 92,000-year-old graves of *H. sapiens*. They believe the lumps of pigment were heated in hearths to achieve a specific hue of scarlet and then used in funerary rituals.

Other finds raise the question of whether symbolism is unique to anatomically modern humans. Neandertal sites commonly contain evidence of systematic ochre processing, and toward the end of their reign in Europe, in the early Upper Paleolithic, Neandertals apparently developed their own cultural tradition of manufacturing body ornaments, as evidenced by the discovery of pierced teeth and other objects at sites such as Quinçay and the Grotte du Renne at Arcy-sur-Cure in France [see "Who Were the Neandertals?" by Kate Wong; SCIENTIFIC AMERICAN, April 2000]. They also interred their dead. The symbolic nature of this behavior in their case is debated because the burials lack grave goods. But this past April at the annual meeting of the Paleoan-thropology Society, Jill Cook of the British Museum reported that digital microscopy of remains from Krapina Rock Shelter in Croatia bolsters the hypothe-sis that Neandertals were cleaning the bones of the deceased, possibly in a kind of mortuary ritual, as opposed to defleshing them for food.

Perhaps the ability to think symbolically evolved independently in Neandertals and anatomically mod-ern *H. sapiens*. Or maybe it arose before the two groups set off on separate evolutionary trajectories, in a primeval common ancestor. "I can't prove it, but I bet [*Homo*] *heidelbergensis* [a hominid that lived as much as 400,000 years ago] was capable of this," White speculates.

For his part, Henshilwood is betting that the dawn of symbol-driven thinking lies in the Middle Stone Age. As this article was going to press, he and his team were undertaking their ninth field season at Blombos. By the end of that period they will have sifted through a third of the cave's 75,000-year-old deposits, leaving the rest to future archaeologists with as yet unforeseen advances in excavation and dating techniques. "We don't really need to go further in these levels at Blom-bos," Henshilwood says. "We need to find other sites now that date to this time period." He is confident that they will succeed in that endeavor, having already identified a number of very promising locales in the coastal De Hoop Nature Reserve, about 30 miles west of Blombos.

Sitting in the courtyard of the African Heritage Research Institute pondering the dainty snail shells in my hand, I consider what they might have represented to the Blombos people. In some ways, it is difficult to imagine our ancient ancestors setting aside basic concerns of food, water, predators and shelter to make such baubles. But later, perusing a Cape Town jew-eler's offerings—from cross pendants cast in gold to diamond engagement rings—it is harder still to con-ceive of *Homo sapiens* behaving any other way. The trinkets may have changed somewhat since 75,000 years ago, but the all-important messages they encode are probably still the same.

MORE TO EXPLORE

The Revolution That Wasn't: A New Interpretation of the Origin of Modern Human Behavior. Sally McBrearty and Alison S. Brooks in *Journal of Human Evolution*, Vol. 39, No. 5, pages 453–563; November 2000.

Emergence of Modern Human Behavior: Middle Stone Age Engravings from South Africa. Christopher S. Hen-shilwood et al. in *Science*, Vol. 295, pages 1278–1280; February 15, 2002.

The Dawn of Human Culture. Richard G. Klein, with Blake Edgar. John Wiley & Sons, 2002.

The Invisible Frontier: A Multiple Species Model for the Origin of Behavioral Modernity. Francesco d'Errico in *Evolutionary Anthropology*, Vol. 12, No. 4, pages 188–202; August 5, 2003.

The Origin of Modern Human Behavior: Critique of the Models and Their Test Implications. Christopher S. Henshilwood and Curtis W. Marean in *Current Anthro-pology*, Vol. 44, No. 5, pages 627–651: December 2003.

Prehistoric Art: The Symbolic Journey of Humankind. Randall White. Harry N. Abrams, 2003.

Nassarius Kraussianus **Shell Beads from Blombos Cave: Evidence for Symbolic Behavior in the Middle Stone Age.** Francesco d'Errico, Christopher Henshilwood, Marian Vanhaeren and Karen van Niekerk in *Journal of Human Evolution*, Vol. 48, No. 1, pages 3–24; January 2005.

PART 7

The Bioanthropology of Modern Human Populations

Hominid evolution did not end with the coming of modern *Homo sapiens*. Although all 6 billion of us on earth today belong to a single species, and although our major adaptive mechanism—and our major adaptations—are cultural, the processes of biological evolution still affect our species and will continue to do so. Moreover, the processes of biological and cultural change can and do interact with one another in both directions. Thus, the anthropological study of the biology of modern humans and human populations is an important one.

We begin with Donald K. Grayson's "Differential Mortality and the Donner Party Disaster." Here, within this fascinating true-life "western" tale of pioneer wagon trains, death, and cannibalism, lies a perfect example of bioanthropology applied to a recent population.

In "Skin Deep," Nina G. Jablonski and George Chaplin describe new research that attempts to explain the evolution and distribution of that most obvious yet vexing of variable human traits—skin color. Contrary to other explanations, theirs focuses on the relationship between ultraviolet radiation, skin color, and key nutrients important to reproduction.

In "Evolution and the Origins of Disease," Randolph M. Nesse and George C. Williams describe the application of evolutionary theory, especially the process of natural selection, to the search for explanations of our vulnerabilities to disease, a new field called Darwinian medicine.

SUGGESTED WEBSITES FOR FURTHER STUDY

http://anthro.palomar.edu/adapt/adapt_4.htm
http://www.utahcrossroads.org/DonnerParty

26

Differential Mortality
and the Donner Party Disaster

Donald K. Grayson

*Donald K. Grayson is a professor of anthropology at the University of Washington.
He specializes in the analysis of human adaptations to past environments. His work
has focused on the arid regions of the American West and southwestern France.*

One of the most famous, and chilling, stories to emerge from this country's period of westward expansion is the tale of the Donner Party, a group of eighty-seven pioneers who left Illinois in 1846 and attempted to cross the Sierra Nevada to California. Trapped by deep snows in the mountains, the remaining eighty-two members (five had already died) had no choice but to camp for the winter. By the next spring, when rescuers reached them, only forty-seven had survived. In the face of almost certain starvation, some had resorted to eating the bodies of the dead. Although this story might seem far removed from the concerns of biological anthropology, it in fact provides a good and interesting example of how population data are organized and of how the principles of evolution may be applied to understanding something about a recent human group. In this selection, Grayson describes the Donner Party in terms of the common parameters of human demography and then looks to see whether our notions of natural selection can be applied to account for who in the party survived and who did not.

As you read, consider the following questions:

1. What factors accounted for the differential mortality between men and women of the Donner Party?

2. How does an individual's sex affect his or her response to cold? How does age relate to cold response?

3. Did the facts about differential mortality among members of the Donner Party coincide with predictions from evolutionary theory?

4. In what ways were human social factors also involved in influencing who died and who survived?

The story of the Donner Party combines powerful American themes. The beginning of the tale is immersed in the romance of the western frontier and in the American dream of improving life by taking bold steps. The end of the tale, in contrast, is awash in death and cannibalism. No wonder Americans learn the story as children; no Grimm's fairy tale can match it. However, detailed analyses of the patterning of Donner Party deaths suggest that the story is even better read as a piece of biology than as a piece of history. Virtually all aspects of Donner Party mortality can now be explained by our knowledge of the factors that cause differential mortality in human societies. The differential fates of these emigrants show us natural selection in action.

In 1845, Lansford W. Hastings published a remarkable piece of propaganda. *The Emigrants' Guide to Oregon and California* was not, as the title might lead the unwary to assume, an impartial discussion of the overland routes heading west from what was then the United States. This was a book with a purpose: to lure emigrants away from Oregon and to California. The route to Oregon from Fort Hall, in what is now southern Idaho (Figure 1), was, said Hastings, "but one continued succession of high mountains, stupendous cliffs, and deep, frightful caverns." In contrast, the road to California "lies through alternate plains, prairies, and valleys, and over hills, amid lofty mountains."[1]

From *Evolutionary Anthropology*, Volume 2, No. 5, 1993. Copyright © 1993 Wiley-Liss, Inc. This material is used by permission of Wiley-Liss, Inc., a subsidiary of John Wiley & Sons, Inc. (excluding map and tables)

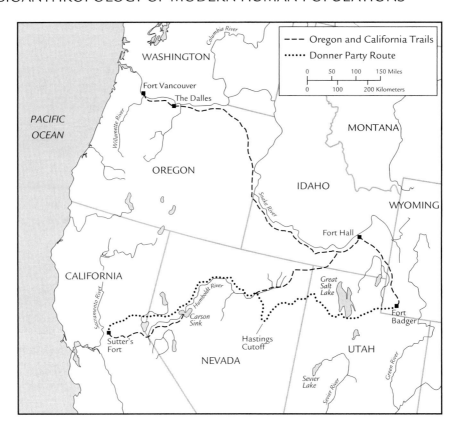

FIGURE 1 Overland trails to Oregon and California during the 1850s; the Donner Party route is indicated by the dotted line.

How foolish it would be to risk material goods and life itself to reach Oregon when wondrous California was so much easier a target.

Prior to the publication of Hastings' book, three attempts had been made to take wagons across something resembling his "California route." In the attempts of 1841 and 1843, the people arrived safely but the wagons were left on the trail. In 1844, the Stevens Party negotiated some of their wagons across the Sierra Nevada, but the effort required was enormous. The party reached what is now Donner Lake on the east slope of the mountains in mid-November, but the last of the group did not reach the Sacramento Valley until March 1, 1845.[2]

The most famous of those who took what came to be called the California Trail, however, were not these vanguard pioneers, but those who followed soon after, drawn in by Hastings. This is the group now referred to as the Donner Party.

THE DONNER PARTY ROUTE

In mid-April 1846, 22 people belonging to three families—those of George and Tamsen Donner, Jacob and Elizabeth Donner, and James and Margaret Reed—left

Springfield, Illinois, heading west for a new life. By July 27, they had reached Fort Badger in southwestern Wyoming, where they made the final decision to follow Hastings' route to California. Leaving July 31, they headed west from Fort Badger to enter the Wasatch Range of northeastern Utah. Here, the party reached its full size: 87 people, 20 wagons, and a wide array of livestock. It was also here that they encountered their first significant difficulties, since the Wasatch Range presented a series of narrow, rugged canyons filled with dense vegetation. Cutting a road through thick aspen, willows, and shrubs, the group finally emerged into Great Salt Lake Valley on August 22. A critical three weeks had been spent traversing what they had believed would be a shortcut.

After passing south of Great Salt Lake, the party had to cross the Great Salt Lake Desert, some 130 waterless and often salt-encrusted kilometers. The quickest of them made it in three days, the slowest in four, but the crossing took its toll. Four wagons had to be abandoned, an estimated 36 cattle were lost, and a week was spent reorganizing and recuperating at the eastern base of the Pilot Range on the Utah-Nevada border.[3]

From here to the Sierra Nevada it was, finally, smooth sailing. Following another of Hastings' shortcuts, the group headed south along the east flank of the

Ruby Mountains, then north along the west flank of the same range. At this point, they met the Humboldt River, which they followed to its sink in western Nevada. From Humboldt Sink, they headed directly to the Sierra Nevada, the last great impediment between them and Sacramento Valley.

By now, however, it was late October, and it was too late for them. Moving up the east flank of the Sierra Nevada, they encountered snows of such depth that they were unable to either go forward or turn back. By November 1, they had established two camps, one adjacent to Donner Lake, another about 8 km to the northeast.[4] Not until April 21, 1847 was the last survivor rescued. By then, however, 40 of the 87 had died, 35 as a direct result of the forced encampment in the Sierran snows.

THE DEMOGRAPHIC STRUCTURE OF THE DONNER PARTY

Because of the intense interest generated by their ordeal, a good deal of information on the geographic origin, age, and sex of the members of the Donner Party is available, much of which was recorded during the nineteenth century. It is known, for instance, that of the 87 people involved, 47 came from Illinois, 16 from Missouri, and 10 from Iowa. The sex of each individual is known, as is the age, or an estimate of the age, of all of the party members except one.

As a result, it is possible to compare the distribution of age and sex in the Donner Party to that in the population from which this sample of emigrants was drawn. Table 1 shows the number of "white" residents of Illinois by age class as reported in the 1850 (7th) United States census, as well as the distribution of males and females across those age classes. Table 2 provides comparable data for the Donner Party. (Details of some of the following analyses have been presented elsewhere,[5] but here I have revised the ages of Patrick Breen and Mrs. Wolfinger using new information provided by King.[6])

Statistical analysis of these data shows that the general age structures of the Donner Party and the "white" population of Illinois in 1850 are quite similar. However, individuals between 15 and 19 years of age are slightly under-represented in the Donner Party, and those between 20 and 29 years are slightly over-represented (both at $p = 0.06$).

There are no significant differences between the 1850 population of Illinois and the Donner Party in the distribution of females across age categories. Males, however, are greatly over-represented among the emigrants. This over-representation is highest for males between 60 and 69, because of the presence of George (62) and Jacob (65) Donner, but it is also pronounced for men between 20 and 39 years of age. This surfeit of men is no surprise, for men constituted a disproportionate number of western emigrants in general.[7] In fact, while the proportion of Donner Party males between 20 and 39 years of age (70.0%) is far higher than that in the population from which these males were drawn (45.9%), it is almost identical to the proportion of "white" males in Oregon in 1850 (72.9%). Although the proportion of young men in the Donner Party was

TABLE 1   Age and Sex Distribution of "White" Illinois Residents in the 7th U.S. Census by 7th Census Age Class

Age Class	Total	%	% Male	% Female
1–4	141,360	16.72	49.11	50.89
5–9	129,905	15.37	48.88	51.12
10–14	112,860	13.35	48.11	51.89
15–19	92,698	10.97	49.34	50.66
20–29	150,044	17.75	47.03	52.97
30–39	102,426	12.12	44.17	55.83
40–49	62,072	7.34	44.60	55.40
50–59	33,828	4.00	43.47	56.53
60–69	14,410	1.71	44.69	55.31
70–79	4,577	0.54	44.79	55.21
80–89	938	0.11	46.27	53.73
90–99	109	0.01	49.54	50.46
100+	15	0.00	33.33	66.67

TABLE 2   Distribution of Males and Females in the Donner Party by 7th Census Age Class

Age Class	N of Males	N of Females	%	% Males	% Females
1–4	7	9	18.61	43.75	56.25
5–9	7	4	12.79	63.64	36.36
10–14	8	5	15.12	61.54	38.46
15–19	2	2	4.65	50.00	50.00
20–29	15	7	25.58	68.18	31.82
30–39	6	2	9.30	75.00	25.00
40–49	2	4	6.98	33.33	66.66
50–59	2	1	3.49	66.66	33.33
60–69	3	0	3.49	100.00	00.00
?	1				
TOTALS	53	34			

distinctly different from that in the population from which these people came, it was distinctly similar to that in the population toward which it was heading.

PREDICTING DONNER PARTY DEATHS

As I mentioned, 40 of the 87 members of the Donner Party died after the group had reached its full size in the Wasatch Range. Of these deaths, 35 occurred after the winter camps had been established in the Sierra Nevada. Although there is no way of knowing the precise cause of death in these 35 cases, cold or starvation or both were clearly to blame. Given that the party consisted of 53 males and 34 females ranging in age from 1 to 65, traveling either alone or in family groups of variable size, can we use general patterns of human mortality to predict who should have died and who should have survived?

THE WEAKER SEX

"Frailty," said Hamlet, "thy name is woman." Measured in terms of mortality, however, frailty is a decidedly male attribute: in most contemporary settings, males die younger than females. In the 35 developed countries analyzed by Lopez,[8] a newborn girl can anticipate an average of 6.4 more years of life than a newborn boy, the difference ranging from 3.9 years in Albania to 10.0 years in the Soviet Union. In Africa as a whole, female life expectancy exceeds that of males by 6.8%.[9] In the United States in 1980, newborn girls could expect to live 77.5 years, 7 years more than newborn boys.[10] The sex differential in mortality has increased dramatically in developed countries during the twentieth century. In the United States in 1920, this differential was on the

order of 2 years, a figure identical to that for Colombia in the mid-1960s.[11–15] However, the differential itself is not a modern phenomenon. For instance, females also outlived males in mid-nineteenth-century America (Table 1). Although it is too much to claim that "women outlive men . . . in all societies"[16]—India, for instance, is a contemporary exception[13]—this statement is at least as accurate as the generalization that, in hunter-gatherer societies, it is the men who hunt and the women who gather.[11,18]

Not only can males expect to have shorter lives than females, but they can also expect to have higher mortality rates at every age, including infancy.[10,14,19] They may even die in greater numbers before birth, although the evidence for this is in dispute.[14,16,20,21] Almost no matter where we look, males are at a longevity disadvantage compared to females.

This difference stems from a diverse set of proximate causes. Males die at a much greater rate than do females from ischemic heart disease,[14,16,22,23] homicide,[24] suicide,[10] motor vehicle and other accidents,[8,25] and a wide variety of infectious diseases, including pneumonia, influenza, and septicemia.[11,19,26] Males are even more susceptible than females to hookworm infection.[27] Indeed, it turns out that human males drop like flies. In fact, they drop very much like house flies (*Musca domestica*), one of many other species in which females outlive males.[28]

Efforts to understand why these proximate causes differentially remove males continue.[29] It is clear, however, that biology is behind nearly all of the longevity gap. Biochemical differences have, for instance, been implicated in the greater male susceptibility to both ischemic heart disease and infectious disease.[11,12,14–16] In addition, in a study of mentally retarded adults who had had the misfortune of being institutionalized at a time when castration was considered an acceptable method of controlling behavior, Hamilton and Mestler found that the life expectancy of castrated males was 13.6 years greater than that of intact males.[30]

Those who study the sex differential in human mortality routinely distinguish between biological and behavioral causes of that differential. Some even argue that if the behavioral causes were eliminated, little difference would remain between the age-specific mortality rates of the sexes.[19] In addition to tobacco smoking, these arguments target homicide, suicide, and accidents, especially motor vehicle accidents, as behavioral causes of death among males.

On the other hand, a substantial body of anthropological, biological, and psychological literature suggests that many of the differences that are drawn between behavior and biology in this realm are artificial. Risk-taking and aggressive behavior are almost universal male attributes. Cross-cultural studies show that even though levels of male aggression vary substantially from society to society, young boys are routinely more aggressive than young girls within particular societies.[31] In addition, females routinely participate in activities that are low in risk compared to those males engage in, just as predicted by evolutionary biology.[32–36] Insofar as these differences are caused by sex hormones,[37–40] the sex differential in mortality resulting from such events as automobile accidents, homicides, and suicides is as biological in origin as biochemically-induced ischemic heart disease.[16] The argument that without gender differences in behavior, the sex differential in mortality would not exist, differs little from arguing that if the sexes were the same, mortality would be the same.

Under usual conditions, then, males are shorter-lived than females and suffer greater mortality across all age classes. What might be expected to happen to this basal pattern under conditions of famine and extreme cold?

Once again, the advantage seems to go to females. Rivers has pointed out that a series of factors should make females less vulnerable to starvation than males: they are smaller (by approximately 17% of body weight[41]); they have a higher percentage of body fat (roughly 27%, compared to about 15% in males, though the absolute figures vary from population to population);[42,43] and, after about the age of five years, they have a lower basal metabolic rate. As a result, males have higher nutrient and energy requirements than do females. Stini, for example, noted that a 70-kg man engaged in moderate physical activity will expend about 300 kcal per hour, 60 kcal more than a woman engaged in the same level of activity.[46] In addition, males use a greater proportion of body protein to meet energy requirements than do females.[47]

All other things being equal, it follows that females, especially adult females, should be more robust in the face of starvation than males, especially adult males, should be. Rivers argues that a higher proportion of females than males may die in any given episode of famine because of "male discrimination" against them.[44,45] Because they are larger and more aggressive, men gain differential access to resources, thus reducing their mortality while increasing the mortality suffered by women. In situations in which both sexes share resources, starvation-induced mortality should differentially remove males from any given human population.

Of the many factors that may play a role in causing differential responses to cold by males and females, subcutaneous fat and body mass seem to be the most important, although regulatory differences stemming from the hypothalamus may also play a role.[41]

Not only do women have a higher proportion of body fat, but a larger proportion of that fat is distributed subcutaneously. For instance, in a study of 214 Japanese men and women, Hattori and his colleagues found the women to have a greater absolute amount of fat (11.4 kg average, compared to 7.7 kg for men), a greater relative amount of fat (20.9% versus 12.4%), and a higher proportion of fat distributed subcutaneously (62.6% versus 53.7%).[43] Poorly vascularized, subcutaneous fat is an effective insulator. Accordingly, several studies have shown that when inactive individuals are exposed to cold, those with greater amounts of subcutaneous fat undergo smaller reductions in core temperature and smaller increases in metabolic rate.[49–51]

Women also maintain a lower skin temperature in response to cold than men do. It is frequently maintained that this difference is a result of the greater insulation provided by body fat,[53,54] but not all studies support this conclusion.[55] No matter what the explanation, however, women's lower skin temperature decreases the temperature differential between body surface and air temperatures, and thus decreases the rate at which body heat is lost.

While the amount and distribution of body fat work in favor of females, body mass would seem to have the opposite effect. Body mass tracks muscle mass, and muscles produce heat when active. As a result, larger-bodied individuals not only have greater thermal inertia, but can also produce more heat than smaller-bodied individuals. In addition, smaller people have a greater surface area/mass ratio; as a result they can lose more heat to the environment than can larger people. Accordingly, it has been argued that women are at a great disadvantage in the cold.[56] Nonetheless, empirical studies have repeatedly shown that under cold conditions, men undergo

TABLE 3   Donner Party Members: Sex and Survivorship by 7th Census Age Class

Age Class	Males: Survived?			Females: Survived?			Totals	% No
	Yes	No	% No	Yes	No	% No		
1–4 (1)[a]	2	5	71.4	4	5	55.6	16	62.5
5–9 (2)	5	2	28.6	4		0.0	11	18.2
10–14 (3)	6	2	25.0	5		0.0	13	15.4
15–19 (4)	1	1	50.0	2		0.0	4	25.0
20–29 (5)	5	10	66.6	6	1	14.3	22	50.0
30–39 (6)	2	4	66.6	2		0.0	8	50.0
40–49 (7)	1	1	50.0	1	3	75.0	6	66.7
50–59 (8)	1	1	50.0		1	100.0	3	66.7
60–69 (9)		3	100.0				3	100.0
?		1					1	
TOTALS	23	30	56.6	24	10	29.4	87	45.0

[a]Numbers in parentheses used to identify age classes in Figure 2.

greater core temperature reductions than do women while maintaining higher skin temperatures, making it fairly clear that men are at a disadvantage in cold settings.

What of the old and very young? In normal situations, relatively high death rates characterize both the oldest and youngest members of human societies. Mortality is generally high between the ages of 1 and 5 years, then it decreases; above the age of about 35 it begins to rise, becoming increasingly higher among older adults.[57]

Conditions of famine or cold, or both, exacerbate this pattern. Young children and older adults routinely suffer greater mortality under starvation conditions than they do when nutrition is adequate,[45] and a variety of studies has shown that these same age groups are far more prone to death from hypothermia than are people of other ages. Young children, for instance, have smaller nutrient and energy stores than do adults;[45] older people are metabolically less responsive to cold; they maintain higher skin temperatures in cold situations; and they are less able to respond to heat loss by vasoconstriction.[51,58–61] The result is that high mortality among the oldest and youngest members of a human population is to be expected under conditions of famine or extreme cold, or both.

What does all this lead us to expect for the Donner Party? Clearly, we should expect that the oldest and youngest members of the group failed to survive. We should also expect that males died not only in greater numbers than females, but sooner.

DONNER PARTY MORTALITY

This, in fact, is exactly what happened. Table 3 provides death and survivorship statistics for the Donner Party by age class. Figure 2 shows mortality rates by age class. Three aspects of these statistics stand out dramatically. First, death fell most heavily on the youngest (ages 1–4, 62.5%) and oldest (ages 50–69, 83.3%) members of the group. In fact, of the nine people (five men, four women) who were 45 years old or older, only Patrick Breen (51) and James Reed (46) survived. Reed, significantly, did not have to deal with the rigors of the forced Sierran encampment. Expelled from the group on October 5 while the party was still along the Humboldt River, Reed crossed the Sierra Nevada alone, well before the snows fell. Later, he assisted in the rescue attempts mounted from Sacramento Valley.

In general, whether male or female, Donner Party survivors were, on average, younger than those who died. Surviving females averaged 15.8 years of age, 6.1 years less than those who died; surviving males averaged 18.2 years of age, 6.2 years less than the average age of those who died (Figure 3). The oldest and youngest members of the Donner Party, then, underwent severe attrition, just as expected from general considerations of human mortality.

In addition, and again as expected, death fell most heavily on the male members of the group. Of the 53 males, 30 (56.6%) succumbed, as compared to 10 (29.4%) of the 34 females. That is, males died at nearly twice the rate of females, and at higher rates across most age groups (Figure 2).

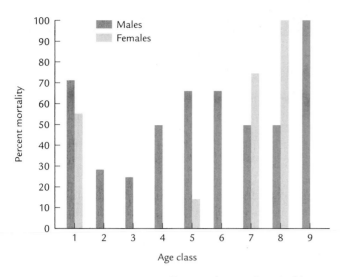

FIGURE 2 Donner Party mortality rates by age class (Table 3 provides the range in years for each numbered age class).

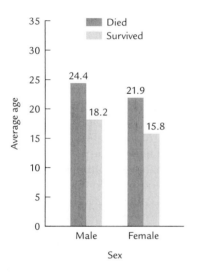

FIGURE 3 The average ages of Donner Party members by sex and survivorship status.

Of the 40 deaths, five occurred before the Sierran encampment. Luke Halloran (25) died of "consumption," presumably tuberculosis, south of the Great Salt Lake on August 28. On October 5, James Reed was provoked into stabbing John Snyder (25), who died of the wound. It was for this reason that Reed was forced to leave the group. Mr. Hardkoop was denied passage in the wagons; 60 years old and forced to walk, he died on or soon after October 8 along the Humboldt River. Mr. Wolfinger (age unknown) was apparently killed by two fellow travelers near Humboldt Sink on or about October 15; William Pike (25) was accidentally shot by his brother-in-law on October 20 while camped at Truckee Meadows, where Reno now sits. Five deaths, all and typically male: infectious disease, aggression, and violence.

Once in the Sierran encampment, not only did males die at far greater rates than females, but they also died more quickly than females. The Sierran camps were established about November 1. The first death among the forced campers occurred about six weeks later. The last occurred five months later, on April 1. Firsthand accounts allow the timing of these deaths to be established either precisely or reasonably securely.[6,62,63] As a result, a chronology of the deaths that occurred after encampment can be constructed. I have presented the raw data for this mortality timetable elsewhere.[64] Here I show the march of death and discuss why it looks the way it does.

Figure 4 displays the chronology of death across the 108 days during which Donner Party members died after the encampment. Males died not only in greater numbers than females, but sooner. The first 14 deaths, beginning on December 15 and continuing through January 30, involved only males. The first female, Harriet McCutcheon (1), succumbed on February 2, after which both males and females lost their lives.

An apparent oddity in this sequence of deaths is the 18-day holiday that death took between January 6 and January 23. Before this lengthy interregnum, only males died; after it, both males and females died. In fact, of the 14 males who died before the first female death, 11 died during the 15-day interval that began December 15 and ended on December 29. During the next 33 days, only 3 additional males lost their lives. Why did the 18-day lull in deaths occur, and why did so many males succumb so quickly?

Figure 5 shows the relationship between age and days-to-death (treating December 15 as the first day-to-death) for all Donner Party males who reached the Sierran encampment. With one significant exception, age and days-to-death are inversely related among these males: the youngest tended to survive longest and the oldest died first.

The exception was 62-year-old George Donner. Donner had cut his hand badly in October, a wound that was never to heal. Once the Donner camp had been established, he could neither attempt to escape nor fend for himself. His wife, Tamsen, refused to leave with rescuers so that she could continue to care for her husband. With Tamsen's help, George survived until about March 26; Tamsen died the next day. George probably survived as long as he did because of Tamsen's care and because he was not engaging in high-energy activities. Indeed, statistical analysis shows him to be a significant outlier (2.7 standard deviations) in the relationship shown in Figure 5. With or without George Donner, the rank order correlation (Spearman's rho, r_s) between age and days-to-death among the males is significant, but it is more significant

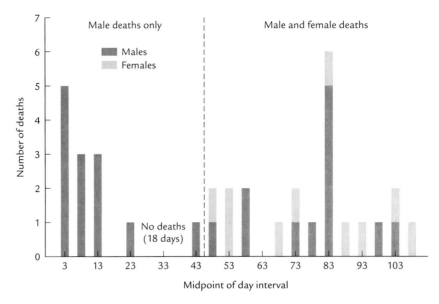

FIGURE 4 The march of death across Donner Party members who reached the Sierran encampment, by five-day intervals.

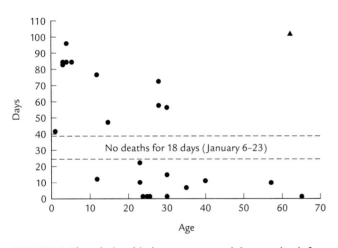

FIGURE 5 The relationship between age and days-to-death for the Donner Party males who reached the Sierran encampment; George Donner is indicated by the triangle in the upper right corner.

without him ($r_s = -.67$, $p < .001$) than with him ($r_s = -.49$, $p = .013$). The average age of males who died before the lull was 32.4 years, and the average age of those who died after it, George Donner included, was 15.4 years. Among the males who died, George Donner was the only one to see the end of February.

Key to understanding both this relationship and the temporary cessation in mortality is the fact that both age and dependency were critical here. Of the 13 males who lost their lives after death had begun again, eight were dependent on others for their care, either because of their age (5 years or under) or because they were injured (George Donner). All of those who lost

their lives during the first bout of death could fend for themselves.

And fend they did. Firsthand accounts make it clear that it was the Donner Party men who bore the brunt of the tremendous physical effort required for the group to negotiate the Wasatch Range, and who performed the heaviest chores in the Sierra Nevada. These, of course, are precisely the chores that males, by virtue of their biology, excel at performing and that, not coincidentally, they were expected to perform in mid-nineteenth-century America. These men had certainly depleted their energy reserves in the Wasatch Range, a situation made worse once they were in the Sierra Nevada. Depleted, the adult males, including prime-aged individuals between 20 and 40 years, were the first to succumb. Once these men were gone, the first episode of death ended; 18 days later, the second episode, involving both males and females, began.

Thus, the initial round of deaths removed people who were doomed by their age and sex. The quick deaths of prime-aged men left the survivors largely without those whose duties would have included such tasks as hunting and wood-cutting. Without a full complement of vigorous adult males to accomplish these tasks, the survivors became far more dependent on rescuers than they otherwise would have been.

THE ROLE OF KIN GROUPS

One other factor was likely to have been critical in determining differential mortality within the Donner Party. Diverse studies have shown that, under normal living conditions, longevity is positively correlated with the size of the social network within which an individual is embedded. This effect has been reported more consistently for men than for women.[65,66] Although it is not clear why this effect exists, Berkman[65] has pointed out that a sense of belonging, access to information, and the availability of timely assistance all seem to play a role, and it is also possible that strong social networks strengthen immune systems.[67] There is no reason to think that the benefits of social networks would not have accrued to the members of the Donner Party, especially given the documented role that family and friends play in providing information and assistance in disaster settings.[68] It is also no surprise that accounts left by members of the Donner Party document that within-family assistance was routine. From this, it follows that mortality in the Donner Party might scale not only to age and sex, but also to the size of the family group in which each individual traveled.

Among individuals between 5 and 40 years of age, for whom age may be assumed to have had a lesser role in causing death, surviving males traveled with families averaging 8.4 people. Males who did not survive traveled with families averaging 5.7 individuals. Surviving females of this age traveled with families whose size averaged 10.1 individuals; the one woman of this age who did not survive, Eleanor Eddy (25), traveled as part of a family of four. Larger kin groups seem to have provided life-enhancing support to members of the Donner Party.

If traveling with larger kin groups decreased the chance of dying, it might also have prolonged the lives of those who did die. Again, this seems to have been the case. The males who succumbed during the initial round of deaths were part of family groups whose size averaged 5.2 individuals; those who died during the second round traveled with families that averaged 9.9 members. As a whole, the chronology of deaths among the Donner Party males who reached the Sierran encampment is significantly, although perhaps not impressively, correlated with family size (r_s = .53, p = .006).

In the United States during the mid-nineteenth century, single women rarely traveled west on their own, while single men routinely made the journey. Within the Donner Party, there were 15 men, but no women, between the ages of 20 and 40 who were traveling alone. Of these 15 men, only 3 survived; nine had died by the time the lull in deaths occurred. Of the 13 males who died after death had resumed, 8 were children 12 years old or younger who, perforce, had to belong to family groups, while another was the dependent George Donner. Could the correlation between days-to-death and family size for males be caused by the early loss of prime-aged single men, coupled with the dependent status of many of those who survived the lull? If so, we would not expect to see a significant positive relationship between days-to-death and family size for females as well. This relationship, however, not only exists, but it is stronger than for males (r_s = .724, p = .018).

Family size thus appears to have played a significant role in mediating death among both the males and females of the Donner Party. The larger the family with which a person traveled, the longer that person survived, many lasting long enough to either escape or be rescued. That family size played a greater role among the females is likely due to the fact that among males, the beneficial effects of being surrounded by family members were overridden by the losses of energy associated with the strenuous tasks they performed. That is, the benefits that male members of the Donner Party gained by belonging to increasingly larger family groups, they tended to lose by virtue of their sex.

CONCLUSIONS

Virtually all the deaths that occurred within the Donner Party can now be explained by what we know about general patterns of human mortality, differences between the sexes in resistance to cold and famine, and the role that social networks play in increasing longevity. Even the timing of Donner Party deaths can now be explained by this knowledge. Death fell most heavily on the youngest and oldest members of the group, on the males, and on those who traveled alone or with smaller support groups. Death came most quickly to prime-aged males, people who, by virtue of their biology, acted as they were expected to act. Death also came more quickly to those who, whether male or female, traveled with smaller support groups than it did to those whose support groups were larger. Far from simply illuminating the fate of a single, albeit famous, emigrant party, this knowledge confirms our understanding of some of the fundamental biological differences between human males and females, and provides us with a case study of natural selection in action within a human group.

ACKNOWLEDGMENTS

My thanks to David B. Madsen for motivation, and to John Fleagle, Walter Hartwig, Kristen Hawkes, Sarah Blaffer Hrdy, and an anonymous reviewer for their assistance.

REFERENCES

1. Hastings LW (1845) *The Emigrants' Guide to Oregon and California*. Cincinnati: Conclin.

2. Grayson DK (1993) *The Desert's Past: A Natural Prehistory of the Great Basin*. Washington: Smithsonian Institution Press.

3. Hawkins BR, Madsen DB (1990) *Excavation of the Donner-Reed Wagons*. Salt Lake City: University of Utah Press.

4. Hardesty DL (1987) The archaeology of the Donner Party tragedy. Nevada Hist Quart 30:246–268.

5. Grayson DK (1991) Donner Party deaths: A demographic assessment. J Anthropol Res 46:223–242.

6. King JA (1992) *Winter of Entrapment: A New Look at the Donner Party*. Toronto: PD Meany.

7. Unruh JD Jr (1979) *The Plains Across: The Overland Emigrants and the Trans-Mississippi West, 1840–1860*. Urbana: University of Illinois Press.

8. Lopez AD (1983) The sex mortality differential in developed countries. In Lopez AD, Ruzicka LT (eds), *Sex Differentials in Mortality: Trends, Determinants and Consequences*, pp 7–32. Misc Ser 4, Department of Demography, Australian National University, Canberra.

9. Ohadike PO (1983) Evolving indications of mortality differentials by sex in Africa. In Lopez AD, Ruzicka LT (eds), *Sex Differentials in Mortality: Trends, Determinants and Consequences*, pp 33–52. Misc Ser 4, Department of Demography, Australian National University, Canberra.

10. Wingard DL (1984) The sex differential in morbidity, mortality, and lifestyle. Ann Rev Public Health 5:433–458.

11. Waldron I (1976) Why do women live longer than men? Soc Sci Med 10:349–362.

12. Seely S (1990) The gender gap: Why do women live longer than men? Int J Cardiol 29:113–119.

13. Heligman L (1983) Patterns of sex differentials in mortality in less developed countries. In Lopez AD, Ruzicka LT (eds), *Sex Differentials in Mortality: Trends, Determinants and Consequences*, pp 7–32. Misc Ser 4, Department of Demography, Australian National University, Canberra.

14. Waldron I (1983) Sex differences in human mortality: The role of genetic factors. Soc Sci Med 17:321–333.

15. Waldron I (1993) Recent trends in sex mortality ratios for adults in developed countries. Soc Sci Med 36:451–462.

16. Hazzard WR (1986) Biological basis of the sex differential in longevity. J Am Geriat Soc 34:455–471.

17. Dahlberg F (1981) Introduction. In Dahlberg F (ed), *Woman the Gatherer*, pp 1–33. New Haven: Yale University Press.

18. Hawkes K (1993) Showing off: Tests of an hypothesis about men's foraging goals. Ethol Sociobiol 12:29–54.

19. Lancaster HO (1990) *Expectations of Life*. New York: Springer-Verlag.

20. McMillen MM (1979) Differential mortality by sex in fetal and neonatal deaths. Science 204:89–91.

21. Stinson S (1985) Sex differences in environmental sensitivity during growth and development. Yearbook Phys Anthropol 28:123–147.

22. Nathanson CA (1984) Sex differences in mortality. Ann Rev Sociol 10:191–213.

23. Short RV (1985) Species differences in reproductive mechanisms. In Austin CR, Short RV (eds), *Reproduction in Mammals, Book 4: Reproductive Fitness*, pp 24–61. Cambridge: Cambridge University Press.

24. Kellerman AL, Mercy JA (1992) Men, women, and murder: Gender-specific differences in rates of fatal violence and victimization. J Trauma 33:1–5.

25. Iskrant AP, Joliet PV (1968) *Accidents and Homicide*. Cambridge: Harvard University Press.

26. Dauer CC, Korns RF, Schuman LM (1968) *Infectious Diseases*. Cambridge: Harvard University Press.

27. Schad GA, Anderson RM (1985) Predisposition to hookworm infection in humans. Science 228:1537–1540.

28. Rockstein M, Lieberman HM (1959) A life table for the common house fly, *Musca domestica*. Gerontologia 3:23–36.

29. Verbrugge AM (1985) Gender and health: An update on hypotheses and evidence. J Health Soc Behav 26:156–182.

30. Hamilton JB, Mestler GE (1969) Mortality and survival: Comparison of eunuchs with intact men and women in a mentally retarded population. J Gerontol 24:395–411.

31. Rohner R (1976) Sex differences in aggression: Phylogenetic and enculturation perspectives. Ethos 4:57–72.

32. Brown J (1970) A note on the sexual division of labor. Am Anthropol 72:1073–1078.

33. Lancaster JB (1985) Evolutionary perspectives on sex differences in higher primates. In Rossi AS (ed), *Gender and the Life Course*, pp 3–27. New York: Aldine.

34. Lancaster JB (1993) The evolutionary biology of women. In Almquist AL, Manyak A (eds), *Milestones in Human Evolution*, pp 21–38. Prospect Heights, Illinois: Waveland Press.

35. Hawkes K (1990) Why do men hunt? Benefits for risky choices. In Cashdan E (ed), *Risk and Uncertainty in Tribal and Peasant Economies*, pp 145–166. Boulder: Westview Press.

36. Kaplan H, Hill K (1992) The evolutionary ecology of food acquisition. In Smith EA, Winterhalder B (eds), *Evolutionary Ecology and Human Behavior*, pp 167–202. New York: Aldine de Gruyter.

37. Meller R (1982) Aggression in primate social groups. In Marsh P, Campbell A (eds), *Aggression and Violence*, pp 118–136. Oxford: Basil Blackwell.

38. Ehrhardt AA (1985) The psychobiology of gender. In Rossi AS (ed), *Gender and the Life Course*, pp 81–96. New York: Aldine.

39. Moir A, Jessel D (1992) *Brain Sex: The Real Difference Between Men and Women.* New York: Dell.

40. Nicholson J (1993) *Men and Women: How Different Are They?* New York: Oxford University Press.

41. Harrison GA, Tanner JM, Pilbeam DR, Baker PT (1988) *Human Biology, Third Edition.* Oxford: Oxford University Press.

42. Wardle MG, Gloss MR, Gloss DS III (1987) Response differences. In Baker MA (ed), *Sex Differences in Human Performance*, pp 107–120. Chichester: Wiley and Sons.

43. Hattori K, Numata N, Ikoma M, Matsuzaka A, Danielson RR (1991) Sex differences in the distribution of subcutaneous and internal fat. Hum Biol 63:53–63.

44. Rivers JPW (1982) Women and children last: An essay on sex discrimination in disasters. Disasters 6:256–267.

45. Rivers JPW (1988) The nutritional biology of famine. In Harrison GA (ed), *Famine*, pp 56–106. Oxford: Oxford University Press.

46. Stini WA (1981) Body composition and nutrient reserves in evolutionary perspective. World Rev Nutr Diet 37:55–83.

47. Widdowson EM (1976) The response of the sexes to nutritional stress. Proc Nutr Soc 35:175–180.

48. Graham TE, Viswanathan M, VanDijk JP, Bonen A, George TC (1989) Thermal and metabolic responses to cold by men and eumenorrheic and amenorrheic women. J Appl Physiol 67:282–290.

49. Buskirk ER, Thompson RH, Whedon GD (1963) Metabolic response to cold air in men and women in relation to total body fat content. J Appl Physiol 18:603–612.

50. Sloan REG, Keatinge WR (1973) Cooling rates of young people swimming in cold water. J Appl Physiol 35:371–375.

51. Keatinge WR (1978) Body fat and cooling rates in relation to age. In Folinsbee LJ, Wagner JA, Borgia JF, Drinkwater BL, Gliner JA, Bedi JF (eds), *Environmental Stress: Individual Human Adaptations*, pp 299–302. New York: Academic Press.

52. Frisancho AR (1979) *Human Adaptation: A Functional Interpretation.* St. Louis: CV Mosby.

53. Haymes EM, Wells CL (1986) *Environment and Human Performance.* Champaign: Human Kinetics Publishers.

54. Wyndham CH, Morrison JF, Williams CG, Bredell GAG, Peter J, Von Rayden MJE, Holdsworth CD, Van Graan CH, Van Rensburg AJ, Munro A (1964) Physiological reactions to cold of Caucasian females. J Appl Physiol 19:877–890.

55. Graham TE, Lougheed TE (1985) Thermal responses to exercise in the cold: Influence of sex differences and alcohol. Hum Biol 57:687–698.

56. Burse RL (1979) Sex differences in human thermoregulatory response to heat and cold stress. Hum Factors 21:687–699.

57. Bogue DJ (1969) *Principles of Demography.* New York: John Wiley & Sons.

58. Wagner JA, Robinson S, Marino RP (1974) Age and temperature regulation of humans in neutral and cold environments. J Appl Physiol 37:562–565.

59. Collins KJ, Dore C, Exton-Smith AN, Fox RH, MacDonald IC, Woodward PM (1977) Accidental hypothermia and impaired temperature homeostasis in the elderly. Br Med J 1:353–356.

60. Seaman J, Leivesley S, Hogg C (1984) *Epidemiology of Natural Disasters.* Basel: Karger.

61. Wagner JA, Horvath SM (1985) Influences of age and gender on human thermoregulatory responses to cold exposures. J Appl Physiol 58:180–192.

62. Thornton JO (1986) *Camp of Death: The Donner Party Mountain Camp, 1846–1847* (reprint of 1849 publication). Golden: Outbooks.

63. Stewart GR (1960) *Ordeal by Hunger: The Story of the Donner Party.* Lincoln: University of Nebraska Press.

64. Grayson DK (n.d.) The timing of Donner Party deaths. In Hardesty DL (ed), *Donner Party Archaeology*, in press. Reno: University of Nevada Press.

65. Berkman LF (1984) Assessing the physical health effects of social networks and social support. Ann Rev Public Health 5:413–432.

66. Kaplan RM, Toshima MT (1990) The functional effects of social relationships on chronic illnesses and disability. In Sarason BR, Sarason IG, Pierce GR (eds), *Social Support: An Interactional View*, pp 427–453. New York: John Wiley & Sons.

67. Kennedy S, Kiecolt-Glaser JK, Glaser R (1990) Social support, stress, and the immune system. In Sarason BR, Sarason IG, Pierce GR (eds), *Social Support: An Interactional View*, pp 253–266. New York: John Wiley & Sons.

68. Neal DM, Perry JB Jr, Green K, Hawkins R (1988) Patterns of giving and receiving help during severe winter conditions: A research note. Disasters 12:366–377.

27

Skin Deep

Nina G. Jablonski and George Chaplin

Nina G. Jablonski is Irvine Chair and curator of anthropology at the California Academy of Sciences in San Francisco specializing in evolutionary adaptations of the primates. George Chaplin, also at the California Academy of Sciences, is a private geographic information systems consultant who specializes in geographic trends in biodiversity.

Skin color is one of our species' most obvious variable traits, and one that is a focus of all manner of misunderstandings, from scientific to social. In this selection, Nina Jablonski and George Chaplin take issue with part of the traditional explanation for the variation in and distribution of skin color and describe evidence for the idea that these are the result of a relationship between skin color, ultraviolet radiation, and nutrients important to reproductive success.

As you read, consider the following questions:

1. How does melanin protect against the ill effects of ultraviolet radiation?

2. What is the authors' objection to the idea that melanin's major function was to protect against skin cancer?

3. How is folate related to reproductive success? How is it related, then, to ultraviolet radiation and skin color?

4. What is the correlation between ultraviolet radiation, skin color, and vitamin D?

5. Why do some populations not fit the predicted skin color pattern?

6. How do men and women differ with regard to skin color?

Among primates, only humans have a mostly naked skin that comes in different colors. Geographers and anthropologists have long recognized that the distribution of skin colors among indigenous populations is not random: darker peoples tend to be found nearer the equator, lighter ones closer to the poles. For years, the prevailing theory has been that darker skins evolved to protect against skin cancer. But a series of discoveries has led us to construct a new framework for understanding the evolutionary basis of variations in human skin color. Recent epidemiological and physiological evidence suggests to us that the worldwide pattern of human skin color is the product of natural selection acting to regulate the effects of the sun's ultraviolet (UV) radiation on key nutrients crucial to reproductive success.

FROM HIRSUTE TO HAIRLESS

The evolution of skin pigmentation is linked with that of hairlessness, and to comprehend both these stories, we need to page back in human history. Human beings have been evolving as an independent lineage of apes since at least seven million years ago, when our immediate ancestors diverged from those of our closest relatives, chimpanzees. Because chimpanzees have changed less over time than humans have, they can provide an idea of what human anatomy and physiology must have been like. Chimpanzees' skin is light in color and is covered by hair over most of their bodies.

Young animals have pink faces, hands, and feet and become freckled or dark in these areas only as they are exposed to sun with age. The earliest humans almost certainly had a light skin covered with hair. Presumably hair loss occurred first, then skin color changed. But that leads to the question, When did we lose our hair?

The skeletons of ancient humans—such as the well-known skeleton of Lucy, which dates to about 3.2 million years ago—give us a good idea of the build and the way of life of our ancestors. The daily activities of Lucy and other hominids that lived before about three million years ago appear to have been similar to those of primates living on the open savannas of Africa today. They probably spent much of their day foraging for food over three to four miles before retiring to the safety of trees to sleep.

By 1.6 million years ago, however, we see evidence that this pattern had begun to change dramatically. The famous skeleton of Turkana Boy—which belonged to the species *Homo ergaster*—is that of a long-legged, striding biped that probably walked long distances. These more active early humans faced the problem of staying cool and protecting their brains from overheating. Peter Wheeler of John Moores University in Liverpool, England, has shown that this was accomplished through an increase in the number of sweat glands on the surface of the body and a reduction in the covering of body hair. Once rid of most of their hair, early members of the genus *Homo* then encountered the challenge of protecting their skin from the damaging effects of sunlight, especially UV rays.

BUILT-IN SUNSCREEN

In chimpanzees, the skin on the hairless parts of the body contains cells called melanocytes that are capable of synthesizing the dark-brown pigment melanin in response to exposure to UV radiation. When humans became mostly hairless, the ability of the skin to produce melanin assumed new importance. Melanin is nature's sunscreen: it is a large organic molecule that serves the dual purpose of physically and chemically filtering the harmful effects of UV radiation; it absorbs UV rays, causing them to lose energy, and it neutralizes harmful chemicals called free radicals that form in the skin after damage by UV radiation.

Anthropologists and biologists have generally reasoned that high concentrations of melanin arose in the skin of peoples in tropical areas because it protected them against skin cancer. James E. Cleaver of the University of California at San Francisco, for instance, has shown that people with the disease xeroderma pigmentosum, in which melanocytes are destroyed by

exposure to the sun, suffer from significantly higher than normal rates of squamous and basal cell carcinomas, which are usually easily treated. Malignant melanomas are more frequently fatal, but they are rare (representing 4 percent of skin cancer diagnoses) and tend to strike only light-skinned people. But all skin cancers typically arise later in life, in most cases after the first reproductive years, so they could not have exerted enough evolutionary pressure for skin protection alone to account for darker skin colors. Accordingly, we began to ask what role melanin might play in human evolution.

THE FOLATE CONNECTION

In 1991 one of us (Jablonski) ran across what turned out to be a critical paper published in 1978 by Richard F. Branda and John W. Eaton, now at the University of Vermont and the University of Louisville, respectively. These investigators showed that light-skinned people who had been exposed to simulated strong sunlight had abnormally low levels of the essential B vitamin folate in their blood. The scientists also observed that subjecting human blood serum to the same conditions resulted in a 50-percent loss of folate content within one hour.

The significance of these findings to reproduction—and hence evolution—became clear when we learned of research being conducted on a major class of birth defects by our colleagues at the University of Western Australia. There Fiona J. Stanley and Carol Bower had established by the late 1980s that folate deficiency in pregnant women is related to an increased risk of neural tube defects such as spina bifida, in which the arches of the spinal vertebrae fail to close around the spinal cord. Many research groups throughout the world have since confirmed this correlation, and efforts to supplement foods with folate and to educate women about the importance of the nutrient have become widespread.

We discovered soon afterward that folate is important not only in preventing neural tube defects but also in a host of other processes. Because folate is essential for the synthesis of DNA in dividing cells, anything that involves rapid cell proliferation, such as spermatogenesis (the production of sperm cells), requires folate. Male rats and mice with chemically induced folate deficiency have impaired spermatogenesis and are infertile. Although no comparable studies of humans have been conducted, Wai Yee Wong and his colleagues at the University Medical Center of Nijmegen in the Netherlands have recently reported that folic acid treatment can boost the sperm counts of men with fertility problems.

Such observations led us to hypothesize that dark skin evolved to protect the body's folate stores from destruction. Our idea was supported by a report published in 1996 by Argentine pediatrician Pablo Lapunzina, who found that three young and otherwise healthy women whom he had attended gave birth to infants with neural tube defects after using sun beds to tan themselves in the early weeks of pregnancy. Our evidence about the breakdown of folate by UV radiation thus supplements what is already known about the harmful (skin-cancer-causing) effects of UV radiation on DNA.

HUMAN SKIN ON THE MOVE

The earliest members of *Homo sapiens*, or modern humans, evolved in Africa between 120,000 and 100,000 years ago and had darkly pigmented skin adapted to the conditions of UV radiation and heat that existed near the equator. As modern humans began to venture out of the tropics, however, they encountered environments in which they received significantly less UV radiation during the year. Under these conditions their high concentrations of natural sunscreen probably proved detrimental. Dark skin contains so much melanin that very little UV radiation, and specifically very little of the shorter-wavelength UVB radiation, can penetrate the skin. Although most of the effects of UVB are harmful, the rays perform one indispensable function: initiating the formation of vitamin D in the skin. Dark-skinned people living in the tropics generally receive sufficient UV radiation during the year for UVB to penetrate the skin and allow them to make vitamin D. Outside the tropics this is not the case. The solution, across evolutionary time, has been for migrants to northern latitudes to lose skin pigmentation.

The connection between the evolution of lightly pigmented skin and vitamin D synthesis was elaborated by W. Farnsworth Loomis of Brandeis University in 1967. He established the importance of vitamin D to reproductive success because of its role in enabling calcium absorption by the intestines, which in turn makes possible the normal development of the skeleton and the maintenance of a healthy immune system. Research led by Michael Holick of the Boston University School of Medicine has, over the past 20 years, further cemented the significance of vitamin D in development and immunity. His team also showed that not all sunlight contains enough UVB to stimulate vitamin D production. In Boston, for instance, which is located at about 42 degrees north latitude, human skin cells begin to produce vitamin D only after mid-March. In the wintertime there isn't enough UVB to do the job. We realized that this was another piece of evidence essential to the skin color story.

During the course of our research in the early 1990s, we searched in vain to find sources of data on actual UV radiation levels at the earth's surface. We were rewarded in 1996, when we contacted Elizabeth Weatherhead of the Cooperative Institute for Research in Environmental Sciences at the University of Colorado at Boulder. She shared with us a database of measurements of UV radiation at the earth's surface taken by NASA's Total Ozone Mapping Spectrophotometer satellite between 1978 and 1993. We were then able to model the distribution of UV radiation on the earth and relate the satellite data to the amount of UVB necessary to produce vitamin D.

We found that the earth's surface could be divided into three vitamin D zones: one comprising the tropics, one the subtropics and temperate regions, and the last the circumpolar regions north and south of about 45 degrees latitude. In the first, the dosage of UVB throughout the year is high enough that humans have ample opportunity to synthesize vitamin D all year. In the second, at least one month during the year has insufficient UVB radiation, and in the third area not enough UVB arrives on average during the entire year to prompt vitamin D synthesis. This distribution could explain why indigenous peoples in the tropics generally have dark skin, whereas people in the subtropics and temperate regions are lighter-skinned but have the ability to tan, and those who live in regions near the poles tend to be very light skinned and burn easily.

One of the most interesting aspects of this investigation was the examination of groups that did not precisely fit the predicted skin-color pattern. An example is the Inuit people of Alaska and northern Canada. The Inuit exhibit skin color that is somewhat darker than would be predicted given the UV levels at their latitude. This is probably caused by two factors. The first is that they are relatively recent inhabitants of these climes, having migrated to North America only roughly 5,000 years ago. The second is that the traditional diet of the Inuit is extremely high in foods containing vitamin D, especially fish and marine mammals. This vitamin D–rich diet offsets the problem that they would otherwise have with vitamin D synthesis in their skin at northern latitudes and permits them to remain more darkly pigmented.

Our analysis of the potential to synthesize vitamin D allowed us to understand another trait related to human skin color: women in all populations are generally lighter-skinned than men. (Our data show that women tend to be between 3 and 4 percent lighter than men.) Scientists have often speculated on the reasons, and most have argued that the phenomenon stems from sexual selection—the preference of men for women of lighter color. We contend that although this is probably part of the story, it is not the original reason for the sexual difference. Females have significantly greater needs for calcium throughout their reproductive lives, especially during pregnancy and lactation, and must be able to make the most of the calcium contained in food. We propose, therefore, that women tend to be lighter-skinned than men to allow slightly more UVB rays to penetrate their skin and thereby increase their ability to produce vitamin D. In areas of the world that receive a large amount of UV radiation, women are indeed at the knife's edge of natural selection, needing to maximize the photoprotective function of their skin on the one hand and the ability to synthesize vitamin D on the other.

WHERE CULTURE AND BIOLOGY MEET

As modern humans moved throughout the Old World about 100,000 years ago, their skin adapted to the environmental conditions that prevailed in different regions. The skin color of the indigenous people of Africa has had the longest time to adapt because anatomically modern humans first evolved there. The skin-color changes that modern humans underwent as they moved from one continent to another—first Asia, then Austro-Melanesia, then Europe and, finally, the Americas—can be reconstructed to some extent. It is important to remember, however, that those humans had clothing and shelter to help protect them from the elements. In some places, they also had the ability to harvest foods that were extraordinarily rich in vitamin D, as in the case of the Inuit. These two factors had profound effects on the tempo and degree of skin-color evolution in human populations.

Africa is an environmentally heterogeneous continent. A number of the earliest movements of contemporary humans outside equatorial Africa were into southern Africa. The descendants of some of these early colonizers, the Khoisan (previously known as Hottentots), are still found in southern Africa and have significantly lighter skin than indigenous equatorial Africans do—a clear adaptation to the lower levels of UV radiation that prevail at the southern extremity of the continent.

Interestingly, however, human skin color in southern Africa is not uniform. Populations of Bantu-language speakers who live in southern Africa today are far darker than the Khoisan. We know from the history of this region that Bantu speakers migrated into this region recently—probably within the past 1,000 years—from parts of West Africa near the equator. The skin-color difference between the Khoisan and Bantu speakers such as the Zulu indicates that the length of time that a group has inhabited a particular region is important in understanding why they have the color they do.

Cultural behaviors have probably also strongly influenced the evolution of skin color in recent human history. This effect can be seen in the indigenous peoples who live on the eastern and western banks of the Red Sea. The tribes on the western side, which speak so-called Nilo-Hamitic languages, are thought to have inhabited this region for as long as 6,000 years. These individuals are distinguished by very darkly pigmented skin and long, thin bodies with long limbs, which are excellent biological adaptations for dissipating heat and intense UV radiation. In contrast, modern agricultural and pastoral groups on the eastern bank of the Red Sea, on the Arabian Peninsula, have lived there for only about 2,000 years. These earliest Arab people, of European origin, have adapted to very similar environmental conditions by almost exclusively cultural means—wearing heavy protective clothing and devising portable shade in the form of tents. (Without such clothing, one would have expected their skin to have begun to darken.) Generally speaking, the more recently a group has migrated into an area, the more extensive its cultural, as opposed to biological, adaptations to the area will be.

PERILS OF RECENT MIGRATIONS

Despite great improvements in overall human health in the past century, some diseases have appeared or reemerged in populations that had previously been little affected by them. One of these is skin cancer, especially basal and squamous cell carcinomas, among light-skinned peoples. Another is rickets, brought about by severe vitamin D deficiency, in dark-skinned peoples. Why are we seeing these conditions?

As people move from an area with one pattern of UV radiation to another region, biological and cultural adaptations have not been able to keep pace. The light-skinned people of northern European origin who bask in the sun of Florida or northern Australia increasingly pay the price in the form of premature aging of the skin and skin cancers, not to mention the unknown cost in human life of folate depletion. Conversely, a number of dark-skinned people of southern Asian and African origin now living in the northern U.K., northern Europe or the northeastern U.S. suffer from a lack of UV radiation and vitamin D, an insidious problem that manifests itself in high rates of rickets and other diseases related to vitamin D deficiency.

The ability of skin color to adapt over long periods to the various environments to which humans have moved reflects the importance of skin color to our survival. But its unstable nature also makes it one of the least useful characteristics in determining the evolutionary relations between human groups. Early Western scientists used skin color improperly to delineate human races, but the beauty of science is that it can and does correct itself. Our current knowledge of the evolution of human skin indicates that variations in skin color, like most of our physical attributes, can be explained by adaptation to the environment through natural selection. We look ahead to the day when the vestiges of old scientific mistakes will be erased and replaced by a better understanding of human origins and diversity. Our variation in skin color should be celebrated as one of the most visible manifestations of our evolution as a species.

MORE TO EXPLORE

The Evolution of Human Skin Coloration. Nina G. Jablonski and George Chaplin in *Journal of Human Evolution*, Vol. 39, No. 1, pages 57–106; July 1, 2000. An abstract of the article is available online at **www.idealibrary .com/links/doi/10.1006/jhev.2000.0403**

Why Skin Comes in Colors. Blake Edgar in *California Wild*, Vol. 53, No. 1, pages 6–7; Winter 2000. The article is also available at **www.calacademy.org/calwild/winter2000/ html/horizons.html**

The Biology of Skin Color: Black and White. Gina Kirchweger in *Discover*, Vol. 22, No. 2, pages 32–33; February 2001. The article is also available at **www.discover .com/feb_01/featbiology.html**

28

Evolution and the Origins of Disease

Randolph M. Nesse and George C. Williams

Randolph M. Nesse is professor of psychiatry and psychology and director of the Evolution and Human Adaptation Program at the Institute for Social Research at the University of Michigan. George C. Williams is professor emeritus of ecology and evolution at the State University of New York at Stony Brook and edits the Quarterly Review of Biology.

Disease is a natural part of the biology of any species, ours included, so it is logical to examine the relationships between our species and those diseases that affect us from an evolutionary perspective. This type of study is referred to as Darwinian medicine. In the selection, Randolph M. Nesse and George C. Williams look at one aspect of Darwinian medicine, the evolution of the characteristics of the human body that make us vulnerable to various ailments.

As you read, consider the following questions:

1. What is the focus of Darwinian medicine as opposed to that of traditional medical research?

2. What are the five evolutionary explanations for our body's "flaws," those things that cause us to fall victim to disease?

3. What are the basic principles of Darwinian medicine?

4. How does Darwinian medicine help us better understand the nature of natural selection? Does susceptibility to disease contradict the basic idea of natural selection?

5. How might the perspective of Darwinian medicine help guide medical research in the future?

Thoughtful contemplation of the human body elicits awe—in equal measure with perplexity. The eye, for instance, has long been an object of wonder, with the clear, living tissue of the cornea curving just the right amount, the iris adjusting to brightness and the lens to distance, so that the optimal quantity of light focuses exactly on the surface of the retina. Admiration of such apparent perfection soon gives way, however, to consternation. Contrary to any sensible design, blood vessels and nerves traverse the inside of the retina, creating a blind spot at their point of exit.

The body is a bundle of such jarring contradictions. For each exquisite heart valve, we have a wisdom tooth. Strands of DNA direct the development of the 10 trillion cells that make up a human adult but then permit his or her steady deterioration and eventual death. Our immune system can identify and destroy a million kinds of foreign matter, yet many bacteria can still kill us. These contradictions make it appear as if the body was designed by a team of superb engineers with occasional interventions by Rube Goldberg.

In fact, such seeming incongruities make sense but only when we investigate the origins of the body's vulnerabilities while keeping in mind the wise words of distinguished geneticist Theodosius Dobzhansky: "Nothing in biology makes sense except in the light of evolution." Evolutionary biology is, of course, the scientific foundation for all biology, and biology is the foundation for all medicine. To a surprising degree, however, evolutionary biology is just now being recognized as a basic medical science. The enterprise of studying medical problems in an evolutionary context has been termed Darwinian medicine. Most medical research tries to explain the causes of an individual's disease and seeks therapies to cure or relieve deleterious conditions. These efforts are traditionally based on consideration of proximate issues, the straightforward study of the body's anatomic and physiological mechanisms as they currently exist. In contrast, Darwinian medicine asks why the body is designed in a way that makes us all vulnerable to problems like cancer, atherosclerosis, depression and choking, thus offering a broader context in which to conduct research.

First, some discomforting conditions, such as pain, fever, cough, vomiting and anxiety, are actually neither diseases nor design defects but rather are evolved defenses. Second, conflicts with other organisms—*Escherichia coli* or crocodiles, for instance—are a fact of life. Third, some circumstances, such as the ready availability of dietary fats, are so recent that natural selection has not yet had a chance to deal with them. Fourth, the body may fall victim to trade-offs between a trait's benefits and its costs; a textbook example is the sickle-cell gene, which also protects against malaria. Finally, the process of natural selection is constrained in ways that leave us with suboptimal design features, as in the case of the mammalian eye.

EVOLVED DEFENSES

Perhaps the most obviously useful defense mechanism is coughing; people who cannot clear foreign matter from their lungs are likely to die from pneumonia. The capacity for pain is also certainly beneficial. The rare individuals who cannot feel pain fail even to experience discomfort from staying in the same position for long periods. Their unnatural stillness impairs the blood supply to their joints, which then deteriorate. Such pain-free people usually die by early adulthood from tissue damage and infections. Cough or pain is usually interpreted as disease or trauma but is actually part of the solution rather than the problem. These defensive capabilities, shaped by natural selection, are kept in reserve until needed.

Less widely recognized as defenses are fever, nausea, vomiting, diarrhea, anxiety, fatigue, sneezing and inflammation. Even some physicians remain unaware of fever's utility. No mere increase in metabolic rate, fever is a carefully regulated rise in the set point of the body's thermostat. The higher body temperature facilitates the destruction of pathogens. Work by Matthew J. Kluger of the Lovelace Institute in Albuquerque, N.M., has shown that even cold-blooded lizards, when infected, move to warmer places until their bodies are several degrees above their usual temperature. If prevented from moving to the warm part of their cage, they are at increased risk of death from the infection. In a similar study by Evelyn Satinoff of the University of Delaware, elderly rats, who can no longer achieve the high fevers of their younger lab companions, also instinctively sought hotter environments when challenged by infection.

A reduced level of iron in the blood is another misunderstood defense mechanism. People suffering from chronic infection often have decreased levels of blood iron. Although such low iron is sometimes blamed for the illness, it actually is a protective response: during infection, iron is sequestered in the liver, which prevents invading bacteria from getting adequate supplies of this vital element.

Morning sickness has long been considered an unfortunate side effect of pregnancy. The nausea, however, coincides with the period of rapid tissue differentiation of the fetus, when development is most vulnerable to interference by toxins. And nauseated women tend to restrict their intake of strong-tasting, potentially harmful substances. These observations led independent researcher Margie Profet to hypothesize that the nausea of pregnancy is an adaptation whereby the mother protects the fetus from exposure to toxins. Profet tested this idea by examining pregnancy outcomes. Sure enough, women with more nausea were less likely to suffer miscarriages. (This evidence supports the hypothesis but is hardly conclusive. If Profet is correct, further research should discover that pregnant females of many species show changes in food preferences. Her theory also predicts an increase in birth defects among offspring of women who have little or no morning sickness and thus eat a wider variety of foods during pregnancy.)

Another common condition, anxiety, obviously originated as a defense in dangerous situations by promoting escape and avoidance. A 1992 study by Lee A. Dugatkin of the University of Louisville evaluated the benefits of fear in guppies. He grouped them as timid, ordinary or bold, depending on their reaction to the presence of smallmouth bass. The timid hid, the ordinary simply swam away, and the bold maintained their ground and eyed the bass. Each guppy group was then left alone in a tank with a bass. After 60 hours, 40 percent of the timid guppies had survived, as had only 15 percent of the ordinary fish. The entire compliment of bold guppies, on the other hand, wound up aiding the transmission of bass genes rather than their own.

Selection for genes promoting anxious behaviors implies that there should be people who experience too much anxiety, and indeed there are. There should also be hypophobic individuals who have insufficient anxiety, because of either genetic tendencies or antianxiety drugs. The exact nature and frequency of such a syndrome is an open question, as few people come to psychiatrists complaining of insufficient apprehension. But if sought, the pathologically non-anxious may be found in emergency rooms, jails and unemployment lines.

The utility of common and unpleasant conditions such as diarrhea, fever and anxiety is not intuitive. If natural selection shapes the mechanisms that regulate defensive responses, how can people get away with using drugs to block these defenses without doing their bodies obvious harm? Part of the answer is that we do, in fact, sometimes do ourselves a disservice by disrupting defenses.

Herbert L. DuPont of the University of Texas at Houston and Richard B. Hornick of Orlando Regional Medical Center studied the diarrhea caused by *Shigella* infection and found that people who took antidiarrhea drugs stayed sick longer and were more likely to have complications than those who took a placebo. In another example, Eugene D. Weinberg of Indiana University has documented that well-intentioned attempts to correct perceived iron deficiencies have led to increases in infectious disease, especially amebiasis, in parts of Africa. Although the iron in most oral supplements is unlikely to make much difference in otherwise healthy people with everyday infections, it can severely harm those who are infected and malnourished. Such people cannot make enough protein to bind the iron, leaving it free for use by infectious agents.

On the morning-sickness front, an antinausea drug was recently blamed for birth defects. It appears that no consideration was given to the possibility that the drug itself might be harmless to the fetus but could still be associated with birth defects, by interfering with the mother's defensive nausea.

Another obstacle to perceiving the benefits of defenses arises from the observation that many individuals regularly experience seemingly worthless reactions of anxiety, pain, fever, diarrhea or nausea. The explanation requires an analysis of the regulation of defensive responses in terms of signal-detection theory. A circulating toxin may come from something in the stomach. An organism can expel it by vomiting, but only at a price. The cost of a false alarm—vomiting when no toxin is truly present—is only a few calories. But the penalty for a single missed authentic alarm—failure to vomit when confronted with a toxin—may be death.

Natural selection therefore tends to shape regulation mechanisms with hair triggers, following what we call the smoke-detector principle. A smoke alarm that will reliably wake a sleeping family in the event of any fire will necessarily give a false alarm every time the toast burns. The price of the human body's numerous "smoke alarms" is much suffering that is completely normal but in most instances unnecessary. The principle also explains why blocking defenses is so often free of tragic consequences. Because most defensive reactions occur in response to insignificant threats, interference is usually harmless; the vast majority of alarms that are stopped by removing the battery from the smoke alarm are false ones, so this strategy may seem reasonable. Until, that is, a real fire occurs.

CONFLICTS WITH OTHER ORGANISMS

Natural selection is unable to provide us with perfect protection against all pathogens, because they tend to evolve much faster than humans do. *E. coli*, for example, with its rapid rates of reproduction, has as much opportunity for mutation and selection in one day as humanity gets in a millennium. And our defenses, whether natural or artificial, make for potent selection forces. Pathogens either quickly evolve a counterdefense or become extinct. Amherst College biologist Paul W. Ewald has suggested classifying phenomena associated with infection according to whether they benefit the host, the pathogen, both or neither. Consider the runny nose associated with a cold. Nasal mucous secretion could expel intruders, speed the pathogen's transmission to new hosts or both [see "The Evolution of Virulence," by Paul W. Ewald; SCIENTIFIC AMERICAN, April 1993]. Answers could come from studies examining whether blocking nasal secretions shortens or prolongs illness, but few such studies have been done.

Humanity won huge battles in the war against pathogens with the development of antibiotics and vaccines. Our victories were so rapid and seemingly complete that in 1969 U.S. Surgeon General William H. Stewart said that it was "time to close the book on infectious disease." But the enemy, and the power of natural selection, had been underestimated. The sober reality is that pathogens apparently can adapt to every chemical researchers develop. ("The war has been won," one scientist more recently quipped. "By the other side.")

Antibiotic resistance is a classic demonstration of natural selection. Bacteria that happen to have genes that allow them to prosper despite the presence of an antibiotic reproduce faster than others, and so the genes that confer resistance spread quickly. As shown by Nobel laureate Joshua Lederberg of the Rockefeller University, they can even jump to different species of bacteria, borne on bits of infectious DNA. Today some strains of tuberculosis in New York City are resistant to all three main antibiotic treatments; patients with those strains have no better chance of surviving than did TB patients a century ago. Stephen S. Morse of Columbia University notes that the multidrug-resistant strain that has spread throughout the East Coast may have originated in a homeless shelter across the street from Columbia-Presbyterian Medical Center. Such a phenomenon would indeed be predicted in an environment where fierce selection pressure quickly weeds out less hardy strains. The surviving bacilli have been bred for resistance.

Many people, including some physicians and scientists, still believe the outdated theory that pathogens necessarily become benign after long association with hosts. Superficially, this makes sense. An organism that kills rapidly may never get to a new host, so natural selection would seem to favor lower virulence. Syphilis, for instance, was a highly virulent disease when it first arrived in Europe, but as the centuries passed it became steadily more mild. The virulence of a pathogen is, however, a life history trait that can increase as well as decrease, depending on which option is more advantageous to its genes.

For agents of disease that are spread directly from person to person, low virulence tends to be beneficial, as it allows the host to remain active and in contact with other potential hosts. But some diseases, like malaria, are transmitted just as well—or better—by the incapacitated. For such pathogens, which usually rely on intermediate vectors like mosquitoes, high virulence can give a selective advantage. This principle has direct implications for infection control in hospitals, where health care workers' hands can be vectors that lead to selection for more virulent strains.

In the case of cholera, public water supplies play the mosquitoes' role. When water for drinking and bathing is contaminated by waste from immobilized patients, selection tends to increase virulence, because more diarrhea enhances the spread of the organism even if individual hosts quickly die. But, as Ewald has shown, when sanitation improves, selection acts against classical *Vibrio cholerae* bacteria in favor of the more benign El Tor biotype. Under these conditions, a dead host is a dead end. But a less ill and more mobile host, able to infect many others over a much longer time, is an effective vehicle for a pathogen of lower virulence. In another example, better sanitation leads to displacement of the aggressive *Shigella flexneri* by the more benign *S. sonnei*.

Such considerations may be relevant for public policy. Evolutionary theory predicts that clean needles and the encouragement of safe sex will do more than save numerous individuals from HIV infection. If humanity's behavior itself slows HIV transmission rates, strains that do not soon kill their hosts have the long-term survival advantage over the more virulent viruses that then die with their hosts, denied the opportunity to spread. Our collective choices can change the very nature of HIV.

Conflicts with other organisms are not limited to pathogens. In times past, humans were at great risk from predators looking for a meal. Except in a few places, large carnivores now pose no threat to humans. People are in more danger today from smaller organisms' defenses, such as the venoms of spiders and snakes. Ironically, our fears of small creatures, in the form of phobias, probably cause more harm than any interactions with those organisms do. Far more dangerous than predators or poisoners are other members of our own species. We attack each other not to get meat but get mates, territory, and other resources. Violent conflicts between individuals are overwhelmingly between young men in competition and give rise to organizations to advance these aims. Armies, again usually composed of young men, serve similar objectives, at huge cost.

Even the most intimate human relationships give rise to conflicts having medical implications. The reproductive interests of a mother and her infant, for instance, may seem congruent at first but soon diverge. As noted by biologist Robert L. Trivers in a now classic 1974 paper, when her child is a few years old, the mother's genetic interests may be best served by becoming pregnant again, whereas her offspring benefits from continuing to nurse. Even in the womb there is contention. From the mother's vantage point, the optimal size of a fetus is a bit smaller than that which would best serve the fetus and the father. This discord, according to David Haig of Harvard University, gives rise to an arms race between fetus and mother over her levels of blood pressure and blood sugar, sometimes resulting in hypertension and diabetes during pregnancy.

COPING WITH NOVELTY

Making rounds in any modern hospital provides sad testimony to the prevalence of diseases humanity has brought on itself. Heart attacks, for example, result mainly from atherosclerosis, a problem that became widespread only in this century and that remains rare among hunter-gatherers. Epidemiological research furnishes the information that should help us prevent heart attacks: limit fat intake, eat lots of vegetables, and exercise hard each day. But hamburger chains proliferate, diet foods languish on the shelves, and exercise machines serve as expensive clothing hangers throughout the land. The proportion of overweight Americans is one third and rising. We all know what is good for us. Why do so many of us continue to make unhealthy choices?

Our poor decisions about diet and exercise are made by brains shaped to cope with an environment substantially different from the one our species now inhabits. On the African savanna, where the modern human design was fine-tuned, fat, salt and sugar were scarce and precious. Individuals who had a tendency to consume large amounts of fat when given the rare opportunity had a selective advantage. They were more likely to survive famines that killed their thinner companions. And we, their descendants, still carry those urges for foodstuffs that today are anything but scarce. These evolved desires—inflamed by advertisements from competing food corporations that themselves survive by selling us more of whatever we want to buy—easily defeat our intellect and willpower. How ironic that humanity worked for centuries to create environments that are almost literally flowing with milk and honey, only to see our success responsible for much modern disease and untimely death.

Increasingly, people also have easy access to many kinds of drugs, especially alcohol and tobacco, that are responsible for a huge proportion of disease, health care costs and premature death. Although individuals have always used psychoactive substances, widespread problems materialized only following another environmental novelty: the ready availability of concentrated drugs and new, direct routes of administration, especially injection. Most of these substances, including nicotine, cocaine and opium, are products of natural selection that evolved to protect plants from insects. Because humans share a common evolutionary heritage with insects, many of these substances also affect our nervous system.

This perspective suggests that it is not just defective individuals or disordered societies that are vulnerable to the dangers of psychoactive drugs; all of us are susceptible because drugs and our biochemistry have a long history of interaction. Understanding the details of that interaction, which is the focus of much current research from both a proximate and evolutionary perspective, may well lead to better treatments for addiction.

The relatively recent and rapid increase in breast cancer must be the result in large part of changing environments and ways of life, with only a few cases resulting solely from genetic abnormalities. Boyd Eaton and his colleagues at Emory University reported that the rate of breast cancer in today's "nonmodern" societies is only a tiny fraction of that in the U.S. They hypothesize that the amount of time between menarche and first pregnancy is a crucial risk factor, as is the related issue of total lifetime number of menstrual cycles. In hunter-gatherers, menarche occurs at about age 15 or later, followed within a few years by pregnancy and two or three years of nursing, then by

another pregnancy soon after. Only between the end of nursing and the next pregnancy will the woman menstruate and thus experience the high levels of hormones that may adversely affect breast cells.

In modern societies, in contrast, menarche occurs at age 12 or 13—probably at least in part because of a fat intake sufficient to allow an extremely young woman to nourish a fetus—and the first pregnancy may be decades later or never. A female hunter-gatherer may have a total of 150 menstrual cycles, whereas the average woman in modern societies has 400 or more. Although few would suggest that women should become pregnant in their teens to prevent breast cancer later, early administration of a burst of hormones to simulate pregnancy may reduce the risk. Trials to test this idea are now under way at the University of California at San Diego.

TRADE-OFFS AND CONSTRAINTS

Compromise is inherent in every adaptation. Arm bones three times their current thickness would almost never break, but *Homo sapiens* would be lumbering creatures on a never-ending quest for calcium. More sensitive ears might sometimes be useful, but we would be distracted by the noise of air molecules banging into our eardrums.

Such trade-offs also exist at the genetic level. If a mutation offers a net reproductive advantage, it will tend to increase in frequency in a population even if it causes vulnerability to disease. People with two copies of the sickle-cell gene, for example, suffer terrible pain and die young. People with two copies of the "normal" gene are at high risk of death from malaria. But individuals with one of each are protected from both malaria and sickle-cell disease. Where malaria is prevalent, such people are fitter, in the Darwinian sense, than members of either other group. So even though the sickle-cell gene causes disease, it is selected for where malaria persists. Which is the "healthy" allele in this environment? The question has no answer. There is no one normal human genome—there are only genes.

Many other genes that cause disease must also have offered benefits, at least in some environments, or they would not be so common. Because cystic fibrosis (CF) kills one out of 2,500 Caucasians, the responsible genes would appear to be at great risk of being eliminated from the gene pool. And yet they endure. For years, researchers mused that the CF gene, like the sickle-cell gene, probably conferred some advantage. Recently, a study by Gerald B. Pier of Harvard Medical School and his colleagues gave substance to this informed speculation: having one copy of the CF gene appears to decrease the chances of the bearer acquiring a typhoid fever infection, which once had a 15 percent mortality.

Aging may be the ultimate example of a genetic trade-off. In 1957 one of us (Williams) suggested that genes that cause aging and eventual death could nonetheless be selected for if they had other effects that gave an advantage in youth, when the force of selection is stronger. For instance, a hypothetical gene that governs calcium metabolism so that bones heal quickly but that also happens to cause the steady deposition of calcium in arterial walls might well be selected for even though it kills some older people. The influence of such pleiotropic genes (those having multiple effects) has been seen in fruit flies and flour beetles, but no specific example has yet been found in humans. Gout, however, is of particular interest, because it arises when a potent antioxidant, uric acid, forms crystals that precipitate out of fluid in joints. Antioxidants have antiaging effects, and plasma levels of uric acid in different species of primates are closely correlated with average adult life span. Perhaps high levels of uric acid benefit most humans by slowing tissue aging, while a few pay the price with gout.

Other examples are more likely to contribute to more rapid aging. For instance, strong immune defenses protect us from infection but also inflict continuous, low-level tissue damage. It is also possible, of course, that most genes that cause aging have no benefit at any age—they simply never decreased reproductive fitness enough in the natural environment to be selected against. Nevertheless, over the next decade research will surely identify specific genes that accelerate senescence, and researchers will soon thereafter gain the means to interfere with their actions or even change them. Before we tinker, however, we should determine whether these actions have benefits early in life.

Because evolution can take place only in the direction of time's arrow, an organism's design is constrained by structures already in place. As noted, the vertebrate eye is arranged backward. The squid eye, in contrast, is free from this defect, with vessels and nerves running on the outside, penetrating where necessary and pinning down the retina so it cannot detach. The human eye's flaw results from simple bad luck; hundreds of millions of years ago, the layer of cells that happened to become sensitive to light in our ancestors was positioned differently from the corresponding layer in ancestors of squids. The two designs evolved along separate tracks, and there is no going back.

Such path dependence also explains why the simple act of swallowing can be life-threatening. Our respiratory and food passages intersect because in an early lungfish ancestor the air opening for breathing at the surface was understandably located at the top of the snout and led into a common space shared by the food passageway. Because natural selection cannot start from scratch, humans are stuck with the possibility that food will clog the opening to our lungs.

The path of natural selection can even lead to a potentially fatal cul-de-sac, as in the case of the appendix, that vestige of a cavity that our ancestors employed in digestion. Because it no longer performs that function, and as it can kill when infected, the expectation might be that natural selection would have eliminated it. The reality is more complex. Appendicitis results when inflammation causes swelling, which compresses the artery supplying blood to the appendix. Blood flow protects against bacterial growth, so any reduction aids infection, which creates more swelling. If the blood supply is cut off completely, bacteria have free rein until the appendix bursts. A slender appendix is especially susceptible to this chain of events, so appendicitis may, paradoxically, apply the selective pressure that maintains a large appendix. Far from arguing that everything in the body is perfect, an evolutionary analysis reveals that we live with some very unfortunate legacies and that some vulnerabilities may even be actively maintained by the force of natural selection.

EVOLUTION OF DARWINIAN MEDICINE

Despite the power of the Darwinian paradigm, evolutionary biology is just now being recognized as a basic science essential for medicine. Most diseases decrease fitness, so it would seem that natural selection could explain only health, not disease. A Darwinian approach makes sense only when the object of explanation is changed from diseases to the traits that make us vulnerable to diseases. The assumption that natural selection maximizes health also is incorrect—selection maximizes the reproductive success of genes. Those genes that make bodies having superior reproductive success will become more common, even if they compromise the individual's health in the end.

Finally, history and misunderstanding have presented obstacles to the acceptance of Darwinian medicine. An evolutionary approach to functional analysis can appear akin to naive teleology or vitalism, errors banished only recently, and with great effort, from medical thinking. And, of course, whenever evolution and medicine are mentioned together, the specter of eugenics arises. Discoveries made through a Darwinian view of how all human bodies are alike in their vulnerability to disease will offer great benefits for individuals, but such insights do not imply that we can

SELECTED PRINCIPLES OF DARWINIAN MEDICINE

A Darwinian approach to medical practice leads to a shift in perspective. The following principles provide a foundation for considering health and disease in an evolutionary context:

Defenses and **defects** are two fundamentally different manifestations of disease.

Blocking defenses has costs as well as benefits.

Because natural selection shapes defense regulation according to the **smoke-detector principle**, much defensive expression and associated suffering are unnecessary in the individual instance.

Modern epidemics are most likely to arise from the mismatch between **physiological design** of our bodies and **novel aspects** of our environment.

Our **desires**, shaped in the ancestral environment to lead us to actions that tended to maximize reproductive success, now often lead us to disease and early death.

The body is a bundle of **compromises**.

There is no such thing as "the **normal** body."

There is no such thing as "the **normal** human genome."

Some **genes** that cause disease may also have benefits, and others are quirks that cause disease only when they interact with novel environmental factors.

Genetic self-interest will drive an individual's actions, even at the expense of the health and longevity of the individual created by those genes.

Virulence is a trait of the pathogen that can increase as well as decrease.

Symptoms of infection can benefit the pathogen, the host, both or neither.

Disease is **inevitable** because of the way that organisms are shaped by evolution.

Each disease needs a **proximate explanation** of why some people get it and others don't, as well as an **evolutionary explanation** of why members of the species are vulnerable to it.

Diseases are not products of natural selection, but most of the **vulnerabilities** that lead to disease are shaped by the process of natural selection.

Aging is better viewed as a **trade-off** than a disease.

Specific clinical recommendations must be based on **clinical studies**; clinical interventions based only on theory are not scientifically grounded and may cause harm.

or should make any attempt to improve the species. If anything, this approach cautions that apparent genetic defects may have unrecognized adaptive significance, that a single "normal" genome is nonexistent and that notions of "normality" tend to be simplistic.

The systematic application of evolutionary biology to medicine is a new enterprise. Like biochemistry at the beginning of this century, Darwinian medicine very likely will need to develop in several incubators before it can prove its power and utility. If it must progress only from the work of scholars without funding to gather data to test their ideas, it will take decades for the field to mature. Departments of evolutionary biology in medical schools would accelerate the process, but for the most part they do not yet exist. If funding agencies had review panels with evolutionary expertise, research would develop faster, but such panels remain to be created. We expect that they will.

The evolutionary viewpoint provides a deep connection between the states of disease and normal functioning and can integrate disparate avenues of medical research as well as suggest fresh and important areas of inquiry. Its utility and power will ultimately lead to recognition of evolutionary biology as a basic medical science.

FURTHER READING

Evolution of Infectious Disease. P. W. Ewald. Oxford University Press, 1994.
Darwinian Psychiatry. M. T. McGuire and A. Troisi. Harvard University Press, 1998.
Evolution in Health and Disease. Edited by S. Stearns. Oxford University Press, 1998.
Evolutionary Medicine. W. R. Trevathan et al. Oxford University Press [1999].

PART 8

Human Biodiversity

A classic example of the interaction of biology and culture is the interpretation by different cultural systems of two areas of our species' biological diversity: sex and regional phenotypic differences. Our sex differences—that is, our identity as male or female—are interpreted by cultural systems and are translated into the cultural categories of man and woman. The biological categories of sex become the cultural categories of gender, with all their norms, expectations, roles, and identities. Similarly, regional biological differences (combined with real and perceived cultural differences) are translated into the cultural categories of race, which vary from society to society and from one time to another. Understanding the difference between the biological realities and the cultural folk taxonomies (cultural classifications) is one of the major contributions of biological anthropology.

We begin with "The Five Sexes" by Anne Fausto-Sterling. She shows that the two familiar sex categories of male and female are not necessarily sufficient to cover biological reality and, as a result, a more complex gender classification is required.

For a historical perspective on race, we look to Carolus Linnaeus (Carl von Linné), the father of taxonomic classification, in "An Early Racial Taxonomy." His 1758 taxonomy of subspecies within *Homo sapiens*, from *Systema naturae*, reflects the true nature of human racial categories and shows how far back some familiar racial stereotypes go.

In "Science and Race," Jonathan Marks explains why race has no biological meaning or utility, looks at the nature of our species' biodiversity, and offers a brief history of how race has been used in social settings.

Matt Cartmill, in "The Third Man," returns to the topic of the debate over modern human origins (see Selection 25) and discusses the perceived connection between these topics and the idea of human racial equality.

SUGGESTED WEBSITES FOR FURTHER STUDY

http://www.racesci.org/in_media/index.html
http://www.isna.org/index.html

29

The Five Sexes:
Why Male and Female Are Not Enough

Anne Fausto-Sterling

Anne Fausto-Sterling is a developmental geneticist and professor of medical science at Brown University. She is the author of Myths of Gender: Biological Theories About Women and Men *(1992: Basic Books).*

Although the majority of people are clearly and unambiguously either biological males or females, thus explaining why most societies recognize two gender categories, about 4 percent of all births involve intersexes or hermaphrodites, people with some mixture of male and female characteristics. In this selection, Anne Fausto-Sterling argues that such people actually fall into at least three categories, with vast variation even within those, and that society needs to recognize more than two sexes and a more complex system of gender roles and identities. Whatever one thinks of her idea, this selection makes clear the distinction between sex and gender and the real complexity of these categories and their interaction within cultural systems. (For a follow-up paper, see Fausto-Sterling's "The Five Sexes, Revisited" in the July/August 2000 issue of *The Sciences*.)

As you read, consider the following questions:

1. What are the three categories of intersexes that Fausto-Sterling suggests and how are they defined?

2. How has the medical community traditionally dealt with the birth of intersexes? How have laws dealt with intersexes? What cultural assumptions are behind the actions of those groups?

3. How does embryology help explain cases of intersexes?

4. What does Fausto-Sterling envision as an ideal cultural situation with regard to these additional sex categories?

In 1843 Levi Suydam, a twenty-three-year-old resident of Salisbury, Connecticut, asked the town board of selectmen to validate his right to vote as a Whig in a hotly contested local election. The request raised a flurry of objections from the opposition party, for reasons that must be rare in the annals of American democracy: it was said that Suydam was more female than male and thus (some eighty years before suffrage was extended to women) could not be allowed to cast a ballot. To settle the dispute a physician, one William James Barry, was brought in to examine Suydam. And,

"The Five Sexes: Why Male and Female Are Not Enough" by Anne Fausto-Sterling. This article is reprinted by permission of the New York Academy of Sciences and is from *The Sciences,* March/April 1993 issue.

presumably upon encountering a phallus, the good doctor declared the prospective voter male. With Suydam safely in their column the Whigs won the election by a majority of one.

Barry's diagnosis, however, turned out to be somewhat premature. Within a few days he discovered that, phallus notwithstanding, Suydam menstruated regularly and had a vaginal opening. Both his/her physique and his/her mental predispositions were more complex than was first suspected. S/he had narrow shoulders and broad hips and felt occasional sexual yearnings for women. Suydam's "feminine propensities, such as a fondness for gay colors, for pieces of calico, comparing and placing them together, and an aversion for bodily labor, and an inability to perform the same, were remarked by many," Barry later wrote. It is not clear whether Suydam lost or retained the vote, or whether the election results were reversed.

Western culture is deeply committed to the idea that there are only two sexes. Even language refuses other possibilities; thus to write about Levi Suydam I have had to invent conventions—*s/he* and *his/her*—to denote someone who is clearly neither male nor female or who is perhaps both sexes at once. Legally, too, every adult is either man or woman, and the difference, of course, is not trivial. For Suydam it meant the franchise; today it means being available for, or exempt from, draft registration, as well as being subject, in various ways, to a number of laws governing marriage, the family and human intimacy. In many parts of the United States, for instance, two people legally registered as men cannot have sexual relations without violating anti-sodomy statutes.

But if the state and the legal system have an interest in maintaining a two-party sexual system, they are in defiance of nature. For biologically speaking, there are many gradations running from female to male: and depending on how one calls the shots, one can argue that along that spectrum lie at least five sexes—and perhaps even more.

For some time medical investigators have recognized the concept of the intersexual body. But the standard medical literature uses the term *intersex* as a catch-all for three major subgroups with some mixture of male and female characteristics: the so-called true hermaphrodites, whom I call herms, who possess one testis and one ovary (the sperm- and egg-producing vessels, or gonads); the male pseudohermaphrodites (the "merms"), who have testes and some aspects of the female genitalia but no ovaries; and the female pseudohermaphrodites (the "ferms"), who have ovaries and some aspects of the male genitalia but lack testes. Each of those categories is in itself complex; the percentage of male and female characteristics, for instance, can vary enormously among members of the same subgroup. Moreover, the inner lives of the people in each subgroup—their special needs and their problems, attractions and repulsions—have gone unexplored by science. But on the basis of what is known about them I suggest that the three intersexes, herm, merm and ferm, deserve to be considered additional sexes each in its own right. Indeed, I would argue further that sex is a vast, infinitely malleable continuum that defies the constraints of even five categories.

Not surprisingly, it is extremely difficult to estimate the frequency of intersexuality, much less the frequency of each of the three additional sexes: it is not the sort of information one volunteers on a job application. The psychologist John Money of Johns Hopkins University, a specialist in the study of congenital sexual-organ defects, suggests intersexuals may constitute as many as 4 percent of births. As I point out to my students at Brown University, in a student body of about 6,000 that fraction, if correct, implies there may be as many as 240 intersexuals on campus—surely enough to form a minority caucus of some kind.

In reality though, few such students would make it as far as Brown in sexually diverse form. Recent advances in physiology and surgical technology now enable physicians to catch most intersexuals at the moment of birth. Almost at once such infants are entered into a program of hormonal and surgical management so that they can slip quietly into society as "normal" heterosexual males or females. I emphasize that the motive is in no way conspiratorial. The aims of the policy are genuinely humanitarian, reflecting the wish that people be able to "fit in" both physically and psychologically. In the medical community, however, the assumptions behind that wish—that there be only two sexes, that heterosexuality alone is normal, that there is one true model of psychological health—have gone virtually unexamined.

The word *hermaphrodite* comes from the Greek names Hermes, variously known as the messenger of the gods, the patron of music, the controller of dreams or the protector of livestock, and Aphrodite, the goddess of sexual love and beauty. According to Greek mythology, those two gods parented Hermaphroditus, who at age fifteen became half male and half female when his body fused with the body of a nymph he fell in love with. In some true hermaphrodites the testis and the ovary grow separately but bilaterally; in others they grow together within the same organ, forming an ovo-testis. Not infrequently, at least one of the gonads functions quite well, producing either sperm cells or eggs, as well as functional levels of the sex hormones—androgens or estrogens. Although in theory it might be possible for a true hermaphrodite to become both father and mother to a child, in practice the appropriate ducts and tubes are not configured so that egg and sperm can meet.

In contrast with the true hermaphrodites, the pseudohermaphrodites possess two gonads of the same kind along with the usual male (XY) or female (XX) chromosomal makeup. But their external genitalia and secondary sex characteristics do not match their chromosomes. Thus merms have testes and XY chromosomes, yet they also have a vagina and a clitoris, and at puberty they often develop breasts. They do not menstruate, however. Ferms have ovaries, two X chromosomes and sometimes a uterus, but they also have at least partly masculine external genitalia. Without medical intervention they can develop beards, deep voices and adult-size penises.

No classification scheme could more than suggest the variety of sexual anatomy encountered in clinical practice. In 1969, for example, two French investigators, Paul Guinet of the Endocrine Clinic in Lyons and

Jacques Decourt of the Endocrine Clinic in Paris, described ninety-eight cases of true hermaphroditism—again, signifying people with both ovarian and testicular tissue—solely according to the appearance of the external genitalia and the accompanying ducts. In some cases the people exhibited strongly feminine development. They had separate openings for the vagina and the urethra, a cleft vulva defined by both the large and the small labia, or vaginal lips, and at puberty they developed breasts and usually began to menstruate. It was the oversize and sexually alert clitoris, which threatened sometimes at puberty to grow into a penis, that usually impelled them to seek medical attention. Members of another group also had breasts and a feminine body type, and they menstruated. But their labia were at least partly fused, forming an incomplete scrotum. The phallus (here an embryological term for a structure that during usual development goes on to form either a clitoris or a penis) was between 1.5 and 2.8 inches long; nevertheless, they urinated through a urethra that opened into or near the vagina.

By far the most frequent form of true hermaphrodite encountered by Guinet and Decourt—55 percent—appeared to have a more masculine physique. In such people the urethra runs either through or near the phallus, which looks more like a penis than a clitoris. Any menstrual blood exits periodically during urination. But in spite of the relatively male appearance of the genitalia, breasts appear at puberty. It is possible that a sample larger than ninety-eight so-called true hermaphrodites would yield even more contrasts and subtleties. Suffice it to say that the varieties are so diverse that it is possible to know which parts are present and what is attached to what only after exploratory surgery.

The embryological origins of human hermaphrodites clearly fit what is known about male and female sexual development. The embryonic gonad generally chooses early in development to follow either a male or a female sexual pathway; for the ovo-testis, however, that choice is fudged. Similarly, the embryonic phallus most often ends up as a clitoris or a penis, but the existence of intermediate states comes as no surprise to the embryologist. There are also uro-genital swellings in the embryo that usually either stay open and become the vaginal labia or fuse and become a scrotum. In some hermaphrodites, though, the choice of opening or closing is ambivalent. Finally, all mammalian embryos have structures that can become the female uterus and the fallopian tubes, as well as structures that can become part of the male sperm-transport system. Typically either the male or the female set of those primordial genital organs degenerates, and the remaining structures achieve their sex-appropriate future. In hermaphrodites both sets of organs develop to varying degrees.

Intersexuality itself is old news. Hermaphrodites, for instance, are often featured in stories about human origins. Early biblical scholars believed Adam began life as a hermaphrodite and later divided into two people—a male and a female—after falling from grace. According to Plato there once were three sexes—male, female and hermaphrodite—but the third sex was lost with time.

Both the Talmud and the Tosefta, the Jewish books of law, list extensive regulations for people of mixed sex. The Tosefta expressly forbids hermaphrodites to inherit their fathers' estates (like daughters), to seclude themselves with women (like sons) or to shave (like men). When hermaphrodites menstruate they must be isolated from men (like women); they are disqualified from serving as witnesses or as priests (like women), but the laws of pederasty apply to them.

In Europe a pattern emerged by the end of the Middle Ages that, in a sense, has lasted to the present day: hermaphrodites were compelled to choose an established gender role and stick with it. The penalty for transgression was often death: Thus in the 1600s a Scottish hermaphrodite living as a woman was buried alive after impregnating his/her master's daughter.

For questions of inheritance, legitimacy, paternity, succession to title and eligibility for certain professions to be determined, modern Anglo-Saxon legal systems require that newborns be registered as either male or female. In the U.S. today sex determination is governed by state laws. Illinois permits adults to change the sex recorded on their birth certificates should a physician attest to having performed the appropriate surgery. The New York Academy of Medicine, on the other hand, has taken an opposite view. In spite of surgical alterations of the external genitalia, the academy argued in 1966, the chromosomal sex remains the same. By that measure, a person's wish to conceal his or her original sex cannot outweigh the public interest in protection against fraud.

During this century the medical community has completed what the legal world began—the complete erasure of any form of embodied sex that does not conform to a male–female, heterosexual pattern. Ironically, a more sophisticated knowledge of the complexity of sexual systems has led to the repression of such intricacy.

In 1937 the urologist Hugh H. Young of Johns Hopkins University published a volume titled *Genital Abnormalities, Hermaphroditism and Related Adrenal Diseases*. The book is remarkable for its erudition, scientific insight and open-mindedness. In it Young drew together a wealth of carefully documented case histories to demonstrate and study the medical treatment of such "accidents of birth." Young did not pass judgment on the people he studied, nor did he attempt to coerce into treatment those intersexuals who rejected that option. And he showed unusual even-handedness in referring to those people who had had sexual experiences as both men and women as "practicing hermaphrodites."

One of Young's more interesting cases was a hermaphrodite named Emma who had grown up as a female. Emma had both a penis-size clitoris and a vagina, which made it possible for him/her to have "normal" heterosexual sex with both men and women. As a teenager Emma had had sex with a number of girls to whom s/he was deeply attracted; but at the age of nineteen s/he married a man. Unfortunately, he had given Emma little sexual pleasure (though *he* had had no complaints), and so throughout that marriage and subsequent ones Emma had kept girlfriends on the side. With some frequency s/he had pleasurable sex with them. Young describes his subject as appearing "to be quite content and even happy." In conversation Emma occasionally told him of his/her wish to be a man, a circumstance Young said would be relatively easy to bring about. But Emma's reply strikes a heroic blow for self-interest:

> Would you have to remove that vagina? I don't know about that because that's my meal ticket. If you did that, I would have to quit my husband and go to work, so I think I'll keep it and stay as I am. My husband supports me well, and even though I don't have any sexual pleasure with him, I do have lots with my girlfriends.

Yet even as Young was illuminating intersexuality with the light of scientific reason, he was beginning its suppression. For his book is also an extended treatise on the most modern surgical and hormonal methods of changing intersexuals into either males or females. Young may have differed from his successors in being less judgmental and controlling of the patients and their families, but he nonetheless supplied the foundation on which current intervention practices were built.

By 1969, when the English physicians Christopher J. Dewhurst and Ronald R. Gordon wrote *The Intersexual Disorders*, medical and surgical approaches to intersexuality had neared a state of rigid uniformity. It is hardly surprising that such a hardening of opinion took place in the era of the feminine mystique—of the post–Second World War flight to the suburbs and the strict division of family roles according to sex. That the medical consensus was not quite universal (or perhaps that it seemed poised to break apart again) can be gleaned from the near-hysterical tone of Dewhurst and Gordon's book, which contrasts markedly with the calm reason of Young's founding work. Consider their opening description of an intersexual newborn:

> One can only attempt to imagine the anguish of the parents. That a newborn should have a deformity . . . [affecting] so fundamental an issue as the very sex of the child . . . is a tragic event which immediately conjures up visions of a hopeless psychological misfit doomed to live always as a sexual freak in loneliness and frustration.

Dewhurst and Gordon warned that such a miserable fate would, indeed, be a baby's lot should the case be improperly managed; "but fortunately," they wrote, "with correct management the outlook is infinitely better than the poor parents—emotionally stunned by the event—or indeed anyone without special knowledge could ever imagine."

Scientific dogma has held fast to the assumption that without medical care hermaphrodites are doomed to a life of misery. Yet there are few empirical studies to back up that assumption, and some of the same research gathered to build a case for medical treatment contradicts it. Francies Benton, another of Young's practicing hermaphrodites, "had not worried over his condition, did not wish to be changed, and was enjoying life." The same could be said of Emma, the opportunistic hausfrau. Even Dewhurst and Gordon, adamant about the psychological importance of treating intersexuals at the infant stage, acknowledged great success in "changing the sex" of older patients. They reported on twenty cases of children reclassified into a different sex after the supposedly critical age of eighteen months. They asserted that all the reclassifications were "successful," and they wondered then whether reregistration could be "recommended more readily than [had] been suggested so far."

The treatment of intersexuality in this century provides a clear example of what the French historian Michel Foucault has called biopower. The knowledge developed in biochemistry, embryology, endocrinology, psychology and surgery has enabled physicians to control the very sex of the human body. The multiple contradictions in that kind of power call for some scrutiny. On the one hand, the medical "management" of intersexuality certainly developed as part of an attempt to free people from perceived psychological pain (though whether the pain was the patient's, the parents' or the physician's is unclear). And if one accepts the assumption that in a sex-divided culture people can realize their greatest potential for happiness and productivity only if they are sure they belong to one of only two acknowledged sexes, modern medicine has been extremely successful.

On the other hand, the same medical accomplishments can be read not as progress but as a mode of discipline. Hermaphrodites have unruly bodies. They do not fall naturally into a binary classification; only a surgical shoehorn can put them there. But why should we care if a "woman," defined as one who has breasts, a vagina, a uterus and ovaries and who menstruates, also has a clitoris large enough to penetrate the vagina of another woman? Why should we care if there are people whose biological equipment enables them to have sex "naturally" with both men and women? The answers seem to lie in a cultural need to maintain clear distinctions between the sexes. Society mandates the control of intersexual bodies because they blur and bridge the great divide. Inasmuch as hermaphrodites literally embody both sexes, they challenge traditional beliefs about sexual difference: they possess the irritating ability to live sometimes as one sex and sometimes the other, and they raise the specter of homosexuality.

But what if things were altogether different? Imagine a world in which the same knowledge that has enabled medicine to intervene in the management of intersexual patients has been placed at the service of multiple sexualities. Imagine that the sexes have multiplied beyond currently imaginable limits. It would have to be a world of shared powers. Patient and physician, parent and child, male and female, heterosexual and homosexual—all those oppositions and others would have to be dissolved as sources of division. A new ethic of medical treatment would arise, one that would permit ambiguity in a culture that had overcome sexual division. The central mission of medical treatment would be to preserve life. Thus hermaphrodites would be concerned primarily not about whether they can conform to society but about whether they might develop potentially life-threatening conditions—hernias, gonadal tumors, salt imbalance caused by adrenal malfunction—that sometimes accompany hermaphroditic development. In my ideal world medical intervention for intersexuals would take place only rarely before the age of reason; subsequent treatment would be a cooperative venture between physician, patient and other advisers trained in issues of gender multiplicity.

I do not pretend that the transition to my utopia would be smooth. Sex, even the supposedly "normal," heterosexual kind, continues to cause untold anxieties in Western society. And certainly a culture that has yet to come to grips—religiously and, in some states,

legally—with the ancient and relatively uncomplicated reality of homosexual love will not readily embrace intersexuality. No doubt the most troublesome arena by far would be the rearing of children. Parents, at least since the Victorian era, have fretted, sometimes to the point of outright denial, over the fact that their children are sexual beings.

All that and more amply explains why intersexual children are generally squeezed into one of the two prevailing sexual categories. But what would be the psychological consequences of taking the alternative road—raising children as unabashed intersexuals? On the surface that tack seems fraught with peril. What, for example, would happen to the intersexual child amid the unrelenting cruelty of the school yard? When the time came to shower in gym class, what horrors and humiliations would await the intersexual as his/her anatomy was displayed in all its non-traditional glory? In whose gym class would s/he register to begin with? What bathroom would s/he use? And how on earth would Mom and Dad help shepherd him/her through the mine field of puberty?

In the past thirty years those questions have been ignored, as the scientific community has, with remarkable unanimity, avoided contemplating the alternative route of unimpeded intersexuality. But modern investigators tend to overlook a substantial body of case histories, most of them compiled between 1930 and 1960, before surgical intervention became rampant. Almost without exception, those reports describe children who grew up knowing they were intersexual (though they did not advertise it) and adjusted to their unusual status. Some of the studies are richly detailed—described at the level of gym-class showering (which most intersexuals avoided without incident); in any event, there is not a psychotic or a suicide in the lot.

Still, the nuances of socialization among intersexuals cry out for more sophisticated analysis. Clearly, before my vision of sexual multiplicity can be realized, the first openly intersexual children and their parents will have to be brave pioneers who will bear the brunt of society's growing pains. But in the long view—though it could take generations to achieve—the prize might be a society in which sexuality is something to be celebrated for its subtleties and not something to be feared or ridiculed.

30

An Early Racial Taxonomy
from *"Systema naturae"* (10th ed., 1758)

Carolus Linnaeus

Carl von Linné (1707–1778), better known to us by his latinized name, Carolus Linnaeus, was a Swedish botanist and physician and a prolific writer, with around 180 published works to his name. His most famous, perhaps, is his Systema naturae *(Natural System), first published in 1735, in which he outlined his scheme for classifying living organisms according to a binomial nomenclature: that is, two names, the first of which indicated a large category and the second of which was the most specific. These are our familiar genus and species names—for example,* Homo sapiens *for our species. He also attempted to lump organisms into larger groups, orders, and families. Although Linnaeus was a creationist, he felt there was a method to God's living creations and one of his projects was to describe what God had in mind. (Linnaeus was never known for his modesty!) Others had attempted such things before, but Linnaeus felt their systems were too human-centered, that they named organisms according to such things as how useful they were to people. He thought species were natural entities (in the sense that they had been created by the mind of God) and should be named and classified according to inherent traits, not perceived ones. Thus, he classified plants by the number and type of their reproductive organs. In subsequent editions of his work, he named other organisms, including mammals (a word he invented, sticking with his emphasis on reproduction). It was in the tenth edition (1758) that he included* Homo sapiens *within the order Primates. It is also noteworthy that, although Linnaeus thought he was describing a static world, he did indicate that he thought perhaps new species could arise through hybridization between existing plant species (which is possible) or due to some environmental influence.*

During Linnaeus's time, European exploration of the world was rapidly increasing knowledge about, among other things, the great variety of peoples that inhabited that world. Sampling groups of people from far-flung corners of the world seemed to clearly indicate that human beings came in a small number of fairly discrete varieties or races, essentially divided by continent. Linnaeus included this variation in his taxonomy, naming five subspecies of *Homo sapiens*, as well as a second species of *Homo*. The second species, *Homo monstrosus*, was to accommodate explorers' yarns of wild "half men" covered with hair and sporting tails. One subspecies, *Homo sapiens ferus* (wild men) was for the probably retarded and aban-doned children who were sometimes found wandering in the woods and who were said to have been raised by animals. The remaining four subspecies should sound familiar. The European taxonomy of human racial groups, which Linnaeus merely formalized within his system, has influenced history down to the present day. Note that Linnaeus's descriptions of each of these races are combinations of physical generalizations, cultural traits, and what anthropologist Stephen Molnar calls "personality profiles." Race to Linnaeus was what it is to us—and to all cultures—today: cultural categories based on a society's interpretation of and attitude toward the people of the world it knows.

Based on translations from Stephen Jay Gould, *The Mismeasure of Man*, rev. and expanded ed., W. W. Norton, 1996, 404–5; and Kenneth A. R. Kennedy, *Human Variations in Space and Time*, Wm. C. Brown, 1976, 25.

As you read, consider the following questions:

1. Linnaeus does not list his racial groups in a ranked order, but his descriptions clearly indicate a hierarchical order to the groups. What is that order; in other words, from Linnaeus's European perspective, how are these four groups ranked?

2. Think about examples of how these groupings, and the cultural attitudes toward them, have influenced world history. How have they influenced American society in particular?

....

Class: **Mammalia**
Order: **Primates**
Genus: *Homo*
Species: *monstrosus*   Varying by climate or art

       sapiens   Diurnal; varying by education and situation

          Varieties:

ferus	Four-footed, mute, hairy
americanus	Red, choleric [angry], upright. Hair black, straight, thick; nostrils wide; face harsh; beard scanty; obstinate, content free. Paints himself with fine red lines. Ruled by habit.
europaeus	White, sanguine [cheerful], muscular. Hair yellow, brown, flowing; eyes blue; gentle, acute, inventive. Covered with cloth vestments. Ruled by custom [or law].
asiaticus	Pale-yellow, melancholy, stiff. Hair black; eyes dark; severe, haughty, covetous. Covered with loose garments. Ruled by belief [or opinions].
afer	Black, phlegmatic [sluggish], relaxed. Hair black, frizzled; skin silky; nose flat; lips tumid [swollen]; crafty, indolent, negligent. Anoints himself with grease. Ruled by caprice [impulse].

31

Science and Race

Jonathan Marks

Besides his specialty in molecular anthropology (see Selection 17), Jon Marks is interested in the question of human biodiversity and race.

One of the most difficult concepts to understand within bioanthropology is the fact that, although the human species displays biological diversity with regional populations showing genetic and phenotypic differences, that diversity cannot be scientifically divided into a given number of subspecies or races. Race, in other words, does not exist for our species on a biological level. Rather, race is a cultural classification. But the confusion of biological variation and cultural categories has been used to establish, maintain, and justify various schemes of social stratification, for example, by making the assertion that different racial groups differ in mental abilities. In this selection, Jonathan Marks explains why race is not a useful biological concept. He also describes the nature of human biodiversity and addresses the issue of variation among populations in intelligence and mental potentials.

As you read, consider the following questions:

1. Is the human species divisible into discrete racial groups? What is the evidence for Marks's answer to that question?

2. How can we tell whether a difference observed between two populations is based on genetic differences?

3. What is the evidence for a biological difference in cognitive ability among human populations? In this regard, what is the distinction Marks makes between performance and ability, and why is it important to the topic of the article?

4. What was the eugenics movement? Have its basic assumptions been verified scientifically?

5. What does Marks mean when he says, "Racial problems are not racial"?

From the standpoint of biological anthropology, there are two general contributions we can make to the discourse of race in America. The first is to understand the empirical pattern of biological or genetic diversity among indigenous human populations, and its relation to structured behavioral or cultural variation. The second involves demonstrating that the focus on human biological variation in American society represents simply one more example of how biology has been regularly recruited into discussions of social issues as a means of falsely justifying a position.

RACE AS AN EMPIRICAL ISSUE

Teaching that racial categories lack biological validity can be as much of a challenge as teaching in the 17th

From *American Behavioral Scientist*, November–December 1996, Vol. 40, No. 2, pp 123–133. Copyright © 1996 by Jonathan Marks. Reprinted by permission of Sage Publications, Inc.

century that the earth goes around the sun—when anyone can plainly see the sun rise, traverse a path along the sky, and set beyond the opposing horizon. How can something that seems so obvious be denied?

Of course, that is the way all great scientific breakthroughs appear, by denying folk wisdom and replacing it with a more sophisticated and analytic interpretation of the same data. We can break down race into four separate empirical issues, each of which has been comprehensively answered by anthropology in [the twentieth] century.

Is the Human Species Naturally Divisible into a Small Number of Reasonably Discrete Groups?

Whether we examine people's bodies or sample their genes, the pattern that we encounter is very concordant. People are similar to those from geographically nearby and different from those far away. We refer to this pattern as *clinal*, a cline being simply a geographic gradient of a particular biological feature (Huxley, 1938; Livingstone, 1962).

Dividing human populations into a small number of discrete groups results in associations of populations and divisions between populations that are arbitrary, not natural. Africa, for example, is home to tall, thin people in Kenya (Nilotic), short people in Zaire (Pygmies), and peoples in southern Africa who are sufficiently different from our physical stereotypes of Africans (i.e., *West* Africans) as to have caused an earlier generation to speculate on whether they had some southeast Asian ancestry (Hiernaux, 1974). As far as we know, all are biologically different, all are indigenously African, and to establish a single category (African/Black/Negroid) to encompass them all reflects an arbitrary decision about human diversity, one that is not at all dictated by nature.

Further, grouping the peoples of Africa together as a single entity and dividing them from the peoples of Europe and the Near East (European/White/Caucasoid) imposes an exceedingly unnatural distinction at the boundary between the two groups. In fact, the "African" peoples of Somalia are far more similar to the peoples of, say, Saudi Arabia or Iran—which are close to Somalia—than they are to the Ghanaians on the western side of Africa. And the Iranis and Saudis are themselves more similar to the Somalis than to Norwegians. Thus associating the Ghanaians and Somalis on one hand and Saudis and Norwegians on the other generates an artificial pattern that is contradicted by empirical studies of human biology.

The reason why this clinal pattern exists lies in the processes of microevolution in the human species. Natural selection adapts people to their environment, yet environments generally change gradually over geography—consequently, adaptive differences in the human species might be expected to track that pattern. In addition, people interbreed with people nearby, who in turn interbreed with people nearby, and over the long run this reinforces the gradual nature of biological distinctions among populations. Indeed, the "isolation" of traditional indigenous peoples is a feature that has been consistently overestimated in the history of anthropology—all peoples trade, and where goods flow, so do genes (Terrell & Stewart, 1996; Wolf, 1972).

We know very little about the time frame in which these clines originated, but genetic and paleontological evidence points to a recent origin for the genetic diversity within our species. For example, we find two randomly chosen chimpanzees or gorillas to be considerably more different genetically than two randomly chosen humans, even though chimps, gorillas, and humans diverged from one another about 7 million years ago and are all consequently the same age

(Ferris, Brown, Davidson, & Wilson, 1981; Ruano, Rogers, Ferguson-Smith, & Kidd, 1992). Genetic diversity in the human species is surprisingly ephemeral— only on the scale of tens of thousands of years—and seems in some large measure to have been replaced by cultural diversity.

The reason why Americans tend to see three "races" of people is simply an artifact of history and statistics. Immigrants to America have come mostly from ports where seafaring vessels in earlier centuries could pick them up—hence our notion of African is actually *West* African, and our notion of Asian is actually *East* Asian (Brace, 1995). When we realize that people originating from very different parts of the world are likely to look very different and combine that with the fact that most European immigrants came from north-central Europe, it is not hard to see why we might perceive three types of people.

If there were a larger immigrant presence in America representing the rest of the world—western Asia, Oceania, East or South Africa, the Arctic—we would be more struck by our inability to classify them easily as representatives of three groups. Perhaps the most obvious example involves the people of South Asia (India and Pakistan), who are darkly complected (like Africans), facially resemble Europeans, and live on the continent of Asia!

To an earlier generation, dividing humans into three types harmonized well with a mythical history that saw humans as descended from Noah's three sons. Although the far reaches of the continents were unknown to them, the ancient Hebrews ascribed the North Africans to the lineage of Ham, central and southern Europeans to the lineage of Japheth, and West Asians (including themselves) to the lineage of Shem, "after their families, after their tongues, in their lands, in their nations" (Genesis 10:20). This origin myth spread in the Roman Empire through the popularity of the *Antiquities of the Jews* by Flavius Josephus (Hannaford, 1996).

However, if there were three geographic types of people in nature, it is difficult to know in the light of modern knowledge what they might represent biohistorically Did one ancestral lineage (Ham) settle near Ghana, one (Shem) settle near Korea, and one (Japheth) settle near Norway, their descendants becoming rather distinct from one another and remaining rather homogenous as they spread outward and mixed at the fringes—as some 19th-century writers essentially believed? No; humans have always been living and evolving in the in-between places, and there is no basis on which to regard the most divergent peoples as somehow the most primordial.

Actually, our racial archetypes represent not some pure ancestors but symbolic representations of the most biologically extreme peoples on earth. We may note in this context that the father of biological classification, Linnaeus, defined Europeans as blond and blue-eyed. Linnaeus, of course, was Swedish. But people with these features are the most *extreme* Europeans, not the most European, nor the most representative.

Dividing and classifying are cultural acts and represent the imposition of arbitrary decisions on natural patterns. This is most evident in the legalities of defining races, so that intermarriage between them could be prohibited—the miscegenation laws (Wright, 1995). In general, a single black great-grandparent was sufficient to establish a person as "Black," whereas seven white great-grandparents were insufficient to establish one as "White." Here, race can be seen as inherited according to a symbolic or folk system of heredity, in contrast to biological inheritance. Thus racial heredity is qualitative, all or nothing, whereas biological heredity is quantitative and fractional.

Can We Compare People from Different Parts of the World?

The primary basis of all science is comparison. Peoples of the world differ from one another, and to understand the nature of those differences we are obliged to compare them. The social issues overlying such comparisons, however, necessitate considerably more introspection than would be taken for granted by a scientist accustomed to comparing spiders or earthworms (Marks, 1995).

The skin, hair, face, and body form all vary across the world's populations. In humans, these biological differences are complemented and exaggerated by differences in language, behavior, dress, and the other components of the cumulative historical stream we call culture. The skeletal differences among the world's most different peoples are actually quite subtle, however, so that although a trained forensic anthropologist can allocate *modern* remains into a small number of given categories, it is virtually impossible to do so with prehistoric remains (Clark, 1963).

The fact that skeletal remains can be sorted into preexisting categories does *not* mean that those categories represent fundamental divisions of the human species (Brace, 1995; Sauer, 1992). When asked to sort blocks of various sizes into large and small, a child can do so easily and replicably, but that is not a testimony to the existence of two kinds of blocks in the universe. It is a testament only to the ease with which distinctions can be imposed on gradients.

By the 18th century, European sailors had demonstrated unambiguously that all known human populations were interfertile and were thus biologically a single taxonomic unit in spite of the perceptible differences among them. Indeed, reconciling the obvious differences among humans to a single creative act in the Bible led 18th-century European scientists (such as Buffon) to the first theories of microevolution. On the other hand, theories of multiple origins of different peoples (polygenism, as opposed to monogenism) persisted in the United States through the Civil War. These biological theories helped to justify the subjugation of non-Whites by emphasizing their biological separation (Stanton, 1960). In the 1920s, geneticists still debated whether race-crossing might be genetically harmful because of the apparently profound differences among human populations (Davenport & Steggerda, 1929; Provine, 1973). Those differences are not so genetically substantial, however, for such interbreeding among human populations has not shown evidence of biologically harmful effects (Shapiro, 1961).

Are Consistently Detectable Differences between Human Populations Genetic?

This is quite possibly the most widely misunderstood aspect of human biology, in spite of nearly a century of study. If I study 1,000 Ibos from Nigeria and 1,000 Danes from Denmark, I can observe any number of differences between the two groups. One group, for example, is darkly complected; the other is lightly complected. This difference would probably be the same whether I selected my sample in the year 1900, 2000, or 2100, and it is presumably genetic in etiology.

On the other hand, one group speaks Ibo and the other speaks Danish. That difference would also be there if I selected my sample in 1900, 2000, or 2100, but it is presumably *not* genetic. At least, generations of immigrants attest to the unlikelihood of a genetic component to it.

How, then, can we know from the observation of a difference whether the difference is biologically based or not?

European explorers were well aware that the people who looked the most different from them also acted the most differently. Linnaeus had invoked broad suites of personality ("impassive, lazy") and culture traits ("wears loose-fitting clothes") in his diagnosis of four geographic subspecies of humans in 1758. The next generation of researchers recognized that these traits were both overgeneralized (if not outright slanderous) and exceedingly malleable, and they sought to establish their formal divisions of the human species solely on biological criteria. (One can also observe that cultural boundaries [political, linguistic, etc.] are generally discrete, in contrast to clinal biological variation, which makes it unlikely that the two are causally connected.)

It was widely assumed by the middle of the 19th century that regardless of the degree of malleability of mental or behavioral traits of human groups, the features of the *body* were fundamentally immutable. Thus traits like the shape of the head could be taken as an indicator of transcendent biological affinity—groups with similarly shaped heads were closely related, and those with differently shaped heads were more distantly related (Gould, 1981).

The first to challenge this assumption empirically was Boas (1912), who measured skulls of immigrants to Ellis Island and compared them to those of relatives already living in the United States. He found that the human body is indeed very sensitive to the conditions of growth and that there was a decided tendency of diverse immigrant groups to become more physically convergent in America—in spite of marrying within their own groups—than they were when they arrived.

In particular, the shape of the head turned out to be very malleable, and not at all a reliable indicator of genetics or race. Subsequent studies of other immigrant groups, notably Japanese immigrants to Hawaii by Shapiro and Hulse (in Shapiro 1939), supported this discovery. Thus the observation of consistent difference between groups of people—even of the body—is not necessarily indicative of a genetic basis for that difference (Kaplan, 1954; Lasker, 1969). This work effectively shifted the burden of proof from those who *question* a genetic basis for the observation of difference to those who *assert* it.

To establish a genetic basis for an observed difference between two populations, therefore, requires more than just observing the difference to be consistent. It requires presumably genetic data. The inference of a genetic difference in the absence of genetic data thus represents not a scientific theory of heredity but a folk theory of heredity. To the extent that behavioral and mental traits—such as test scores and athletic performances—are even more developmentally plastic than are strictly physical traits, the same injunction must hold even more strongly for them. Genetic inferences require genetic data.

Do Different Groups Have Different Potentials?

One of the catch-phrases of 1995's best-selling *The Bell Curve* (Herrnstein & Murray, 1994) was "cognitive ability." Eluding a scientifically rigorous definition, the phrase is left to be explained by a commonsense or folk definition—cognitive ability presumably means the mental development possible for a person under optimal circumstances. But it would take an extraordinarily naive or evil scientist to suggest seriously that such circumstances are, in fact, broadly optimized across social groups in our society. Consequently, not only can we not establish *that* abilities are different, we have no reliable way even to measure such an innate property in the first place. What we have is performance—on tests or just in life—which is measurable, but which is the result of many things, only one of which is unmeasurable innate ability.

Once again, we encounter the problem of a burden of proof for a biological assertion. If the concept itself is metaphysical, the burden of proof must obviously be very heavy. On one hand, it is not at all unreasonable to suggest that different people have different individual "gifts"—we all possess unique genetic constellations, after all. On the other hand, those gifts are not amenable to scientific study, for they are only detectable by virtue of having been developed or cultivated. Thus no scientific statements can be responsibly made about such genetic gifts in the absence of the life history of the person to whom they belong.

In other words, ability is a concept that is generally easy to see only in the past tense. I know I had the ability to be a college professor, because I *am* one; but how can I know in any scientifically valid sense whether I *could have been* a major-league third baseman? I can't, so it is simply vain for me to speculate on it. A life is lived but once, and what it could have been—while fascinating to contemplate—is not a scientific issue.

There is also an important asymmetry about the concept of ability. A good performance indicates a good ability, but a poor performance need not indicate poor ability. As noted above, many factors go into a performance, only one of which is ability. Thus, when we encounter the question of whether poor performance—even over the long term—is an indication of the lack of cognitive ability, the only defensible position from the standpoint of biology is agnosticism. We do not know whether humans or human groups differ in their potentials in any significant way. More than that, we *cannot* know—so this question lies outside the domain of scientific discourse and within the domain of folk knowledge.

Further, this raises a darker question: What are we to make of scientists who assert the existence of constitutional differences in ability? If we cannot gauge differences in ability in any reliable manner, it is a corruption of science to assert in its name that one group indeed has less ability than another. From the mouth or pen of a politician, the assertion might reflect ignorance or demagoguery; from that of a scientist, it reflects incompetence or irresponsibility. Scientists are subject to the cultural values of their time, place, and class and historically have found it difficult to disentangle those values from their pronouncements as scientists. We now recognize the need to define the boundaries of science in order to distinguish the authoritative voice of scientists speaking as scientists from the voice of scientists speaking as citizens. This distinction is vital to keeping science from being tarnished by those few scientists who have chosen to invoke it as a validation of odious social and political doctrines.

A reliable inference of differences in ability from the observation of differences in performance requires the control of many cultural and life history variables. The first step toward controlling those variables is to develop a society in which children from diverse social groups and upbringings have equal opportunities to cultivate their diverse gifts.

HUMAN BIOLOGY THROUGH THE LENS OF HISTORY

Because ability is a metaphysical concept, there is no valid evidence from the fields of science that groups of people have similar abilities, any more than there is evidence that they have different abilities.

There is evidence bearing on this issue from the humanities, however—namely, history. Ours is not the first generation in which the claim has been put forward that human groups are of unequal worth, ostensibly based on science. Leading geneticists of the 1910s and 1920s avidly promoted the recent discoveries of chromosomes and Mendel's laws. Breakthroughs in genetics suggested that it might be fruitful to look there for a solution to America's social problems. Crosscutting political lines, Americans widely embraced a social philosophy known as eugenics, whose cardinal tenet was that antisocial traits represented the effects of a gene for "feeblemindedness," which had a very uneven distribution in the world (Davenport, 1911). It was found commonly among the rural and urban poor, and across the world in the techno-economically backward nations.

Among the most widely cited data was the pseudonymous Kallikak family, whose 18th-century genitor had sired a child by a "feebleminded tavern girl" and another by his lawful Quaker wife. Several generations later, the descendants of the illegitimate son were primarily social outcasts, whereas those of the legitimate son were upstanding citizens (Goddard, 1912). This was cited for decades, even in genetics textbooks, as evidence for the transmission of feeblemindedness through one side of the family—in spite of the fact that it could hardly be diagnosed as a biological trait.

Scientific solutions to America's problems readily presented themselves on this basis: (a) restriction of immigration for the "feebleminded" hoping to enter the country and (b) sterilization for the "feebleminded" already here (Grant, 1916). The latter was upheld by the Supreme Court's 1927 decision in *Buck v. Bell*, in which the right of the state to sterilize the feebleminded, who "sap the strength of our nation," was upheld, on the grounds that "three generations of imbeciles are enough." This was not about enabling the poor to control their own reproduction, by giving them both the life options and the technology to implement them, but rather about the elimination of the gene pool of the poor, on the basis that it was irredeemably corrupt. Immigration restriction was enacted by the Johnson Act of 1924 and had an ultimate effect of denying asylum to many who would later suffer at the hands of the Nazis. Both were based on the expert voices of geneticists (Allen, 1983; Kevles, 1985; Paul, 1995).

The eugenics movement was not so much racist as classist—asserting the genetic superiority of the rich over the poor—but the Depression showed widely that economic status was not a reliable basis on which to infer genetic constitution. It was, curiously enough, geneticists themselves whose blind faith in (and promotion of) their subject proved them to be the least able to distinguish their own science from the folk prejudices that merely claimed that particular science as its basis.

Nearly a century later, however, some of these ideas are undergoing a renaissance. Promoting the Human Genome Project, James Watson declared that "we used to think our fate was in the stars. Now we know, in large measure, our fate is in our genes" (Jaroff, 1989, p. 67). With such a blank check for the power of genetics, it is no wonder we now hear routinely about hypothetical genes for crime, personality, intelligence, and sexual preference—often with evidence no more substantive than was presented in the 1920s (Nelkin & Lindee, 1995).

The eugenics movement was predicated on the apocalyptic fear that high reproductive rates in the lower classes would doom the nation to ever-growing numbers of constitutionally stupid people. And yet the descendants of those poor people became educated and socially mobile, and they have shown themselves indeed capable of running the nation. Ironically, the group targeted most strongly by I.Q. zealots of that era—poor immigrant Ashkenazi Jews—are now identified in *The Bell Curve* as comprising a "cognitive elite." With such extraordinary intellectual leapfrogging documentable in the history of this subject, we are consequently obliged to regard skeptically any broad criticisms of the gene pools of large classes of people. The issue revealed itself to be a social one—how to allow the children of the poor access to the means to develop their abilities—not a biological one, their lack of abilities.

CONCLUSIONS

Racial classifications represent a form of folk heredity, wherein subjects are compelled to identify with one of a small number of designated human groups. Where parents are members of different designated groups, offspring are generally expected to choose one, in defiance of their biological relationships.

Differing patterns of migration, and the intermixture that accompanies increasing urbanization, are ultimately proving the biological uselessness of racial classifications. Identification with a group is probably a fundamental feature of human existence. Such groups, however, are genetically fluid, and to the extent that they may sometimes reflect biological populations, they are defined locally. Races do not reflect large fundamental biological divisions of the human species, for the species does not, and probably never has, come packaged that way.

Merely calling racial issues "racial" may serve to load the discussion with reified patterns of biological variation and to focus on biology rather than on the social inequities at the heart of the problem. Racism is most fundamentally the assessment of individual worth on the basis of real or imputed group characteristics. Its evil lies in the denial of people's right to be judged as individuals, rather than as group members, and in the truncation of opportunities or rights on that basis. But this is true of other "isms"—sexism, anti-Semitism, and prejudices against other groups—and points toward the most important conclusion about human biology: Racial problems are not racial. If biologically diverse peoples had no biological differences but were marked simply on the basis of language, religion, or behavior, the same problems would still exist. How do we know this? Because they *do* exist, for other groups. The problems of race are social problems, not biological ones; and the focus on race (i.e., seemingly discontinuous bio-geographic variation) is therefore a deflection away from the real issues (Montagu, 1963).

The most fundamental dichotomy we can emphasize from the standpoint of biology is that between identity and equality. Identity is a relationship defined by biology; equality is a relationship conferred by culture and society. Genetic processes operate to guarantee that we are not biologically identical to others, although we are more or less similar to others; however, our laws guarantee equality, independently of biology (Dobzhansky, 1962). A society in which individual talents can be cultivated without regard to group affiliations, social rank, or other a priori judgments will be a successful one—acknowledging biological heterogeneity while developing the diverse individual gifts of its citizenry.

FOR FURTHER INFORMATION

Marks, J. (1995). *Human biodiversity.* Explores the overlap between genetics and anthropology, searching for areas of mutual illumination.

Montagu, A. (1963). *Man's most dangerous myth.* A classic work by an outstanding and outspoken scholar.

Nelkin, D., & Lindee, M. S. (1995). *The DNA mystique.* A popular account of the American infatuation with heredity, and the ways in which it has been exploited by science in this century.

REFERENCES

Allen, G. (1983). The misuse of biological hierarchies: The American eugenics movement, 1900–1940. *History and Philosophy of the Life Sciences, 5*, 105–127.

Boas, F. (1912). Changes in the bodily form of descendants of immigrants. *American Anthropologist, 14*, 530–562.

Brace, C. L. (1995). Region does not mean "race"—Reality versus convention in forensic anthropology. *Journal of Forensic Sciences, 40*, 171–175.

Buck v. Bell, 274 U.S. 200 (1927).

Clark, W. E. Le Gros. (1963, January 12). How many families of man? *The Nation,* pp. 35–36.

Davenport, C. B. (1911). *Heredity in relation to eugenics.* New York: Henry Holt.

Davenport, C. B., & Steggerda, M. (1929). *Race crossing in Jamaica* (Publication No. 395). Washington, DC: Carnegie Institution of Washington.

Dobzhansky, T. (1962). *Mankind evolving.* New Haven: Yale University Press.

Ferris, S. D., Brown, W. M., Davidson, W. S., & Wilson, A. C. (1981). Extensive polymorphism in the mitochondrial DNA of apes. *Proceedings of the National Academy of Sciences, USA, 78*, 6319–6323.

Goddard, H. H. (1912). *The Kallikak family: A study in the heredity of feeblemindedness.* New York: Macmillan.

Gould, S. J. (1981). *The mismeasure of man.* New York: Norton.

Grant, M. (1916). *The passing of the great race.* New York: Scribner.

Hannaford, I. (1996). *Race: The history of an idea in the West.* Baltimore: Johns Hopkins University Press.

Herrnstein, R., & Murray, C. (1994). *The bell curve.* New York: Free Press.

Hiernaux, J. (1974). *The people of Africa.* London: Weidenfeld & Nicolson.

Huxley, J. (1938). Clines: An auxiliary taxonomic principle. *Nature, 142*, 219–220.

Jaroff, L. (1989, March 20). The gene hunt. *Time,* 62–67.

Johnson Act (Immigration) ch. 190, 43 Stat. 153 (May 26, 1924).

Kaplan, B. A. (1954). Environment and human plasticity. *American Anthropologist, 56*, 780–800.

Kevles, D. J. (1985). *In the name of eugenics.* Berkeley: University of California Press.

Lasker, G. W. (1969). Human biological adaptability. *Science, 166*, 1480–1486.

Livingstone, F. (1962). On the non-existence of human races. *Current Anthropology, 3*, 279.

Marks, J. (1995). *Human biodiversity: Genes, race, and history.* Hawthorne, NY: Aldine.

Montagu, A. (1963). *Man's most dangerous myth: The fallacy of race.* Cleveland: World Publishing.

Nelkin, D., & Lindee, M. S. (1995). *The DNA mystique: The gene as cultural icon.* New York: Freeman.

Paul, D. B. (1995). *Controlling human heredity.* Atlantic Highlands, NJ: Humanities Press.

Provine, W. (1973). Geneticists and the biology of race crossing. *Science, 182*, 790–796.

Ruano, G., Rogers, J., Ferguson-Smith, A. C., & Kidd, K. K. (1992). DNA sequence polymorphism within hominoid species exceeds the number of phylogenetically informative characters for a HOX2 locus. *Molecular Biology and Evolution, 9*, 575–586.

Sauer, N. (1992). Forensic anthropology and the concept of race: If races don't exist, why are forensic anthropologists so good at identifying them? *Social Science and Medicine, 34*, 107–111.

Shapiro, H. (1939). *Migration and environment.* London: Oxford University Press.

Shapiro, H. (1961). Race mixture. In *The race question in modern science* (pp. 343–389). New York: Columbia University Press/UNESCO.

Stanton, W. H. (1960). *The leopard's spots: Scientific attitudes toward race in America, 1815–59.* Chicago: University of Chicago Press.

Terrell, J. E., & Stewart, P. J. (1996). The paradox of human population genetics at the end of the twentieth century. *Reviews in Anthropology, 25*, 13–33.

Wolf, E. (1972). *Europe and the people without history.* Berkeley: University of California Press.

Wright, L. (1995, July 25). One drop of blood. *The New Yorker*, pp. 46–55.

32

The Third Man

Matt Cartmill

Matt Cartmill is professor of biological anthropology and anatomy at Duke University.
He has written a number of essays on our cultural perceptions of various issues in
human evolution, including our ideas about hunting and its place in our history.

As a demonstration of the holistic nature of anthropology, Matt Cartmill adds a new dimension to the fossil record issues: the role that the topic of race can play in other aspects of biological anthropology. From early interpretations of the place of *Homo erectus* in human evolution to the current debate over the origin of modern *Homo sapiens*, prevailing ideas and concerns about race and racial issues have had a decided influence. Cartmill concludes with the argument that concepts of racial equality are irrelevant to the dispute over modern human origins.

As you read, consider the following questions:

1. What did *Homo erectus* look like, and where and when did they exist?

2. Describe the two basic models of human evolution: the regional-continuity (or multiregional) model and the out-of-Africa model. What are the data Cartmill mentions that support and that argue against the latter model?

3. What are the implications of the new and very recent dates (56,000 to 21,000 years ago) for *Homo erectus* in Java?

4. How did early concepts of racial difference influence the depiction of the human evolutionary tree?

5. What was the premise of Carleton Coon's 1962 book, *The Origin of Races*? What was the reaction in the anthropological community to this book?

6. How has the issue of racial equality been connected to the regional-continuity and out-of-Africa models of human evolution? What does Cartmill say about these connections?

From *Discover*, September 1997. Copyright © 1997 by Matt Cartmill. Reprinted by permission of the author.

Java is a big, densely populated tropical island northwest of Australia. To most of us, it's just another word for coffee, but to scientists who study human origins, Java is more richly evocative as the first place ancient human fossils were discovered in the 1890s. Recently, some of those dusty fossils have come off the museum shelves and, after more than a century, started to make headlines again. New techniques for dating fossils indicate that some of those Javanese remains are a lot older, and others are a lot younger, than we had thought. These new dates pose problems for all our big-picture theories about human evolution—though the news is worse for some theories than for others.

The story of Java in paleoanthropology goes back to 1891, when a young Dutch army doctor named Eugène Dubois found the top of a simian-looking skull in a Javanese riverbank near the town of Trinil. At first he thought he had found a chimpanzee fossil. Like a chimpanzee, the Trinil creature had a low braincase with a steeply sloping forehead and big bony ridges over the eye sockets. But the braincase was a bit too large, and the forehead a bit too bulging, to belong to an ape.

The next year Dubois dug up a human-looking thighbone a few yards away from where he had found the skullcap. He put the two specimens together and announced that he had found the missing link between apes and humans: a primate that had long legs and an upright gait like ours, but whose brain was only about 50 percent larger than a big gorilla's. Dubois named his creature *Pithecanthropus erectus*, meaning upright ape-man.

Other Dutch scientists went back to the area in 1931 and uncovered 11 more skulls from a site near the town of Ngandong, downriver from Trinil. The Ngandong skulls were younger than the Trinil skullcap and somewhat less primitive-looking. Although they too had thick bones, big brows, and receding foreheads, their braincases were 21 percent bigger than Trinil's, averaging around 1,100 cubic centimeters—which is at the low end of today's normal human range.

Over the years, more *Pithecanthropus* fossils have emerged. We now have a dozen more-or-less fragmentary skulls, several lower jaws, and a number of smaller bits and loose teeth. The deposits they come from had been dated from more than a million years ago to around 700,000 years ago—about midway through the Pleistocene Epoch (1.6 million to 10,000 years ago). *Pithecanthropus* skulls are found throughout the sequence. They didn't change much through the years, although on average, the more ancient skulls have slightly smaller braincases.

Nowadays, anthropologists consider *Pithecanthropus* a species in our own genus, *Homo*. We are *Homo sapiens*, and *Pithecanthropus erectus* is now *Homo erectus*. Experts argue over which species the Ngandong skulls belong to; and they argue even more vigorously about the precise relationship between the two species. Many scientists, from Dubois's time to the present, have embraced *Homo erectus* as our direct ancestor. Others have dismissed it as merely a retarded cousin and have searched for more ancient people with bigger brains to put at the base of the human family tree.

The basic facts about human origins are pretty much agreed upon these days. Around 2.5 million years ago in Africa, *Homo* evolved from one of the smaller-brained, bipedal man-apes called *Australopithecus*. The first stone tools also show up in Africa around this time, and some researchers think the two events are connected. There were probably two species of early *Homo*—*H. rudolfensis* and *H. habilis*. The former had bigger brains than *Australopithecus*; the latter had smaller molars. These advanced traits suggest that one or both early *Homo* species were making those tools, since toolmaking takes brains, and using them takes some of the load off your teeth.

By 1.9 million years ago, these two species had been joined in Africa by a third: our old Javanese acquaintance, *Homo erectus*. The newcomer had a thoroughly human body build, with relatively long legs and short arms that made it look less apelike than previous hominids. *H. erectus* also had a bigger brain—around 900 cubic centimeters, versus 600 to 700 for the earlier *Homo*. But its skull is curiously brutish, with thickened braincase walls, massive browridges, and evidence of powerful neck muscles. All in all, *H. erectus* fits the familiar stereotype of the chinless, thick-headed, beetle-browed, bullnecked caveman. It must have been a fearsome competitor for the earlier *Homo* types, which disappeared some 300,000 years after erectus arrived on the scene.

After its competitors died out, African *Homo erectus* made two important breakthroughs. One was a new kind of stone technology. Earlier toolmakers had just banged a couple of pebbles together to get a short broken edge. The new tools were made more economically and artfully, by flaking big flat chips off boulders and then reworking the detached flakes, yielding a sharp edge all around.

The other breakthrough was moving out of Africa. By one million years ago, *Homo erectus* was in China and Asian Georgia. By 500,000 years ago, there were *erectus*-like populations throughout the Old World, from Germany to the Far East and down into Africa. These creatures were improvements on the original *H. erectus*, sporting enlarged, 1,200-cubic-centimeter brains under their persistently low foreheads and thick skull bones. Some people call this new, improved model archaic *Homo sapiens*. Others call it advanced *Homo erectus*, and still others put it into a species of its own, *Homo heidelbergensis*. In Europe this intermediate type seems to have evolved into the distinctive-looking, bigger-brained Neanderthal. The first fossils recognized as modern *Homo sapiens* of our own sort, with proper foreheads and protruding chins, showed up in the Middle East around 90,000 years ago.

All the experts agree on the fundamentals of this story. But they disagree on what it all means. The simplest interpretation of the fossils is that all the *Homo erectus* populations, from Africa to Java, evolved together as a single entity into modern *Homo sapiens*. By this so-called regional-continuity interpretation, there's no real distinction between *sapiens* and *erectus*, and *Homo heidelbergensis* is just a vague label for the populations in the middle of this process.

The other leading interpretation is the out-of-Africa theory, which sees human evolution as a series of two or three waves of advancement emanating from Africa. In this view, *erectus* populations were replaced by a wave of *heidelbergensis* populations, including their Neanderthal offshoot in Europe. All these were replaced in turn by a wave of fully modern *Homo sapiens*—with no interbreeding between the old natives and the new immigrants.

The out-of-Africa theory has some shortcomings. The biggest problem with it is that nobody can reliably distinguish all these supposed species—*Homo erectus, heidelbergensis, neanderthalensis,* and *sapiens*—from one another. There are a lot of fossils that straddle the lines between them, and no two experts agree on just where one species ends and another starts. But the theory also has some facts on its side. Several lines of evidence suggest that the genetic differences between human populations today date back no further than some 200,000 years. As many geneticists see it, their data just don't fit the picture of a gradual, million-year-long evolution of *erectus* into *sapiens* throughout the whole Old World. To these researchers, the genetic facts suggest that modern populations (or at least modern genes) spread more recently from a single center, just as the out-of-Africa model would have it.

One piece of paleontological evidence for the out-of-Africa theory is that some archaic *Homo* populations seem to have lingered beyond their time, alongside more modern-looking people—implying that the two types weren't interbreeding and therefore must have belonged to different species. And this brings us back to the new dates from Java.

Determining just how old the Javanese fossils are has always been a problem. Most of the early finds were unearthed by local laborers who were paid for each fossil brought in—and therefore had financial incentive to conceal the exact spot where they had struck pay dirt. As a result, none of the early finds can be placed exactly in the local stratigraphy. And even knowing exactly where a Javanese fossil came from is no guarantee of its age. When a river cuts through ancient deposits, the fossils that weather out of its banks can tumble downslope, fall into the river, and get reburied in new sediments. If you date them from those fresh sediments, you underestimate their age. All the Javanese fossils come from riverbank deposits, and a lot of them look as if they were knocked around for some time in a flowing river. If that's indeed the case, they may originally have been buried and fossilized in sediments older than the ones they were found in.

In 1971, Garniss Curtis from the University of California at Berkeley put a date on some volcanic minerals found around one of the oldest *Pithecanthropus* fossils from Java, the skull of a child from a site called Mojokerto. He analyzed how the potassium in the rock had changed over time into argon and came up with a surprisingly ancient date—around 1.9 million years ago. In 1992, Curtis and his colleague Carl Swisher used a more sophisticated technique to date the minerals taken from inside the skull itself and got an age of 1.8 million years.

These dates are almost a million years older than most experts had expected. If the new dates are correct, *Homo erectus* appears in the fossil record of Java around the same time it first shows up in Africa. This is hard to square with any of our theories about early human evolution. If *erectus* evolved in Africa, why doesn't it show up there before we encounter it in Java? And if *erectus* evolved somewhere in between Africa and Java and spread from there to reach both Africa and Java 1.9 million years ago, then why haven't any earlier fossil hominids been found outside Africa?

Having dropped their Mojokerto bombshell, Curtis and Swisher went back to take a look at the other, upper end of the Javanese fossil record—those later but still primitive-looking braincases from Ngandong. (The Ngandong deposits don't contain the volcanic minerals needed for argon dating, so the researchers used other techniques. Buried teeth pick up uranium salts from groundwater, and by measuring the ratio of uranium to the products of its fission in tooth enamel, you can estimate how long the teeth have been buried.) For these fossils they obtained age estimates ranging from 56,000 to only 21,000 years ago.

These dates are stunningly late. By 20,000 years ago, Neanderthals were long gone and humans around the world were essentially indistinguishable from people living today. By 10,000 years ago, people in the Middle East and Southeast Asia were starting to experiment with agriculture. But if the new dates for Ngandong are correct, a lonely surviving population of backward, slope-headed creatures that most experts would call *Homo erectus* was still clinging to a Lower Pleistocene way of life in Java long after the last continental glaciers had melted and everybody else had straightened up their foreheads and started painting pictures on cave walls. Like any other date from Java, these new dates are subject to various doubts; but if Curtis and Swisher are right, it's a blow to the regional-continuity theory.

The blow isn't necessarily a crushing one. Pleistocene Java might be the Land That Time Forgot: a primitive pocket, colonized early on and then cut off from all the currents of gene flow that were steadily transforming the rest of *erectus* into modern *sapiens.* One reason for thinking that Java might have been a peculiar backwater is that there are almost no stone tools in the *erectus* deposits. Everywhere else in the world where we find *Homo* fossils, they're far outnumbered by the stone tools found alongside them. But the only tools ever found with Javanese *erectus* are a few dubiously associated flakes and hammerstones. Some scientists argue that *erectus* didn't need stone tools in Java because they could make all the knives, spears, and scrapers they needed out of the flinty stems of bamboo. But then what were they using to cut the bamboo?

Why do anthropologists get so excited about these questions? Why should any of us care whether we're descended from late-surviving archaic humans, or from equally primitive types who lived somewhat earlier and somewhere else? The electricity surrounding these issues flows partly from the clash of scientific egos and partly from the sheer fascination of stories about things long ago and far away. But it also flows out of the long, sordid history of scientific racism.

The study of human evolution has been contaminated with the politics of race from its very beginnings. In the late 1800s, it seemed pretty clear to most educated Europeans that white folks were taking over the world because they were better than everybody else. Naturally, Darwinians saw this as the survival of the fittest. Many scientists regarded the native peoples of colonial Africa, Australia, and the New World as living fossils: leftovers from earlier stages in human evolution, doomed by Nature's iron laws of competition to go down to extinction with the Tasmanian wolf and the Tasmanian aborigines.

It was easy to turn this racist thought the other way around and apply it to the fossils. If the Tasmanian natives had been exterminated because they were too low and primitive to compete, then still lower and more primitive extinct forms like *Pithecanthropus* must have been wiped out because they couldn't compete, either. And whoever wiped them out must have been the ancestors of modern humans. Therefore we can't be descended from *Pithecanthropus*. Nobody ever laid this argument out quite so nakedly as that, but a lot of experts were thinking along similar lines. Down through the late 1940s, leading textbooks of human evolution portrayed almost all the Pleistocene human fossils as doomed, blind-alley offshoots of the mainstream (white European) human lineage. Some depicted the tree of human evolution as fir-shaped, with a thick central trunk leading to the Europeans, and a lot of mostly extinct side branches coming off: first *Pithecanthropus* (which dies out), then the Neanderthals (which die out), and then the native Australians and Africans, who haven't died out—yet.

After World War II, in the aftermath of Nazi horror, anthropologists hastened to throw out all these ideas about racial hierarchy. The collapse of the European empires in Africa and Asia also helped cure white scientists of the old habit of thinking of themselves as members of the master race. By 1960, no reputable anthropologists were still talking about racial differences in evolutionary status.

The old hierarchical interpretation of the fossil record—and the prehistoric genocides implicit in it—got thrown out as well. During the 1950s and 1960s, it came to be regarded as vaguely racist to exclude any fossil humans from our own ancestry. All the taxonomic doors flew open. *Australopithecus* joined the human family, *Pithecanthropus* was welcomed into the genus *Homo*, and the Neanderthals were recognized as just an extreme racial variant of modern *Homo sapiens*. And if the low-browed Neanderthals were the ancestors and equals of today's Europeans, it was ludicrous to think of assigning a lower status to the high-browed modern natives of Africa, Australia, or America. Scientific racism looked like a thing of the past.

It wasn't. In his 1962 book *The Origin of Races*, the American anthropologist Carleton Coon came along and turned all this blossoming egalitarianism upside down. Coon accepted regional continuity and agreed that all the *erectus* fossils were our ancestors. But by juggling his dates and his taxonomy, he made out that the transition from *erectus* to *sapiens* had happened at different times for different races. Not surprisingly, he thought that whites had gotten sapienized first, then the Oriental peoples (probably by gene flow from Europe), and finally the Africans and Australians out on the periphery of Eurasia, who were the last people to become fully human. Coon hinted that these dark-skinned latecomers are still a bit retarded when compared with whites and Asians. His book features side-by-side photos of a small-headed Native Australian woman and a big-domed "Chinese sage," captioned "The Alpha and Omega of *Homo sapiens*."

Coon's book aroused furious controversy. Dismayed by the racial hierarchy implicit in his model, many anthropologists attacked it as a theoretical impossibility. They insisted that a single interbreeding population couldn't belong to one species at one end and a different species at the other. (In fact, several examples of this sort of arrangement have been described in some species of birds, salamanders, and other animals, although scientists argue about the truth of these descriptions.) The upshot of the controversy over Coon's book was that some anthropologists began to view the whole regional-continuity model of human origins as a theory tainted by racism.

For this reason, some fossil experts hail every piece of evidence for the out-of-Africa theory as further proof of modern human equality. (If we're all descended from an African "Eve" who lived just 100,000 years ago, we can't be very different from one another, can we?) Others see the regional-continuity model, with its ages-long pattern of gene flow back and forth among all human populations, as a bulwark against racial typology. And some of us, who were trained back in the sixties and got all those old tree diagrams of racial divergence stuck in our heads, still have a vague feeling that real egalitarians shouldn't discriminate against Neanderthals. (If Neanderthals are fully human, the differences between modern races are too trivial to bother about, aren't they?) This debate may be more vehement than it needs to be because partisans on each side see themselves as defending the unity and equality of the Family of Man against attacks by the opposing camp.

The scientific jury is still out on those dates from Java. But while we wait for fresh evidence, we would do well to remember that the equality of today's human beings is not really on the line. We are what we are, not what our ancestors were. If my grandmother had type A blood, that doesn't mean I have it or am even carrying a gene for the A blood group. And even if my great-great-to-the-nth-power grandfather 30,000 years ago was a Neanderthal, that doesn't change the slope of my own forehead by a single degree or imply that I'm carrying some taint of Nean-derthal "blood." The truth of racial egalitarianism hinges on the facts about living people. Their genealogies are irrelevant.

Understanding these simple truths might help alleviate some of the uneasiness many people feel about human evolution. A lot of that uneasiness springs from a mistaken notion that deep down, underneath all the cultural varnish, we are still what our ancestors were—that if we're descended from apes, we must somehow *be* apes and have license to behave like apes whenever we feel like it. We aren't, and we don't. Knowing where we come from doesn't tell us where we are right now. If we can all accept that principle, it may help make future debates about human origins less heated and more illuminating.

PART 9

Bioanthropology and the Human Genome

In the not too distant past of biological anthropology, studies of our evolution, biodiversity, and biocultural history relied on phenotypic features as data. About the closest we could come to studying our genetic code was to look at phenotypes that were direct products of genes, such things as blood proteins. In an amazingly short time, new technologies have allowed us to delve into the most specific details of the human genome—the very sequence of base pairs in the DNA that make up the code. This has opened up new avenues of research and, although there is much left to study and discover, we have already learned a great deal about our species, some of it very surprising indeed.

In "The Mosaic That Is Our Genome," Svante Pääbo shows how, if we look at the human genome as a mosaic of discrete segments, new light can be shed on the relationships among modern human populations, on the relationships between humans and our closest relatives, and on the history of our species.

In "The Chimpanzee and Us," Wen-Hsiung Li and Matthew A. Saunders report on the publication of the draft sequence of the chimpanzee genome and what it tells us about the differences between our two species.

Sally Lehrman, in "Trace Elements," discusses new and popular services that offer to trace one's roots through DNA samples. A commentary by Jonathan Marks on the scientific reliability of these services follows.

SUGGESTED WEBSITES FOR FURTHER STUDY

http://www.wellcome.ac.uk/en/genome
http://www.genome.gov

33

The Mosaic That Is Our Genome

Svante Pääbo

Svante Pääbo is director of the Department of Genetics at the Max Planck Institute
for Evolutionary Biology in Leipzig, Germany. He has written extensively on many
aspects of genetics and holds several patents for technologies for DNA analysis.

The publication in February 2001 of the human genome heralded one of the most important events in the history of science. Since then, our knowledge of the genetic code, its functions, and its products has accumulated at an accelerating pace. In this selection, geneticist Svante Pääbo applies our new understanding of the human genome as a "mosaic," arranged in different segments with different histories. Especially important are segments that show variation within the species. These come in "blocks" called haplotypes and are particularly useful in comparing modern humans and human populations, in tracing our species' evolutionary history, and in tracking the genetic origins of particular human traits.

As you read, consider the following questions:

1. What can we say about the genetic similarities between humans and the great apes?

2. What has recent genetic research shown us regarding the differences in DNA sequences among living humans?

3. What might genetic research tell us about our relationship with the Neandertals?

4. How has recent genetic research questioned the idea of biological races within our species?

5. How does current research provide us with a potential means of determining which genes are unique to our species?

The discovery of the structure of DNA,[1] and the realization that the chemical basis of mutations is changes in the nucleotide sequence of the DNA, meant that the history of a piece of DNA could be traced by studying variation in its nucleotide sequence found in different individuals and in different species. But it was not until rapid and inexpensive methods became available for probing DNA sequence variation in many individuals that the efficient study of molecular evolution in general—and of human evolution in particular—became feasible. Thus, the development in the 1980s of techniques for efficiently scoring polymorphisms with restriction enzymes and amplifying DNA[2,3] enabled the study of molecular evolution to become a truly booming enterprise.

What follows is a personal and, by necessity, selective attempt to consider what the accelerating pace of exploration of human genetic variation over the past two decades has taught us about ourselves as a species, as well as some suggestions for what may be fruitful areas for future studies.

PRIMATE RELATIONS

The first insight of fundamental importance for our understanding of our origins came from comparisons of DNA sequences between humans and the great apes. These analyses showed that the African apes, especially the chimpanzees and the bonobos, but also the gorillas, are more closely related to humans than are the orangutans in Asia.[4] Thus, from a genetic standpoint, humans are essentially African apes. Although there had been hints of this from molecular comparisons of proteins,[5,6] it was a marked shift from the earlier common belief that humans represented their own branch separate from the great apes.

Our sense of uniqueness as a species was further rocked by the revelation that human DNA sequences differ by, on average, only 1.2 percent from those of the chimpanzees,[7] as a consequence of humans and apes

From *Nature*, January 23, 2003, Vol. 421, pp. 409–411. Copyright © 2003 Macmillan Magazines Ltd. Reprinted with permission from the publisher and the authors.

sharing a recent common ancestry. It should be noted that the dating of molecular divergences has uncertainties of unknown magnitude attached, not least because of calibration based on palaeontological data. Nevertheless, it seems clear that the human evolutionary lineage diverged from that of chimpanzees about 4–6 million years ago, from that of gorillas about 6–8 million years ago, and from that of the orangutans about 12–16 million years ago.[7] Before the advent of molecular data, the human–chimpanzee divergence was widely believed to be about 30 million years old.

In fact, we have recently come to realize that the relationship between humans and the African apes is so close as to be entangled. Although the majority of regions in our genome are most closely related to chimpanzees and bonobos, a non-trivial fraction is more closely related to gorillas.[7] In yet other regions, the apes are more closely related to each other than to us. This is because the speciation events that separated these lineages occurred so closely in time that genetic variation in the first ancestral species, from which the gorilla lineage diverged, survived until the second speciation event between the human and chimpanzee lineages.[8] Thus, there is not one history with which we can describe the relationship of our genome to the genomes of the African apes, but instead different histories for different segments of our genome. In this respect, our genome is a mosaic, where each segment has its own relationship to that of the African apes.

MODERN HUMANS

The mosaic nature of our genome is even more striking when we consider differences in DNA sequence between currently living humans. Our genome sequences are about 99.9 percent identical to each other. The variation found along a chromosome is structured in "blocks" where the nucleotide substitutions are associated in so-called haplotypes. These "haplotype blocks" are likely to result from the fact that recombination, that is, the re-shuffling of chromosome segments that occurs during formation of sex cells (meiosis), tends to occur in certain areas of the chromosomes more often than in others.[9–11] In addition, the chance occurrence of recombination events at certain spots and not at others in the genealogy of human chromosomes will influence the structure of these blocks. Thus, any single human chromosome is a mosaic of different haplotype blocks, where each block has its own pattern of variation. Although the delineation of such blocks depends on the methods used to define them, they are typically 5,000–200,000 base pairs in length, and as few as four to five common haplotypes account for most of the variation in each block.

Of 928 such haplotype blocks recently studied in humans from Africa, Asia and Europe,[12] 51 percent were found on all three continents, 72 percent in two continents and only 28 percent on one continent. Of those haplotypes that were on one continent only, 90 percent were found in Africa, and African DNA sequences differ on average more among themselves than they differ from Asian or European DNA sequences.[13] Therefore, within the human gene pool, most variation is found in Africa and what is seen outside Africa is a subset of the variation found within Africa.

Two parts of the human genome can be regarded as haplotype blocks where the history is particularly straightforward to reconstruct, as no recombination occurs at all. The first of these is the genome of the mitochondrion (the cellular organelle that produces energy and has its own genetic material), which is passed on to the next generation from the mother's side; the second is the Y chromosome, which is passed on from the father's side. Variation in DNA sequences from both the mitochondrial genome[14–16] and the Y chromosome,[17] as well as many sections of the nuclear genome,[13,18–20] have their geographical origin in Africa. Because other evidence suggests that humans expanded some 50,000 to 200,000 years ago[21] from a population of about 10,000 individuals, this suggests that we expanded from a rather small African population. Thus, from a genomic perspective, we are all Africans, either living in Africa or in quite recent exile outside Africa.

ANCIENT HUMANS

What happened to the other hominids that existed in the Old World from about 2 million years ago until about 30,000 years ago? For instance, the Neanderthals are abundant in the fossil record and persisted in western Europe until less than 30,000 years ago. Analysis of Neanderthal mitochondrial DNA has shown that, at least with respect to the mitochondrial genome, there is no evidence that Neanderthals contributed to the gene pool of current humans.[22–25] It is possible, however, that some as yet undetected interbreeding took place between modern humans and archaic hominids, such as *Homo erectus* in Asia or Neanderthals in Europe.[22,26,27]

But any interbreeding would not have significantly changed our genome, as we know that the variation found in many haplotype blocks in the nuclear genome of contemporary humans is older than the divergence between Neanderthals and humans. Thus, the divergence of modern humans and Neanderthals was so recent that Neanderthal nuclear DNA sequences were probably more closely related to some current human DNA sequences than to other Neanderthals. In other words, the overlapping genetic variation that is likely to have existed between different ancient hominid forms makes it difficult to resolve the extent to which any interbreeding occurred.

Nevertheless, the limited variation among humans outside Africa, as well as palaeontological evidence,[28] suggest that any contribution cannot have been particularly extensive. Thus, it seems most likely that modern humans replaced archaic humans without extensive interbreeding and that the past 30,000 years of human history are unique in that we lack the company of the closely related yet distinct hominids with which we used to share the planet.

HUMAN VARIATION AND "RACE"

Comparisons of the within-species variation among humans and among the great apes have shown that humans have less genetic variation than the great apes.[29,30] Furthermore, early data that only about 10 percent of the genetic variation in humans exist between so-called "races"[31] is borne out by DNA sequences which show that races are not characterized by fixed genetic differences. Rather, for any given haplotype block in the genome, a person from, for example, Europe is often more closely related to a person from Africa or from Asia than to another person from Europe that shares his or her complexion (for example, see ref. 32).

Claims about fixed genetic differences between races (see ref. 33, for example) have proved to be due to insufficient sampling.[34] Furthermore, because the main pattern of genetic variation across the globe is one of gene-frequency gradients,[35] the contention that significant differences between races can be seen in frequencies of various genetic markers[36] is very likely due to sampling of populations separated by vast geographical distances. In this context it is worth noting that the colonization history of the United States has resulted in a sampling of the human population made up largely of people from western Europe, western Africa and southeast Asia. Thus, the fact that "racial groups" in the United States differ in gene frequencies cannot be taken as evidence that such differences represent any true subdivision of the human gene pool on a worldwide scale.

Rather than thinking about "populations," "ethnicities" or "races," a more constructive way to think about human genetic variation is to consider the genome of any particular individual as a mosaic of haplotype blocks. A rough calculation reveals that each individual carries in the order of 30 percent of the entire haplotype variation of the human gene pool.

Although not all of our genome may show a typical haplotype-block structure and more research is needed to fully understand the haplotype landscape of our genome, this perspective clearly indicates that each of us contain a vast proportion of the genetic variation found in our species. In the future, we therefore need to focus on individuals rather than populations when exploring genetic variation in our species.

TRACKING HUMAN TRAITS

What are the frontiers ahead of us in human evolutionary studies? One of them, to my mind, is to identify gene variants that have been selected and fixed in all humans during the past few hundred thousand years. These will include genes involved in phenotypic traits that set humans apart from the apes and at least some archaic human forms (for example, genes involved in complex cognitive abilities, language and longevity). However, an important obstacle in this respect is that there is little detailed knowledge of many of the relevant traits in the great apes. For example, only recently has the extent to which apes possess the capability for language[37] and culture[38] begun to be comprehensively described. As a consequence, we have come to realize that almost all features that set humans apart from apes may turn out to be differences in grade rather than absolute differences.

Many such differences are likely to be quantitative traits rather than single-gene traits. To have a chance to unravel the genetic basis of such traits, we will need to rigorously define the differences between apes and humans—for instance, how we learn, how we communicate and how we age. In the next few years, geneticists will therefore need to consider insights from primatology and psychology, and more studies will be required that directly compare humans to apes.

There are, however, ways in which we can contribute towards the future unravelling of functionally important genetic differences between humans and apes. For example, we can identify regions of the human genome where the patterns of variation suggest the recent occurrence of a mutation that was positively selected and swept through the entire human population. The sequencing of the chimpanzee genome, as well as the haplotype-map project, will greatly help in this. Further prerequisites include the capability to determine the DNA sequence of many human genomes and the development of tools and methods to analyse the resulting data; in particular, a more realistic model of human demographic history is required.

Collectively these studies will allow us to identify regions in the human genome that have recently been acted upon by selection and thus are likely to contain genes contributing to human-specific traits. Other interesting candidate genes for human-specific traits are genes duplicated or deleted in humans,[39] genes that have changed their expression in humans,[40] and genes responsible for disorders affecting traits unique to humans, such as language[41] and a large brain size.[42]

A problem inherent in studying genes that are involved in traits unique to humans, such as language, is that functional experiments cannot be performed, as no animal model exists, and transgenic humans or chimpanzees cannot be constructed. A further difficulty is that many genes that enable humans to perform tasks of interest may exert their effects during early development where our ability to study their expression both in apes and humans is extremely limited.

A challenge for the future is therefore to design ways around these difficulties. This will involve *in vitro* as well as *in silico* approaches that study how genes interact with each other to influence developmental and physiological systems. As these goals are achieved, we will be able to determine the order and approximate times of genetic changes during the emergence of modern humans that led to the traits that set us apart among animals.

1. Watson, J. D. & Crick, F. H. C. A structure for deoxyribose nucleic acid. *Nature* 171, 737–738 (1953).

2. Botstein, D., White, R. L., Skolnick, M. & Davis, R. W. Construction of a genetic linkage map in man using restriction fragment length polymorphisms. *Am. J. Hum. Genet.* 32, 314–331 (1980).

3. Saiki, R. K. *et al.* Enzymatic amplification of β-globin genomic sequences and restriction site analysis for diagnosis of sickle cell anemia. *Science* 230, 1350–1354 (1985).

4. Miyamoto, M. M., Slightom, J. L., & Goodman, M. Phylogenetic relations of humans and African apes from DNA sequences in the ψη-globin region. *Science* 238, 369–373 (1987).

5. Mayr, E. *Animal Species and Evolution* (Harvard Univ. Press, Cambridge, MA, 1963).

6. Wilson, A. C. & Sarich, V. M. A molecular time scale for human evolution. *Proc. Natl Acad. Sci. USA* 63, 1088–1093 (1969).

7. Chen, F. C., Vallender, E. J., Wang, H., Tzeng, C. S. & Li, W. H. Genomic divergence between human and chimpanzee estimated from large-scale alignments of genomic sequences. *J. Hered.* 92, 481–489 (2001).

8. Nei, M. *Molecular Evolutionary Genetics* (Columbia Univ. Press, New York, 1987).

9. Daly, M. J., Rioux, J. D., Schaffner, S. F., Hudson, T. J. & Lander, E. S. High-resolution haplotype structure in the human genome. *Nature Genet.* 29, 229–232 (2001).

10. Jeffreys, A. J., Kauppi, L. & Neumann, R. Intensely punctuated meiotic recombination in the class II region of the major histocompatibility complex. *Nature Genet.* 29, 217–222 (2001).

11. Patil, N. *et al.* Blocks of limited haplotype diversity revealed by high-resolution scanning of human chromosome 21. *Science* 294, 1719–1723 (2001).

12. Gabriel, S. B. *et al.* The structure of haplotype blocks in the human genome. *Science* 296, 2225–2229 (2002).

13. Yu, N. *et al.* Larger genetic differences within Africans than between Africans and Eurasians. *Genetics* 161, 269–274 (2002).

14. Cann, R. L., Stoneking, M. & Wilson, A. C. Mitochondrial DNA and human evolution. *Nature* 325, 31–36 (1987).

15. Vigilant, L., Stoneking, M., Harpending, H., Hawkes, K. & Wilson, A. C. African populations and the evolution of human mitochondrial DNA. *Science* 253, 1503–1507 (1991).

16. Ingman, M., Kaessmann, H., Pääbo, S. & Gyllensten, U. Mitochondrial genome variation and the origin of modern humans. *Nature* 408, 708–713 (2000).

17. Underhill, P. A. *et al.* Y chromosome sequence variation and the history of human populations. *Nature Genet.* 26, 358–361 (2000).

18. Stoneking, M. *et al.* Alu insertion polymorphisms and human evolution: evidence for a larger population size in Africa. *Genome Res.* 7, 1061–1071 (1997).

19. Tishkoff, S. A. *et al.* Global patterns of linkage disequilibrium at the CD4 locus and modern human origins. *Science* 271, 1380–1387 (1996).

20. Takahata, N., Lee, S. H. & Satta, Y. Testing multiregionality of modern human origins. *Mol. Biol. Evol.* 18, 172–183 (2001).

21. Harpending, H. & Rogers, A. Genetic perspectives on human origins and differentiation. *Annu. Rev. Genomics Hum. Genet.* 1, 361–385 (2000).

22. Krings, M. *et al.* Neandertal DNA sequences and the origin of modern humans. *Cell* 90, 19–30 (1997).

23. Ovchinnikov, I. V. *et al.* Molecular analysis of Neanderthal DNA from the northern Caucasus. *Nature* 404, 490–493 (2000).

24. Krings, M., Geisert, H., Schmitz, R. W., Krainitzki, H. & Pääbo, S. DNA sequence of the mitochondrial hypervariable region II from the Neandertal type specimen. *Proc. Natl Acad. Sci. USA* 96, 5581–5585 (1999).

25. Krings, M. *et al.* A view of Neandertal genetic diversity. *Nature Genet.* 26, 144–146 (2000).

26. Nordborg, M. On the probability of Neanderthal ancestry. *Am. J. Hum. Genet.* 63, 1237–1240 (1998).

27. Pääbo, S. Human evolution. *Trends Cell Biol.* 9, M13–M16 (1999).

28. Stringer, C. Modern human origins: progress and prospects. *Phil. Trans. R. Soc. Lond. B* 357, 563–579 (2002).

29. Deinard, A. & Kidd, K. Evolution of a HOXB6 intergenic region within the great apes and humans. *J. Hum. Evol.* 36, 687–703 (1999).

30. Kaessmann, H., Wiebe, V., Weiss, G. & Pääbo, S. Great ape DNA sequences reveal a reduced diversity and an expansion in humans. *Nature Genet.* 27, 155–156 (2001).

31. Lewontin, R. C. The problem of genetic diversity. *Evol. Biol.* 6, 381–398 (1972).

32. Kaessmann, H., Heissig, F., von Haesler, A. & Pääbo, S. DNA sequence variation in a non-coding region of low recombination on the human X chromosome. *Nature Genet.* 22, 78–81 (1999).

33. Harris, E. E. & Hey, J. X chromosome evidence for ancient human histories. *Proc. Natl Acad. Sci. USA* 96, 3320–3324 (1999).

34. Yua, N. & Li, W.-H. No fixed nucleotide difference between Africans and non-Africans at the pyruvate dehydrogenase E1 α-subunit locus. *Genetics* 155, 1481–1483 (2000).

35. Cavalli-Sforza, L. L., Menozzi, P. & Piazza, A. *The History and Geography of Human Genes* (Princeton Univ. Press, Princeton, NJ, 1993).

36. Risch, N., Burchard, E., Ziv, E. & Tang, H. Categorization of humans in biological research: genes, race and disease. *Genome Biol.* 3, 2007.1–2007.2 (2002).

37. Tomasello, M. & Call, J. *Primate Cognition* (Oxford Univ. Press, New York, 1997).

38. Whiten, A. *et al.* Cultures in chimpanzees. *Nature* 399, 682–685 (1999).

39. Eichler, E. E. Recent duplication, domain accretion and the dynamic mutation of the human genome. *Trends Genet.* 17, 661–669 (2001).

40. Enard, W. *et al.* Intra- and interspecific variation in primate gene expression patterns. *Science* 296, 340–343 (2002).

41. Enard, W. *et al.* Molecular evolution of *FOXP2*, a gene involved in speech and language. *Nature* 418, 869–872 (2002).

42. Jackson, A. P. *et al.* Identification of microcephalin, a protein implicated in determining the size of the human brain. *Am. J. Hum. Genet.* 71, 136–142 (2002).

ACKNOWLEDGMENTS

My work is funded by the Max Planck Society, the Bundesministerium für Bildung und Forschung and the Deutsche Forschungsgemeinschaft. I thank B. Cohen, H. Kaessmann, D. Serre, M. Stoneking, C. Stringer, L. Vigilant and especially D. Altshuler for helpful comments on the manuscript.

34

The Chimpanzee and Us

Wen-Hsiung Li and Matthew A. Saunders

Wen-Hsiung Li and Matthew A. Saunders are in the Department of Ecology
and Evolution, University of Chicago

In Selection 17 Jonathan Marks addressed the commonly held wisdom that humans and chimpanzees are 98 percent genetically identical. Now, with the draft sequence of the chimpanzee genome (about 94 percent of the total genome), we can be more specific as to just *what* parts of our genomes are similar or different and, if different, *how*. In this selection, Wen-Hsiung Li and Matthew Saunders give some of these details and also conjecture as to how our genetic differences from the chimpanzee give us the phenotypic traits that "make us human."

As you read, consider the following questions:

1. What are the specific differences between the human and chimpanzee genomes that generate the famous "98 percent identical" figure?

2. What are the three current hypotheses proposed to explain how the genetic differences between us and chimpanzees have led to our "humanness"?

Publication of the draft DNA sequence of the chimpanzee genome is an especially notable event: the data provide a treasury of information for understanding human biology and evolution.

What genetic changes make us so different from the chimpanzee, our closest relative? Scientists have been trying to answer this challenging question for decades, and publication of the draft of the chimpanzee genome (page 69 of this issue)[1] is a significant step forward. The species studied is the common chimpanzee, *Pan troglodytes*; its only 'sister' species is the pygmy chimpanzee or bonobo, *Pan paniscus*.

The draft tells us that the DNA sequence of our genome and that of the chimpanzee differ by only a few per cent. This still amounts to tens of millions of differences because each genome contains some 3 billion nucleotides. One way to determine what the important differences are is to identify evolutionary changes that are specific to us, *Homo sapiens*. Another is to look for signatures of positive natural selection in the sequences of the two genomes. Both of these approaches, and other comparative analyses, are described in the draft-genome paper[1] and the companion papers (pages 88–104)[2-4].

The assembly of a complete genome requires multiple rounds of sequencing. The chimpanzee genome draft represents a sequencing coverage of about 3.5 times, lower than that in the initial publication of other genomes, such as those of human, mouse and rat. Nonetheless, the draft is extremely useful for showing general differences between the chimpanzee and human genomes. The new data show that they differ by only 1.23% in terms of nucleotide substitutions. This is identical to a previous estimate from a mere 53 regions, each of about 500 base pairs, randomly chosen from the genome[5].

The sequence divergence varies among genomic regions, presumably because of regional variations in mutation rate, selective constraints and the rate of sequence exchange (recombination) between chromosome pairs during cell division. The highest divergence is found for the Y chromosome and the lowest for the X chromosome. This is expected, because the Y chromosome is present only in males, which have a higher germ-line mutation rate than females, whereas the X chromosome is carried in both females and males.

Natural selection is commonly thought to operate mainly at the protein level. For this reason, nucleotide changes in protein-coding regions are usually classified into two groups: 'synonymous changes' (which do not cause any change in amino acids) and 'non-synonymous changes' (which do cause amino-acid changes). If a coding region is subject to strong selective constraints, then the non-synonymous substitution rate (K_A) will be considerably lower than the synonymous substitution rate (K_S); that is, the K_A/K_S ratio will be less than 1. On the other hand, if a gene is subject to very weak selective constraints or continued positive selection, K_A/K_S may be close to 1 or even higher.

Comparison[1] of 13,454 human–chimpanzee gene pairs gives an average K_A/K_S of 0.23, much lower than previously estimated from more limited data sets of human–chimpanzee (0.63)[6] and human–baboon (0.34)[7] comparisons. This ratio is twice that estimated from the mouse–rat comparison (0.13): this is probably due to less effective purifying selection, a process that eliminates deleterious mutations, in species with relatively small population sizes such as primates. Importantly, the new estimate is similar to the K_A/K_S from data on variation among humans (~0.20–0.23), suggesting that the proportion of advantageous mutations along the human lineage is lower than previously estimated[7,8]. A total of 585 genes (more than that expected at random) do, however, display a higher K_A than the substitution rate in non-coding sequence (K_I). The highest K_A/K_I examples include the genes that encode glycophorin C, granulysin, protamine and semenogelin, proteins that are involved in immunity or reproduction.

DUPLICATIONS, INSERTIONS AND DELETIONS

Although single-nucleotide substitutions are commonly considered when quantifying sequence divergence, insertions/deletions (indels) and recent duplications of DNA segments account for a markedly larger proportion of the difference between the human and chimpanzee genomes (3% and 2.7%, respectively). More than a third of the indels are due to repeated sequences, and about a quarter to transposable elements. These are DNA sequences that can move to different genomic regions, two of the major classes being Alu elements (short transposable sequences about 300 base pairs long) and L1 elements (long transposable sequences).

There are approximately 7,000 Alu elements in the human genome but only about 2,300 in the chimpanzee genome, indicating that these elements have been less active in the chimpanzee. L1 elements, however, have been equally active in the two genomes—against the

previous estimate of two- to three-fold higher activity in the chimpanzee[9]. The functional importance, if any, of these differences remains unknown. Recent segmental duplications (of longer than 20 megabases and greater than 94% sequence identity) are common in both genomes[2]. But although about 33% of human duplicated segments are human-specific, only about 17% of chimpanzee duplicated segments are chimpanzee-specific. Interestingly, about half of the genes in the human-specific duplicated regions exhibit significant differences in gene expression relative to the chimpanzee, and are most often upregulated.

HUMAN GENETIC VARIATION

The chimpanzee genome places the wealth of data on existing genetic variation in humans into evolutionary context. It now becomes possible to determine the ancestral states of that variation, and, with the aid of gene-frequency data in human populations, we may uncover 'footprints' of positive selection that occurred recently (less than 250,000 years ago, say) in humans. Under selective neutrality, new variants should rarely be found at high frequency, and between-species divergence should be correlated with the level of within-species genetic variation. The current analyses identify only six genomic regions that display significantly less variation than expected from the divergence between the *Homo* and *Pan* lineages, which split about 6 million years ago; each of these regions suggests the recent action of positive selection in humans. The power of such a method will increase substantially with the completion of genome drafts of a more distantly related primate such as an Old World monkey or the orang-utan, both of which are in progress.[10] . . .

WHAT MAKES US HUMAN?

The question of what genetic changes make us human is far more complex. Although the two genomes are very similar, there are about 35 million nucleotide differences, 5 million indels and many chromosomal rearrangements to take into account. Most of these changes will have no significant biological effect, so identification of the genomic differences underlying such characteristics of 'humanness' as large cranial capacity, bipedalism and advanced brain development remains a daunting task. Given the short time since the human–chimpanzee split, it is likely that a few mutations of large effect are responsible for part of the current physical—phenotypic—differences that separate humans from chimpanzees and other great apes.

There are three prevailing hypotheses to account for the evolution of 'humanness traits': protein evolution, the 'less-is-more' hypothesis[11], and changes in the regions of the genome that regulate gene activity.[12] . . . Preliminary analyses of the human and chimpanzee genomes provide some clues about the relative contributions of these effects.

First, consider protein evolution. Are amino-acid changes that have contributed to 'humanness' to be found in rapidly evolving proteins? Most of those genes that do show a K_A/K_S of more than 1 are not involved in processes related to supposed humanness traits. In fact, genes related to brain function and neuronal activity show lower-than-average K_A/K_S values. The genes that display high K_A/K_S are mostly related to host–pathogen interaction, immunity and reproduction. This pattern is also found in rats, mice and other mammals. This suggests that protein evolution may not be a major contributor to the evolution of traits unique to humans. But before dismissing this possibility, we must bear in mind that the K_A/K_S test is biased towards genes that experience repeated amino-acid replacements. Genes involved in immunity and reproduction are particularly affected by these processes. But a gene that experiences a 'selective sweep' as a result of only a few changes—because those changes are strongly advantageous—would not leave a significant signal on K_A/K_S. For example, two amino-acid changes alone in the highly conserved FOXP2 protein, a gene-transcription factor, might have contributed to the human capacity for speech[13]. Finally, the role of indels and gene duplications in human-chimpanzee protein evolution remains largely unexplored.

Second, the 'less-is-more' hypothesis posits that loss-of-function changes relative to the 'prototypical ape' traits are characteristic of certain humanness traits—for example, lack of body hair, preservation of some juvenile traits into adulthood and expansion of the cranium. Such loss-of-function changes could be caused by non-synonymous substitutions, indels, loss of coding regions and deletion of entire genes. The comparisons to the chimpanzee have unveiled 53 human genes with disruptive indels in the coding regions, and genes in this category may be associated with intriguing phenotypes[14–16]. Indels could plausibly be major contributors to human–chimpanzee phenotypic differences, especially given that these mutations can also influence the two other proposed mechanisms for the evolution of humanness. . . .

Third, there is the long-standing hypothesis that the phenotypic differences between humans and chimpanzees primarily arise from changes in gene-regulatory regions. The current analyses[1] do not address this issue in detail, because it is still notoriously difficult to identify such regions. Most of our current knowledge about regulatory regions comes from identifying similarities between distantly related species. The matter could be addressed further in a comparative genomic framework by identifying conserved regulatory regions among relatively closely related species[17], including Old World monkeys, in conjunction with a comparison to the chimpanzee sequence and with microarray expression studies that can provide functional validation. The hypothesis invoking evolution in gene-regulating regions is currently the hardest to test. Yet it may be the most promising, given what we know of human biology relative to that of apes.

The draft of the chimpanzee genome is an exciting addition to the list of sequenced vertebrate genomes. Next to the human genome itself, it is the most useful for understanding human biology and evolution. But the data still leave many questions unanswered about what genetic modifications underlie the major features distinguishing *Homo sapiens* from the great apes. The next stages of this grand project will involve finer-scale investigation of individual regions and genes to reveal the details of the general patterns now uncovered at the genomic level.

1. The Chimpanzee Sequencing and Analysis Consortium *Nature* **437,** 69–87 (2005).
2. Cheng, Z. *et al. Nature* **437,** 88–93 (2005).
3. Linardopoulou, E.V. *et al. Nature* **437,** 94–100 (2005).
4. Hughes, J. F. *et al. Nature* **437,** 101–104 (2005).
5. Chen, F. C. & Li, W.-H. *Am. J. Hum. Genet.* **68,** 444–456 (2001).
6. Eyre-Walker, A. & Keightley, P. D. *Nature* **397,** 344–347 (1999).
7. Fay, J. C., Wyckoff, G. J. & Wu, C. I. *Genetics* **158,** 1227–1234 (2001).
8. Clark, A. G. *et al. Science* **302,** 1960–1963 (2003).
9. Mathews, L. M., Chi, S. Y., Greenberg, N., Ovchinnikov, I. & Swergold, G. D. *Am. J. Hum. Genet.* **72,** 739–748 (2003).
10. http://www.genome.gov/10002154.
11. Olson, M. V. & Varki, A. *Nature Rev. Genet.* **4,** 20–28 (2003).
12. King, M. C. & Wilson, A. C. *Science* **188,** 107–116 (1975).
13. Enard, W. *et al. Nature* **418,** 869–872 (2002).
14. Stedman, H. H. *et al. Nature* **428,** 415–418 (2004).
15. Hahn, Y. & Lee, B. *Bioinformatics* **21,** I186–I194 (2005).
16. International Human Genome Sequence Consortium. *Nature* **431,** 931–945 (2004).
17. Boffelli, D. *et al. Science* **299,** 1391–1394 (2003).

35

Genetic Ancestry Services

Sally Lehrman and Jonathan Marks

Sally Lehrman is an award-winning reporter and writer specializing in medical and science policy reporting. She serves as national diversity chair for the Society of Professional Journalists and is active in several organizations that promote diversity in the media. Jonathan Marks (see Selection 17) specializes in molecular anthropology, the application of genetics to human evolution and diversity.

There are nearly a dozen companies now offering the service of tracing one's ancestral roots using the new technologies of DNA analysis. The offers range from finding out what percentage of your DNA comes from various geographic regions to finding out if you are descended from an ancient Jewish priestly clan or even Genghis Khan. In this selection, Sally Lehrman describes some of these services, focusing on one in particular that specializes in tracing African ancestry. She notes some of the scientific cautions and limitations of such analyses but also the popularity of the services based on their fulfilling a "critical social need" to link living peoples to their ancestry, to "recover family ties."

The limitations of these services, however, are more severe than is implied by the article. Following the main selection are some comments on the issue by Jonathan Marks, from a paper he presented at the 2005 annual meeting of the American Anthropological Association.

As you read, consider the following questions:

1. What services do the described companies offer? What is the specific service offered by the highlighted company, African Ancestry?
2. What is the "critical social need" that African Ancestry is trying to meet?
3. What limitations of such DNA analyses does the article point out?
4. Do you think analyses such as those described cause confusion about the nonexistence of human biological races (see Selection 31); that is, do they imply that races exist genetically?
5. What are the more severe limitations of these analyses and services that Marks points out?

Trace Elements: Reconnecting African-Americans to an Ancestral Past *by Sally Lehrman*

Even as population geneticists battle over the meaning of race, cline and "biogeographical ancestry," a small industry has emerged out of the quest to understand human migration and identity. At least 11 companies offer individuals the ability to trace their African, Native American, Asian or European roots through

DNA markers. One, Oxford Ancestors, will even help men learn if they carry the "heroic Y chromosome that flowed through the veins of the High Kings of Ireland" or inherited it "directly from Genghis Khan."

Hyperbolic promises aside, many population geneticists urge caution in interpreting these ancestry tests. Detractors say these companies rarely clarify that they are tracing just a tiny fraction of ancestry or that many lineages might share the same markers. And taken together, critics emphasize, the claims made for this technology misleadingly convey the sense of race and family as a matter of biological precision.

Rick Kittles, a geneticist at Ohio State University, acknowledges these pitfalls but has pressed forward with his firm, African Ancestry, because of what he considers a critical social need. The Washington, D.C.–based company compares a client's DNA with that of ethnic groups now living mainly in West and Central Africa, aiming to recover the family ties destroyed by the slave trade. Like the other firms, its technicians examine either a section of mitochondrial DNA or markers on the Y chromosome and then try to match them up with databases of maternal and paternal lineages.

With 13,690 maternal and 11,747 paternal lineages, African Ancestry offers unusually rich detail. Even so, Kittles acknowledges that each of the tests follows only a single ancestral line out of as many as 1,024 over 250 to 300 years (10 generations). The analysis cannot detect all the historical groups that may have contributed to a person's ancestry or even trace a single line beyond the populations Kittles has sampled so far.

But unlike other firms, Kittles is careful to say he is helping his clients connect to modern Africans, not historical figures or tribes, and he is not trying to categorize ethnicity or race. Instead of boiling identity down to genetics, he aims to highlight the interweaving of biology, history and culture. One concrete link to a part of Africa can be deeply healing, he says. Otherwise, most African-Americans can follow their history back only to enslavement. "It creates this void in the psyche of African-Americans, this missing piece of their identity," Kittles explains.

African Ancestry is also adding 200 lineages every few months, broadening out geographically from the original population samples. Kittles hopes that this expanding database may illuminate migration patterns from east and south African regions into the west and central areas, which had been the heart of the transatlantic slave trade. By tapping into the continent's high genetic diversity, this approach might overcome the difficulty of interpreting DNA markers shared across populations on the continent.

Besides technical improvements, with anthropologist Mark Shriver, Kittles has called for a code of conduct that would require companies offering personalized genetic histories to explain both the promises and limitations of their science. "He's careful and responsive to the ethical concerns," says Duana Fullwiley, a medical anthropologist at Harvard University. Still, Fullwiley and others remain cautious. For one thing, they see Kittles's desire to bridge the injury of slavery as overly idealistic. Ancestry tracing "may heal certain wounds," she acknowledges. But "it doesn't give us lost history back." Moreover, rather than resolving questions about identity, the test may open up new questions about genetic pedigree.

With his extensive database, Kittles has pinpointed African-American ancestry in more detail than other scientists thought possible, according to Joanna Mountain, a Stanford University population geneticist. Africa "is not just one homogeneous pot of people," Mountain says. Furthermore, individual African-Americans, who have a very mixed ancestry in their genomes, may be more similar to one another than to any group within Africa. "It's a neat story that's arising," she observes.

Some Comments on Genetic Ancestry Services by Jonathan Marks, from "Is Creationism Worse Than Genetic Essentialism?"

Presented at the 104th Annual Meeting of the American Anthropological Association, Washington, D.C., December 1, 2005.

The two most well-known approaches [to the ancestry services] are: first, racial ancestry using nuclear DNA, in which (for example) your percentage of African ancestry (plus or minus a double-digit number) is computed as your similarity, judged by your DNA markers, to a cell panel derived from a few dozen Nigerians and Congolese, who stand for the African gene pool. A humanist calls this synecdoche, and a scientist calls it unbelievably bad sampling.

The other marketable genetic approach to kinship involves the use of mitochondrial or Y chromosomal DNA to identify your kinfolk. Now mitochondrial DNA and most of the Y have the property of being clonally inherited: mother to sons and daughters in the case of mitochondrial DNA, and father to sons in the case of the Y. The bad news is that this tracks the inheritance of perhaps 1/50 of your genome, and it leaves most of your ancestors in any generation invisible.

So for example, if you go back three generations, we can know something about one of your eight great-grandparents from your mitochondrial DNA, and if you're a man, we know one more from your Y chromosome, but six of the eight of them are still invisible. And every generation backwards the number of invisible ancestors doubles, and the number of visible ancestors stays the same: two. So if, for example, you are an African-American and you think that mitochondrial or Y chromosome DNA is going to help you find your roots in Africa, we can do a simple calculation to help you.

Let's say your ancestors arrived on these shores 300 years ago, in 1705. Let's generously assume 25 years per generation, so your ancestry in this hemisphere goes back 12 generations.

How many ancestors did you actually have 12 generations ago? Simple: two to the twelfth power, or 4096. Assuming a perfect and unique match of the DNA sequences, how many of your 4096 ancestors 12 generations ago have you located? If you're a woman, one; and if you're a man, two [using both mitochondrial and Y chromosome DNA]. How many of those ancestors do you have absolutely no knowledge of? If you are lucky, 4094; if you're not lucky, 4095. And if you're especially not lucky, all 4096. In what postmodern universe can knowing less than one-tenth of one percent of something—this case, ancestry—count as positive scientific knowledge? Sure it's better than nothing, but not by much—in fact, it seems to be a lot closer to nothing than it is to something.

In other words, these genetic tests are using high technology to produce knowledge about a culturally constituted form of kinship, expressed in idioms of the seeming naturalness of DNA. They are putting an authoritative voice on relatedness that transcends biology.

Note: Even if, as Marks puts it, you get "a perfect and unique match of the DNA sequences" with some ancestor, famous or not, it still doesn't tell you much. The farther back in time you go, the more ancestry people have in common. That is, if Genghis Khan (a currently popular ancestor to trace to) was your grandfather thirty-two generations ago, he was also the grandfather of a lot of other people. So you really haven't learned much about your overall roots or about family trees. Moreover, in terms of DNA sequences, for the few variable sequences there are anyway (humans are over 99 percent genetically identical), there are very few that are unique to specific populations, so a match of DNA might not be a match in terms of your ancestry.

PART 10

Biological Anthropology: Applied and Considered

The best way to see how biological anthropology works, and to appreciate how it can contribute to our knowledge of ourselves on many levels, is to look at some specific studies that apply the methods and perspective of the field to practical and ethical situations.

In "Babies Need Their Mothers Beside Them," James J. McKenna presents a broad anthropological and cross-cultural perspective in support of the practice of co-sleeping, a controversial practice in Western societies.

Karen R. Rosenberg and Wenda R. Trevathan consider "The Evolution of Human Birth" and tell why humans are the only primate species that regularly seeks help during labor and delivery.

In "The Iceman Reconsidered," James H. Dickson, Klaus Oeggl, and Linda L. Handley show how many areas of inquiry, working together, have provided us with the latest information on the diet, age, health, place of origin, and cause of death of the famous mummy from the Italian Alps.

Douglas W. Owsley, Davor Strinović, Mario Šlaus, Dana D. Kollmann, and Malcolm L. Richardson bring the specialty of forensic anthropology to bear on some recent events in "Recovery and Identification of Civilian Victims of War in Croatia."

In "The Ethics of Research on Great Apes," Pascal Gagneux, James J. Moore, and Ajit Varki consider this ethical issue and conclude, in part, that ape subjects should be treated similarly to "human subjects who cannot give informed consent."

In "Saartje Baartman," Phillip V. Tobias recounts the story of the so-called Hottentot Venus, a South African woman who was taken to Europe and exhibited and studied between 1810 and her death in 1816, after which her body was dissected and her skeleton and some of her organs preserved. The story ends only in 2002. In telling this chilling tale, Tobias in effect surveys the history of scientific thinking on the subject of race.

Finally, Michael Balter addresses the question "Are Humans Still Evolving?" He shows that the answer is affirmative and gives examples of research to explain why.

SUGGESTED WEBSITES FOR FURTHER STUDY

http://www.forensicanthro.com
http://www.darwinianmedicine.org
http://www.nd.edu/~jmckenn1/lab
http://www.ncrr.nih.gov/compmed/cm_chimp.asp

36

Babies Need Their Mothers Beside Them

James J. McKenna

James J. McKenna is professor of anthropology and director of the Center for Behavioral Studies of Mother-Infant Sleep at Notre Dame University.

Some health officials and child-care specialists in Western societies have advocated that infants and mothers sleep separately, claiming that this decreases the chances of sudden infant death syndrome (SIDS), infant dependency, and the risk of suffocation. But anthropological data, including cross-cultural studies, indicate otherwise. In this selection, James McKenna, one of the foremost experts on the subject, details the arguments for co-sleeping.

As you read, consider the following questions:

1. What are the benefits McKenna lists for co-sleeping?

2. What are the ill effects that some authorities cite for separate sleeping? What might be the origin of this argument against co-sleeping? Can you think of any other reasons this has been discouraged in Western societies?

3. What is it about humans in particular that argues for co-sleeping?

Throughout human history, breast-feeding mothers sleeping alongside their infants constituted a marvelously adaptive system in which both the mothers' and infants' sleep physiology and health were connected in beneficial ways. By sleeping next to its mother, the infant receives protection, warmth, emotional reassurance, and breast milk—in just the forms and quantities that nature intended.

This sleeping arrangement permits mothers (and fathers) to respond quickly to the infant if it cries, chokes, or needs its nasal passages cleared, its body cooled, warmed, caressed, rocked or held. This arrangement thus helps to regulate the infant's breathing, sleep state, arousal patterns, heart rates and body temperature. The mother's proximity also stimulates the infant to feed more frequently, thus receiving more antibodies to fight disease. The increased nipple contact also causes changes in the mother's hormone levels that help to prevent a new pregnancy before the infant is ready to be weaned. In this way, the infant regulates its mother's biology, too; increased breast-feeding blocks ovulation, which helps to ensure that pregnancies will

not ordinarily occur until the mother's body is able to restore the fat and iron reserves needed for optimal maternal health.

It is a curious fact that in Western societies the practice of mothers, fathers and infants sleeping together came to be thought of as strange, unhealthy and dangerous. Western parents are taught that "co-sleeping" will make the infant too dependent on them, or risk accidental suffocation. Such views are not supported by human experience worldwide, however, where for perhaps millions of years, infants as a matter of course slept next to at least one caregiver, usually the mother, in order to survive. At some point in recent history, infant separateness with low parental contact during the night came to be advocated by childcare specialists, while infant-parent interdependence with high parental contact came to be discouraged. In fact, the few psychological studies which are available suggest that children who have "co-slept" in loving and safe environments become better adjusted adults than those who were encouraged to sleep without parental contact or reassurance.

The fear of suffocating infants has a long and complex cultural history. Since before the Middle Ages "overlying" or suffocating infants deliberately was common, particularly among the poor in crowded cities. This form of infanticide led local church

---

"Babies Need Their Mothers Beside Them" by James J. McKenna, Ph.D., from *World Health*, March–April 1996. Reprinted by permission of the author.

authorities to make laws forbidding parents to let infants sleep next to them. The practice of giving infants alcohol or opiates to get them to sleep also became common; under such conditions, babies often did not wake up, and it was presumed that the mothers must have overlaid them. Also, in smoke-filled, underventilated rooms, infants can easily succumb to asphyxia. Unfortunately, health officials in some Western countries promote the message that sleep contact between the mother and infant increases the chances of the infant dying from sudden infant death syndrome (SIDS). But the research on which this message is based only indicates that bed sharing can be dangerous when it occurs in the context of extreme poverty or when the mother is a smoker. Some researchers have attempted to export this message to other cultures. However, in Japan, for example, where co-sleeping is the norm, SIDS rates are among the lowest in the world, which suggests that this arrangement may actually help to prevent SIDS.

Human infants need constant attention and contact with other human beings because they are unable to look after themselves. Unlike other mammals, they cannot keep themselves warm, move about, or feed themselves until relatively late in life. It is their extreme neurological immaturity at birth and slow maturation that make the mother-infant relationship so important. The human infant's brain is only about 25% of its adult weight at birth, whereas most other mammals are born with 60–90% of their adult brain size. The young of most other mammals become independent of their parents within a year, whereas humans take 14 to 17 years to become fully developed physically, and usually longer than that to be fully independent.

Apart from being a natural characteristic of our species, constant proximity to the mother during infancy is also made necessary by the need to feed frequently. Human milk is composed of relatively low amounts of protein and fat, and high amounts of quickly absorbed and metabolized sugars. Therefore the infant's hunger cycle is short, as is the time spent in deep sleep. All of these factors seem to indicate that the custom of separating infants from their parents during sleep time is more the result of cultural history than of fundamental physiological or psychological needs. Sleep laboratory studies have shown that bed-sharing, instead of sleeping in separate rooms, almost doubled the number of breast-feeding episodes and tripled the total nightly duration of breast-feeding. Infants cried much less frequently when sleeping next to their mothers, and spent less time awake. We think that the more frequently infants are breast-fed, the less likely they are to die from cot death.

Our scientific studies of mother and infants sleeping together have shown how tightly bound together the physiological and social aspects of the mother-infant relationship really are. Other studies have shown that separation of the mother and infant has adverse consequences. Anthropological considerations also suggest that separation between the mother and infant should be minimal. Western societies must consider carefully how far and under what circumstances they want to push infants away from the loving and protective co-sleeping environment. Infants' nutritional, emotional and social needs as well as maternal responses to them have evolved in this environment for millennia.

37

The Evolution of Human Birth

Karen R. Rosenberg and Wenda R. Trevathan

Karen R. Rosenberg is a paleoanthropologist at the University of Delaware and specializes in pelvic morphology. Wenda R. Trevathan is a biological anthropologist at New Mexico State University with interests in childbirth and related areas. The original article points out that both authors have firsthand experience in their subject: Rosenberg is the mother of two daughters and Trevathan is a trained midwife.

Human childbirth is particularly difficult and risky, and seeking assistance during labor and birth is nearly a "universal" human custom. In this selection, Karen Rosenberg and Wenda Trevathan explain that this is the evolutionary price we have paid for two of our species' defining traits—bipedalism and big brains—and that assisted childbirth might have appeared at the very beginnings of hominid evolution.

As you read, consider the following questions:

1. Why is human childbirth more difficult and risky than the same process in other primates?
2. What is it specifically about the shape of the human birth canal that makes childbirth so problematic?
3. What do the authors mean when they say that assisted birth is a "universal" human custom?
4. What evidence from the fossil record suggests that assisted birth might be a very old practice for the hominids? How old?

Giving birth in the treetops is not the normal human way of doing things, but that is exactly what Sophia Pedro was forced to do during the height of the floods that ravaged southern Mozambique in March 2000. Pedro had survived for four days perched high above the raging floodwaters that killed more than 700 people in the region. The day after her delivery, television broadcasts and newspapers all over the world featured images of Pedro and her newborn child being plucked from the tree during a dramatic helicopter rescue.

Treetop delivery rooms are unusual for humans but not for other primate species. For millions of years, primates have secluded themselves in treetops or bushes to give birth. Human beings are the only primate species that regularly seeks assistance during labor and delivery. So when and why did our female ancestors abandon their unassisted and solitary habit?

The answers lie in the difficult and risky nature of human birth.

Many women know from experience that pushing a baby through the birth canal is no easy task. It's the price we pay for our large brains and intelligence: humans have exceptionally big heads relative to the size of their bodies. Those who have delved deeper into the subject know that the opening in the human pelvis through which the baby must pass is limited in size by our upright posture. But only recently have anthropologists begun to realize that the complex twists and turns that human babies make as they travel through the birth canal have troubled humans and their ancestors for at least 100,000 years. Fossil clues also indicate that anatomy, not just our social nature, has led human mothers—in contrast to our closest primate relatives and almost all other mammals—to ask for help during childbirth. Indeed, this practice of seeking assistance may have been in place when the earliest members of our genus, *Homo*, emerged and may possibly date back to five million years ago, when our ancestors first began to walk upright on a regular basis.

TIGHT SQUEEZE

To test our theory that the practice of assisted birth may have been around for millennia, we considered first what scientists know about the way a primate baby fits through the mother's birth canal. Viewed from above, the infant's head is basically an oval, longest from the forehead to the back of the head and narrowest from ear to ear. Conveniently, the birth canal—the bony opening in the pelvis through which the baby must travel to get from the uterus to the outside world—is also an oval shape. The challenge of birth for many primates is that the size of the infant's head is close to the size of that opening.

For humans, this tight squeeze is complicated by the birth canal's not being a constant shape in cross section. The entrance of the birth canal, where the baby begins its journey, is widest from side to side relative to the mother's body. Midway through, however, this orientation shifts 90 degrees, and the long axis of the oval extends from the front of the mother's body to her back. This means that the human infant must negotiate a series of turns as it works its way through the birth canal so that the two parts of its body with the largest dimensions—the head and the shoulders—are always aligned with the largest dimension of the birth canal.

To understand the birth process from the mother's point of view, imagine you are about to give birth. The baby is most likely upside down, facing your side, when its head enters the birth canal. Midway through the canal, however, it must turn to face your back, and the back of its head is pressed against your pubic bones. At that time, its shoulders are oriented side to side. When the baby exits your body it is still facing backward, but it will turn its head slightly to the side. This rotation helps to turn the baby's shoulders so that they can also fit between your pubic bones and tailbone. To appreciate the close correspondence of the maternal and fetal dimensions, consider that the average pelvic opening in human females is 13 centimeters at its largest diameter and 10 centimeters at its smallest. The average infant head is 10 centimeters from front to back, and the shoulders are 12 centimeters across. This journey through a passageway of changing cross-sectional shape makes human birth difficult and risky for the vast majority of mothers and babies.

If we retreat far enough back along the family tree of human ancestors, we would eventually reach a point where birth was not so difficult. Although humans are more closely related to apes genetically, monkeys may present a better model for birth in prehuman primates. One line of reasoning to support this assertion is as follows: Of the primate fossils discovered from the time before the first known hominid, *Australopithecus*, one possible remote ancestor is

Proconsul, a primate fossil dated to about 25 million years ago. This tailless creature probably looked like an ape, but its skeleton suggests that it moved more like a monkey. Its pelvis, too, was more monkeylike. The heads of modern monkey infants are typically about 98 percent the diameter of the mother's birth canal—a situation more comparable with that of humans than that of chimps, whose birth canals are relatively spacious.

Despite the monkey infant's tight squeeze, its entrance into the world is less challenging than that of a human baby. In contrast to the twisted birth canal of modern humans, monkeys' birth canals maintain the same cross-sectional shape from entrance to exit. The longest diameter of this oval shape is oriented front to back, and the broadest part of the oval is against the mother's back. A monkey infant enters the birth canal headfirst, with the broad back of its skull against the roomy back of the mother's pelvis and tailbone. That means the baby monkey emerges from the birth canal face forward—in other words, facing the same direction as the mother.

Firsthand observations of monkey deliveries have revealed a great advantage in babies' being born facing forward. Monkeys give birth squatting on their hind legs or crouching on all fours. As the infant is born, the mother reaches down to guide it out of the birth canal and toward her nipples. In many cases, she also wipes mucus from the baby's mouth and nose to aid its breathing. Infants are strong enough at birth to take part in their own deliveries. Once their hands are free, they can grab their mother's body and pull themselves out.

If human babies were also born face forward, their mothers would have a much easier time. Instead, the evolutionary modifications of the human pelvis that enabled hominids to walk upright necessitate that most infants exit the birth canal with the back of their heads against the pubic bones, facing in the opposite direction as the mother (in a position obstetricians call "occiput anterior"). For this reason, it is difficult for the laboring human mother—whether squatting, sitting, or lying on her back—to reach down and guide the baby as it emerges. This configuration also greatly inhibits the mother's ability to clear a breathing passage for the infant, to remove the umbilical cord from around its neck or even to lift the baby up to her breast. If she tries to accelerate the delivery by grabbing the baby and guiding it from the birth canal, she risks bending its back awkwardly against the natural curve of its spine. Pulling on a newborn at this angle risks injury to its spinal cord, nerves and muscles.

For contemporary humans, the response to these challenges is to seek assistance during labor and delivery. Whether a technology-oriented professional, a lay midwife or a family member who is familiar with the birth process, the assistant can help the human mother do all the things the monkey mother does by herself. The assistant can also compensate for the limited motor abilities of the relatively helpless human infant. The advantages of even simple forms of assistance have reduced maternal and infant mortality throughout history.

ASSISTED BIRTH

Of course, our ancestors and even women today can and do give birth alone successfully. Many fictional accounts portray stalwart peasant women giving birth alone in the fields, perhaps most famously in the novel *The Good Earth*, by Pearl S. Buck. Such images give the impression that delivering babies is easy. But anthropologists who have studied childbirth in cultures around the world report that these perceptions are highly romanticized and that human birth is seldom easy and rarely unattended. Today virtually all women in all societies seek assistance at delivery. Even among the !Kung of southern Africa's Kalahari Desert—who are well known for viewing solitary birth as a cultural ideal—women do not usually manage to give birth alone until they have delivered several babies at which mothers, sisters or other women are present. So, though rare exceptions do exist, assisted birth comes close to being a universal custom in human cultures (see box on p. 200).

Knowing this—and believing that this practice is driven by the difficulty and risk that accompany human birth—we began to think that midwifery is not unique to contemporary humans but instead has its roots deep in our ancestry. Our analysis of the birth process throughout human evolution has led us to suggest that the practice of midwifery might have appeared as early as five million years ago, when the advent of bipedalism first constricted the size and shape of the pelvis and birth canal.

A behavior pattern as complex as midwifery obviously does not fossilize, but pelvic bones do. The tight fit between the infant's head and the mother's birth canal in humans means that the mechanism of birth can be reconstructed if we know the relative sizes of each. Pelvic anatomy is now fairly well known from most time periods in the human fossil record, and we can estimate infant brain and skull size based on our extensive knowledge of adult skull sizes. (The delicate skulls of infants are not commonly found preserved until the point when humans began to bury their dead about 100,000 years ago.) Knowing the size and shape of the skulls and pelvises has also helped us and other researchers to understand whether infants were born facing forward or backward relative to their mothers—in turn revealing how challenging the birth might have been.

WALKING ON TWO LEGS

In modern humans, both bipedalism and enlarged brains constrain birth in important ways, but the first fundamental shift away from a nonhuman primate way of birth came about because of bipedalism alone. This unique way of walking appeared in early human ancestors of the genus *Australopithecus* about four million years ago [see "Evolution of Human Walking," by C. Owen Lovejoy; SCIENTIFIC AMERICAN, November 1988]. Despite their upright posture, australopithecines typically stood no more than four feet tall, and their brains were not much bigger than these of living chimpanzees. Recent evidence has called into question which of the several australopithecine species were part of the lineage that led to *Homo*. Understanding the way any of them gave birth is still important, however, because walking on two legs would have constricted the maximum size of the pelvis and birth canal in similar ways among related species.

The anatomy of the female pelvis from this time period is well known from two complete fossils. Anthropologists unearthed the first (known as Sts 14 and presumed to be 2.5 million years old) in Sterkfontein, a site in the Transvaal region of South Africa. The second is best known as Lucy, a fossil discovered in the Hadar region of Ethiopia and dated at just over three million years old. Based on these specimens and on estimates of newborns' head size, C. Owen Lovejoy of Kent State University and Robert G. Tague of Louisiana State University concluded in the mid-1980s that birth in early hominids was unlike that known for any living species of primate.

The shape of the australopithecine birth canal is a flattened oval with the greatest dimension from side to side at both the entrance and exit. This shape appears to require a birth pattern different from that of monkeys, apes or modern humans. The head would not have rotated within the birth canal, but we think that in order for the shoulders to fit through, the baby might have had to turn its head once it emerged. In other words, if the baby's head entered the birth canal facing the side of the mother's body, its shoulders would have been oriented in a line from the mother's belly to her back. This starting position would have meant that the shoulders probably also had to turn sideways to squeeze through the birth canal.

This simple rotation could have introduced a kind of difficulty in australopithecine deliveries that no other known primate species had ever experienced.

CHILDBIRTH ACROSS CULTURES

The complicated configuration of the human birth canal is such that laboring women and their babies benefit—by lower rates of mortality, injury and anxiety—from the assistance of others. This evolutionary reality helps to explain why attended birth is a near universal feature of human cultures. Individual women throughout history have given birth alone in certain circumstances, of course. But much more common is the attendance of familiar friends and relatives, most of whom are women. (Men may be variously forbidden, tolerated, welcomed or even required at birth.) In Western societies, where women usually give birth in the presence of strangers, recent research on birth practices has also shown that a doula—a person who provides social and emotional support to a woman in labor—reduces the rate of complications.

In many societies, a woman may not be recognized as an adult until she has had a baby. The preferred location of the delivery is often specified, as are the positions that the laboring women assume. The typical expectation in Western culture is that women should give birth lying flat on their backs on a bed, but in the rest of the world the most prevalent position for the delivery is upright—sitting, squatting or, in some cases, standing.

—K.R.R. AND W.R.T.

Depending on which way the baby's shoulders turned, its head could have exited the birth canal facing either forward or backward relative to the mother. Because the australopithecine birth canal is a symmetrical opening of unchanging shape, the baby could have just as easily turned its shoulders toward the front or back of its body, giving it about a 50–50 chance of emerging in the easier, face-forward position. If the infant were born facing backward, the australopithecine mother—like modern human mothers—may well have benefited from some kind of assistance.

GROWING BIGGER BRAINS

If bipedalism alone did not introduce into the process of childbirth enough difficulty for mothers to benefit from assistance, then the expanding size of the hominid brain certainly did. The most significant expansion in adult and infant brain size evolved subsequent to the australopithecines, particularly in the genus *Homo*. Fossil remains of the pelvis of early *Homo* are quite rare, and the best-preserved specimen, the 1.5-million-year-old Nariokotome fossil from Kenya, is an adolescent often referred to as Turkana Boy. Researchers have estimated that the boy's adult relatives probably had brains about twice as large as those of australopithecines but still only two thirds the size of modern human brains.

By reconstructing the shape of the boy's pelvis from fragments, Christopher B. Ruff of Johns Hopkins University and Alan Walker of Pennsylvania State University have estimated what he would have looked like had he reached adulthood. Using predictable differences between male and female pelvises in more recent hominid species, they could also infer what a female of that species would have looked like and could estimate the shape of the birth canal. That shape turns out to be a flattened oval similar to that of the australopithecines. Based on these reconstructions, the researchers determined that Turkana Boy's kin probably had a birth mechanism like that seen in australopithecines.

In recent years, scientists have been testing an important hypothesis that follows from Ruff and Walker's assertion: the pelvic anatomy of early *Homo* may have limited the growth of the human brain until the evolutionary point at which the birth canal expanded enough to allow a larger infant head to pass. This assertion implies that bigger brains and roomier pelvises were linked from an evolutionary perspective. Individuals who displayed both characteristics were more successful at giving birth to offspring who survived to pass on the traits. These changes in pelvic anatomy, accompanied by assisted birth, may have allowed the dramatic increase in human brain size that took place from two million to 100,000 years ago.

Fossils that span the past 300,000 years of human evolution support the connection between the expansion of brain size and changes in pelvic anatomy. In the past 20 years, scientists have uncovered three pelvic fossils of archaic *Homo sapiens*: a male from Sima de los Huesos in Sierra Atapuerca, Spain (more than 200,000 years old); a female from Jinniushan, China (280,000 years old); and the male Kebara Neandertal—which is also an archaic *H. sapiens*—from Israel (about 60,000 years old). These specimens all have the twisted pelvic openings characteristic of modern humans, which suggests that their large-brained babies would most likely have had to rotate the head and shoulders within the birth canal and would thus have emerged facing away from the mother—a major challenge that human mothers face in delivering their babes safely.

The triple challenge of big-brained infants, a pelvis designed for walking upright, and a rotational delivery in which the baby emerges facing backward is not merely a contemporary circumstance. For this reason, we suggest that natural selection long ago favored the behavior of seeking assistance during birth because such help compensated for these difficulties. Mothers probably did not seek assistance solely because they predicted the risk that childbirth poses, however. Pain, fear and anxiety more likely drove their desire for companionship and security.

Psychiatrists have argued that natural selection might have favored such emotions—also common during illness and injury—because they led individuals who experienced them to seek the protection of companions, which would have given them a better chance of surviving [see "Evolution and the Origins of Disease," by Randolph M. Nesse and George C. Williams; SCIENTIFIC AMERICAN, November 1998]. The offspring of the survivors would then also have an enhanced tendency to experience such emotions during times of pain or disease. Taking into consideration the evolutionary advantage that fear and anxiety impart, it is no surprise that women commonly experience these emotions during labor and delivery.

Modern women giving birth have a dual evolutionary legacy: the need for physical as well as emotional support. When Sophia Pedro gave birth in a tree surrounded by raging floodwaters, she may have had both kinds of assistance. In an interview several months after her helicopter rescue, she told reporters that her mother-in-law, who was also in the tree, helped her during delivery. Desire for this kind of support, it appears, may well be as ancient as humanity itself.

MORE TO EXPLORE

Human Birth: An Evolutionary Perspective. Wenda R. Trevathan. Aldine de Gruyter, 1987.

Birth as an American Rite of Passage. Robbie Davis-Floyd. University of California Press, 1993.

Bipedalism and Human Birth: The Obstetrical Dilemma Revisited. Karen R. Rosenberg and Wenda R. Trevathan in *Evolutionary Anthropology*, Vol. 4, No. 5, pages 161–168; 1996.

On Fertile Ground: A Natural History of Human Reproduction. Peter T. Ellison. Harvard University Press, 2001.

38

The Iceman Reconsidered

James H. Dickson, Klaus Oeggl, and Linda L. Handley

James H. Dickson is professor of archaeobotany and plant systematics at the University of Glasgow. Klaus Oeggl is professor of botany at the University of Innsbruck, Austria, and has co-edited a book on the Iceman, The Iceman and His Natural Environment *(2000, Springer-Verlag). Linda L. Handley is an ecophysiologist at the Scottish Crop Research Institute in Invergowrie, Scotland.*

On rare occasions, science is provided with a piece of evidence that opens new windows into our understanding of some aspect of our world. In 1991, the nearly intact naturally mummified body of a 5,000-year-old man was discovered in the Italian Alps and has become a virtual "time traveler," giving us heretofore unheard-of glimpses into the past. In this selection, Dickson, Oeggl, and Handley tell the story of the Iceman and bring us up to date on the latest research into his life and times. The Iceman is now in a special chamber in the South Tyrol Museum of Archaeology in Bolzano, Italy.

As you read, consider the following questions:

1. What do we know about the Iceman's physical traits while alive, especially anomalies and illnesses?

2. What artifacts were found with the Iceman's body?

3. Where was the Iceman from and what did he eat, and how do we know?

4. How did the Iceman die, and when?

On a clear day in September 1991 a couple hiking along a high ridge in the Alps came upon a corpse melting out of the ice. When they returned to the mountain hut where they were staying, they alerted the authorities, who assumed the body was one of the missing climbers lost every year in the crevasses that crisscross the glaciers of the region. But after the remains were delivered to nearby Innsbruck, Austria, Konrad Spindler, an archaeologist from the university there, ascertained that the corpse was prehistoric. The victim, a male, had died several thousand years ago. Spindler and other scientists deduced that his body and belongings had been preserved in the ice until a fall of dust from the Sahara and an unusually warm spell combined to melt the ice, exposing his head, back and shoulders.

No well-preserved bodies had ever been found in Europe from this period, the Neolithic, or New Stone

Age. The Iceman is much older than the Iron Age men from the Danish peat bogs and older even than the Egyptian royal mummies. Almost as astounding was the presence of a complete set of clothes and a variety of gear.

In the ensuing excitement over the discovery, the press and researchers offered many speculations about the ancient man. Spindler hypothesized an elaborate disaster theory. He proposed that the man had fled to safety in the mountains after being injured in a fight at his home village. It was autumn, Spindler went on, and the man was a shepherd who sought refuge in the high pastures where he took his herds in summer. Hurt and in a state of exhaustion, he fell asleep and died on the boulder on which he was found five millennia later. The beautiful preservation of the body, according to this account, was the result of a fall of snow that protected the corpse from scavengers, followed by rapid freeze-drying.

Because the uniqueness of the discovery had not been immediately evident, the corpse was torn from the ice in a way that destroyed much archaeological information and damaged the body itself. A more thorough archaeological excavation of the site took place in the summer of 1992 and produced much valuable evidence, including an abundance of organic material (seeds, leaves, wood, mosses). This material added greatly to the plant remains, especially mosses, already washed from the clothes during the conservation process. Now, after a decade of labor-intensive research by us and other scientists on these plant remains and on samples taken from the Iceman's intestines, some hard facts are revising those first, sketchily formed impressions and replacing them with a more substantiated story.

WHO WAS HE?

The hikers had discovered the body at 3,210 meters above sea level in the Ötztal Alps, which led to the popular humanizing nickname Ötzi. A mere 92 meters south of the Austrian-Italian border, the shallow, rocky hollow that sheltered the body is near the pass called Hauslabjoch between Italy's Schnalstal (Val Senales in Italian) and the Ventertal in Austria. Ötzi lay in an awkward position, draped prone over a boulder, his left arm sticking out to the right, and his right hand trapped under a large stone. His gear and clothing, also frozen or partially frozen in the ice, were scattered around him, some items as far as several meters away. Radiocarbon dates from three different laboratories made both on plant remains found with the body and on samples of Ötzi's tissues and gear all confirm that he lived about 5,300 years ago.

Certain other features of Ötzi were relatively easy to discover as well. At 159 centimeters (5'2.5"), he was a small man, as many men in the Schnalstal vicinity are today. Bone studies show he was 46 years old, an advanced age for people of his time. DNA analysis indicates his origin in central-northern Europe, which may seem obvious, but it differentiates him from Mediterranean people, whose lands lie not too far distant to the south.

In an unusual congenital anomaly, his 12th ribs are missing. His seventh and eighth left ribs had been broken and had healed in his lifetime. According to Peter Vanezis of the University of Glasgow, his right rib cage is deformed and there are possible fractures of the third and fourth ribs. These changes happened after he died, as did a fracture of the left arm. That these breakages occurred after death is among the considerable evidence that casts doubt on the early disaster theory. So does the finding that an area of missing scalp was caused by pressure, not by a blow or decay.

Holding aside the unanswered questions concerning Ötzi's death and whether it was violent or not, several sound reasons suggest that he had not been in the best of health when he died. Although most of his epidermis (the outer layer of the skin), hair and fingernails are gone, probably having decayed as a result of exposure to water during occasional thaws, his remains still offer something of a health record for modern investigators. Examination of the only one of his fingernails to have been found revealed three Beau's lines, which develop when the nails stop growing and then start again. These lines show that he had been very ill three times in the last six months of his life and that the final episode, about two months before his death, was the most serious and lasted at least two weeks. Horst Aspöck of the University of Vienna found that he had an infestation of the intestinal parasite whipworm, which can cause debilitating diarrhea and even dysentery, although we do not know how bad his infestation was.

Moreover, many simple, charcoal-dust tattoos are visible on the layer of skin under the missing epidermis. These marks were certainly not decorative and were probably therapeutic. Several are on or close to Chinese acupuncture points and at places where he could have suffered from arthritis—the lower spine, right knee and ankle. This coincidence has led to claims of treatment by acupuncture. Yet, according to Vanezis and Franco Tagliaro of the University of Rome, x-rays show little if any sign of arthritis.

The little toe of his left foot reveals evidence of frostbite. Ötzi's teeth are very worn, a reflection of his age and diet. Remains of two human fleas were found in his clothes. No lice were seen, but because his epidermis had been shed, any lice may have been lost.

WHAT WAS HIS GEAR LIKE?

Turning to Ötzi's clothing and gear, scientists have learned not only abut Ötzi himself but about the community in which he lived. The items are a testament to how intimately his people knew the rocks, fungi, plants and animals in their immediate surroundings. And we can see that they also knew how to obtain resources from farther afield, such as flint and copper ore. This knowledge ensured that Ötzi was extremely well equipped, each object fashioned from the material best suited to its purpose.

He had been warmly dressed in three layers of clothing—leggings, loincloth and jacket made of the hide of deer and goat, and a cape made of grass and bast, the long, tough fibers from the bark of the linden tree. His hat was bearskin, and his shoes, which were insulated with grass, had bearskin soles and goatskin uppers.

He had carried a copper ax and a dagger of flint from near Lake Garda, about 150 kilometers to the south. The handle of the dagger was ash wood, a material still used for handles today because it does not splinter easily. His unfinished longbow was carved from yew, the best wood for such a purpose because of its great tensile strength. The famous English longbows used to defeat the French at Agincourt some 4,000 years later were made of yew. A hide quiver contained 14 arrows, only two of which had feathers and flint arrowheads attached, but these two were broken. Thirteen of the arrow shafts were made of wayfaring tree, which produces long, straight, rigid stems of suitable diameter; one was partly of wayfaring tree and partly of dogwood.

A belted pouch contained a tinder kit, which held a bracket fungus that grows on trees, known as the true tinder fungus, and iron pyrites and flints for making sparks. A small tool for sharpening the flints was also found with the body. On hide thongs, Ötzi carried two pierced pieces of birch bracket fungus; it is known to contain pharmacologically active compounds (triterpens) and so may have been used medicinally. There were also the fragments of a net, the frame of a backpack, and two containers made of birch bark; one held both charcoal and leaves of Norway maple—perhaps it originally transported embers wrapped in the leaves.

WHERE WAS HE FROM?

In this part of the Alps, the valleys run north and south between towering ranges of mountains. Thus, the question of Ötzi's homeland resolves itself into north versus south rather than east versus west. The botanical evidence points to the south. A Neolithic site has been discovered at Juval, a medieval castle at the southern end of the Schnalstal, more than 2,000 meters lower but only 15 kilometers from the hollow as the crow flies. Archaeologists have not excavated the site in modern times, and there has been no radiocarbon dating, but Juval is the nearest place to the hollow where a number of the flowering plants and mosses associated with Ötzi now grow. We have no reason to suppose that they did not grow there in prehistoric times, and so perhaps that is the very place where Ötzi lived.

When his clothes were conserved, the washing revealed many plant fragments, including a mass of the large woodland moss *Neckera complanata*. This moss and others he had carried grow to the north and to the south of where he was found, but the southern sources are much closer. *N. complanata* grows in some abundance near Juval. Wolfgang Hofbauer of the Fraunhofer Institute for Building Physics in Valley, Germany,

has discovered that this moss grows, in more moderate amounts, at Vernagt (Vernago), just 1,450 meters lower than the site and only five kilometers away. And most recently, Alexandra Schmidl of the University of Innsbruck Botanical Institute discovered small leaf fragments of the moss *Anomodon viticulosus* in samples taken from the stomach. This woodland moss grows with *N. complanata* in lowermost Schnalstal.

If Juval was not his home, signs of Neolithic occupation at other locations in the immediately adjacent Vinschgau (Val Venosta), the valley of the River Etsch (Adige), offer other possibilities. In contrast, to the north, the nearest known Stone Age settlements are many tens of kilometers away, and we are not aware of any Neolithic settlements in the Ventertal or elsewhere in the Ötztal. If Ötzi's home was indeed in lowermost Schnalstal or in Vinschgau, then his community lived in a region of mild, short, largely snow-free winters, especially so if the climate was then slightly warmer.

Investigations by Wolfgang Miller of the Australian National University of the isotopic composition of the Iceman's tooth enamel suggest that he had grown up in one area but spent the last several decades of his life in a different place. Investigating stable isotopes and trace elements, Jurian Hoogewerff of the Institute of Food Research in Norwich, England, and other researchers have claimed that Ötzi probably spent most of his final years in the Ventertal or nearby valleys to the north. If these deductions can be substantiated, they are intriguing developments.

WHAT DID HE EAT?

The ongoing studies of the plant remains in samples taken from the digestive tract provide direct evidence of some of Ötzi's last meals. One of us (Oeggl) has detected bran of the primitive wheat called einkorn, so fine that it may well have been ground into flour for baking bread rather than having been made into a gruel. Microscopic debris of as yet unidentified types shows that he had eaten other plants as well. And Franco Rollo and his team at the University of Camerino in Italy, in the DNA studies of food residues in the intestines, have recognized both red deer and alpine ibex (wild goat). Splinters of ibex neck bones were also discovered close to Ötzi's body. A solitary but whole sloe lay near the corpse as well. Sloes are small, bitter, plumlike fruit, and Ötzi may have been carrying dried sloes as provisions.

Several types of moss were recovered from the digestive tract. There is virtually no evidence that humans have ever eaten mosses, certainly not as a staple of their diet. But 5,000 and more years ago no materials were manufactured for wrapping, packing, stuffing or wiping. Mosses were highly convenient for such purposes, as many archaeological discoveries across Europe have revealed: various mosses in Viking and medieval cesspits were clearly used as toilet paper. Had Ötzi's provisions been wrapped in moss, that would neatly explain, as an accidental ingestion, the several leaves and leaf fragments of *N. complanata* recovered from the samples taken from the gut.

Analyzing archaeological remains of bone and hair for their abundances of the stable isotopes of carbon and nitrogen (carbon 13 and nitrogen 15) can provide information about a person's diet. Nitrogen 15 can reveal the extent to which the individual relied on animal or plant protein. Carbon 13 can indicate the type of food plant the person ate and whether seafood or terrestrial carbon was an important part of the diet.

The isotopic data agree with the other evidence that Ötzi ate a mixed diet of plants and animals. He obtained about 30 percent of his dietary nitrogen from animal protein and the rest from plants. This value is consistent with those found in hunter-gatherer tribes living today. The data also indicate that seafood was probably not a component of his diet, a finding that makes sense because of the great distance to the sea.

WHAT WAS HE DOING THERE?

To this day, in what may be an ancient custom, shepherds take their flocks from the Schnalstal up to high pastures in the Ötztal in June and bring them down again in September. The body was found near one of the traditional routes, which is why early theories held that he was a shepherd. Nothing about his clothing or equipment, however, proves that he had done such work. No wool was on or around his person, no dead collie by his feet, no crook in his hand. Some support for the shepherd hypothesis comes from the grass and bast cape, which has modern parallels in garments worn by shepherds in the Balkans, but that alone is not conclusive; for all we know, it was standard dress for travelers at that time.

Analysis of the few strands of Ötzi's hair that survived reveals very high values of both arsenic and copper. The published explanation (also given independently on television) was that he had taken part in the smelting of copper. But Geoffrey Grime of the University of Surrey in England now considers that these exceptional levels may have resulted from the action of metal-fixing bacteria after Ötzi died and that the copper was *on*, not *in*, the hair. Further support for the possibility of copper having attached itself to the hair after death comes from the presence of the moss *Mielichhoferia elongata*, called copper moss, which spreads preferentially on copper-bearing rocks. It has

been found growing at the site by one of us (Dickson) and, independently, by Ronald D. Porley of the U.K. government agency English Nature.

Another hypothesis is that Ötzi was a hunter of alpine ibex; the longbow and quiver of arrows may support this notion. If, however, he had been actively engaged in hunting at the time of his death, why is the bow unfinished and unstrung and all but two of the arrows without heads and feathers and those two broken?

Other early ideas about Ötzi are that he was an outlaw, a trader of flint, a shaman or a warrior. None of these has any solid basis, unless the pieces of bracket fungus he was carrying had medicinal or spiritual use for a shaman.

HOW DID HE DIE?

In July 2001 Paul Gostner and Eduard Egarter Vigl of the Regional Hospital of Bolzano in Italy announced that x-rays had revealed an arrowhead in Ötzi's back under the left shoulder. This assertion has led to numerous statements in the media that Ötzi was murdered and to claims from Gostner and Egarter Vigl that it is "now proven that Ötzi did not die a natural death, nor due to exhaustion or frostbite alone." Although three-dimensional reconstructions of the object, which is 27 millimeters long and 18 millimeters wide, exist, requests by Vanezis and Tagliaro for the object to be removed to show convincingly that it is an arrowhead are still unanswered. Furthermore, it must be removed in a way that makes clear what fatal damage it might have done.

The arrowhead need not have caused death. Many people stay alive after foreign objects such as bullets have entered their bodies. A notable archaeological example is the Cascade spear point in the right pelvis of the famous Kennewick Man in North America; it had been there long enough for the bone to begin healing around it.

Even more recently, in a statement to the media, Egarter Vigl has reported that Ötzi's right hand reveals a deep stab wound. No scientific publication of this finding has been made yet.

AT WHAT TIME OF YEAR?

Initial reports placed the season of death in autumn. The presence of the sloe, which ripens in late summer, near the body and small pieces of grain in Ötzi's clothing, presumed to have lodged there during harvest threshing, formed the basis for these reports. But strong botanical evidence now indicates that Ötzi died in late spring or early summer. Studies by Oeggl of a tiny sample of food residue from Ötzi's colon have revealed the presence of the pollen of a small tree called hop hornbeam. Strikingly, much of that pollen has retained its cellular contents, which normally decay swiftly. This means that Ötzi might have ingested airborne pollen or drunk water containing freshly shed pollen shortly before he died. The hop hornbeam, which grows up to about 1,200 meters above sea level in the Schnalstal, flowers only in late spring and early summer.

As for the sloe found near his body, if Ötzi had been carrying sloes dried like prunes, the drying could have taken place some time before his journey. Small bits of grain also keep indefinitely, and a few scraps could have been carried inadvertently in his clothes for a long period.

WHAT WE KNOW

More than 10 years after the discovery of the oldest, best-preserved human body, interpretations about who he was and how he came to rest in a rocky hollow high in the Alps have changed greatly. Just as important, we see that much careful research still needs to be done. The studies of the plant remains—the pollen, seeds, mosses and fungi found both inside and outside the body—have already disclosed a surprising number of Ötzi's secrets. We are aware of his omnivorous diet, his intimate knowledge of his surroundings, his southern domicile, his age and state of health, the season of his death, and something of his environment. Perhaps one of the most surprising reinterpretations is that Ötzi

did not die on the boulder on which he was found. Rather, he had floated there during one of the temporary thaws known to have occurred over the past 5,000 years. The positioning of the body, with the left arm stuck out awkwardly to the right and the right hand trapped under a stone, and the missing epidermis both suggest this conclusion. So does the fact that some of his belongings lay several meters distant, as if they had floated away from the body.

But we do not know and may never know what reason Ötzi had for being at a great altitude in the Alps. And we may never understand exactly how he died. An autopsy would be too destructive to be carried out. In the absence of this kind of proof, we cannot completely exclude the possibility that perhaps Ötzi died elsewhere and was carried to the hollow where the hikers found him 5,000 years later.

MORE TO EXPLORE

The Omnivorous Tyrolean Iceman: Colon Content (Meat, Cereals, Pollen, Moss and Whipworm) and Stable Isotope Analyses. James H. Dickson et al. in *Philosophical Transactions of the Royal Society of London, Series B*, Vol. 355, pages 1843–1849; December 29, 2000.

INSIGHT: Report of Radiological-Forensic Findings on the Iceman. Paul Gostner and Eduard Egarter Vigl in *Journal of Archaeological Science*, Vol. 29, No. 3, pages 323–326; March 2002.

Ötzi's Last Meals: DNA Analysis of the Intestinal Content of the Neolithic Glacier Mummy from the Alps. Franco Rollo et al. in *Proceedings of the National Academy of Sciences USA*, Vol. 99; No. 20, pages 12594–12599; October 1, 2002.

39

Recovery and Identification
of Civilian Victims of War in Croatia

Douglas W. Owsley, Davor Strinović, Mario Šlaus,
Dana D. Kollmann, and Malcolm L. Richardson

Douglas W. Owsley is a forensic anthropologist and curator at the National Museum of Natural History, Smithsonian Institution. Davor Strinović is a forensic pathologist with the Department of Forensic Medicine and Criminology at the University of Zagreb, School of Medicine. Mario Šlaus is a physical anthropologist with the Zavod du Arheologiju, HAZU, Zagreb. Dana D. Kollmann is a criminologist with the Forensic Investigation Division of the Baltimore County Police Department. Malcolm L. Richardson is an archaeologist affiliated with the Archaeological Society of Virginia.

Forensic anthropological techniques were used on the Iceman (Selection 38) and have become common in various criminal and missing persons cases. They are also valuable in situations of war to document atrocities and identify victims. There have been numerous examples of such activities in the areas of the former Yugoslavia. They continue to this day. In this selection, Douglas Owsley and colleagues tell of their efforts in Croatia.

As you read, consider the following questions:

1. What sorts of information about human remains are forensic anthropologists able to supply? What were the specific goals of Owsley's team in Croatia?

2. How did the team go about locating burials?

3. Once a burial was located, what procedures were used to recover and record its contents?

4. What information was recorded about each individual set of human remains, and what techniques were used?

5. How were individuals identified?

$\mathbf{A}$n hour after leaving Zagreb and traveling south toward the current border between Croatia and Bosnia, we were overwhelmed by the devastation caused by the conflict that began in August 1991. The Croatian military had regained this territory from Serbian forces in August 1995. Small villages consist almost entirely of ruins of former homes; partially destroyed walls of concrete and terra cotta blocks are the remnants of sturdy houses that are generations old. Roofless and without doors or windows, the houses bear the scars of war created by rockets and artillery.

Also visible are the pockmarks from grenade fragments and automatic weapons.

Fires consumed all the combustible parts of the homes, including the furniture and other comforts and keepsakes. In the early spring of 1996, the fields of these farming communities remain untilled because they are still seeded with land mines. Although a few residents are beginning to return and rebuild, most are still absent, having fled to places of safety. Other villagers are absent because they lost their lives during acts of brutality when they would not desert their homes.

These were our first impressions as part of a joint Croatian–United States forensic investigation team during its initial visit to the area around the small town

From *Cultural Resource Management*, 1996, No. 10, pp 33–36. Reprinted by permission of the publisher.

of Glina to search for burials, systematically recover the remains, determine the cause of death, and identify the victims. The three-person team representing the Smithsonian Institution was headed by a forensic anthropologist (Dr. Douglas Owsley), accompanied by an archeologist and a criminalist on loan from the Baltimore County Police Department's Crime Laboratory. The Croatian contingent was led by forensic pathologist Dr. Davor Strinović, Department of Forensic Medicine and Criminology at the University of Zagreb, and physical anthropologist Mario Šlaus of the Zavod du Arheologiju at Zagreb. The recovery effort was sponsored by the Croatian-American Joint Science Board. The goal is to aid the development of forensic anthropology in Croatia by demonstrating techniques and instrumentation employed in the discovery, excavation, and examination of human remains. Depending on the preservation and completeness of the remains, forensic anthropologists can supply information on age at death, sex, race, stature, time elapsed since death, dental and osteological pathology, perimortem trauma (injuries occurring at the time of death), and cause of death. In some instances, skeletal attributes also provide clues to lifestyle, occupation, habitual patterns of activity, and other sociobehavioral characteristics.

The primary objective in Croatia was to establish the identification of the deceased and to determine the cause of death. The forensic team also recorded cranial and postcranial skeletal measurements for an osteometric data bank being developed for this region, which will aid future personal identifications by providing important comparative data. This initiative is patterned after the forensic anthropological data bank that has been developed for North America by the Department of Anthropology of the University of Tennessee, Knoxville.

Prior to assembling the joint team, Croatian government investigators interviewed friends, relatives, and neighbors of persons that are missing. Files have been created on those reported killed or missing, including detailed physical descriptions, photographs, and data about the time and circumstances of their death or disappearance. The investigators were thorough in collecting evidence, and when the government teams visited areas of reported atrocities, they successfully located the aftermath of many multiple or mass burials.

The roads leading from the village of Glina to these scenes of tragedy were single-lane dirt tracks that were deeply rutted and eroded. They are rarely used, as the former inhabitants are gone and the roads have received no maintenance. In most areas, formerly cultivated fields on both sides of these roads were delineated with plastic tape warning of the danger of mines. Many of these fields were on fire, their owners hoping that the heat would explode mines and release or expose trip-wired booby-traps. Several abandoned bunkers and rifle pits held commanding positions along the rude roads. The bunkers were constructed of sand-filled ammunition boxes with roofs of logs or planks covered with sod.

During the fieldwork, the many liaison matters were expertly dealt with by a military commander and a high-level civilian government official; both, along with their personnel, were dedicated to the task of investigating all such burials in Croatia. The crews were escorted to and protected at every location by Croatian police. Military personnel successfully led the vehicle convoy over unmined roads and paths past areas cordoned with razor wire. Upon arrival at a reported burial site, a military explosive ordnance disposal team first cleared the work area for mines. While the forensic team was occupied with their tasks, these specialists continually broadened their search area and, in addition to finding and collecting mines, also gathered live but unexploded grenades, rockets, and mortar and artillery shells. Loud explosions attested to their success in locating and disposing of these remnants of war that are retarding the return of former inhabitants to the area and their pursuit of a peaceful livelihood.

The first clues to soil disturbances were visual surface anomalies such as depressions, unusual soil concentrations, changes in vegetation, or the presence of sub-surface soils. There are a variety of remote-sensing techniques that can be used for validating surface features or for detection of soil disturbances when such clues are not present. These tools range from the simple to the complex and include probes, resistivity meters, magnetometers, and sophisticated ground penetrating radar devices. Considering that our areas of investigation were remote, and often in rugged terrain accessible only by foot and with no available electrical power, the highly portable and effective stainless steel probe was the obvious choice for our field studies. The investigator determines the amount of resistance to the probe in undisturbed soil. When inserted in the less compacted soils resulting from previous excavations, the ease of entry is apparent. Disturbed soil stratigraphy was verified by examining a soil coring sample.

Once a burial was delineated, the upper soils were removed by supervised military personnel with shovels. The pyrotechnic specialists regularly checked for booby-traps. After exposure, the remains were photographed and detailed notes taken and drawings made of the positions of the bodies and their coverings and clothing. A precise method of control was employed that included the assignment of identifying numbers and provenances to the remains of these victims. The bodies were carefully removed from their temporary graves for transport to Zagreb. The soil around and beneath the individuals was thoroughly checked for additional evidence.

Our first investigation was of a burial reported to contain five victims. The pit was deep, having been dug through several stratigraphic layers of heavy clay soils. It appeared to have been excavated mechanically, probably with a backhoe. The grave contained the bodies of four men in various positions and the skeleton of a dog. Several possessed identifying cards and papers, and one man's trouser pocket contained a large sum of money. One individual had the end of a length of chain attached to his ankles, possibly used to drag the body to the burial place. All had been shot. Near the burials was a one-man bunker protected with banked earth and a look-out or sniper's perch in a tree. The men reportedly had been killed in the adjacent house, and an examination of a ground-floor room disclosed the pockmarks left by weapons fire on the concrete walls. On the floor were numerous 7.62 mm shell casings that can be fired from an SKS or AK-47 automatic weapon.

While the first multiple grave was being excavated, a second crew was dispatched to the reported site of another burial about a half mile away. This second site was accessible only by foot over a cleared path through the mined fields. Located at the base of a gentle slope along the edge of a swampy field, the grave was evident by a boot that protruded up through the soil and by a cloth-covered object that later proved to be the knee of another victim. The grave was a shallow burial sparsely covered by soil. Three individuals were found covered by a plastic sheet. Two were reported to be brothers and the third a cousin. They had been shot and some body parts were missing. Local people reported that the men had decided not to abandon their farm and home by fleeing and shortly thereafter were gunned down in a field and left there. Unfortunately, feral pigs attacked the bodies before villagers could safely return and attend to their dead relatives and neighbors. Approximately a week later, the decomposing and partly scavenged bodies were transported into the woods and quickly buried.

A third site was investigated and contained the remains of a woman. Her death was caused by gunshot wounds and had resulted from her refusal to leave her home. She was buried in front of her house which had been vandalized with graffiti that served to identify the perpetrators. Having died during December, this woman and all of the men in the other burials wore multiple layers of heavy winter clothing, i.e., long underwear, several pairs of long pants, skirts, an apron, shirts, vests, sweaters, a scarf or shawl, and heavy coats.

The first day of fieldwork culminated with the investigation of a purported slaying and burial of a woman on her farm. She was said to have been buried in front of a brick and tile milk house. Probing identified a potential burial shaft, and diligent digging in the early evening began to expose a rectangular pit. It was extraordinarily deep, but the bottom was eventually reached. To our surprise and emotional relief, we did not find the remains of the missing woman but instead the complete skeleton of a cow.

Subsequent plans called for exploring a deep well reported to contain the remains of a large family and for also investigating the burned remnants of the nearby house. Croatian government officials excavated the well prior to the arrival of the full forensic team. Excavation of the well required heavy equipment before the bottom was reached. The information obtained from local residents was inaccurate; the well contained no bodies.

Unlike most houses that are made of concrete and terra cotta block in this part of Croatia, this house had been a small, wooden structure with a clay tile roof and packed clay floors, except for a concrete floor in the kitchen. The house was burned in late 1991 and remained untouched since that time. The larger, charred pieces of the burned structure and the noncombustible furnishings, appliances, and equipment were carefully removed to expose the underlying debris. The floor of the entire structure was then closely inspected for human remains. Small, calcined fragments of human bone were found among the ashes in the kitchen. Two clusters of small animal bones were located in other rooms of the house. These bones were identified as belonging to an immature pig; a neighbor reported that the family had been butchering a pig on the day of the attack. The kitchen was isolated for special treatment. The remaining rooms were carefully cleaned with flat-blade shovels; no other osteological evidence was found.

The kitchen was then sectioned into quadrants for purposes of control and the exact positioning of pertinent artifacts. Excavation of the quadrants was accomplished in two levels. The upper level contained large charred fragments of the building, segments of the clay-tiled roof, and curved pieces of whitewash that at first glance resembled burned bone fragments. The lower level consisted of fine ash particles among which were scattered kitchen implements and a large concentration of small human bone fragments that had been calcined from extreme heat. The commingled bone fragments were from two adult females, one significantly older than the other. Among the bone fragments were several metal dental crowns, one of gold, and personal articles including metal eyeglass frames, a chain that once held wooden rosary beads and the metal fasteners of a coin purse.

The neighbors believed that the family had been killed by knives or axes, as no gunshots were heard. However, expended shell casings and spent bullets from a 7.62 mm assault weapon and two different caliber pistols, a 9 mm and a 32 automatic, were recovered.

While excavation of the kitchen ashes was underway, Croat team members investigated a rumor which circulated among the neighbors. It was said that the matron of the house had buried a chest containing family heirlooms and keepsakes under the floor. Using probes, two buried objects were found: a wooden chest and a glazed steel box containing national costumes, laces, shawls, pictures and family papers and documents that were considerably damaged by moisture. Examinations were conducted in the morgue and laboratory facilities in the Anatomy Department of the Medical School of the University of Zagreb. Various states of deterioration among the remains reflected differences with respect to the acidity of the soil, burial depth, and length of time since interment. Many consisted of bones having small segments of soft and connective tissue still covered by clothing. Adipocere was present in some remains; and in several cases, the tissues had almost totally saponified on the skeleton and as such, they resembled figures constructed of plaster of paris.

The autopsies and forensic examinations were conducted jointly by the pathologist and forensic anthropologist who continuously dictated notes to a nearby member of the team equipped with a notebook computer. A vast amount of information about each individual was recorded relating to clothing, age, sex, stature, antemortem injuries and diseases, perimortem trauma, and postmortem damage when present. Important observations were recorded by the ever-present camera of a full-time photographer. Portable photographic studio equipment had been brought from the Smithsonian Institution in order to photograph all bones that showed trauma and other burial artifacts. Also photographed were bones that revealed diseases, mended bones, surgically implanted devices, and those showing past health problems.

The remains of each individual were carefully examined by plotting the position of bullet entrance and exit holes in their clothing or damage to the bones. Each of the multiple garments was described and cataloged as it was removed and the contents of garment pockets were inventoried. As outer layers were removed, the continuity of bullet holes was verified in lower garments and finally matched with entrance and exit wounds in the body or with projectile-fractured bones.

Time-consuming attention was given to the analysis of the bone fragments of the women burned in the house, as they were the most difficult from which to extract data for identification. The two sets of fragmented remains could be effectively sorted on the basis of bone size and robusticity, osteoporotic changes in the older woman, and perceptible differences in the color of the calcined pieces of bone of each woman. The rewards were significant: by determining their ages, health conditions, past diseases, dental work (the gold crown), and the metal framed eyeglasses, the identities of the two women could be established.

The identities of others were ascertained by matching forensic data with information collected by officials during earlier interviews. In North America, personal identification is often confirmed by the comparing and matching of detailed bone and dental features seen in antemortem radiographs with those present in the skeleton or dentition being examined. In Croatia and Bosnia, however, even when such records originally existed, medical facilities were often targeted and destroyed. As a consequence, identification criteria depend heavily on descriptive information provided by friends and relatives. As a supplement to the information contained in the antemortem data base, when probable identifications were indicated, family members were brought to Zagreb to discuss the findings of each investigation with the forensic team. Friends and relatives attending these conferences were shown photographs of clothing and personal items and relatives often recognized apparel belonging to a missing individual based on the garment's color, style, or pattern.

Through this collaborative effort, a tremendous amount of work in the field and laboratory was accomplished. Croatians and Americans worked side by side, sharing their expertise and knowledge to complete these unpleasant but necessary tasks. All were rewarded by knowing that the results of their work provided the relatives of the missing villagers with important facts concerning the fate of their loved ones as well as providing data to the Croatian government concerning the circumstances surrounding the deaths of some of its citizens.

Support from the United States–Croatian Science and Technology Program, the Smithsonian Institution's Department of Anthropology and its Office of International Relations, and the University of Zagreb School of Medicine made this recovery and forensic investigation possible.

40

The Ethics of Research on Great Apes

Pascal Gagneux, James J. Moore, and Ajit Varki

Pascal Gagneux is at Conservation and Research for Endangered Species, Zoological Society of San Diego. James J. Moore is in the Department of Anthropology and Ajit Varki in the Department of Medicine and Cellular and Molecular Medicine, University of California, San Diego.

There are some 3,000 great apes in captivity in the United States, many in research institutions. How these research apes should be treated is a matter of much debate. Some see them as simply research tools. Others—noting that they *are* used for research because they are so similar to us—feel that all such research is unethical. In this selection, Pascal Gagneux, James Moore, and Ajit Varki discuss the issue and suggest both an overriding philosophy and some very specific guidelines.

As you read, consider the following questions:

1. What is the philosophical premise for the suggested treatment of captive research apes? Do you think this should be applied to other research animals as well (such as monkeys, dogs, cats, and rats) or limited to apes?

2. What is the authors' overriding guideline for the treatment of apes?

3. What specific goals and objectives do they suggest?

4. What do they say about the breeding of apes in captivity?

5. How might these considerations apply to the plight of wild apes?

Publication of the draft sequence of the chimpanzee genome is an exciting event; it opens the door to learning a great deal about our closest evolutionary cousins—and about ourselves in the process. But unlike the human genome project, the chimpanzee sequencing effort was not accompanied by studies addressing ethical, legal and social issues[1]. Meanwhile, there is continuing debate over the future of captive 'great apes' (chimpanzees, bonobos, gorillas and orang-utans)*.

What does the publication of the chimpanzee genome mean for the thousands of great apes in captivity in the United States? Some fear the potential for increased invasive research on these individuals. Others are concerned that our limited knowledge of chimpanzee physiology and biology will constrain the usefulness of the chimpanzee sequence for understanding both humans and great apes. For example, critical resources required for comparative genetic and biological studies, such as messenger RNA or complementary DNA libraries, are almost non-existent for great apes. Here, we advance a proposal that addresses these and related issues, to lead, we hope, to a mutually beneficial outcome for all, including the great apes (see Box for a summary of proposed goals and objectives). We emphasize that this article relates only to great apes, and not to other primates, nor other animals. Also, this piece is not about animal 'rights' but about ethical and scientific challenges specific to great apes in captivity.

*'Great apes' is used here in its colloquial sense. In the commonly used classification, these species are grouped alongside humans in the family Hominidae, and humans belong to the tribe Hominini, along with chimpanzees and bonobos.

BORN IN CAPTIVITY

Opinions and attitudes regarding captive great apes span from the view that they are just expensive research animals to the idea that they should be accorded equal 'rights' with humans. Such views are in the minority, but there is need for continued dialogue among the majority spanning the middle ground.

The current ethical status of the great apes also varies among nations. US research on great apes is regulated by local 'animal-subjects' committees. And although national guidelines for breeding and long-term care have been proposed[2,3], there is still much disagreement. Some believe that our close similarity to the great apes means that they should never be kept in captivity, but for the ones now living in US facilities, it is too late.

While great ape numbers in the wild have fallen to tens of thousands, captive populations have expanded, especially in the United States, where past government support for breeding programmes was aimed at producing subjects for research into the human immunodeficiency virus (HIV). Today the United States is home to roughly 3,000 captive great apes (mostly west African chimpanzees) in research institutions, sanctuaries, zoos, private hands or the entertainment industry. Most of these individuals were born in captivity and never learned how to forage for survival or avoid predators. Thus, with few exceptions, attempts at returning captive great apes to the wild have proven extremely demanding—logistically and financially.

Regardless, we agree with those who say the biomedical-research community has special ethical responsibilities towards captive great apes. In our view, the great apes share traits—including, but not limited to, their genetic similarity to humans, the ability to use and modify tools and a sense of 'self'—that collectively justify this special status. (Individually, such traits are not unique to great apes; for example, bottle-nosed dolphins may also have a sense of self.)

PAUSE FOR THOUGHT

But there are other reasons to re-evaluate the situation for captive great apes. Their current medical care often assumes physiological and pathological identity with humans. But despite genetic and biological similarities, humans and apes differ markedly in their susceptibility to some major diseases, including AIDS (ref. 3). Working out the reasons for such biomedical differences will benefit all concerned, including the great apes, by allowing more species-appropriate medical care. Understanding how our genetic differences give rise to these

---

A SUMMARY OF PROPOSED GOALS AND OBJECTIVES

Community Issues

- Promote funding for an ELSI (ethical, legal and social issues) component of the chimpanzee genome project, as was done with the human genome project.
- Encourage dialogue on ethical standards and guidelines for research on great apes, following principles generally similar to those used in research on humans.
- Promote institutional and individual recognition of, and support for, the connection between the care and use of captive apes and their conservation in the wild.

Research Issues

- Encourage exploration of genetic, biological and medical similarities and differences between great apes and humans, especially in the context of providing medical care.
- Promote development of standardized databases of individual genotypic and phenotypic information about all captive great apes.
- Encourage funding for standardized collection and banking of tissues, fluids, imaging and biometric data obtained during medical care and autopsies. And make such data available to the scientific community for genetic, biochemical, histological and morphological studies.
- Encourage funding for the production of high quality cDNA libraries.
- Encourage funding for expanded programmes focused on understanding cognitive functions in great apes.
- Encourage development of mechanisms for sharing data, while respecting individual and institutional privacy concerns.

Care Issues

- Encourage greater fiscal support to ensure optimal living conditions for captive great apes.
- Suggest mechanisms to ensure and support the best possible medical care for captive great apes.

and other biological differences has been a long-term interest of some researchers.

Sequencing of the chimpanzee genome is likely to motivate many further studies of ape biology and physiology. But how such research should proceed needs careful thought. Given the diversity of opinions (including among the three of us), it is impossible to define a single clear-cut principle that can guide this discussion. We do suggest, however, that the study of great apes should follow ethical principles generally similar to those currently used in studies on human subjects who cannot give informed consent. Of course, many complex questions arise, such as who acts as the advocate for a great ape in agreeing on what are appropriate studies? And there are many grey areas. For example, is it acceptable to do reversible harm, such as causing a mild treatable infection (as is done with adult human volunteers), or to sedate a chimpanzee (as you would a child) to allow a therapeutic or research procedure?

Captive great apes have been subject to experimental procedures with the potential for irreversible damage or death, such as infections with human pathogens, vital-organ biopsies, multiple inoculations for vaccine testing, transfections for virus production and so on. Development of the widely used hepatitis B vaccine and understanding of the hepatitis C virus would not have been possible without the use of captive chimpanzees—and may still not be possible using other technologies. In retrospect, however, many of these expensive studies (for example, on HIV/AIDS, *Plasmodium falciparum* malaria and influenza A) turned out to have limited benefits for improving human health.

We suggest that alternatives to the use of whole chimpanzees be sought as soon as possible, and that substantial new funding be directed towards finding such alternatives. And, as with humans, we believe that the newly emerging genomic data should never be used to attempt germline genetic modifications in great apes (to produce 'transgenic' apes, as is routinely done with mice). Additionally, we recommend that any new biomedical studies on great apes be carried out in a manner that supports further improvements to their care.

The time has come to establish broadly accepted guidelines for systematic, humane and ethical studies of captive great ape populations. These studies should be carried out at all levels, from genetics to biochemistry to physiology to behaviour and culture. A previous US National Research Council report[2] addressed many issues regarding the care of captive chimpanzees, and a follow-up 2005 Federal Register Notice emphasized that they deserve the best and most humane care possible. For example, they should be maintained in groups that respect existing social bonds, with opportunities for physical, intellectual and social activities. Moreover,

euthanasia is specifically excluded as a means of population control[2]. Although opinions vary about the benefits of contact with human caretakers, there is generally wider agreement regarding human intervention for the control of escalating aggression within or between groups.

PRECIOUS RESOURCE

There is currently a moratorium on the breeding of chimpanzees at facilities funded by the National Institutes of Health (NIH). Although this may seem inhumane to some, it must be remembered that each birth in captivity can represent a 50-year or longer commitment on the part of human society. Facilities that do allow great apes to breed should avoid large numbers of births, as well as inbreeding and the mixing of subspecies.

As long as great ape facilities provide a safe, healthy and humane environment, it seems reasonable that captive great apes should remain a source of basic knowledge—which, in turn, may benefit both them and us. Understanding the normal biology, physiology and behaviour of the great apes provides a unique approach to understanding ourselves, even if we do not suffer from all the same diseases. Much of this can be accomplished through simple observational studies and by giving high-quality medical care to diseased individuals, as occurs routinely in human medicine. Experiments involving physical intervention with no long-term consequences could also be considered, provided that there is due consideration to the individual personalities of each ape, and that comparisons to normal humans are made wherever possible.

When a captive ape dies of natural causes (or is humanely killed to end incurable suffering), a thorough autopsy and rapid collection of organ samples for genomic, transcriptomic (gene expression), proteomic, biochemical and histological studies should be done, to generate an extremely valuable and sorely needed resource. There is also much to learn by careful preservation and analysis of the remaining musculoskeletal system. Partly due to inadequate funding, personnel, and facilities, many great ape deaths now occur without such analysis, translating into numerous wasted opportunities to learn more about their biology. Being responsible for great ape captivity, we must maximize the information from them, rather than treating them as single-use, disposable tools. Likewise, body fluid and tissue samples that are collected during routine medical care are often discarded or inadequately archived. Such detailed studies of living and deceased humans have long benefited our species by providing valuable medical and scientific knowledge.

Indeed, some humans approve postmortem donation of their entire bodies to science.

MUTUAL GAINS

In 2000, the US Congress passed a Chimpanzee Health Improvement, Maintenance, and Protection Act mandating the establishment of the NIH Chimpanzee Management Program[4] (ChiMP) and federal funding of sanctuaries for chimpanzees from research institutions, such as Chimp Haven (www.chimphaven.org). We suggest that these and many other ongoing efforts be bolstered by a federally and philanthropically supported collaborative network in which facilities housing captive great apes could choose to participate.

This would generate interactions among interested scientists from fields such as comparative biomedicine, psychology or biological anthropology. Already, leaders from US institutions holding most chimpanzees have come together to establish a National Chimpanzee Resource Committee, which meets regularly to discuss issues of mutual interest. The increased cost of supporting all such facilities will be more than justified by the knowledge gleaned from the study of healthy, socially integrated great apes—information that could potentially contribute to the ultimate survival of some of these species in their natural habitat.

Such a national network could also help train and support scientists interested in the standardized accumulation of all relevant biological information on healthy captive great apes. Each great ape should continue to be accounted for, by a name and unique identifier. Complete medical records should be collected in a standardized fashion into electronically searchable databases, in a way that maintains the privacy of researchers and institutions. Samples, such as body fluids, taken from live apes during routine physical examinations should also be collected and archived. In this way, we can create a great ape tissue bank of flash-frozen and archived samples for use by the scientific community—which could eventually result in (among other payoffs) the production of high quality cDNA libraries.

In some cases, therapeutic medical care could be extended to include data collection for research purposes (for example, standardized brain magnetic resonance imaging protocols appended to diagnostic imaging procedures). Increased funding will be needed to enhance existing medical facilities and expertise, and the ability to perform complete autopsies with tissue collection.

As for newly proposed research studies on live great apes, we suggest that these be reviewed and approved by specialized ethical oversight groups that incorporate appropriate aspects of the separate human-subject and animal-subject committees found at most institutions. Cooperation by the great ape research subjects will be critical for many studies, and will only be possible if there is also adequate funding for behavioural training of the animals.

We fully recognize that our proposal is unlikely to please everyone interested in great apes, and that this is only an initial contribution to a much-needed dialogue among all interested parties. Many changes and adjustments will be required to develop a mutually acceptable solution for all concerned, including the great apes.

Meanwhile, there is a deep irony in the fact that the sequencing of the chimpanzee genome coincides with the potential demise of great apes in the wild. We urge all scientists studying great apes, or tissues and samples derived from them, to contribute not only to the care of captive apes, but also to develop mechanisms by which studies of captive great apes would help generate a revenue stream to support the conservation of populations in the wild. While recommending improved care of captive great apes, we recognize that the remaining wild great apes may end up living in strictly managed reserves, depending on increased human intervention for their survival. In the long run, even our ability to care for wild populations could benefit from an increased understanding of great ape cognition, behaviour, physiology, biology, pathology and medicine.

NOTES

1. Human Genome Project Information www.ornl.gov/sci/techresources/Human_Genome/elsi/elsi.shtml (2004).

2. The National Academies Press http://books.nap.edu/catalog/5843.html (1997).

3. Olson, M. & Varki A. *Nature Rev. Genet.* 4, 20–28 (2003).

4. National Center for Research Resources www.ncrr.nih.gov/compmed/cm_chimp.asp

ACKNOWLEDGEMENTS

We are grateful to the following readers for very helpful comments and suggestions: A. Zihlman, C. Tutin, D. Povinelli, D. Rumbaugh, F. B. M. de Waal, J. Goodall, J. Allman, K. Semendeferi, K. Benirschke, M. Goodman, O. Ryder, R. Wrangham, S. Boysen, S. Blaffer Hrdy, S. Savage-Rumbaugh, T. Matsuzawa, T. Murray, and W. McGrew. We also gratefully acknowledge the support of the G. Harold and Leila Y. Mathers Charitable Foundation.

41

Saartje Baartman: Her Life, Her Remains, and the Negotiations for Their Repatriation from France to South Africa

P. V. Tobias

Phillip V. Tobias is professor emeritus of anatomy and human biology at the University of the Witwatersrand Medical School, Johannesburg, South Africa, an institution he has served for over fifty years. He is an honorary professorial research associate and director of the Sterkfontein Research Unit at the School of Anatomical Sciences. Best known for his research on early hominid fossils from South Africa, Tobias has also studied subjects ranging from mammalian chromosomes to living peoples of Africa to the origins of spoken language. He has published over one thousand works and is an ardent spokesman for racial equality and a leader in the anti-apartheid fight. For a more complete biography of this remarkable scientist, see www.roundtable.wits.ac.za/tobias.htm.

As Phillip Tobias recounts in this selection, from 1810 to 1816, a South African woman, Saartje Baartman, was literally exhibited in Europe as the "Hottentot Venus," where she was also studied by, among others, the famous anatomist Georges Cuvier. At her death in 1816 a body cast was made, her body was dissected, her skeleton mounted, and portions of her anatomy preserved. These were displayed, until quite recently, in the Musée de l'Homme in Paris. After nearly two centuries, Baartman's remains, thanks in large part to Professor Tobias, have finally been repatriated to South Africa. (The film mentioned in the article, *The Life and Times of Sara Baartman*, is available in the United States from First Run/Icarus Films, 153 Waverly Place, New York, NY 10014.)

As you read, consider the following questions:

1. Why was Baartman dubbed the "Hottentot Venus"? Address both words of her title. In other words, why was she considered such an exotic attraction?

2. What was the attitude, in nineteenth-century Europe, about the place of Baartman and others like her in the kingdom of living things? What did Cuvier conclude after studying her remains?

3. What case was made for repatriating Baartman's remains to South Africa?

4. What do you think, in general, of the issues of the repatriation of human remains?

Negotiations are complete for the repatriation, after nearly two centuries, of the remains of a Khoisan woman, Saartje Baartman, from Paris to South Africa. This article summarizes the facts and recommendations contained in the documentation presented to the French and South African governments to motivate this repatriation.

From *South African Journal of Science*, 2002. Reprinted with permission.

INTRODUCTION

Saartje Baartman[1] (1789–1816) was a tragic victim of the colonial era and has become a symbol of its oppressions. Of South African Khoisan extraction, she was taken from Cape Town to England in 1810 to be exhibited. In 1814, she was removed from England to France, where she died on New Year's day 1816. Those parts of her body that were preserved after her death have stayed in Paris until this day. There is a strong feeling within the South African government, Khoisan organizations and academe that these remains should be repatriated.

The author of this article was invited by South Africa's Department of Arts, Culture, Science and Technology (DACST) to negotiate with the French authorities, especially Henry de Lumley, director of the Musée de l'Homme and the Muséum National d'Histoire Naturelle in Paris. As director, he was the custodian of Baartman's remains. Negotiations took place from 1996 until 2001.[2]

The following is a summary of the researches and negotiations, and the author's recommendations made to the South African and French governments.

A BIOGRAPHICAL SKETCH OF SAARTJE BAARTMAN

Sara Baartman ("Saartje" is a Dutch diminutive form of "Sara" or "Sarah") was born in or about 1789 near the Gamtoos River, about the easterly limit to which Dutch settlers had penetrated (in the Eastern Cape Province of South Africa). Although no documentation about her birth has been traced, she is commonly believed to have been of KhoiKhoi (or KhoeKhoe) affinity (to which southern African populace the pejorative name "Hottentot" was formerly applied). The term "Khoi" or "Khoe" is often linked to the word "San" which is commonly applied to those formerly called "Bushmen," which term is also considered derogatory today. Thus, Khoisan (or Khoesan) is the term in widest use today.

About the time of the First British Occupation of the Cape of Good Hope (1795) or of the Second British Occupation (1806), Baartman moved to the area near Cape Town. By 1810, aged about 20 or 21 years, she was working as a servant on the farm of Peter Cezar. Hendrik Cezar, Peter's brother, brought an English ship's surgeon, Alexander (or William) Dunlop, to the farm. They were so impressed by features of Baartman's anatomy that Hendrik persuaded her to go to England with him and Dunlop, to exhibit herself to the public.

In 1810, Cezar began exhibiting Miss Baartman in London, as the "Hottentot Venus," evidently with great success. *The Times* of London described how during one such "show" she was ordered to come out from a cage: "The Hottentot was produced like a wild beast, and ordered to move backwards and forwards, and come and go into her cage, more like a bear on a chain than a human being. And one time, when she refused

Note added in proof: Saartje Baartman's remains were returned to South Africa in May 2002, and she was buried, near where she was born, in August of that year.

for a moment to come out of her cage, the keeper let down the curtain, went behind, and was seen to hold up his hand to her in a menacing posture; she then came forward at his call, and was perfectly obedient."[3] Such degradation led the African Association in London to take Cezar and Dunlop to court, claiming that "this unfortunate female was exhibited to the public under circumstances of peculiar disgrace to a civilized country."[3] They alleged that she must have been brought from her own country without her consent, that she doubtless had no desire to be exhibited, and that her appearance of compliance was the result of menace and ill-treatment.

In the testimony that Baartman offered, during a three-hour interview conducted in Dutch, she said she had agreed of her own free will to come to England for six years. She confirmed that she had appeared before the British Governor at the Cape (the Earl of Caledon, 1807–1811) and obtained permission; that she had been persuaded by the prospect held out by Dunlop and Cezar that she would make much money; that she was under no restraint and was happy in England. She wanted neither to go back nor to see her brothers and sisters. In the South African film researched and directed by Zola Maseko, *The Life and Times of Sara Baartman* (1998), a speaker declares that there is room for reservations about the degree to which she had freedom of choice.[4]

On Baartman's evidence, the case was dismissed, as it appeared she was under no restraint. "If, however, there was any indecency in the exhibition," the Court added, "the law would afford another remedy."[5]

After the court case, Baartman disappeared from the public gaze in London, but whether or not she was exhibited in other English cities (as some aver) is not known. She was baptized in Manchester, England, on 1 December 1811, and appears to have married a West Indian by whom she had two children. Nothing more is known about her from 1811 to 1813.

About the middle of 1814, Hendrik Cezar took Baartman to Paris and sold her to an animal trainer, who exhibited her in the rue Neuve des Petits-Champs and hired her out for dinner parties. Her working day extended from 11:00 to 22:00. Her working conditions were claimed to be much improved: there were no cage, no chain, no cruel keeper. According to one Parisian journal, she was treated in a manner befitting a lady: "The doors of the salon open, and the 'Hottentot Venus' is seen to enter. Some sweets are given to her in order to induce her to leap and sing, and she is informed that she is the prettiest woman in society."

The French public were as captivated by Baartman as the English had been. As in England, she featured in satirical cartoons and was even portrayed in a musical melodrama in a Parisian theatre.

She drew the attention of several French savants, particularly Georges Cuvier, Henri de Blainville and Etienne Geoffroy Saint-Hilaire. Cuvier arranged for her to be examined in the Jardin du Roi in March 1815. There, as Saint-Hilaire and Frédéric Cuvier (a younger brother of Georges) reported, "she was obliging enough to undress and to allow herself to be painted in the nude." These paintings, as well as Georges Cuvier's scientific observations on her,[6] were reproduced in *Histoire Naturelle des Mammifères* (1820–1842) by Saint-Hilaire and Frédéric Cuvier. Georges Cuvier's description was at pains to point out supposed "monkey-like" and "orang-utan-like"[8] features,[7,8] but, as Stephen Jay Gould indicates, Cuvier also stated that Saartje was an intelligent woman, possessed an excellent memory, and (apart from her own Khoi or Khoe language), spoke Dutch rather well, had some command of English, and was learning French. Cuvier even spoke of *sa main charmante* (her charming hand).[9] Carmel Schrire, of the Department of Anthropology at Rutgers University, New Jersey, U.S.A., concluded that "despite all that he knew of her accomplishments, Cuvier could not entirely shake off the animalistic implications of Saartje's nether regions. He was, after all descended intellectually, if not directly, from a long line of European observers, all of whom itched to examine the Khoikhoi sex [external genitalia], partly to see whether these were fully human and partly for their own sake."[10]

Ill-health beset Baartman in her last year or two, but whether it started in England or in France is not certain. Some assert it was smallpox, others speak of an inflammatory and eruptive illness. Georges Cuvier wrote, "What flattered her taste more than anything else was brandy. I might even ascribe her death to an excess of drink to which she gave herself up during her last illness." Bernth Lindfors believes that brandy might have been simply the *coup de grâce*.[11] (Recent press reports that, at the time of her death, she was a prostitute are without corroboration.) The terminal illness occurred in 1815, and Baartman died in Paris on 1 January 1816, at the probable age of 26 years.

THE POSTHUMOUS DISSECTION OF BAARTMAN'S BODY

Georges Cuvier obtained permission to study and dissect Baartman's body. He made a total body cast in wax and from this "negative impression," a "positive" cast was made. This still reposes in the Musée de l'Homme, where it was seen in recent times by, among others, South Africa's former ambassador to France, Barbara Masekela, and by the author.

Cuvier dissected the body, paying especial attention to the buttocks and external genitalia. Her buttocks were characterized by *steatopygia* (great enlargement), a common feature in Khoisan populations, but occurring also in some non-Khoisan populations. He was, it seems, the first to dissect a Khoi person and steatopygous buttocks. He studied, cast and dissected the enlarged labia minora (known scientifically as *tablier* or *macronympha*, and in vulgar parlance as the "Hottentot apron"). Of it he wrote: "there is nothing more celebrated in natural history."[12] His preoccupation with the sexual characteristics is strikingly brought out by the fact that over half (nine pages) of his 16-page report dealt with Baartman's genitalia, breasts, buttocks and pelvis. The external genitalia were removed and preserved in a bottle. The brain-case was cut across horizontally and the brain removed.

At the time, European anatomists and anthropologists were trying to define the supposed line between human and animal. To their biased eyes the "Hottentot" was closest in bodily structure, behaviour and even language to non-human animals. It was seriously doubted by some whether they belonged to the same species, *Homo sapiens*, as the rest of humankind. Cuvier and his contemporaries believed that the brain and the genital anatomy (and presumed sexual behaviour) would provide convincing answers to the question: were the Khoisan human or subhuman?

Such attitudes survived even into the twentieth century. In South Africa, in the earlier part of the last century, a church synod seriously questioned whether the Gospels were applicable to the Khoisan—implying their doubt as to whether the Khoisan were human. At the Empire Exhibition in Johannesburg from September 1936 to January 1937, a group of living/Auni and /Khoimani San from the southern Kalahari were among the exhibits, and this was apparently deemed acceptable.

While such ideas did not survive in the science of the late twentieth century, the early nineteenth century questioned the Khoisan's human status. Cuvier, however, while drawing attention to those of Baartman's anatomical features as he supposed resembled the corresponding traits of monkeys and apes, nevertheless concluded that she *was* a human being[6]—as much from her behaviour, which he had observed in her lifetime in March 1815, as from her anatomy, which he dissected in 1816.

In those days, for body casts, brain casts and face masks to be made of remarkable people was common practice. The death mask of Napoleon I is in the Paris Military Museum, for example, while Descartes's skull and Buffon's and Broca's brains are in the Muséum National d'Histoire Naturelle.

THE SURVIVING REMAINS

The following remains of Saartje Baartman were retained. Access to them has for some years been strictly limited to those authorized to see them by the museum's director and on the recommendation of the ambassador of South Africa in France.

The complete skeleton was freed of muscles, tendons and ligaments, reassembled, articulated and mounted on a stand. It is in a storeroom of the Muséum National d'Histoire Naturelle. It was on public display when shown to the author in 1955. It was seen by Gould in 1982 and 1985,[13,14] by Penny Siopis of the Department of Fine Arts, University of the Witwatersrand in 1989, by Schrire in 1995[15] and again by the author in 1996/97. It is shown in the film *The Life and Times of Sara Baartman*.

The complete death-cast of Baartman's body is in the Muséum National d'Histoire Naturelle. It has been seen recently and is shown also in Maseko's film.

Until recently, *Baartman's preserved organs* remained a mystery, and their fate and whereabouts were not known. As far as we can ascertain, apart from the skeleton, only two parts of Baartman's body were preserved: her brain and her external genitalia. These were kept in embalming fluid in sealed glass jars. They were on public display in the Muséum National d'Histoire Naturelle in 1955, when they were shown to the author by the French palaeontologist, Camille Arambourg. In August 1996, the South African writer Stephen Gray reported having seen Baartman's "decanted brain" alongside her skeleton in the late 1960s.[16] At some stage, the bottled specimens were removed from public display and placed in the museum's storerooms.

Gould saw Baartman's genitalia, along with two other bottled specimens of female external genitals, when he was shown Broca's brain by Yves Coppens in April or May 1982.[17]

In 1989, Schrire was shown the bottled external genitalia of the "Hottentot Venus" on a storeroom shelf.[18] Penny Siopis studied the iconography of Baartman. She was given access to the original cartoons and caricatures of Miss Baartman when she visited the Musée de l'Homme between 16 and 20 December 1988. She informed the author on 24 August 1998 that she had been told that the genitalia of the "Hottentot Venus" had been moved to the Muséum National d'Histoire Naturelle, and that it could not be arranged for her to see them there.

Regarding the whereabouts of the bottled parts, de Lumley stated that Baartman's viscera had suffered destruction in 1983 or 1984, when several shelves laden with glass jars had supposedly collapsed and the jars had then broken. He did not indicate whether the specimens in question were retrieved and re-bottled. The head of the Laboratory of Anthropology, André Langaney, told the author that he had found no trace of them when he assumed his position as head of the laboratory about the late 1980s, and he repeated this in the film *The Life and Times of Sara Baartman*.

There are several conflicting accounts, therefore, of what happened to these preserved parts. At present there is no certainty as to the whereabouts or even the continued existence of Baartman's brain and external genitalia. (It was reported to the author, in April 2002, by an officer of DACST, that they had been located and seen by Deputy Minister Mabandla and the South African Ambassador to France at the time of the debate in the French Parliament in January/February 2002.)

SOUTH AFRICA'S REQUEST FOR REPATRIATION

The South African government committed itself six years ago to seek the return of Saartje Baartman's remains. Its request for the repatriation arises from its dedication to the advancement of the heritage of the various peoples that make up the nation's population. One marginalized group of South Africans comprises the Khoisan peoples. Anxious to preserve the culture and heritage of Khoisan peoples, DACST set up a small advisory committee on the Khoisan peoples, comprising persons who have specialized knowledge of them, their languages, culture, history and prehistory.

Hundreds of human skulls, skeletons and cultural objects were removed from South Africa during the colonial period, always, it may be assumed, without the informed consent of the indigenous peoples concerned. These objects are in the museums of Europe, North America and elsewhere. If all of them were to be repatriated, it would be impossible for them to be accommodated, curated and handled, within the existing museum institutions of South Africa.

The South African parties have stated that they do not intend to seek the repatriation of other cultural and skeletal remains. They regard the case of Saartje Baartman as special and, indeed, unique. Unlike the anonymous skulls and skeletons of victims of commando forays by settlers from Cape Town and surrounding areas in the eighteenth and nineteenth centuries and unlike those that were exhumed for archaeological and anthropological study, Baartman's identity was known in life; she was baptized, married, and the mother of children, and many details of her life history are known. There are living Baartmans in South Africa who may belong to the same lineage. In her lifetime she was the object of an outcry by anti-slavery abolitionists in London, and she remains an icon, and the subject of films, books, exhibitions and articles that deplore the degrading treatment to which she was subjected after her removal to Europe in 1810. Baartman has become, in South Africa and internationally, a symbol of colonial and imperial excesses.

For these reasons (and not for any political advantage) the South African parties concerned wish to see her remains repatriated.

BAARTMAN, THE MUSÉUM NATIONAL D'HISTOIRE NATURELLE AND THE FRENCH GOVERNMENT

The Muséum National d'Histoire Naturelle, following the custom and academic purposes of earlier days, preserves remains of many remarkable persons, among whom is Saartje Baartman. Neither the museum nor the French government can be held responsible for the attitudes of racial superiority and inferiority that prevailed in earlier times or for the typological approaches that characterized anthropological researches and judgments in 1816 (when Cuvier dissected Baartman's body).

France was not responsible for removing Baartman from South Africa, nor for shameful conditions inflicted on her. The return of her remains to South Africa, therefore, would not imply that France was to blame but would be seen, rather, as a humanitarian gesture towards the peoples of South Africa and a reaffirmation of France's historic role as an upholder of human rights.[19]

During the negotiations, the museum's director affirmed his duty to safeguard the integrity of the museum's collections. Baartman's remains were defined as part of the French national collection and, he stated, under French law, items in these collections were inalienable. The director himself had not the power to de-accession Baartman's remains.[20] Their transfer to South Africa required permission from the French Parliament, and the museum's director indicated that he would be bound by parliament's decision.

RECOMMENDATIONS

As a result of the negotiations, it was recommended that Baartman be regarded as a symbol of all the victims of her period and that her remains be repatriated to South Africa, there to be handled with respect and dignity. The South African government needed to reassure the French government that this case was not the first of a series of requests for the return of other remains removed from South Africa during colonial times.

The remains requested for repatriation are as follows:

a. The mounted articulated skeleton of Saartje Baartman, including her skull and teeth;

b. Her bottled body parts (brain and external genitalia), if and when they can be found;

c. A cast of the total body cast that was made in 1816.

In addition, as a record of the ignominious treatment meted out to Saartje Baartman, a further request was to be made for good-quality photocopies of the cartoons that appeared in the French press when she was in Paris.

It was strongly recommended that Baartman's remains be handed over by the French government directly to the South African government, and that no group should seek to gain political advantage from the repatriation. South Africa and its people would see the return of Baartman's remains as belated recognition of her essential humanity and a gesture of reconciliation after the appalling treatment meted out to her and to the Khoisan in general.

The South African government should decide upon the disposition of Baartman's remains, after approaching various competent bodies in the country, including those representing the Khoisan themselves such as the National Khoisan Consultative Conference of South Africa, and researchers studying the Khoisan peoples.

It was not recommended that the remains be buried in the ground, as they would thereby be forever lost to scientific and forensic analysis. It may for instance be important to determine the genetic relationship between Baartman's DNA and that of living descendants of her brothers and sisters, or to confirm her age at death, or to verify that the returned bottled organs indeed belong to the same individual as did the skeleton, or to seek evidence bearing on the diagnosis of her final illness. It was proposed that, as an alternative, South Africa consider building a dignified tomb for housing the remains, designed as a shrine of remembrance open to visitors, with an illustrated account of Baartman's life and death on the walls. It was further suggested that members of the Khoisan communities might be invited to serve as the custodians of the proposed Saartje Baartman memorial shrine.

THE REPATRIATION OF THE BAARTMAN REMAINS FROM FRANCE TO SOUTH AFRICA

In a three-stage procedure the French Parliament in January and February 2002 approved a Bill to permit the return of Baartman's remains as requested by the South African government.

The proposal was moved in the French Senate by Senator Nicolas About on 29 January 2002 and was unanimously approved the same day. The Bill was then passed to a committee of the National Assembly which, on 14 February 2002, unanimously supported it and passed it on to the National Assembly. It came before the full National Assembly on 20 February 2002 and again was passed unanimously.[21]

South Africa's deputy minister of Arts, Culture, Science and Technology, Brigitte Mabandla, and the ambassador of South Africa in France were present at the National Assembly for the debate, and Mabandla stated afterwards that "it was moving to see the French people admit that this was a travesty of justice," and that in the debate "there was a consistent affirmation of human rights." She added, "Sooner rather than later the remains will be at our Embassy and then in South Africa."[22]

The French minister of research, Roger Gérard Schwartzenberg, has underlined the symbolic and political importance of the gesture which, he stated, aims to restore her dignity to Saartje Baartman and to enable her to rest in peace in her native land. The legislation then went to the French Cabinet for approval, the text stipulating that the remains be returned within two months. The administrative authority approved the bill and the appropriate arrangements are now being made for Baartman's remains to be returned to South Africa.[21]

The enticement of Saartje Baartman to England, to exhibit her body and supposedly become a rich woman, exemplifies the attitudes of the day towards subject peoples. It incorporates attitudes of racial superiority and inferiority, and of a prurient sexism, for the London and Paris audiences who paid to see her were inordinately curious about her sexual features. The history of this Khoisan woman epitomizes an entire epoch of racial repression and colonial subjugation. It is meet that her remains be returned to the land of her birth.

The author of this note and of the memorandum wishes to thank the following for help of various kinds. In France, the Ministry of Foreign Affairs, Cultural Division; Henry de Lumley; Andre Langaney; at the Embassy of South Africa, former ambassador Barbara Masekela, the present ambassador, Thuthukile Skweyiya, Lincoln Marais, Natalie Africa and other staff members; the Muséum National d'Histoire Naturelle; the Musée de l'Homme; the late Camille Arambourg, and the late Henri V. Vallois. In South Africa, thanks are due to Minister Ben Ngubane and Deputy Minister Brigitte Mabandla, Director-General Rob Adam; the ambassador of France, Tristan d'Albis; the Scientific Attaché at the French Embassy, Patrick Le Fort; Zola Maseko and Dumisani Dlamini; Henry Bredenkamp; Cecil Le Fleur; Penny Siopis; Terry Borain; Heather White; Peter Faugust; the University of the Witwatersrand and the School of Anatomical Sciences. Thanks are due also to Stephen Jay Gould and Carmel Schrire.

The National Khoi-San Consultative Conference of South Africa declared in a statement adopted at a Council meeting on 18 February 2002 that it "would like the world to know that we accept that the dignified return of her remains and the body cast for burial is a matter of national heritage interest."[23]

It now rests with the South African government to consult all interested and concerned parties and scholars, and then determine the most appropriate manner of disposal of her remains—whether by burial or by entombment—and the most suitable locale for such a final resting place.

NOTES

1. The spelling of the surname used here, Baartman, is the one used in contemporary documents and by living members of the Baartman family in the Oudtshoorn and Uniondale districts. On Saartje Baartman's baptismal certificate, however, issued in Manchester, England, the name was spelled Bartman.

2. The South African Cabinet entrusted the negotiations to DACST which, in turn, invited the author to carry out the mediation with the relevant museum authorities in Paris. The Memorandum written by the author gave details of the life and death of Baartman, the treatment of her in life and her body after death, the reasons why the repatriation was being requested, an outline of the negotiations and a set of recommendations. This Memorandum was available in the last phase of government-to-government negotiations and reached the Senate and National Assembly in Paris. In addition to the author's researches on Baartman's life and remains, and letters and telephonic discussions between the author, de Lumley, and South Africa's ambassador to France, meetings were held as follows: in Paris on 29 November 1996, in Pretoria on 25 April 1997, in Paris on 24 June 1997, and in Pretoria on 26 January 1998. The author was present at all four meetings and de Lumley at three. Other participants at various times included representatives of DACST, the French Ministry of Foreign Affairs, the Embassy of France in South Africa, the Embassy of South Africa in France, and officers of the Muséum National d'Histoire Naturelle.

3. African Association statement, published in *The Times* (London), 1810.

4. Maseko K. (director) and Gavshon H. (producer) (1998). *The Life and Times of Sara Baartman: The*

Hottentot Venus. Dola Bill Productions, Johannesburg.

5. *The Morning Post* (London), 29 November 1810.

6. Part of *Histoire Naturelle des Mammifères* by E. G. Saint-Hilaire and F. Cuvier.

7. Schrire C. (1995). *In Digging through Darkness: Chronicles of an Archaeologist*, pp. 177–178. University Press of Virginia and Witwatersrand University Press, Johannesburg.

8. Gould S. J. (1982). The Hottentot Venus. *Natural History* 10, 20–24. This article was reproduced in Gould's book *The Flamingo's Smile: Reflections in Natural History* (1985), chap. 19, pp. 291–301.

9. Gould (1982), p. 21; (1985), p. 296.

10. Schrire (1995), p. 177.

11. Linfors B., cited by Gray S. (1996).

12. Gould (1982), p. 23.

13. Gould S. J. (1985). The Hottentot Venus. In *The Flamingo's Smile: Reflections in Natural History* (1985), chap. 19, pp. 291–301. See also Postscript to chap. 19, pp. 302–305.

14. Gould S. J. (1998). Letter to P. V. Tobias, 6 October 1998.

15. Schrire C. (1998). Letter to P. V. Tobias (undated, received 21 August 1998).

16. Gray S. (1996). To celebrate Saartje. *Review of Books*: Literary Supplement to the *Mail and Guardian* (Johannesburg), August, pp. 1–2.

17. Gould (1982), p. 20.

18. Schrire (1995), p. 176.

19. Xaba A. (2002). Saartjie Baartman remains back in South Africa: statement by B. Mabandla, Deputy Minister of Arts, Culture, Science and Technology. Communication from DACST, Pretoria.

20. De Lumley H. (1999). Press statement issued in Paris, quoted by Liesl Louw: "It's unlikely that Saartjie's remains will return to SA." *Saturday Star* (Johannesburg), 20 February 1999.

21. Agence France Presse (2002). Le "Vénus hottentote" va pouvoir rentrer chez elle en Afrique du Sud. 21 February 2002. From the Embassy of France in South Africa.

22. Mabandla B. (2002). Media release by the Deputy Minister of Arts, Culture, Science and Technology. February 2002.

23. Le Fleur C. (2002). National Khoi-San Consultative Conference of South Africa media statement on the Sarah Bartmann issue, 18 February 2002.

42

Are Humans Still Evolving?

Michael Balter

Michael Balter is a contributing correspondent for Science International.

Certainly our ability to alter our environments through culture, especially in terms of improving survival rates, has relaxed natural selection in our species. But we are far from halting evolution. By definition, if mutation, flow, and drift are still occurring, we are still evolving. But we have also been and are still at the mercy of natural selection, since reproductive success is still linked to certain adaptive situations over which we have less cultural control—diseases, for example. In this selection, Michael Balter discusses some of the evidence for the recent and continued evolution of modern *Homo sapiens*.

As you read, consider the following questions:

1. In a general sense, how do we know that humans *must* still be evolving, as we have defined evolution?

2. How are some aspects of our body form—such as our faces, stature, and head shape—the result of evolutionary forces?

3. How are researchers using new technology in genetics to investigate the relative roles of drift and selection in modern humans?

4. How is lactase persistence an example of natural selection?

5. How are malaria and AIDS also examples of natural selection?

6. What are the genetic studies of Icelanders indicating about the relative frequencies of a particular genetic variant?

7. What can we say about our future evolution?

T he news made headlines around the world: Blonds were going extinct. According to CNN and other media, a World Health Organization (WHO) study concluded that the gene for blond hair, which was described as recessive to dominant genes for dark hair, would disappear in 200 years. The BBC announced that the last natural blond would be born in Finland and suggested that those who dyed their hair might be to blame, because "bottle blonds" were apparently more attractive to the opposite sex than natural blonds were and thus had more children.

Fortunately for blonds, the whole story turned out to be a hoax—"a pigment of the imagination," as the *Times of India* later put it. WHO announced that it had never conducted such a study, and hair color is probably determined by several genes that do not act in a simple dominant-recessive relationship. The story, which may have originally sprung from a German women's magazine, apparently simply leaped from one media outlet to another.

Although the story was untrue, the ease with which it spread reflects popular fascination with the evolutionary future of our species, as well as the media's appetite for evolutionary pop science. Today, Oxford University geneticist Bryan Sykes is receiving voluminous coverage for his book, *Adam's Curse*, which predicts that continuing degeneration of genes on the Y chromosome will leave men sterile or even extinct in 125,000 years. Many biologists say that the question they most often receive from students and the public is "Are humans still evolving?"

To many researchers, the answer is obvious: Human biology, like that of all other living organisms on Earth, is the result of natural selection and other evolutionary mechanisms. Some say the question itself betrays a misunderstanding of how evolution works. "The very notion that . . . we might not be evolving derives from a belief that all other life forms were merely stages on the way to the appearance of humans as the intended end point," says primatologist Mary Pavelka of the University of Calgary in Canada.

But other scientists point out that in developed countries, culture, technology, and especially medical advances have changed the evolutionary rules, from survival of the fittest to the survival of nearly everyone. The result, they say, is a "relaxation" of the selective pressures that might have operated 50 or 100 years ago. "Biologically, human beings are going nowhere," says anthropologist Ian Tattersall of the American Museum of Natural History in New York City. University College London geneticist Steven Jones agrees. "The central issue is what one means by 'evolving,'" Jones says. "Most people when they think of evolution mean natural selection, a change to a different or better adapted state. In that sense, in the developed world, human evolution has stopped."

Yet millions of people in developing countries continue to live under the combined stresses of poverty and disease. Under these conditions, even skeptics of ongoing human evolution agree that natural selection may be favoring genes that confer resistance to disease or enhance reproductive fitness in other ways. Indeed, researchers are now tracking how deadly maladies such as AIDS and malaria exert selective pressure on people today. "As long as some people die before reproducing or reaching reproductive age, selection is likely to be acting," says geneticist Chris Tyler-Smith of the Sanger Institute near Cambridge, United Kingdom.

Even in developed countries, where survival tends to be prolonged for almost all, recent studies suggest that there are still genetic differences among people in fertility and reproductive fitness, an indication that natural selection is operating. "The question 'Are humans still evolving?' should be rephrased as 'Do all people have the same number of children?'" says Pavelka. "The answer is that we do not make equal contributions to the next generation, and thus we are still evolving."

Over the past few years, a wealth of new data has begun to illuminate how natural selection has shaped—and may still be shaping—humanity. The human genome project and genetic data from people around the world have powered an explosion of research seeking signs of natural selection in human DNA. "A lot of the tools we are now using to search for selection were developed by people working on flies and other organisms," says evolutionary geneticist Bruce Lahn of the University of Chicago. "But once

researchers began to discover examples of ongoing selection in humans, it opened the door and gave them confidence that they could find even more."

So far, the number of confirmed cases of genes under recent selective pressure is only "a handful," says Tyler-Smith. But that is likely to change once the results of the International HapMap Project, a multination effort to determine worldwide variation in the human genome, are released later this year. Because genetic variation is the raw material on which natural selection works, favoring certain alleles over others, Tyler-Smith says the HapMap should "give us an overall view of the regions of the genome that have been under selection."

DRIFTING TOWARD MODERNITY?

To science-fiction fans, the future of human evolution conjures up visions of dramatic changes in our bodies, such as huge brains and skulls. "Many people see us continuing on the righteous path of increasing intelligence," says Pavelka. "But we will not head in the direction of larger brains and crania as long as infants are required to pass through a woman's pelvis to get into the world."

Whatever lies in our evolutionary future, scientists agree that the modern human body form is largely the result of evolutionary changes that can be traced back millions of years. The uniquely human lineage dates from about 6 million years ago, and many studies have demonstrated that our divergence from chimpanzees was accompanied by strong selective pressure, for example on the human brain. Yet researchers caution that not all morphological changes—the ones we can see in body shape and size—are the result of natural selection; some may not be due to genetic evolution at all. For example, the increase in average height seen in many developed nations over the past 150 years or so is probably due mostly to better diets rather than natural selection.

Even very early evolutionary changes in the hominid line were not necessarily due to natural selection. Take the hominid face, which has changed dramatically in the past 3 million years from the heavy-jawed mugs of the australopithecines to the relatively small and gracile skulls of modern humans. Anthropologist Rebecca Ackermann of the University of Cape Town in South Africa and anatomist James Cheverud of the Washington University School of Medicine in St. Louis, Missouri, analyzed hominid faces over time, using formulas that model natural selection as well as random genetic drift, in which some traits or alleles become more common simply through chance. They concluded last December in the

Candidates for Recent Selection in Humans

GENE OR GENETIC LOCUS	HYPOTHESIZED SELECTIVE PRESSURE
Lactase	Improved nutrition from milk
G6PD	Protection against malaria
Duffly blood group	Protection against malaria
Hemoglobin C	Protection against malaria
TNFSF5	Protection against malaria
CCR5	Protection against smallpox and AIDS
H2 haplotype	Unknown but only in Europe
DRD4	Cognition and behavior
MAOA	Cognition and behavior
AGT	Protection against hypertension
CYP3A	Protection against hypertension
TAS2R38	Bitter taste perception

Proceedings of the National Academy of Sciences (*PNAS*) that natural selection probably drove the evolution of facial form up to the birth of early *Homo*. But they also found that genetic drift could explain most of the changes in the human face after the birth of *Homo* about 2.5 million years ago. "Selective pressures on the face may have been released" when humans began using tools and so did less biting and chewing, says Ackermann.

The take-home lesson, she says, is that "genetic drift has played an important role in shaping human diversity. This is evolution, too." Drift has continued to shape modern human faces and skulls in the more recent past, according to other studies. For example, researchers have examined regional differences in head shape—parameters such as width of the skull, height of the nose, and length of the jaw—to see whether certain traits were favored by natural selection in response to differences in climate or environment. In most cases, the differences among populations turned out to be no more than expected due to random drift. But there are a few exceptions: Anthropologist Charles Roseman of Stanford University in California last year reported in *PNAS* that the skulls of the Buriat people of Siberia are broader than predicted by random drift. Broad skulls have smaller surface areas and so may be an adaptation to cold climates. That fits with previous work by anthropologist John Relethford of the State University of New York College at Oneonta. Relethford concludes that random drift and migration can explain cranial differences in "most cases," with the exception of people like the Buriat and Greenland Eskimos, who live in very cold environments.

Although the evolution of measurable traits such as modern human skull shape may be due to random drift, some changes in human body form may have more to do with cultural and environmental factors such as diet. "Over the past 10,000 years, there has been a significant trend toward rounder skulls and smaller, more gracile faces and jaws," notes anthropologist Clark Larsen of Ohio State University in Columbus. Most of the change, says Larsen, is probably due to how we use our jaws rather than genetic evolution. With the rise of farming, humans began to eat much softer food that was easier to chew. The resulting relaxation of stress on the face and jaw triggered changes in skull shape, Larsen says. He adds that the dramatic and worldwide increase in tooth malocclusion, tooth crowding, and impacted molars are also signs of these changes: Our teeth are too big for our smaller jaws. Numerous studies show that non-Western people who eat harder textured foods have very low rates of malocclusion, he notes. Similar changes are found in monkeys fed hard and soft diets. "With the reduction in masticatory stress, the chewing muscles grow smaller, and thus the bone grows smaller," Larsen says. "It is not genetic but rather reflects the great plasticity of bone. It is a biological change but heavily influenced by culture."

SIGNS OF SELECTION

Even if random drift and other nongenetic forces have helped shape modern humans, there is growing evidence that natural selection has also played an important role, even if its effects have been more subtle. Human evolution researchers are now mining the riches of genomic data to spot genes subject to recent selective pressures (*Science*, 15 November 2002, p. 1324). Geneticists have a large arsenal of "tests of selection" at their disposal, all of which exploit the genetic diversity of human populations to determine whether individual alleles or larger blocks of the genome—called haplotypes—are behaving as would be expected if they were only subject to random drift and were not under selection.

Some tests look for evidence that mutations in an allele that alter the protein it codes for have been favored over those that cause no change; others examine whether certain alleles are more common than expected. A fairly new and powerful approach compares the frequency of an allele in a population with the genetic diversity within a haplotype to which it belongs. If the allele is common due to random drift over a long time, the adjacent region of the genome should show considerable variation due to genetic recombination, the exchange of DNA between chromosomes during meiotic cell divisions. But if the variation is less than expected, the allele may have risen to high frequency in a much shorter period of time—a telltale sign of selection. "These tools are powerful," says Lahn. "Where we are lagging behind is in good data."

By deploying such methods, geneticists have identified more than two dozen genes that appear to have come under selective pressures since the rise of *Homo*, and several of them may still be subject to such pressures today. Some of these favored alleles apparently arose at highly critical periods in human evolution. Such is the case of *FOXP2*, the so-called speech gene, which is implicated in the ability to talk, shows signs of strong selection, and arose no more than 200,000 years ago, coinciding closely with the first appearance of *Homo sapiens* (*Science*, 16 August 2002, p. 1105). Other genes under selection are linked to cognition and behavior, and still others are involved in defense against diseases such as hypertension, malaria, and AIDS (see table, p. 224).

In some cases, the new tests for selection have helped nail down long-suspected cases of evolutionary adaptation. One classic example is lactase persistence, the inverse condition of so-called lactose intolerance. Most adults cannot drink milk because they produce little lactase, the enzyme that breaks down lactose, which is the major sugar in milk. But a sizable number of people can, and their geographical distribution correlates closely with the spread of domesticated cattle out of the Near East. Thus, more than 70% of Europeans, who have a long history of drinking milk, have lactase persistence, as do some African pastoralists. In contrast, the percentage is very low in most of sub-Saharan Africa and Southeast Asia.

Last year, researchers clinched the case for selection at the lactase gene. A team led by genome researcher Joel Hirschhorn of Harvard Medical School in Boston identified a haplotype more than 1 million nucleotide base pairs long that includes the lactase gene and confers lactase persistence on people who carry it. This form of the haplotype is found in nearly 80% of Europeans and Americans of European ancestry but is absent in the Bantu of South Africa and most Chinese populations. Hirschhorn and colleagues concluded from the unusual length of the DNA block that it is young, because it has not yet been broken up by genetic recombination. They calculate in the June 2004 issue of the *American Journal of Human Genetics* that this haplotype came under very strong selective pressure beginning between 5000 and 10,000 years ago, corresponding to the rise of dairy farming. Thus a cultural and technological change apparently fostered a genetic one. "This is one of the best examples of recent selection in humans," says Tyler-Smith.

Although being able to drink milk as an adult has its pleasant side, as any chocolate-shake lover can testify, most people in the world get along fine without the beverage. Yet in some cases, having a certain allele can be a matter of life or death. Thus, the genes most likely to be under strong selective pressure today are probably those involved in providing resistance to infectious disease, says Sarah Tishkoff, a geneticist at the University of Maryland, College Park. "In Africa, people are dying daily [of infectious disease], and those who have genotypes that confer some resistance are going to have more offspring. That is natural selection in action."

AIDS and malaria are arguably the worst scourges of humankind today, and they may both be exerting selective pressure on African genomes. Several genes have alleles that provide resistance to malaria, including those that code for hemoglobin C and an allele of the so-called Duffy blood group found only in sub-Saharan Africa; accumulating evidence suggests that they have both been under recent selective pressure. Four years ago, Tishkoff and colleagues showed that two different alleles of a gene called *glucose-6-phosphate dehydrogenase* (*G6PD*) have also been favored by strong selective pressure. The mutant alleles, A^- and Med, are found only where malaria is or recently was a problem and offer resistance against malaria, although they can cause blood diseases.

Tishkoff and her co-workers used the known geographical variations in the *G6PD* gene to estimate that the A^- allele probably arose in Africa about 6300 years ago and then spread rapidly across the continent; the Med allele, found in southern Europe, the Middle East, and India, is estimated to be only about 3300 years old (*Science*, 20 July 2001, pp. 442 and 455). These estimates are consistent with archaeological evidence that malaria only became a major health problem after the invention of farming, when the clearing of forests left standing pools of water in which the vector for the disease, the *Anopheles* mosquito, could breed. Thus a cultural change again led to a genetic one.

The case of AIDS, and the virus that causes it, HIV, suggests that the selective advantage of a gene can shift over time. As HIV infects T cells in the blood, it docks onto a cell surface receptor called CCR5. In the mid-1990s researchers discovered that a mutation in the *CCR5* gene provides strong protection against AIDS in homozygotes, people who have two copies of the protective allele. The mutation, called delta 32, is found in up to 13% of European populations but is extremely rare in other groups, including Africans. Researchers dated the origins of the delta 32 mutation in humans to about 700 years ago and concluded that a strong selective event resulted in its spread; this finding was confirmed in 2001 using sophisticated selection tests.

Yet because the AIDS epidemic dates only from the late 1970s at the earliest, researchers believe that the selective pressure on the delta 32 mutation must have been from some other factor. Researchers have debated whether the plague or smallpox, both of which ravaged European populations in the past, is more likely, although some recent studies have leaned toward smallpox.

ICELANDERS EVOLVING?

Although researchers scouring the human genome for signs of natural selection have uncovered a few examples, direct evidence that a particular allele actually boosts reproduction—the sine qua non of natural selection—is hard to come by in humans. But that's just what researchers were able to do in one dramatic study in Iceland. For the past several years, scientists at deCODE Genetics, a biotechnology company based in Reykjavik, Iceland, have been gathering genetic information on the nation's 270,000 citizens, in a government-approved effort to isolate disease genes (*Science*, 24 October 1997, p. 566). In the course of this research, deCODE researchers discovered a variant of human chromosome 17 in which a 900,000-nucleotide-base-pair stretch of DNA was inverted; this inversion was associated with a previously identified haplotype called H2, which they estimate arose 3 million years ago. H2 carriers make up about 17.5% of Icelanders and 21% of Europeans, but only about 6% of Africans and 1% of Asians.

To see whether the relatively high frequencies in Europeans represented natural selection, the team genotyped 29,137 Icelanders born between 1925 and 1965. When these data were correlated with the island's extensive genealogical database, the evidence

for positive selection was stunning: As the team reported in the February 2005 issue of *Nature Genetics*, female H2 carriers had about 3.5% more children than H1 carriers. "This study has large implications," says anthropologist Osbjorn Pearson of the University of New Mexico, Albuquerque. "The European version of the H2 haplotype could sweep the entire human population if it conveyed the same reproductive advantage in other people and environments." But deCODE CEO and research team co-leader Kári Stefánsson says the low frequencies of H2 outside Europe suggest that for some reason, its advantages are limited to that continent. "Why, I can't tell you," he says.

There are several genes in the H2 region, but it is not at all clear which ones cause H2 carriers to have more children; one nearby gene is implicated in pregnancy complications. The deCODE team is looking at the genes to see whether differences in expression might create the selective advantage. One lead, Stefánsson says, is that H2 carriers also show a higher rate of recombination during meiosis. In an earlier study, his team found that mothers with high oocyte recombination rates also tend to have more children, possibly because this genetic shuffling helps protect against errors in meiosis, which are a major cause of miscarriage in older mothers. H2 carriers also appear to live longer on average. "It is fascinating to think that there might be an advantage associated with a DNA variant at both ends of life," Stefánsson says.

OUR EVOLUTIONARY FUTURE

To many researchers, the limited but growing evidence that natural selection is currently acting on the human genome means that humans are still evolving, even if in subtle ways. But can we actually predict the course of future evolution, à la Sykes's disappearing males or the vanishing blonds? Most researchers' predictions are considerably more narrow and cautious and are tied to known selective pressures.

For example, researchers predict that delta 32 and other protective CCR5 mutations may become more common in populations widely infected with HIV, especially in Africa. "If there are no more advances in the treatment of AIDS and people continue to die, we would expect selection pressure to increase [the mutations'] frequency over time," says Tyler-Smith, who adds that he sees "no reason why they should not go to fixation"—that is, replace all other alleles of the gene.

Whether or not these patterns will make a significant difference in the way humans look or live is another question. "There will be minor fluctuations over time and space in the makeup of local human gene pools as humans respond to local conditions," predicts Tattersall, "but they won't be directional. I find it hard to foresee that under current conditions a qualitatively new kind of human is ever likely to emerge. But if conditions change, all bets are off."

Evolutionary predictions are tied to speculation about just what kind of environment we may face. Some researchers suggest that changing climate conditions may diminish the benefits of culture and medicine, creating a new era of natural selection. "There has been a relaxation in selective pressures in industrialized societies," says evolutionary geneticist Peter Keightley of the University of Edinburgh, U.K. "But our ability to sustain that relaxation is probably temporary. We are using up our energy resources, our population is growing, and the climate is changing. All this is bound to lead to greater difficulties and renewed selective pressures."

Despite such concerns, however, most scientists remain leery of long-term forecasts, in part because of the way evolution works. "Evolution is not directed towards a goal," says Tyler-Smith. "It always takes the short-term view, operating just on what allows us to survive and reproduce better in this generation." For now, predicting humanity's evolutionary future may be little more than crystal ball gazing—better suited to science fiction than scientific research.

Glossary

¹⁴C dating A dating technique using the decay rate of a radioactive isotope of carbon found in organic remains. Also called radiocarbon dating.

Acheulean The toolmaking tradition of *Homo erectus* in Europe and Africa, including the hand axe.

adapted A state of adjustment to a particular environment through a species' anatomy, physiology, and behavior.

adipocere A waxy substance produced in decomposing bodies exposed to moisture.

alleles Variants of a gene.

alpha male The dominant male in a group, usually used with regard to nonhuman mammals or birds.

altruism An act performed for the benefit of others with no regard to the welfare of the performer.

amino acids The chief components of proteins.

analogies Traits shared by two or more species that are similar in function but unrelated evolutionarily.

antemortem Before death.

arboreal Adapted to life in the trees.

artifact A natural object modified for a specific use.

australopithecines A group of extinct African hominids, dated from 4.4 to about 1 million years ago, characterized by ape-sized brains and facial morphology, but who walked upright.

bases In genetics, chemicals that constitute the genetic code, analogous to the letters in an alphabet.

bipedal The ability to walk on the hind limbs.

carnivore An organism that specializes in eating meat.

chromosome Strands of DNA, the molecule carrying the genetic code, in the nuclei of cells.

cline In biology, a variable species characteristic that changes gradually over geographic space.

coelacanth A primitive type of fish (called lobefin) once thought to be extinct but discovered still living in the Indian Ocean.

congenital condition An unusual condition present from birth.

Cro-Magnon Specifically, an early modern human site in France, but used generally as a synonym for modern humans in Europe.

culture In general, nongenetic means of adaptation. Ideas and behaviors that are invented, learned, and shared.

Darwinian medicine The study of disease from an evolutionary perspective, focusing on the human traits that make us susceptible to various ailments.

demography The study of the size and makeup of populations.

dimorphic Literally, occurring in two forms. Usually with reference to physical differences between the sexes of species not directly related to reproductive anatomy.

Down syndrome A condition caused by an extra twenty-first chromosome, resulting in variable mental deficiencies, heart and intestinal problems, immune system deficiencies, and characteristic (though variable) facial features.

egalitarian A social situation in which members of a group treat one another as equals.

endemic Referring to a disease that is constantly present in a population.

epidemic Referring to a disease that spreads quickly to a large number of individuals.

epidemiology The study of the geography and population patterns of diseases.

estrus The period of female fertility. Also, the signals indicating this condition to males and which stimulate mating behavior.

etiology The study of causes, usually with reference to the causes of disease.

eugenics The improvement of the human species through the control of mating and heredity.

fitness The relative adaptiveness of an individual organism, measured by reproductive success.

flint A type of stone that flakes easily and has been used to make tools for most of human history.

folk taxonomy Cultural categories used to organize important facts and ideas.

foragers Peoples who rely on naturally occurring food sources. The same as hunter-gatherers.

forensic Referring to legal matters; in anthropology, to the identification of human remains and the determination of time and cause of death.

fossils Any remains of life forms from the past.

founder effect Genetic differences between populations produced by the fact that genetically different individuals established (founded) those populations.

gangrene A decay of tissue when the blood supply is obstructed by injury or disease.

gene A sequence of DNA that codes for the production of functional product, usually a particular protein.

gene flow The exchange of genes among populations through interbreeding.

gene frequency The percentage of times a particular allele appears in a population.

genetic drift Changes in gene frequency from generation to generation as a result of random fluctuations.

genome The total genetic endowment of a species.

genomics The study of a set of genes and their interactions, as opposed to single genes or gene products.

genotype An individual's particular complement of genes.

grooming The cleaning of the fur of another animal, common among the primates, that functions as well to promote social cohesion.

hand axe A bifacial, all-purpose stone tool first produced by *Homo erectus*.

haplotype Specific combination of alleles of two or more linked genes. Haplotypes are useful in population comparisons.

herbivore   An organism that specializes in eating plants.

hermaphrodite   A general term for an individual with a mixture of male and female characteristics.

heterozygote advantage   An adaptive advantage conferred on individuals who possess a pair (or pairs) of genes made up of different alleles.

heterozygous   Having two different alleles in a genetic pair.

holistic   Assuming an interrelationship among the parts of a subject.

hominid   Traditionally, modern humans and our ancestors, defined as the upright-walking primate. (A more current definition, although not accepted by everyone, is based on genetic closeness and includes the African great apes—the chimpanzee, the bonobo, and the gorilla.)

hominoid   The taxonomic group that includes all apes and humans.

homologies   Traits shared by two or more species through inheritance from a common ancestor. These traits may not share the same function.

homozygous   Having two of the same allele in a genetic pair.

hunter-gatherers   Peoples who rely on naturally occurring food sources. The same as foragers.

hypothermia   The condition of having a body temperature below normal.

hypothesis   Educated guess to explain a natural phenomenon. In science, a hypothesis must be testable.

indels (insertions and deletions)   Mutations where one or more nucleotides are inserted into or deleted from a sequence of DNA.

infanticide   The killing of infants, especially by members of the same species.

inheritance of acquired characteristics   The incorrect idea that an organism can acquire adaptive traits during its lifetime and pass them on to its offspring.

intelligent design   The idea that an intelligent designer played a role in some aspect of the evolution of life, usually the origin of life itself. It is a form of scientific creationism, not a scientific concept.

intersexual   A person of mixed or ambiguous biological sex.

iridium   A metallic element, almost nonexistent in surface rocks on earth, but found in extraterrestrial sources like comets, meteorites, and asteroids. A layer of rock higher than expected in iridium and dated at 65 million years ago is evidence for a massive impact at that time.

isolating mechanism   Any difference that prevents the production of fertile offspring between members of two populations.

kin selection   The idea that fitness is measured by the success of one's genes, whether possessed by the individual or that individual's close relatives.

knuckle walking   A form of locomotion, typical of African apes, in which the backs of the knuckles of the hand make contact with the ground.

law of independent assortment   In genetics, the principle that genes for different traits operate independently of one another such that the presence of one trait does not predict the presence of another.

law of segregation   In genetics, the breaking up of gene pairs in the production of the cells of reproduction (e.g.,

sperm and egg) so that each such cell carries only one copy of each gene.

macroevolution   The level of evolutionary change at which new species branch off from existing ones.

matrilineage   A kinship system in which descent is figured through the females.

matrix   The rock in which a fossil is enclosed or embedded.

medical genetics   The study of diseases with known or suspected genetic bases.

meiosis   The production of gametes (reproductive cells), each of which has only one of each chromosome pair and thus only one of each gene pair.

microbe   A microscopic organism, usually single-celled.

microevolution   Evolutionary change within a single species.

mitochondrial DNA (mtDNA)   The genetic material found in a cell's mitochondria, the structures that supply energy to the cell.

molecular evolution   The evolution of the genetic code itself and the investigation of the evolution of species by examining their genetic code.

monogamous   Literally, pertaining to single marriage, one husband and one wife. Also used to describe nonhuman species where a group consists of pairs of males and females.

monogenism   The idea that all human races had a single origin.

monomorphic   Literally, occurring in one form. Usually with reference to a lack of physical differences between the sexes of a species not related to reproductive anatomy.

morphology   Physical appearance, usually with reference to anatomy.

mutation   Any mistake in an organism's genetic code.

natural selection   Evolutionary change based on the differential reproductive success of individuals within a species.

Neandertals   Populations of "archaic" humans who lived in Europe and the Near East from about 125,000 to about 35,000 years ago. Some authorities consider them a group of *Homo sapiens*, while others think them a separate species of genus *Homo*.

neocortex   The part of the brain responsible for memory and thought.

nondisjunction   Failure of chromosome pairs to separate and go to different gametes during meiosis. The result is a gamete with a pair of chromosomes and therefore the possibility of a new individual with three copies, instead of two, of a chromosome. This is the cause of Down syndrome.

nuclear DNA   The genetic material found in the nucleus of a cell.

nucleotide   The basic chemical building block of DNA and RNA, made up of a sugar, a phosphate, and, most important, one of the four bases of the genetic code.

obsidian   A volcanic glass used to make cutting tools.

osteology   The study of the skeleton and the biology of bone.

ovulation   In mammals, the maturation of an egg in the female marking the beginning of the period during which she may conceive.

paleoanthropologist   An anthropologist who specializes in the study of the human fossil record.

Paleolithic   The "Old Stone Age," normally dated from 2.5 million years ago to about 10,000 years ago.

paradigm   A general perspective underlying the methodology and theories of a particular science.

paranormal phenomenon   A phenomenon beyond the scope of normal scientific investigation.

paraphyletic   Referring to a set of species that contains the ancestral species but not all of its descendants. The included species are those that resemble the ancestral species; excluded species have evolved away from a resemblance to the ancestor.

particulate   In genetics, the idea that traits are controlled separately by individual factors rather than all together by a single hereditary agent.

pastoralists   Societies that rely on herds of animals for their subsistence.

pathogens   Organisms that cause disease.

pathologist   One who studies the origin, nature, causes, and development of disease.

patrilineage   A kinship system in which descent is figured through the males.

patrilocal   Refers to a society where a married couple lives with the family of the husband.

perimortem   At or about the time of death.

phenotype   The chemical or physical results of the genetic code. Measurable, observable traits of a genetic origin.

phylogenies   Evolutionary relationships.

physiological   Having to do with the bodily functions and processes of living things.

plasticity   The ability of organisms to change biology or behavior in response to environmental changes.

pleiotropic   A gene or set of genes that influence more than one phenotypic trait.

Pleistocene   The geological time period dated from 1.6 million years ago to 10,000 years ago, characterized by a series of glacial advances and retreats. The "Ice Ages."

polyandrous   Usually referring to marriages of one female and several males. Also used to describe groups of nonhumans consisting of one female and several males with whom they mate.

polygenism   The refuted idea that human races had separate evolutionary origins.

polygynous   Usually referring to marriages of one male and several females. Also used to describe groups of nonhumans consisting of single males and a group of females with whom they mate.

postcranial   Referring to anatomy from the head down.

postmortem   After death.

potassium-argon dating   A dating technique based on the decay of radioactive potassium into stable argon gas, usually used to date rock of volcanic origin.

predation   Hunting behavior.

primate   One of a group of large-brained, tree-dwelling mammals with three-dimensional vision and grasping hands. Humans, despite our terrestrial life, are primates.

progressive evolution   In evolution, the now discounted idea that all change is toward increasing complexity and perfection.

proteins   Molecules that make cells and carry out cellular functions. Constructed of amino acids and coded for by genes.

proteomics   The study that determines the proteins encoded by the genome.

pseudohermaphrodite   An individual whose external sexual characteristics do not match their chromosomal or gonadal sex.

pseudoscience   A scientifically testable idea that is taken on faith, even if tested and shown to be invalid.

punctuated equilibrium   The view that species tend to remain stable and that new species arise fairly suddenly.

quadrupedal   Walking on all fours.

race   In biology, the same as subspecies. In culture, cultural categories used to classify and account for human diversity.

radiocarbon   A dating technique using the decay rate of radioactive carbon (^{14}C) found in organic remains.

reciprocal altruism   An altruistic act performed with the expectation that the beneficiaries may someday aid the performer.

recombination   In genetics, genetic change resulting from sections of chromosomes switching during cell division.

sagittal crest   A ridge of bone running front to back along the top of the skull for the attachment of chewing muscles. Seen in gorillas and some extinct primate species, including some early hominids.

saponify   To undergo chemical changes that produce a soaplike appearance, as with tissue in a dead body.

savanna   The open grasslands of the tropics, especially with reference to Africa.

scientific creationism   The belief in a literal biblical interpretation regarding the creation of the universe, the earth, and life on earth, with the connected belief that this view is supported by scientific evidence.

sedentism   Refers to a population with limited movement.

sequence   In genetics, the process of determining the exact arrangement of bases (the individual letters) of the genetic code.

shaman   A part-time, supernaturally chosen religious specialist who can manipulate the supernatural.

SIDS (sudden infant death syndrome)   The sudden and unexplained death of an infant while sleeping.

slash-and-burn agriculture   A farming practice that involves the cutting down and burning of native plants to make way for cultivated plants.

sociobiology   The scientific study that examines evolutionary explanations for social behaviors.

speciation   The process of the evolution of new species.

species   A group of organisms that can produce fertile offspring among themselves but not with members of other groups.

steatopygia   The accumulation of large amounts of fat on the buttocks, especially in women.

stratigraphy   The arrangement of layers of rock and soil, used in anthropology for dating remains.

subspecies   Geographically distinct populations within a species.

symbolic   With reference to communication, any system that uses arbitrary but agreed-on sounds and signs for meaning.

syntax   In language, the rules of word order.

tetrapod   Group of organisms made up of birds, mammals, reptiles, and amphibians; four-limbed animals.

theory   A set of ideas to explain some natural phenomenon that have been well supported by evidence and scientific testing.

vasoconstriction   A response to low temperature in which the blood vessels constrict to help conserve body heat.

virus   A simple, single-celled organism consisting basically of a small amount of genetic material within a protein sheath. Viruses appropriate the genes of a host cell in order to carry out life functions, including reproduction.

X chromosome   The chromosome that carries genes for female characteristics as well as for many other traits.

Y chromosome   The chromosome that carries genes for male characteristics.

Index